Social Class in America and Britain

Social Class in America and Britain

FIONA DEVINE

EDINBURGH UNIVERSITY PRESS

To my mother, with love

© Fiona Devine, 1997

Edinburgh University Press
22 George Square, Edinburgh

Typeset in Linotype Plantin Light
by Bibliocraft, Dundee, and
printed and bound in Great Britain

A CIP record for this book is available from the British Library.

ISBN 0 7486 0666 1

Contents

List of Tables

Preface

This book is a comparative study of social class in America and Britain. In the 1990s, there has been a debate among American and British sociologists as to whether social class is declining in importance or remains a significant form of structured inequality in a period of rapid economic, social and political change. What is paradoxical about the debate is that it is being conducted among sociologists in two nations which are often portrayed as being at opposite ends of the spectrum. That is, America is invariably characterised as a classless society while Britain is frequently portrayed as a class-bound society. The debate on class, however, challenges these somewhat stereotypical images of the two nations. The controversy suggests that the stereotypes of America and Britain should be subject to critical sociological enquiry. The dispute, for example, begs a number of questions. Is America a classless society? Was it a land of abundant opportunity in the past? Is it an open society today? Is Britain a class-bound society? Was it a closed society in the past? Is it a closed society now? Are America and Britain as different as popular images of the two nations imply? Do they share any similarities? The answers to these questions, of course, can only be found in a comparative analysis of the two nations.

There has been a huge amount of historical and contemporary research on class embracing America and Britain. Indeed, the literature on international comparisons of social class is now so vast that it is increasingly difficult to keep abreast of the full range of newly published empirical findings. Few texts, however, introduce this comparative research to a student audience in an accessible way. Reference is sometimes made to another nation in passing although the focus is on one country. The limitation of these texts is that they do not have a genuinely comparative focus. Alternatively, the net is cast so wide across a number of nations that it is difficult to form an overall picture of what the evidence shows. Comparative research, in other words, has been drawn upon in only a limited fashion or the overall findings remain inaccessible to students in need of an introduction to the theoretical debates and empirical research.

This book seeks to rectify this omission with a focused comparison of social class in America and Britain. It has been written with a student audience in mind. It reviews a large body of sociological literature with reference to the general debate on social class and with reference to specific debates on different social classes in the two nations. The main theoretical controversies in America and Britain, therefore, have been summarised as succinctly as possible. More importantly, the book draws on a wide range of empirical results from both nations which are reported upon and sometimes reproduced in each of the chapters throughout the text. Special attention has been given to examining research on social class which has drawn on quantitative and qualitative methods of enquiry as a way of considering macro and micro sociological issues. The central argument of the book is that popular stereotypes of America and Britain do not stand up to systematic empirical scrutiny. America is not a classless society and Britain is not a class-bound society. In other words, popular images overstate differences and mask important similarities between the two nations. They also highlight the static nature of class inequalities and overlook how social class changes over time and space. In America and Britain, social class remains an important form of structured social inequality in the late twentieth century. In this respect, social class has proved remarkably persistent in both nations. At the same time, however, it is argued that class divisions are constantly changing and being re-formed in sometimes familiar and sometimes novel ways. The book emphasises both the continuities and changes in social class over the twentieth century.

The writing of this book was greatly facilitated by a research visit to the University of Chicago in 1995. Funds for the trip were made available by the University of Manchester for which I am duly grateful. I would like to thank Professor Ken Roberts of the University of Liverpool who supported the application for funds and to Professor Robert Moore, also of Liverpool University, who initiated the process by which I became a visiting scholar at Chicago. I am very grateful to Professor William Julius Wilson, of the Center for the Study of Urban Inequality, who sponsored my application and to Professor Marta Tienda who, as Head of the Department of Sociology, processed it through the University. Similar thanks should go to members of the Department of Sociology at Chicago for their willingness to talk about social class in America. My gratitude also extends to Jim Quane, Associate Director of the Center for the Study of Urban Inequality, for introducing me to all sides of the City of Chicago, to Jeff Rice for acquainting me with some of its restaurants and to Jerome and Anna Coakley for their generous hospitality.

A number of colleagues commented on drafts of individual chapters, and I am very thankful for the time and effort which they gave to my work. I should like to acknowledge the help of David Lockwood, David Rose, Peter Saunders, Mike Savage and John Scott. Special thanks are due to Ken Roberts who read all of the chapters as I wrote them and to Graham Crow who commented on all of them on more than one occasion. I should also like to thank Gordon Marshall who read the draft manuscript in its entirety and who provided some important suggestions for improving upon the book as a whole. I am especially grateful to Ken, Graham and Gordon who have performed this role for me before although their own research, teaching and administrative commitments are probably greater now than they were in the past. Colleagues at the Universities of Liverpool and Manchester provided a supportive environment while I completed this book. Special thanks should go to Lynne Brydon (and Tom and Anna McCluskie), Helen Jones and Tony Lane at Liverpool and to Sue Heath, Stephanie Linkogle, Rosemary Mellor, Simon Miller, Nikos Papastergiadis and Mike Savage at Manchester. Ann Cronley and Lesley Jones worked on chapters and tables for me at a late stage which I appreciate very much.

Finally, I should like to acknowledge the support and encouragement of long-standing friends and family. Once again, I should like to thank Graham Crow for his loyal friendship spanning many years. I should like to express my heartfelt thanks to Karen Wallace-Smith, Rob, Rohhss, Chloe and Casey Chapman and Tom, Jo, Hester and Reuben Clarke for their long friendship and support especially in the last stages of completing the book. A very, very special vote of thanks is due to Jo Clarke in this respect. I should also like to express by appreciation to my parents-in-law, Philomena and Gerald Smith, for their calmness and unfailing good sense about work and a lot more besides over many years. Special thanks should go to my immediate family – Barbara, John, Shirley, Shauna, Deirdre and Matthew – who I know are greatly looking forward to reading this book. Last but not least, I should like to thank my mother – Martha Devine – for everything. It is to her that I dedicate this book.

Fiona Devine
Manchester

Introduction

Is social class a major source of structured inequality in post-industrial societies? Does it shape people's life-chances? Does it influence the social identities which people adopt and the political beliefs they hold? These questions have generated a debate among American and British sociologists as to whether class is declining in importance or remains a significant form of stratification in a period of rapid economic, social and political change. The future of class analysis has also become the focus of debate. Some commentators have argued that the concept of class is no longer a useful explanatory tool in sociology while others have argued that sub-field of class analysis has an important part to play in the study of contemporary societies.

THE DEBATE IN AMERICA

The debate on class among American sociologists can be found in the journal *International Sociology*. Clark and Lipset (1991), for example, have argued that 'class is an increasingly outmoded concept' as traditional class hierarchies have died and new social divisions have emerged. Social strati-fication, in other words, is now fragmented. They examined the decline of class across three situs: politics, the economy and the family. In the domain of politics, class voting has declined and the old left-right spectrum of political beliefs has changed. A new, second left of young, educated and affluent people has emerged who are more preoccupied with social issues – life-styles, amenities and so on – than with traditional class political issues. Drawing on data from the Fiscal Austerity and Urban Innovation (FAUI) Project, they showed that older French mayors who are fiscally liberal are also socially liberal while younger French mayors and US mayors of all ages show no relationship between fiscal and social liberalism. The changing relationship between fiscal issues and social issues, demonstrates that 'hierarchy and class effects have declined dramatically in just a few years' (Clark and Lipset 1991: 405).

Turning to the economic sphere, Clark and Lipset argued that growth has undermined hierarchical class stratification. The rise in incomes has fuelled 'more elaborate and varied tastes' met by niche markets in which small firms are more competitive than large firms. Unfettered by traditional management structures, small firms have been able to explore their technology and knowledge base in such areas as computers, biological engineering and robotics. Highly educated technical and professional employees are increasingly making autonomous decisions heralding the emergence of 'egalitarian, collegial decisions. In the context of the growth of markets and the demise of family businesses, there has been a decline in traditional authority, hierarchy and class relations (Clark and Lipset 1991: 406). Finally, in the social sphere, a slimmer family has emerged in which personal relations are more equal and more flexible. The family no longer influences the life-chances of individual members in terms of education and jobs. Education, rather than family background, increasingly shapes the prospects of social mobility. The family, therefore, is less important as a vehicle for stratification and indicates, once again, the weakening of hierarchical stratification. Overall, the trends in all three spheres of life demonstrates that 'social classes are dying' and 'new patterns of social stratification are emerging'. The key trend may be described as the 'fragmentation of stratification' (Clark and Lipset 1991: 407–8).

Clark and Lipset offer a wide-ranging theory of change to account for the death of social change. The argument, of course, has a familiar ring echoing earlier theories of change proposed by liberal theorists such as Daniel Bell and Ronald Inglehart. Bell argued in *The Coming of Post-Industrial Society* (1973) that economic growth and technical change had led to an up-grading of the occupational structure with the decline of unskilled manual employment and the growth of high-specialised nonmanual employment. These changes in the structure of employment facilitated a high level of social mobility on the basis of merit so that post-industrial societies were becoming more egalitarian and open. Rigid class structures would become more fluid hierarchies. In the sphere of politics, Inglehart in *The Silent Revolution* (1977) argued that as societies have become more affluent, the nature of politics has changed from materialist concerns of a class nature to post-materialist concerns of a non-class kind. Political debates no longer revolve around economic issues which preoccupy the working class but focus on issues of life-style, the environment, peace and so forth which concern the middle class. These theories are not all of a piece but they share a somewhat benign and optimistic view of social change. Clark and Lipset's arguments are a re-statement of these liberal accounts of industrial society and demonstrate their continued popularity over the second half of the twentieth century.

In reply, Hout, Brooks and Manza (1993) have argued for the persistence of class in post-industrial societies. They do not deny that changes are taking place but the social and political implications of these trends are not inevitable. The concept of class 'remains indispensable' to sociologists and they 'turn away from class at their own peril' (Hout *et al.* 1993: 261). Hout and his associates noted that Clark and Lipset's discussion of the concept of class interchangeably with the concept of hierarchy has led to some misunderstandings. It is not clear whether they are describing the decline of status distinctions rather than class distinctions. Defining classes in terms of material interest rooted in the economic order, they argue that the unequal distribution of wealth and growing income inequality in America demonstrate the persistence of class. Drawing on data from the 1991 US follow-up to the *Class Structure and Class Consciousness* surveys conducted by Wright in the 1980s, they found that class differences in income are statistically and substantively significant. Employing Wright's class schema, they found that the ratio of earnings from the top to the bottom was 4.2: 1 for men and 2.5: 1 for women while the Erikson-Goldthorpe schema produced similar patterns of 4.9: 1 among men and 3.6: 1 among women. The evidence, therefore, demonstrates that 'changes in the class structure have not eroded the important effects of class on earnings' (Hout *et al.* 1993: 263). Alongside evidence of extreme poverty, they concluded that predictions 'about the impending death of classes is premature'. Such evidence, largely ignored by Clark and Lipset, demonstrates the persistence of class.

Clark and Lipset's evidence on the declining significance of class was also found wanting. The Alford Index has its shortcomings since it is highly sensitive to the arrival of new parties and candidates in the political sphere. The relevance of data on the ideologies of French and American mayors is not obviously relevant to the debate on class since it focuses on an elite, and the relationship between fiscal and social liberalism and class politics is not clear. The empirical evidence, therefore, does not support their claims about the death of class in the political arena. Moreover, Clark and Lipset did not demonstrate the link between changes in the economy – the growth of markets, the increase in small firms and so on – and changes in class stratification. Nor did they provide evidence to back up their assertions about the growth of the slimmer family and the growth of egalitarian family relations. Their interpretation of trends in social mobility were misguided (Hout *et al.* 1993: 270). Overall, Hout and his colleagues concluded that while the class structure of post-industrial societies is changing with the decline in manual employment and the rise of nonmanual employment, there is no evidence of classes dying. It is to the persistence of class, therefore, that sociologists should turn their attention. The task in hand is to offer explanations of why classes are so persistent and the extent to which politics is a cause rather than a consequence of the class structure and class mobility. Class, therefore, remains an important source of structured inequality within contemporary societies and the task of sociologists in the field of class analysis is to explain its continued significance despite rapid economic, social and political change.

The robustness of Hout *et al.*'s reply led Clark, Lipset and Rempel to qualify their earlier assertions. They argued 'Social classes have not died, but their political significance has declined substantially: this justifies a shift from class-centred analysis towards multi-causal explanations of political behaviour and related social phenomena'. Again, they drew on evidence from the FAUI project to demonstrate the political importance of the young, affluent members of the middle class who are preoccupied with social value issues (in line with Inglehart). Moreover, they argued that as class distinctions have become less rigid, other cleavages such as those based on race and gender have become the basis of polarisation in the political sphere (Clark *et al.* 1993: 313). Even their qualified account of the death of class, however, has been rejected. Analysing data from the Political Action surveys (Barnes and Kaase 1983; Jennings 1991), Brooks and Manza (1994) refuted Inglehart's post-materialist thesis. They found no evidence of a commitment to new types of social values. Nor did they find that post-materialism leads to a rejection of the state as an agent of change. Instead, they found evidence of 'value pluralism' in that people are concerned with economic and social issues and continue to see the state as an important institution for achieving political outcomes. Clark *et al.*'s more cautious account of the demise of class, in other words, was rejected. The protagonists in the American debate continue to differ on the importance of class in post-industrial society.

THE DEBATE IN BRITAIN

The debate on class – and especially the limitations of class analysis – among British sociologists can be found principally in the journal, *Sociology*. Pahl (1989) has argued that 'class as a concept is ceasing to do any useful work for sociology' because of the inadequate theorising about the relationship between structure, consciousness and action (SCA). The links in the chain have been theorised in an overly-deterministic fashion as if consciousness and action can be 'read off' from structure. It is widely assumed, for example, that the deprived are the most likely radicals in society. Moreover, sociologists have become increasingly preoccupied with analysing class structure and have failed to explore the consequences for consciousness and action. Sociologists have become absorbed, for example, with competing class schemas and the socio-economic criteria which define and explain them. Thus, the notion of 'class as a force for political and social change' is problematic but given their preoccupation with class structures, sociologists have increasingly ignored the problem anyway (Pahl 1989: 715).

Pahl was highly critical, therefore, of the faith placed in the concept of class in sociological investigation. Its weakness as an explanatory tool has a number of origins. First, the study of class developed in the nineteenth century when manufacturing industry was dominant and the exploitative relationship between the bourgeoisie and proletariat was stark. However, this class-based model is less relevant for a service-based economy at the end of the twentieth century. Second, interest in class developed when the nation state was all important and obtaining control of the state was a plausible way of overthrowing exploitative relationships. The globalisation of economic relations, however, has meant that the nation state is no longer the arena of class struggle. In this context, 'other forms of identity and social consciousness are coming to have greater practical relevance' (Pahl 1989: 716). Thus, class has become a catch-all concept which has undermined its usefulness. Finally, Pahl argued that the decentralisation of production means that a collective consciousness based on the workplace is unlikely to carry over into the private sphere. While the sphere of consumption has not yet been the source of new forms of collective consciousness, it is an increasingly important dimension of late twentieth-century Britain which sociologists should analyse. Furthermore, great attention should be paid to issues of locality, race, religion, gender and nation, formal and informal groups, kinship groups and so on in the study of consciousness and action. It is in relation to these cleavages that a more sophisticated theoretical understanding of the relationship between SCA will be found. Class, therefore, is no longer a key explanatory variable and reference to class actually inhibits the analysis of important phenomena in a changing society.

While it might be inappropriate to characterise Pahl's argument as a variant of liberal accounts of industrial society, there are a number of parallels between his views and those of Clark and Lipset. Like them, he sets great store by the argument that rapid change has fundamentally undermined the class structure, class inequalities, class identities and class politics. Echoing Clark and Lipset's thesis about the fragmentation of stratification, for example, he calls for research on other cleavages such as race, gender and locality as the most likely basis of collective consciousness and action. He also attaches considerable importance to the sphere of consumption as the basis of consciousness and action with the decline of manufacturing and the rise of the service economy. Unlike his American counterparts, Pahl is also critical of sociological analyses of class. The absence of theory to explain why the notion of class might be useful absorbs much of his attention. However, like Clark and Lipset, the overall thrust of his argument is that class is no longer helpful for understanding contemporary society in the face of rapid economic, social and political change.

Pahl's work generated a number of immediate responses (Crompton 1991; Marshall 1991; Mullins 1991). The principal reply to Pahl's argument came from Goldthorpe and Marshall (1992). They argued that Pahl's criticism of class analysis – and Sorensen's (1991) somewhat similar critique that Goldthorpe's analysis of social mobility lacked a satisfactory theory of how class generates inequality within the labour market – were misplaced because they had failed to distinguish Marxist and non-Marxist class analysis. Goldthorpe and Marshall affirmed their commitment to a non-Marxist analysis of class which is different from the class analysis of Marxist sociology in four respects. First, they assume no theory of history in which class conflict is the motor of social change to avoid the historicism of such accounts of development. Second, there is no expectation that relationships are inherently exploitative to allow an exploration of class compromises. Third, no assumption is made of a link between structure and agency to acknowledge the difficulties of collective action. Fourth, they reject reductionist theories of politics in order to explore the crucial role of political organisations in mobilising class identities and class interests (Goldthorpe and Marshall 1992: 385). Their analysis of class, in contrast, has three requirements. First, it requires that classes are as sharply defined as possible since the categorisations employed effect the substantive findings which emerge from research. Second, the multivariate approach should be the main method of inquiry as a way of assessing the relative significance of class and other structural cleavages and the processes behind their influence and effects. Finally, they argue that class analysis should have a time dimension drawn from longitudinal research on which to evaluate claims that class is no longer important as a result of profound economic, social and political changes (Goldthorpe and Marshall 1992: 387). If conceived in this way, criticisms levelled against class analysis are misplaced.

Goldthorpe and Marshall went on to make the case for the continuing relevance of class analysis by reviewing the findings from three substantive areas: social mobility, class and education and class politics. The study of social mobility is a way of investigating the processes of class formation or decomposition. Research on class and education addresses the extent to which society is becoming more open or closed. The study of class politics offers the opportunity to explore whether class influences partisanship and voting. The findings from each area demonstrate the continued importance of class in sociology. Finally, they stressed that their proposed research programme provides the sub-discipline with new substantive areas. They concluded that the major finding from more than three decades of research was the 'stability rather than the dynamism of class relations' and the 'remarkable persistence' of class even during periods of rapid economic, social and political change (Goldthorpe and Marshall 1992: 393). The stability of class relations, they argued, has two implications. First, it undermines liberal theories of the death of class and Marxist theories of the dynamism of class. Second, theoretical concerns need to be 'radically reoriented' since, 'They must focus, not on the explanation of social change via class relations, but rather on understanding the processes that underlie the profound resistance to change that such relations offer'. Like Hout and his associates, therefore, Goldthorpe and Marshall emphasised the persistence of class and the need to offer explanations of the mechanisms by which stability is maintained.

Goldthorpe and Marshall's response did not, however, satisfy Pahl (1993). He expressed his continued dissatisfaction with the absence of theory in class analysis, and Goldthorpe and Marshall's emphasis on methodological rigour. Their argument demonstrates their preoccupation with correlations rather than explanations. While Goldthorpe has identified classes as demographic entities, for example, he has failed to justify their being called classes. Pahl concluded that Goldthorpe and Marshall's programme of research is limited for without theory there is no theoretical debate, and without theoretical debate in class analysis, the concept of class is of little use (Pahl 1993: 256). Other participants in the debate have also called for a more theoretically informed analysis of class (Holton and Turner 1994; Lee 1994; Scott 1994b). The most recent contributors to the controversy, however, have acknowledged Pahl's critique (Breen and Rottman 1995b). They developed Goldthorpe's implicit (rational choice) theory of class. Classes are defined in terms of advantage and power and individual behaviour is rationally shaped by the command of such resources. Thus, those with advantages employ strategies for retaining their privileged position while the disadvantaged seek ways of alleviating their deprivation. Breen and Rottman (1995: 453b) also conceded that class analysis has had 'little difficulty' in establishing an association between class and a range of outcomes, but it has experienced 'very great difficulties' in specifying the mechanisms by which class is associated with certain outcomes. The future task of class analysis is to design research to test existing theories of class which explain 'how class comes to have the effects it has' (Breen and Rottman 1995: 468b). Overall, the major issue at stake is the extent to which rapid economic, social and political change has affected class structures, class inequalities, class identities and class politics, and how sociologists might capture the changes which have occurred and the continuities which persist in contemporary societies.

What is somewhat surprising about the debate on the demise or persistence of class is that it is being conducted among sociologists in two countries which are often portrayed as being at opposite ends of the spectrum. That is, America is characterised as a classless society while Britain is portrayed as a class-bound society. America, for example, has long been described as 'exceptional' in exhibiting high levels of mobility and openness in comparison with European nations (de Tocqueville 1848). The high level of flux within American society has been used to explain the weakness of the working class and the absence of socialism in the US. A national culture embodying the notions of unlimited opportunities and classlessness of a distinctly new society developed instead (Sombart 1906). The idea of American exceptionalism remains popular having recently been restated, for example, by Lipset and other contributors to Shafer's (1991) edited collection *Is America Different: A New Look at American Exceptionalism*. Similarly, Hochschild's (1995) study of race and class, *Facing Up to the American Dream*, has noted that beliefs about opportunity and classlessness remain a central ideology of Americans. The American Dream – 'the promise that all Americans have a reasonable chance to achieve success as they define it – material or otherwise – through their own efforts, and to attain virtue and fulfilment through success' – still captures the view that Americans have of themselves and non-Americans have of America (Hochschild 1995: xvi).

In contrast, Britain has long been portrayed as a class-bound society. While opportunities for mobility have been plentiful at least since the Second World War and Britain is far from being a closed society, the prevailing view is that it is a society still heavily structured by class. As Halsey *et al.* demonstrated in *Origins and Destinations* (1980), family background still exerts a considerable influence on occupational outcomes. The relative chances of entering the middle class remain unequal (Goldthorpe *et al.* 1980) Moreover, Britain is a highly unequal society in that class inequalities are to be found in all spheres of life (Reid 1989). Finally, as Marshall and his colleagues found in *Social Class in Modern Britain*, people are well aware of class inequalities and may even be described as 'class conscious' in that their objective class position and subjective perceptions of class are an important influence on socio-political attitudes and behaviour (Marshall *et al.* 1988). The national culture is thus informed by class. Thus, while America is often held up to be the ultimate example of a classless society, Britain is the exemplar of a class society. The controversy over class, however, undermines these somewhat stereotypical images of America and Britain. Some American sociologists, after all, argue that class is becoming more important while some British sociologists argue that class is becoming less important. The debate is not what popular images of the two nations would lead us to expect forcing us, in turn, to question those images. Was America an open society? Is it a land of opportunity now? Was Britain a closed society? Is it class-bound today? What are the main differences and similarities between the two countries? These questions, of course, can only be answered through comparative research on the two countries. Now, it could be argued that there is a huge amount of historical and contemporary on class embracing the US, Britain and a whole host of other nations (Brooks 1994; Erikson and Goldthorpe 1992a, Esping-Andersen 1993; Mann 1986). However, there are very few books which introduce this comparative research in an easily accessible way to students. The focus of attention is either on one country with only a passing reference to another nation (Scase 1992; Edgell 1993; Crompton 1993). These texts are not genuinely comparative in design. Otherwise, the net is cast very wide to include a large number of countries (Hamilton and Hirzowicz 1993; Breen and Rottman 1995b). It is often hard, as a result, to establish a coherent picture. In other words, comparative research has been drawn upon in a limited fashion or the empirical findings reported in such a way that students find them difficult to digest.

This book is a focussed comparison of social class in America and Britain. It is an introductory text which has been written with students in mind. It reviews the general debates on social class discussed above and specific debates and specific debates on different social classes in the two countries. The main theoretical debates in America and Britain are summarised and evaluated. The book also draws on empirical research from both nations and some of the key findings are reproduced as tables in the text. Special attention has been given to examining research on social class which has drawn on quantitative and qualitative methods of enquiry. The sub-discipline of class analysis has become increasingly associated with the statistical analysis of large data-sets (Crompton 1991; 1993; Savage 1996). For students using this material, however, the task of evaluating the material is extremely daunting, and it is sometimes difficult to see the wood for the trees. Nevertheless, quantitative data is extremely important for examining macro trends in one or more nations. Erikson and Goldthorpe's (1992a) international research on social mobility is a case in point. Care, therefore, has been taken to present the most important statistical findings on social class in America and Britain which students might find useful. At the same time, the findings from qualitative research have also been examined for the micro-sociological processes at work in both nations. Historical and case study research, after all, provides important insights into the actions of people who constitute social classes and whose strategies, values and beliefs, and attitudes and behaviour play a crucial part in class formation (Crompton 1993; Devine 1996a). DiPrete's (1989) historical research on the professionalisation of high-level nonmanual work in the US comes to mind. The aim throughout the book has been to draw on the complimentary strengths of each research tradition as a means of addressing debates and controversies within class analysis from a variety of different angles. This book, therefore, has been written as an accessible introduction to students on debates about social class in America and Britain. The comparison is particularly appropriate since America is frequently seen as an exemplar of classlessness while Britain is usually held to be the class society *par excellence*.

Sociology, of course, is inherently comparative. As Durkheim (1938: 157) famously asserted, 'comparative sociology is not a particular branch of sociology, it is sociology itself, in so far as it ceases to be purely descriptive and aspires to account for facts'. There is, then, no distinctive comparative method within the discipline. That said, comparative analysis is increasingly associated with the study of social phenomena across two or more nation states (Kohn 1987). Its advantage lies in the ability to compare and contrast the patterns and trends in a social phenomenon like social class and to explore the general conditions under which it is found and the particular form which it takes across countries like America and Britain. As Kohn has argued, comparative research is indispensable for 'establishing the generality of findings and the validity of interpretations derived from single-nation studies' and for 'forcing us to revise our interpretations to take account of cross-national differences and inconsistencies that could never be uncovered in single-nation research (Kohn 1987: 713). Comparative research, however, is far from easy. The main difficulty is that of juggling the twin demands of examining the similarities and differences between two countries simultaneously (Przeworski and Teune 1970). On the one hand, the search for comparisons between nations often leads to a neglect of context in the search for potential universal features. On the other hand, the search for contrasts invariably leads to a focus on context and a neglect of universal explanations. Most comparative research draws on quantitative analysis but there are problems with such methods of investigation. It is invariably difficult to obtain comparative data which have been collected and analysed using similar methods. Nor is it easy to be confident that different sources of data enjoy the same level of adequacy (Scott 1986). There is also the problem of investigating social phenomena which might be objectively the same although subjectively different across varied cultural contexts (Mackie and Marsh 1995). Comparative research, in other words, has its disadvantages, and there are competing views of how such difficulties might be overcome (Oyen 1990; Ragin 1987; Ragin 1991).

Arguably, however, the advantages of comparative research still out-weigh its disadvantages. Comparative analysis also provides the opportunity to compare and contrast research traditions. In the US, for example, the 'status attainment' tradition has been dominant in the study of social mobility. The focus of attention is on the extent to which such factors as educational attainment or socio-economic prestige affect individual success (Blau and Duncan 1967; Featherman and Hauser 1978). In contrast, social mobility in Britain has been studied from a 'class structural' perspective which assumes that individual and group life-chances are shaped by relationships in the economic sphere (Goldthorpe *et al.* 1987; Marshall *et al.* 1988). Examining the varied ways in which research questions are posed and the manner in which they are answered forces the sociologist to think in novel ways rather than always be bound by a specific national research tradition. A comparative perspective, therefore, challenges the researcher to think explicitly about how social phenomena might be conceptualised theoretically and operationalised empirically. It is also useful to note how sociological debates in one country influence debates in another. The controversy surrounding the underclass in America and Britain is a case in point. After all, the main proponent of the underclass thesis in the US has been more than happy to comment on the phenomenon in Britain. Murray's (1990; 1994) predictions about the rise of an underclass stimulated an important debate on poverty, deprivation and social polarisation (Morris 1994). His most recent pronouncements on the emergence of a 'new rabble' (Murray 1995) will, no doubt, fuel controversy. The debates over intelligence and meritocracy in America (Herrnstein and Murray 1994; Fraser 1995) and Britain (Marshall and Swift 1993; Saunders 1995) is the most recent example of a debate taking place simultaneously across America and Britain. An appreciation of the international flavour to these controversies also provides a strong vantage point from which to evaluate whether America can be portrayed as a classless society and the extent to which Britain can be characterised as a class-bound nation.

There are, of course, well-known similarities and differences between the two nations. They have similar economic histories. Britain industrialised somewhat before America but the US soon experienced the growth of large enterprises which quickly outstripped their British counterparts in size (Scott 1986). Both nations have witnessed industrial change with the decline of manufacturing and the growth in services. Both of them have witnessed occupational change such as the growth of high-level technical personnel including professional scientists and engineers (*Statistical*

Abstract of the US 1994; IER 1995). To a greater or lesser degree, they have similar trends in income inequality over the last ten years (Harrison and Bluestone 1988; Levy 1987). Finally, in the 1980s and 1990s, both countries have seen the dominance of a political economy in which the free operation of the market has been paramount. Such principles were translated into policies by the governments of Reagan and Bush in the US and Thatcher and Major in the UK. These policies – including cuts to mothers on welfare – were pursued with renewed vigour by Newt Gingrich under the auspices of his 'Contract with America' (*New York Times* 19 April 1995). The politics of the two nations over the last ten to fifteen years, therefore, have been remarkably similar.

The differences in the economics and politics of the two countries are also well known. While Britain has competed in the world economy for some time (Gamble 1990), the American economy has long been a protected market, and it is only recently that it has experienced foreign competition (Esping-Andersen 1993). Britain remains more of an industrial economy than the US which has a larger service sector. Britain has a higher rate of unemployment than in America because there are more low-level 'junk jobs' in the consumer services sector (Jacobs 1993). Many of these poorly-paid jobs with few fringe benefits are filled by young people and members of various ethnic minorities. It is for this reason that the unemployment rate in America is half that of Britain, although the nature of the labour market also explains why poverty is such an endemic feature of America in comparison to Britain (Phillips 1990; Townsend 1993). The prevalence of poverty in the US can also be explained with reference to the limited welfare state which grew out of the New Deal in the 1930s in comparison with the more extensive welfare state which developed under the Labour Government of 1945–51 (Skocpol 1992; 1995). Finally, of course, the Democratic Party was able to establish a broad coalition of voters to elect Bill Clinton into presidential office in 1992 and 1996 while an increasingly social democratic Labour Party has failed to gain widespread support to obtain office in the early 1990s. Differences in the economics and politics of the two countries, therefore, are plain to see.

RATIONALE OF THE BOOK

These impressions of the similarities and differences between America and Britain, however, do not provide a comprehensive picture of the nature of structured social inequality in the two countries. This book is a *systematic* sociological investigation of class in the two nations. It is divided into two parts. Part I focuses on general debates in class analysis surrounding class structures, class processes and class consciousness. Part II is devoted to specific debates on each of the five major classes which can be identified in each country: namely social power (the capitalist class and the petty bourgeoisie), social closure (the upper middle class), proletarianisation (the lower middle class), embourgeoisement (the working class) and social exclusion (the underclass). It will be argued that both America and Britain may be characterised as class societies. They have broadly similar class structures, class processes and class consciousness. With similar economic histories, it is not surprising to find that the overall shape of the class structure in the two countries is quite similar. Both countries have experienced an increase in absolute mobility since the Second World War. Finally, Americans and Britons are well aware of class in their respective nations although it does not necessarily shape their socio-political proclivities.

There are notable differences as well. The size of the different classes, and the occupations which comprise them, vary across the two countries. The *de facto* rates of social mobility are higher in America than Britain. Lastly, class awareness in America does not translate into political behaviour to the same extent as in Britain. These differences, however, are not as great as are often supposed. America is not as 'open' and Britain is not as 'closed' as popular images of the two nations imply. Americans are not unconscious of class and Britons are not exclusively class conscious. The differences between the two countries, in other words, are not as great as less systematic enquiries suggest. Thus, despite rapid economic, social and political change, social class remains a major form of structured inequality in the two nations under investigation. Indeed, against the background of hardening inequalities in America and Britain (Westergaard 1995), the stability and persistence of class in each nation should feature highly on the research agenda of class analysis. The need to examine the mechanisms by which classes are constantly being remade in sometimes similar and sometimes different ways across the two nations is addressed in the concluding chapter.

This book is primarily about class stratification. No comparison of America or Britain, however, could fail to consider other sources of structured inequality; namely, race and gender. After all, America comprises many ethnic groups as a result of a long history of immigration. In 1990, African Americans comprised 12 per cent of the total population and are estimated to rise to 12.5 per cent by 1995. Hispanics (especially Mexicans who have comprised the biggest wave of immigrants into America in the last ten years) comprised 8.8 per cent of the total population in 1990, and the figure is expected to rise to 9.9 per cent by 1995 (*Statistical Abstract of the US 1994*). Not surprisingly, the relative significance of race and class has been a source of major controversy among American sociologists (Wilson 1978; 1987). Britain's ethnic minorities, in contrast, constitute a smaller proportion of the population. An analysis of the 1991 census showed that they comprised only 5.5 per cent of the total population, over half of them coming from South Asia, with Indians comprising the largest group (Owen 1992: 1–2). That said, there is a growing interest in the different occupational profiles of ethnic minority groups – principally South Asian, Blacks, Chinese and others – and, by implication, the varied class positions which they may occupy (Jones 1993; Robinson 1988; Sarre 1989). The controversy on the rise of the black middle class in America is now the source of debate in Britain (Daye 1994; Phillips and Sarre 1995; Small 1994). This debate in addressed in Chapter 6 while the debate on the black underclass is considered in Chapter 9. Rather than neglect issues of race, therefore, the book seeks to examine the complex interdependence of class and race.

The interdependence of class and gender is also considered in each of the chapters in this book. America and Britain have witnessed the increasing participation of women in the labour market since the Second World War (Dex and Shaw 1986; Jacobs 1989; Reskin and Hartmann 1986; Reskin and Padavic 1994; Stockman *et al.* 1995). Women now constitute over half of the labour force in each country in that 58 per cent of American women and 53 per cent of British women were economically active in 1993 (*Statistical Abstract of the US 1994*; *Social Focus on Women* 1995). This trend has led feminist sociologists on both sides of the Atlantic to call for the integration of women into class analysis (Sorensen 1994). The debate has been especially trenchant in Britain where sociologists such as Crompton (1992; 1993) have maintained a dual interest in class analysis and gender relations in contrast to America where the study of women's employment is somewhat divorced from the status attainment tradition, despite the preoccupation with income (England and Farkas 1986). That said, the debate on gender and class has focused on a narrow range of questions: principally, what is the unit of class analysis? This controversy is addressed in Chapter 2 although issues of gender are also prominent in the discussions on patterns and trends in social mobility and class attitudes and class politics. The position of women in each of the social classes is also addressed with reference to debates on the under-presentation of women in the middle class (Crompton 1995; Witz 1995) and the feminisation and deskilling of clerical work (Fine 1990; Strom 1992). As with issues of race, therefore, interest in class divisions among women is growing, and promises to widen the scope and rationale of class analysis. Finally, of course, it has been argued that race and gender have become more important forms of stratification in contemporary society than class stratification. A book which purports to examine the *relative* significance of class as a form of structured social inequality, therefore, cannot ignore the relationship between class, race and gender.

This book draws on a wide range of empirical material of a quantitative and qualitative kind from both countries in order to evaluate the debates on the relative significance of class in post-industrial or post-modern societies. It may not be as theoretically informed as some critics of class analysis might like. This is not to suggest, however, that the book is atheoretical. On the contrary, it draws on a general theory of social classes which are defined in terms of differential amounts of power and advantage. The economic, cultural and social resources which members of classes command shape the opportunities and constraints which influence their life-styles, identities, interests, attitudes and behaviour to a greater or lesser degree. Those in advantaged positions, for example, seek to maintain their privileges while those in disadvantaged positions try to obtain some privileges for themselves. The powerful, however, enjoy ample opportunities while the powerless face numerous constraints. The self-maintaining properties of the class structure, therefore, explain the remarkable stability and persistence of class relations although the mechanisms by which classes are constantly being remade vary over time and place (Breen and Rottman 1995a; Erikson and Goldthorpe 1992a; Goldthorpe *et al.* 1987). The book also addresses specific theoretical debates about each of the classes and the extent to which they have disappeared, changed or remained the same. The controversies surrounding the nature of the capitalist class and the working class in the late twentieth century are a case in point. Theoretical debates tend to lose their momentum, however, in the absence of relevant empirical evidence. It is the empirical evaluation of theoretical issues which provides the momentum which class analysis in particular and sociology in general requires if the sub-discipline and the discipline as a whole can be described as a progressive social science (Pawson 1989; 1993).

The sociological literature on social class in America and Britain is vast. As a result, it is extremely difficult to do justice to all of the debates and controversies in class analysis across the two nations. Nevertheless, an attempt has been made to explore a wide range of material from a comparative perspective, and to present it to students in an accessible way. Readers in each country, no doubt, will sometimes feel that some issues should have been covered in more depth. It is an enterprise which I hope to fulfil in the future. In the meantime, this book offers a critical evaluation of the major debate on the demise or persistence of class in the two nations, and the wider implications for stereotypical views of America as a classless society and Britain as a class-bound society. In doing so, some new areas for research in the sub-discipline have been identified with an emphasis on the study of change and continuity in class relations in comparative perspective. This book, therefore, shows that class analysis has a 'promising future' in America and Britain.

Part I

Chapter 2

Class Structures

The study of class structures which involves placing people into objective class locations has been one of the most contentious issues in class analysis in America and Britain over the last twenty years. Dissatisfaction with class categorisations used by government officials and market researchers (Rose 1995) has led sociologists to devise a variety of theoretically-informed schemas which have produced different maps of the class structure. The different findings about the overall shape of the class structure and the specific boundaries between the classes have been hotly contested. Considerable debate has also surrounded the choice of the unit of class since the use of different approaches in the allocation of men and women to class positions has also led to different results. Both debates, as we shall see, have raised fundamental questions about the rationale of class analysis. Much of the controversy surrounding these issues has taken the form of theoretical debate in terms of conceptual clarifications and re-clarifications. Rather than become embroiled in essentialist debates about class, however, this chapter will focus on the empirical results arising from attempts to place men and women into a structure of class positions in America and Britain.

This chapter is divided into three parts. First, the class schemas devised by the American sociologist Erik Olin Wright (1985; 1989) and the British sociologist John H. Goldthorpe (1987; Erikson and Goldthorpe 1992a) are outlined, and particular attention is paid to their empirical findings regarding the shape of the class structure in America and Britain. We shall see that their class schemas produce different pictures of the class structure although each class schema produces remarkably similar findings across the two countries. Wright identifies a substantial proletariat amounting to nearly half of the working population in America and Britain while the middle classes and the bourgeoisie are relatively small in comparison. Goldthorpe, in contrast, identifies a much smaller working class constitut- ing approximately a third of the employed and much larger middle classes across the two countries. Wright and Goldthorpe also differ on their explanations of the shape of the class structures they found. Wright argues that the working class is large as a result of proletarianisation. Any trend towards the upgrading of the occupational structure has been countered by the absorption of sections of the middle class into the working class. Goldthorpe, however, argues that there has been an upgrading of the occupational structure as manual employment has declined and low-level and high nonmanual employment has increased in the second half of the twentieth century. Their divergent findings, in other words, have produced different interpretations of the shape of the class structure over time.

Second, attention turns to the inclusion of women in class analysis. It will be seen that Wright collected information on women's employment but his class categories fail to capture the diversity of women's labour market experiences. The majority of women are relegated to the proletariat in both countries. Goldthorpe did not collect information on women's employment so they are excluded from his analysis of the class structure altogether. However, in Marshall *et al.* the analysis of women's individual employment characteristics using Goldthorpe's class categories illustrates that the shape of the class structure and the size of different classes is highly 'gendered'. Women, for example, dominate routine nonmanual employment. Revisions are required, however, to Goldthorpe's essentially 'male' class schema to capture the nature of women's conditions and relations of employment. Further thought also needs to be given to how static class structures embody the dynamic nature of women's employment across the family life-cycle by including non-employed groups like housewives who are usually excluded from conventional class analysis.

Third, the evaluation of the competing class schemas in Marshall *et al.* (1988) will be considered as will subsequent criticisms of their adjudication procedures. It will be seen that Goldthorpe's class schema is superior to Wright's class schema in terms of internal (criterion) validity and external (construct) validity. That said, Goldthorpe's class schema is not above criticism since the procedures by which men and women are allocated to class positions from information on occupational title and employment status is not entirely clear. Direct information on individual conditions and relations of employment might offer a more accurate picture of the class structure than the proxy indicators currently used. However, Marshall *et al.*'s evaluation of the competing schemas has also been subject to a variety of criticisms. The adjudication process has been accused of bias (Pawson 1990) and dismissed as a worthless exercise (Crompton 1993). It will be argued that the task of clearly defining concepts of class, operationalising them for empirical research and evaluating different approaches to the study of the class structure is important. That said, it is also important not to lose sight of the fact that class schemas are heuristic devices which have their limitations in capturing the dynamic nature of the class structure and the diverse forms which class action might take. Overall, however, the study of class structures via class schemas is a serious exercise for those who argue that social class is a powerful form of structured social inequality in post-industrial or post-modern societies like America and Britain.

AMERICAN AND BRITISH CLASS SCHEMAS

The most prominent American sociologist who has concerned himself with mapping the class structure is the neo-Marxist Erik Olin Wright. His work has come to occupy such a prominent position within class analysis since he has been firmly committed 'to develop empirical research agendas firmly rooted within not only the categories, but the logic, of Marxist theory' (Wright 1976: 10). To this end, he coordinated the *Comparative Project on Class Structure and Class Consciousness* in the late 1970s and early 1980s. Wright has also written numerous books over the last twenty years including *Class, Crisis and the State* (1976), *Classes* (1985), *The Debate on Classes* (1989a) and *Interrogating Inequality* (1994), and many articles written alone or with various collaborators (see, for example, Wright 1976; 1980; Wright and Singlemann 1982; Wright and Martin 1987).

One of the major themes in Wright's work has been 'how to analyze the class location of those positions in the social structure which are often labelled middle class' (Wright 1978: 27). The theoretical development of Wright's class schema – from six classes distinguished on the basis of control and autonomy to twelve classes defined in terms of the exploitation of different assets – has been extensively discussed elsewhere (Breen and Rottman 1995a; Crompton 1993; Edgell 1993; Marshall *et al.* 1988). Suffice to say, Wright argued that classes are defined by the assets they control 'which lead them to adopt certain strategies within exchange relations, and which in turn determine the outcomes of those market transactions' (Wright 1985: 73). The owners of the means of production exploit their property assets while the nonowners exploit their organisational assets or skill/credential assets to varying degrees. On this basis, Wright distinguished between three owning classes and three nonowning classes (see Table 2: 1).

Using data from a national telephone survey conducted by the University of Michigan Survey Research Centre in 1980, Wright used his second class map to outline the shape of the American and Swedish class structures. He operationalised ownership assets by collecting information on self employment and number of employees, organisational assets by collecting information on decision-making and supervisory authority and skills assets in terms of occupation, educational credentials and job autonomy (Wright 1985: 150). He found that the proletariat is the largest class consisting of

Table 2.1. Distribution of the labour force in the class matrix using the exploitation-centered concept of class[1]

Assets in the means of production			
Owners	Non-owners (wage labourers)		
1 Bourgeoisie	4 Expert managers	7 Semi-credentialled managers	10 Uncredentialled managers
USA 1.8%	USA 3.9%	USA 6.2%	USA 2.3%
Sweden 0.7%	Sweden 4.4%	Sweden 4.0%	Sweden 2.5%
Britain 2.0%	Britain 5.6%	Britain 7.9%	Britain 3.2%
2 Small employers	5 Expert supervisors	8 Semi-credentialled supervisors	11 Uncredentialled supervisors
USA 6.0%	USA 3.7%	USA 6.8%	USA 6.9%
Sweden 4.8%	Sweden 3.8%	Sweden 3.2%	Sweden 3.1%
Britain 4.5%	Britain 2.2%	Britain 3.8%	Britain 3.4%
3 Petty bourgeoisie	6 Expert non-managers	9 Semi-credentialled workers	12 Proletarians
USA 6.9%	USA 3.4%	USA 12.2%	USA 39.9%
Sweden 5.4%	Sweden 6.8%	Sweden 17.8%	Sweden 43.5%
Britain 6.0%	Britain 4.1%	Britain 14.4%	Britain 42.9%

Skill/credential assets

USA N = 1487   Sweden N = 1179   Britain N = 1315

[1] Distribution are of people working in the labour force, thus excluding unemployed, housewives, pensioners etc.

Sources: Wright (1985), Table 6.1, p. 195; Marshall *et al.* (1988), Table 3.1, p. 36.

approximately 40 per cent of the labour force in both countries. Adding together those contradictory locations which have marginal control over organisation and skill assets (categories 9 and 11) to this total, proletarians constitute about 60 per cent of the labour force. Wright also found that the owners of the means of production are small in amounting to 13 per cent. The bourgeoisie amounts to less than 2 per cent in both countries. The class distributions were found to be the same in the US and Sweden (Wright 1985: 194–5). Wright also pointed to differences in the two classes structures. First, he noted that there is a higher proportion of people engaged in supervision in the US compared with Sweden. Second, he noted that the working class is larger in Sweden (61 per cent compared with 52 per cent) than in the US if pure proletarians are combined with semi-credentialed workers (cells 9 and 12). Third, he found twice as many non-managerial experts in Sweden than the US (7 per cent compared with 3 per cent). Finally, he found more self-employed in the US than in Sweden (15 per cent compared with 11 per cent). Looking closely at the different cells, therefore, highlighted some of the differences in the class structures of the two countries (Wright 1985: 196–7).

Overall, Wright highlighted the similarities between America and Sweden since both countries had a large proletariat, a small bourgeoisie and small middle-class groupings. The dominance of the proletariat in the second half of the twentieth century, he argued, was the result of proletarianisation. That is, sections of the middle class were being absorbed into the working class as a result of deskilling. Proletarianisation has led to a growth in the size of the proletariat in the overall class structure (Braverman 1974: Wright and Singlemann 1982). With reference to differences between the US and Sweden, he argued that 'the differences in the authority distributions in the two societies and the linkage between authority and credentials accounts for most of the differences in the distributions of contradictory class locations in the two societies' (Wright 1985: 222). Wright noted that the supervisory aspects of managerial functions had been delegated to effectively working-class occupations. This was the result, he argued, of the limited power of the labour movement (and especially that of managerial employees) in the US which had in turn led American capitalists to integrate skilled workers into supervisory positions thereby weakening the labour movement still further. Moreover, the strong unions in Sweden controlled workers while supervisors performed the same function in the US (Wright 1985: 224–5). It is the varying political power of capital and labour in the two countries which explains their different class structures.

For comparative purposes, British data collected by Marshall *et al.* (1988: 36) under the auspices of Wright's project have been included in Table 2: 1. The evidence shows that America and Britain have remarkably similar class structures. Again, the proletariat is the largest class consisting of 42 per cent of the working population (rising to 69 per cent if uncredentialled supervisors and semi-credentialled workers are included). Similarly, the owning classes are approximately the same size (14.7 per cent in the US compared with 12.5 per cent in Britain). The major difference lies in the number of managers and supervisors in each country. While the US has a relatively high number of supervisors as Wright noted with reference to Sweden, Britain has a high number of managers. While managers constitute 12.4 per cent of employed respondents in America, they constitute 16.7 per cent of employed respondents in Britain. The most notable difference within this category is that of semi-credentialled managers (6.2 per cent in the US compared with 7.9 per cent in Britain). In other words, there is a weaker link between authority and credentials in Britain than in America. Overall, however, it is similarities rather than differences which are most striking between America, Britain and, for that matter, Sweden.

Wright's monograph was well reviewed and generated much excitement (Mann 1986: 839). Some of the flavour of interest in his book is captured in *The Debate on Classes* edited by Wright (1985). Numerous commentators (Carter 1986; Rose and Marshall 1986), however, noted the similarities between Wright's Marxist class schema and a Weberian analysis of the middle classes. His characterisation of the middle classes as internally differentiated according to different assets bore a striking resemblance to Weberian concerns with conditions and relations of employment. Wright initially rebuffed such critics, emphasising the superiority of the Marxist approach over the Weberian approach on political, theoretical and methodological grounds (Wright 1989: 319–20). More recently, however, he has acknowledged that the two traditions 'may not be so divergent'. He has conceded that 'as Marxist accounts of these 'middle class' categories have become more sophisticated, the line of demarcation between these two traditions has become somewhat less sharply drawn' (Wright 1994: 92).

At this juncture, it is appropriate to look more closely at a neo-Weberian analysis of the class structure as embodied in the work of British sociologist, John H. Goldthorpe although the label 'Weberian' is one which he reluctant to take on (Goldthorpe 1990). He devised a map of the class structure in order to address issues of social mobility; namely, the movement of people between distinct social classes. His most famous publications include *Social Mobility and Class Structure in Modern Britain* which was published in collaboration with Catriona Llewellyn and Clive Payne in 1980 and as a second edition in 1987. More recently, his comparative research on social mobility with Robert Erikson has seen the publication of *The Constant Flux* (Erikson and Goldthorpe 1992a). Like Wright, Goldthorpe has also published an extensive range of articles alone (Goldthorpe 1984; 1990) and with colleagues (Erikson and Goldthorpe 1985; Erikson *et al.* 1979; 1982).

The theoretical development of Goldthorpe's class schemas has also been widely discussed elsewhere (Breen and Rottman 1995b; Clarke *et al.* 1990; Crompton 1993; Marshall 1990). Needless to say, Goldthorpe abandoned the Hope-Goldthorpe scale of social desirability as a means of distinguishing between classes in preference for the occupational groups and employment statuses by OPCS in the 1980s. His comparative work, embracing countries with large proportions of farmers and farm labourers, led him to increase the number of classes from seven to twelve. Indeed, the recent publication of the cumulative findings of the comparative research programme has seen Goldthorpe and his colleague Erikson reformulate the rationale for his class schema. The aim of the schema, they argue, 'is to differentiate positions within *labour markets* and *production units*, or more specifically, one could say, to differentiate such positions in terms of the *employment relations* that they entail' (Erikson and Goldthorpe 1992a: 37). Drawing on Marx and Weber, they go on to argue that 'employment relations are crucial to the delineation of the structure of class positions within modern society' (Erikson and Goldthorpe 1992a: 37). On this basis, they distinguish between a basic threefold division of class positions – employers, self-employed workers and employees – and then divide these groups further into large employers, small employers (distinguishing between industry and agriculture), self-employed workers employed in industry and agriculture, and employees who are differentiated according to a range of market and work situations. The main line of division based on the form of regulation of employment is between employees engaged in a service relationship and those employees on a labour contract with a range of intermediate positions in between (Erikson and Goldthorpe 1993: 41–2). The basic threefold division of class positions in terms of employment relations is more explicitly developed than before but the detailed structure of Goldthorpe's class schema, especially in relation to employees, remains much the same.

Erikson and Goldthorpe recoded respondents from a variety of data sets including America (the 1973 'Occupational Change in a Generation Replicate' by Featherman and Hauser (1978)) and England and Wales (the 1972 'Oxford National Occupational Mobility Enquiry' by Goldthorpe (1980)) into his class schema. Table 2.2 shows the shape of the class structure in each country employing the seven-class version of the schema. The US and England and Wales have broadly similar class structures. America has a somewhat larger category of non-manual workers than England and Wales (46 per cent compared with 42 per cent). England and Wales, however, have a larger class of manual workers in the two countries (55 per cent compared with 50 per cent). It is also notable within this class that England and Wales have a high proportion of skilled manual workers (33 per cent) while the US has a high proportion of non-skilled manual workers (26 per cent) (Erikson and Goldthorpe 1992a: 328). The common features of the class structures of the two countries can be explained with reference to the shared economic history of the rise of the nonmanual employment and the decline of manual employment since the Second World War. The differences within classes can be explained with reference to the expansion and contraction of occupational groups over time which is related to the

Table 2.2. The class structure of Britain, the USA and other nations in the
CASMIN project

Goldthorpe Classes	ENG[1]	FRA	FRG	HUN	IRL	NIR	POL	SCO	SWE	USA	AUS	JAP
Service class	25	21	28	15	14	18	18	21	24	28	27	24
Routine non-manual	09	10	05	07	09	09	02	09	08	11	08	16
Petty bourgeoisie	08	10	07	02	08	10	02	06	08	07	12	13
Farmers	02	11	04	01	22	10	25	03	05	03	07	10
Skilled workers	33	24	37	31	20	26	31	33	30	24	27	20
Non-skilled workers	22	21	18	30	21	24	19	25	22	26	16	14
Agricultural labourers	02	03	01	14	07	03	03	03	02	01	02	03
Total	100	100	100	100	100	100	100	100	100	100	100	100

[1] ENG – England and Wales; FRA – France; FRG – Federal Republic of Germany;
HUN – Hungary; IRL – Ireland; NIR – Northern Ireland; POL – Poland; SCO –
Scotland; SWE – Sweden; USA – United States of America; AUS – Australia;
JAP – Japan.

Source: Erikson and Goldthorpe (1992a), Table 6.2, p. 193; Table 9.3, p. 328,
Table 10.3, p. 353.

overall social division of labour. Goldthorpe's class schema, therefore,
produced a very different picture of the class structures of America and
Britain to those of Wright. Goldthorpe's portrayal of both countries having
relatively large middle classes and small working classes is in sharp contrast,
of course, to Wright's picture of a large proletariat and small middle classes
in America and Britain.

Goldthorpe's class schema been subject to much criticism over the years
(Ahrne 1990; Barbalet 1980; Binns 1977; Crompton 1980; Penn 1981),
and Erikson and Goldthorpe's recent reformulation has not escaped critical
comment either. Their argument that it is possible to distinguish as many
classes 'as it proves empirically useful to distinguish for the analytical
purposes in hand' (Erikson and Goldthorpe 1992a: 46) has met with
much criticism (Rose 1995). More recently, it has been argued that the
class schema no longer has a conceptual rationale. Rather, Goldthorpe's
research programme has become degenerative rather than progressive as
he has increasingly focused on nominal categories and justified them on
pragmatic predictive grounds. These nominal categories have become ends
in themselves rather than a provisional step in an analysis of the demographic formation of social classes (Scott 1996; Morris and Scott 1996;
Crompton 1996). These issues will be discussed further in due course. A
fundamental criticism which has been levelled against Goldthorpe has been
his failure to incorporate women into his class schema. Since both Wright

and Goldthorpe have commented on this issue, attention now turns to the debate on women and class analysis.

WOMEN AND CLASS ANALYSIS

Despite the recasting of his theoretical ideas, Wright (1978; 1985; 1989b) has constantly argued that (male) workers and their (female) spouses do not have divergent interests and that the family is the unit of analysis. Information on the male head of household is an appropriate indicator of a family's class position. Nevertheless, he actually allocated the male and female respondents of his survey to a class position according to their individual social relations of production in practice. The small number of housewives (170) in his American sample (who only featured because no employed person in the household was available for interview) were omitted from the analysis. Wright found that the class distribution between men and women differed in both the United States and Sweden in that 'women in the labour force are disproportionately in the working class, while men are disproportionately in exploiting class positions, particularly the capitalist class and managerial positions' (Wright 1985: 197). As Table 2.3 shows, he found that women formed a 'clear majority' of the proletariat in that 60 per cent of all workers were women in both countries. Wright concluded, 'The image which is still present in many Marxist accounts that the working class consists primarily of male factory workers simply does not hold true any longer (if one adopts the concept of class proposed here)' (Wright 1985: 198).

Examining the class distribution within sexes, Wright also found that a third of all men in America and Sweden are exploiters (employers, managers and experts) while only a fifth of women occupied such positions. Over half (52.8 per cent) of the women in gainful employment are in the working class compared with less than a third (29 per cent) of men (Wright 1985: 198). Finally, looking at the class distribution of men and women within age groups, he found that the proportion of women who are working class does not vary across age groups while the proportion of men in the working class declines until middle age and rises slightly among older men. Conversely, the number of men who are managers increases in middle age while there is a substantial decrease in the number of women in managerial positions among the older age groups. The findings suggest 'that men have much greater probabilities of promotional mobility from working-class positions into managerial positions than women do, particularly during the early and middle stages of careers' (Wright 1985: 199).

Again, data on the position of men and women in Wright's class categories from the British class project have been included in Table 2.3 for comparative purposes (Marshall *et al.* 1988: 90-2). Women are a

Table 2.3. Distribution of sexes within classes and distribution of class within sexes: the USA, Sweden and Britain

	Distribution of sexes within classes						Distribution of classes within sexes					
	USA		Sweden		Britain		USA		Sweden		Britain	
Class Categories	Men	Women	Men	Women	Men	Women	Men	Women	Men	Women	Men	Women
1 Capitalists	79.3	20.7	100.0	0.0	88.6	11.5	2.7	0.8	1.2	0.0	3.0	0.6
2 Small employers	66.7	33.3	80.7	19.3	84.7	15.3	7.4	4.4	7.0	2.1	6.5	1.7
3 Petty Bourgeois	50.3	49.7	75.7	24.3	68.4	31.6	6.4	7.5	7.3	3.0	7.0	4.6
4 Expert manager	75.0	25.0	87.4	12.6	71.6	28.4	5.4	2.1	6.8	1.3	6.9	3.9
5 Expert supervisor	70.3	29.7	42.9	57.1	51.7	48.3	4.8	2.4	2.9	4.9	1.9	2.6
6 Expert non-manager	47.7	52.3	56.1	43.9	37.0	63.0	3.0	3.9	6.8	6.8	2.6	6.3
7 Semi-credentialled manager	77.4	22.6	84.2	15.8	85.6	14.4	8.8	3.0	6.1	1.4	11.5	2.8
8 Semi-credentialled supervisor	75.6	24.4	76.7	23.3	78.0	22.0	9.5	3.6	4.4	1.7	5.1	2.0
9 Semi-credentialled worker	73.6	26.4	63.4	36.5	73.5	26.5	16.6	7.1	20.2	14.8	18.0	9.2
10 Uncredentialled manager	31.0	69.0	51.2	48.8	42.9	57.1	1.3	3.5	1.3	3.5	2.3	4.4
11 Uncredentialled supervisor	41.4	58.6	76.1	23.9	53.3	46.7	5.2	8.8	4.2	1.7	3.1	3.9
12 Proletarian	39.5	60.5	39.8	60.2	43.8	56.2	29.0	52.8	30.9	59.6	32.0	58.3
Totals	54.3	45.7	56.0	44.0	58.6	41.4						
Weighted N	807	680	660	519	771	544						

Sources: Wright (1985), Table III.1, p. 324; Marshal; et al. (1988), Table 4.13, pp. 91–2.

majority in the proletariat although less so than in America (56.2 per cent compared with 60.5 per cent). That said, women are more dominant in the category of expert non-manager – in Britain 63 per cent – while women predominate in the uncredentialled manager category – 69 per cent in the US. It appears that women exploit their skill/credential assets more in Britain than America. Finally, it should be noted that men are dominant in the exploiting class categories in both countries although their presence is more notable in Britain than America. That is, men dominate both the capitalist class (88.5 per cent compared with 79.3 per cent) and the semi-credentialled manager category (85.6 per cent compared with 77.4 per cent). Semi-credentialled managers who are, as we noted, a larger category in Britain than in America are, therefore, predominately men with low levels of education. Turning to the distribution of classes within the sexes, the evidence shows that men dominate the exploiting classes while women dominate the exploited classes. Women, for example, are concentrated into the working class (58.3 per cent) while less than a third of men (32.0 per cent) occupy working-class positions. The position of men and women within the class structure according to Wright's class categories is virtually the same across America and Britain. The British evidence also shows that gender segregation of the labour market effects the distribution of men and women within classes.

Wright went on to consider issues of class and family since individuals are invariably part of families. Since the family is the unit of consumption, Wright argued, the class composition of the family has important implications for class interests and class formation. Wright found that 39% of households in the US were homogeneously working class (compared with 44 per cent in Sweden). Looking at contradictory locations, Wright found that credentialed managers, uncredentialed managers and non-managerial experts all live in families which are much less class homogeneous than is the case for the working class or the capitalist class. Half in each of these class locations are in homogeneous families so that the class homogeneity of households rises to 68 per cent among American middle-class households (Wright 1985: 229). While the number of 'mixed class families' is not insignificant (25 per cent), most workers 'live in unambiguously working-class families' (Wright 1985: 230).

Wright's attempt to incorporate women into class analysis has been criticised. Dex (1985), for example, has argued that Wright's method of excluding women not employed (at the time of the research) is 'only a partial solution to the problem of recognising women in the class structure'. She argued, 'His solution incorporates women who happen to be employed when he decides to describe the class structure. Since most women are likely to be employed at some time in their lives, Wright's approach does not capture the dynamics of women's employment' (Dex 1985: 162). More importantly, it is also questionable whether Wright has seriously considered the class position of women in employment. We have seen that the majority of employed women in America (52.8 per cent) and Britain (58.3 per cent) are located in Wright's proletarian category. Thus, while he went to considerable lengths to capture the diversity of men's class positions in the development of his class schema, the diversity of women's class positions was ignored. The varied career trajectories of women – be they teachers, nurses, clerical workers or manual workers – is almost entirely neglected in his class schema (Dex 1987; Marshall *et al.* 1988). For these reasons, critics have agreed that Wright's analysis failed to incorporate women satisfactorily into class analysis.

In response to charges of intellectual sexism (Acker 1973; Delphy 1981), Goldthorpe also defended the conventional approach of using the male head of household as a proxy for the class position of the family. He became embroiled in a heated exchange in the journal *Sociology*, with Heath and Britten (1984) who advocated a joint approach (taking wives characteristics into account in the study of class) and Stanworth (1984) who proposed the individual approach (assigning men and women to a class according to their own market and work positions). Goldthorpe (1984) was unconvinced by the critics and remains an 'entirely unrepentant supporter of the conventional view'. In their recent study of comparative social mobility, for example, Erikson and Goldthorpe (1992a: 275) employed the family as the unit of analysis and concluded that patterns and trends in women's marital mobility indicates 'how little women's experience of class mobility differs from that of men'. Thus, the exclusion of women from class analysis has not undermined their findings on the shape of the class structure and class processes in comparative perspective.

There were extensive commentaries (Crompton and Mann 1986) on the debate on women and class analysis and contributions to the controversy continue (Leiulfrud and Woodward 1987; Graetz 1990). However, the debate was propelled forward by the development of the individual approach by Marshall and his colleagues in *Social Class in Modern Britain* (1988). Using Goldthorpe's class schema, they allocated the men and women respondents of their nationally representative survey to class positions according to their individual market and work situations. They found that women were distributed across the class structure in different ways to men. A greater proportion of men than women were to be found in class I (13 per cent compared with 4 per cent), in class V (11 per cent compared with 4 per cent) and class VI (17 per cent compared with 6 per cent). In contrast, more women than men were found in class IIIa (28 per cent compared with 6 per cent) and class IIIb (10 per cent compared with

Table 2.4. Distribution of respondents by Goldthorpe social class and sex

Count Row (%) Column (%) Total Class	Male	Female	Total
1	101 82.1 13.1 7.7	22 17.9 4.0 1.7	123 9.4
II	132 56.2 17.1 10.0	103 43.8 18.9 7.8	235 17.9
IIIa	44 22.2 5.7 3.3	154 77.8 28.3 11.7	198 15.1
IIIb	2 3.4 0.3 0.2	56 96.6 10.3 4.3	58 4.4
IVa	40 85.1 5.2 3.0	7 14.9 1.3 0.5	47 3.6
IVb	40 67.8 5.2 3.0	19 32.2 3.5 1.4	59 4.5
IVc	10 90.9 1.3 0.8	1 9.1 0.2 0.1	11 0.8
V	87 82.1 11.3 6.6	19 17.9 3.5 1.4	106 8.1
VI	134 81.2 17.4 10.2	31 18.8 5.7 2.4	165 12.5
VIIa	176 57.5 22.8 13.4	130 42.5 23.9 9.9	306 23.3
VIIb	5 71.4 0.6 0.4	2 28.6 0.4 0.2	7 0.5
Total	771 58.6	544 41.4	1315 100.0

Source: Marshall *et al.* (1988), Table 4.6 p. 74.

0.3 per cent). A similar proportion of men and women were to be found in the other classes (II, IVa, IVb, IVc, VIIb and VIIb) (Marshall *et al.* 1988). Overall, men dominated the top and bottom of the class structure while women were found in the middle and bottom of the structure. Allocating respondents according to their own occupations, therefore, provided a somewhat different picture of the class structure inflating the relative size of the intermediate classes (which are dominated by women) and deflating the size of men in classes I, VI, VI and VII (dominated by men). They noted, 'Given this degree of class segmentation by sex one can feasibly claim that the distribution of male life-chances is conditioned by the highly particular location of women within the overall structure'(Marshall *et al.* 1988: 75).

Marshall *et al.* (1988) also found a considerable number of cross-class families within the class structure. Half of the conjugal units (where husbands and wives were employed) constituted cross-class families. They found a similar proportion of cross-class families within Goldthorpe's service class, intermediate class and working class (16 per cent, 16 per cent and 18 per cent respectively). They also found that women usually share the same position as their spouses or they occupy lower positions than them. Half of the men in service-class positions were married to women in the same class while the other half were married to women in the intermediate class or working class. In this respect, Marshall and his colleagues concurred with Goldthorpe's view that women share the same class positions as their husbands or occupy a lower position (Marshall *et al.* 1988: 68–9).

Overall, Marshall and his colleagues rejected the charges of intellectual sexism levelled against Goldthorpe although they disagreed with Goldthorpe's views on the objectives of class analysis which underlie his theoretical position and empirical research. That is, for Goldthorpe the study of class formation involves an investigation of demographic class formation and socio-political class formation. His interest in demographic class formation, however, is restricted to its implications for socio-political class formation. For Marshall *et al.*, this overriding concern limits the study of class formation by, for example, affecting the questions which are asked and the answers that are found. The 'gendered' nature of the occupational division of labour should fall within the remit of class analysis. They argued,

> It is not social actors that are distributed via the market through the places of the structure: it is men and women. Their differing experiences are interdependent, so that the distribution and situations of men are powerfully influenced by those of women, as well as vice versa. The fact that women are routinely constrained in this way serves only to highlight the obverse side of the structure: namely, that the collective effect of women's

employment on the occupational system would seem to be one
of privileging men. (Marshall *et al.* 1988: 84)

With reference to issues of the unit of class analysis, the Essex team concluded that 'social classes are neither families nor individuals but individuals
in families'. Thus, the study of class should be conducted at different levels
of analysis to embrace the issue of 'the collective effects of women's limited
access to economic and political power on the reproduction of positions
within the structure' and 'the complex determination of life-chances
accruing to individuals in conjugal units' (Marshall *et al.* 1988: 85)

The Essex team's conclusions have been widely endorsed by other
commentators on the women and class debate (Dale *et al.* 1986; Dex 1990;
Marsh 1986) although, arguably, the implications of their argument have
yet to be followed through. As Dex (1985: 171) suggests, 'There appear
to be a large set of class related questions which now necessitate women's
earnings and occupations being considered'. The role of women in both demographic and socio-political class formation offers huge potential for class
analysis. Moreover, it is widely agreed that there is plenty of room to employ
different units of analysis, and the choice of unit should be governed by
the social phenomena under investigation. Dale and her associates (1986:
388), for example, have argued that the family might be an appropriate
unit of analysis in the study of consumption since 'the relationship of the
individual to the labour market cannot be used to predict life-styles and
life-chances, for they depend upon the inputs and demands of all family
members, whether or not directly involved in the economic sphere'. The
choice of unit of analysis should be governed by the dimensions of class
under consideration.

However, it is also widely recognised that using different units of analysis
facilitates change on only one side of the coin. Given that men and women
have different career trajectories (as Heath and Britten noted), further work
is required to re-conceptualise the occupational and class classifications
so they which are more appropriate to women (Murgatroyd 1982; 1983;
Roberts and Barker 1989). Dale *et al.* (1986), for example, have noted
that the market situation of men and women in similar occupations is
often different. Training is narrowly defined in terms of apprenticeship
so that skilled jobs performed by women are invariably defined as semi- or
unskilled. Female-dominated occupations such as clerical work and personal service work are also lumped together with no attempt to distinguish
between skilled, semi- and unskilled jobs. Dale *et al.* subsequently developed
an occupational classification for women by examining the patterning of
the market power of each occupation according to a variety of variables as
a means of establishing empirically discrete classes. Their work provides

some valuable insights into the different experiences of men and women as well as differences between women in the labour market. Nevertheless, their classification is an *occupational* classification rather than a *class* classification which incorporates men and women. Their class clusters, for example, do not embrace any notion of work situation operationalised via employment status. In this respect, Dale *et al.*'s work lacks a theoretical rationale in which to place both men and women into a structure of class positions. Other researchers (Dex 1987) have made extensive use of the occupational classification specifically designed for the *Women and Employment* survey (Martin and Roberts 1984) which distinguishes between a range of occupations dominated by women. Again, however, these refinements to occupational classifications have not facilitated the development of distinct classes.

A more systematic way of incorporating women into class analysis may be to revise Goldthorpe's class categories. This exercise could be undertaken by examining men's and women's different conditions and relations of employment and amending the class schema accordingly. This is not a novel suggestion but one which both Goldthorpe and Marshall *et al.* have already made. In his analysis of the class mobility of women, for example, Goldthorpe wanted to reallocate semi or unskilled clerical workers such as copy-typists, audio-typists and office machine operators into sub-class IIIb (and in the working class when using his three-fold classification) when he reallocated shop assistants and so forth into this new category. However, his attempt to make his class schema more suitable to the class allocation for women was thwarted by the limited information on these groupings provided by the 1980 OPCS Classification of Occupations (Goldthorpe and Payne 1986b: 551). Marshall *et al.* were not able to incorporate Goldthorpe's revised class schema into their analysis. Nevertheless, in a brief 'coda', they vindicated Goldthorpe's and Payne's amendments (Marshall *et al.* 1988: 307). They looked at the market and work situations of the men and women in Goldthorpe's classes. Men were found to have better market situations, defined in terms of pay and promotion prospects, and work situations, defined in terms of autonomy, decision-making and supervisory responsibilities. At each occupational level, men receive higher incomes than women, they have greater chances of promotion than women and they enjoy greater levels of autonomy, decision-making and control over their work routines than women. The Essex team hinted that, 'It may well be the case, for example, that rather more extensive revisions are required before Goldthorpe's class categories can cope fully with the peculiarities of women's employment situations' (Marshall *et al.* 1988: 307).

Secondary analysis of men and women's conditions and relations of employment using the Essex data has now been conducted by Evans (1992a; 1996). His analysis confirms the need to re-allocate women low-skilled nonmanual workers into the working class. The possibilities of re-allocating some women in low-level nonmanual employment (from class IIIa to class VII) may now exist with publication of the 1990 Standard Occupational Classification (SOC). The SOC was explicitly revised to make finer distinctions between skilled and semi and unskilled nonmanual work, and these distinctions could be used to revise Goldthorpe's class schema. The re-allocation of women in low-level clerical work from the intermediate class into the working class would have important substantive implications. Placing lowly-skilled women clerical workers into the working class would reduce the number of cross-class families (ie families where wives occupy intermediate class positions while their husbands occupy working-class positions) in survey research. This substantive finding is one which Goldthorpe (1984) would happily embrace since he has always viewed the notion of cross-class families as largely an artefact of the methods used and not a sociologically meaningful concept. As he has noted, women clerical workers do not have as favourable conditions and relations of employment as skilled manual workers. It is appropriate that women occupying low-level nonmanual jobs should be classified as working class.

A case could also be made for reallocating some female-dominated occupations in class II (the lower echelons of the service class) such as administrators and supervisors of nonmanual employees into Class IIIa (the intermediate class). The task might not be so difficult since men and women tend to occupy different jobs. The suggestion would also have substantive implications for the definition of the service class. A more tightly-defined service class would overcome the heterogeneity of occupations currently incorporated in the service class for which Goldthorpe was criticised (Ahrne 1990; Crompton 1980; Penn 1981). The size of the service class would be reduced to include a more homogeneous group of occupational positions. Thus, a revised class schema would capture the gender segregation of the labour market and the disadvantaged labour market position of women in comparison to men while retaining a picture of the diversity of women's conditions and relations. Revisions to Goldthorpe's class schema to incorporate men and women would also go some way to tackling other problems with the classification as it currently stands.

Finally, the position of women who do not participate in the labour market needs to be considered further since Marshall *et al.*, like Wright, confined their analysis to men and women in employment at the time of their survey. Other research (Dex 1987) suggests that housewives could be incorporated into class analysis by allocating them to a class position according to their previous employment. Fortunately, attention is now being turned to those people usually excluded from conventional class analysis (Marshall *et al.* 1996). Further thought also needs to be given to the differences between women in full-time and part-time employment. In this way, an analysis of class structures would not be confined to those in employment in any one point in time but incorporate people who move in and out of the labour market over their life-time. It might then capture the dynamism of men and women's employment as they move through the family life-cycle. The status of class schemas will be considered again in due course.

COMPARING CLASS SCHEMAS

Attention has focused on the different class schemas developed by Wright and Goldthorpe and the contribution of each to the women and class debate. The focus will now turn to a comparison of the two schemas by returning to the work of Marshall and his associates. They studied the class structure in Britain by using the class schemas devised by Wright and Goldthorpe, and examined the 'operational procedures by which modern class analysts allocate individuals to the various social classes' (Marshall *et al.* 1988: 10). Overall, the aim of fitting their data to the contrasting approaches was to offer a 'more systematic and empirical assessment of their alternative conceptions of the class structure and class processes in modern capitalist societies in order to complement the theoretical discussion already available' (Marshall *et al.* 1988: 26).

Not surprisingly, fitting the data to the two class schemas using different operational procedures produced different results. Focusing on the discrepancies between the two schemas (as shown by cross-classifying the sample according to the different class algorithms), the Essex team found, that 12% of Wright's expert managers and 33% of semi-credentialed managers fell outside Goldthorpe's service class. Some of Wright's semi-credentialed and uncredentialed managers appeared in Goldthorpe's service class (classes I and II) and in the intermediate classes (class V). Wright's semi-credentialed workers were spread across all of Goldthorpe's employee classes. Finally, they found that Wright's proletariat was still split by Goldthorpe's skilled manual and routine nonmanual distinction (Marshall *et al.* 1988: 48). There was, therefore, substantial disagreement between the two classifications.

Marshall *et al.* (1988: 50) decided to unpack the discrepancies between the two schemas. First, in relation to the proletariat, the most extreme discrepancy was the appearance of eight respondents in Wright's proletariat in Goldthorpe's service class. These respondents turned out to be a buying officer, a purchasing officer, an investment broker, a retail supervisor, a secretarial supervisor, a hospital matron and two clerical supervisors. They

Table 2.5. Wright II (revised) classes by Goldthorpe classes

				Goldthorpe				
	I	II	III	IV	V	VI	VII	Total
B	1.4 (18)	0.5 (6)	0.0 (0)	0.2 (2)	0.0 (0)	0.0 (0)	0.0 (0)	2.0 (26)
SE	0.5 (7)	0.5 (6)	0.0 (0)	3.4 (45)	0.0 (0)	0.0 (0)	0.1 (1)	4.5 (50)
PB	0.3 (4)	0.5 (7)	0.0 (0)	5.2 (68)	0.0 (0)	0.0 (0)	0.0 (0)	6.0 (79)
EM	2.7 (35)	2.3 (30)	0.5 (7)	0.0 (0)	0.2 (2)	0.0 (0)	0.0 (0)	5.6 (74)
ES	0.9 (12)	0.8 (11)	0.5 (6)	0.0 (0)	0.0 (0)	0.0 (0)	0.0 (0)	2.2 (29)
ENM	0.8 (10)	1.9 (25)	1.4 (19)	0.0 (0)	0.0 (0)	0.0 (0)	0.0 (0)	4.1 (54)
SCM	1.9 (25)	3.4 (45)	0.4 (5)	0.0 (0)	1.9 (25)	0.2 (3)	0.1 (1)	7.9 (104)
SCS	0.5 (7)	1.4 (18)	0.1 (1)	0.0 (0)	1.7 (23)	0.1 (1)	0.0 (0)	3.8 (50)
SCW	0.3 (4)	4.0 (52)	0.5 (7)	0.0 (0)	1.5 (20)	7.8 (102)	0.3 (4)	14.4 (189)
UM	0.0 (0)	1.1 (14)	0.6 (8)	0.0 (0)	1.1 (15)	0.2 (3)	0.2 (2)	3.2 (42)
US	0.0 (0)	1.1 (14)	0.3 (4)	0.0 (0)	1.4 (19)	0.0 (0)	0.6 (8)	3.4 (45)
P	0.1 (1)	0.5 (7)	15.1 (199)	0.0 (0)	0.2 (3)	4.3 (56)	22.7 (298)	42.9 (564)
Total	9.4 (123)	17.9 (235)	19.5 (256)	8.7 (115)	8.1 (107)	12.5 (165)	23.9 (314)	100.0 (1315)

Wright (row label, left of class rows)

Key: B Bourgeoisie; SE Small employers; PB Petit bourgeoisie; EM Expert managers; ES Expert supervisors; ENM Expert non-managers; SCM Semi-credentialled managers; SCS Semi-credentialled supervisors; SCW Semi-credentialled workers; UM Uncredentialled managers; US Uncredentialled Supervisors; P Proletarians.

Source: Marshall *et al.* (1988), Table 3.5, p. 49.

appeared in Wright's proletariat because they were non-owners of capital, non-managers engaged in clerical sales and white-collar work, had low educational credentials and reported little job autonomy. This extreme aside, the major difference between Wright's proletariat and Goldthorpe's working class is that the former includes routine nonmanual workers as well as manual workers while the latter includes only manual workers, routine nonmanual workers being allocated to a distinct intermediate class position of their own. It is for this reason that Wright's schema produces such a large proletariat (43 per cent) compared with Goldthorpe's smaller working class (36 per cent) using the Essex data.

Second, turning to Wright's capitalist classes, Marshall *et al.* found that most of Wright's small employers (59 respondents or 5 per cent of the total Essex sample) were indistinguishable from his petty bourgeoisie (79 respondents constituting 6 per cent of the sample), the only difference between them being the number of employees they had. There was little point, they argued, in making the distinction between the categories. Furthermore, they found that only twenty-six of their respondents could be allocated to Wright's bourgeoisie constituting a mere 2 per cent of the employed population. Many of these respondents were senior executives whose shares in the company were part of their remuneration package. They were employees rather than capitalists. Indeed, no capitalists engaged in the money markets appeared in the sample who might have been classified as members of the contemporary bourgeoisie. On this basis, the Essex team concluded that Wright's three owning classes were less useful class categories than Goldthorpe's service class in the survey of Britain's class structure (Marshall *et al.* 1988: 59).

Third, Wright's contradictory class locations diverged considerably from Goldthorpe's classificatory scheme. Marshall *et al.* found that one hundred and eighty nine respondents appeared in Wright's category of semi-credentialed workers constituting 14 per cent of the sample in paid employment. 30 per cent of these respondents appeared in Goldthorpe's service class, 15 per cent appeared in his intermediate class while 55 per cent appeared in the working class. Among the respondents classified as semi-credentialed workers according to Wright, they found two roofers, a metal worker and a slinger (who would have appeared in Goldthorpe's working class) and two quantity surveyors and two buying and purchasing officers (who would have appeared in Goldthorpe's service class). They argued that such workers should be not be classified together as Wright's schema demanded but should be given a variety of class locations along the lines of Goldthorpe's classificatory scheme (Marshall *et al.* 1988: 60).

The Essex team concluded that Wright's class categories were too hetero-geneous. Wright's objective criteria for defining the common attributes of his various classes – especially the measures used to denote skill assets – were found wanting. The Essex team argued 'Prima facie, therefore, the class schema proposed by John Goldthorpe seems to be more robust than those of Erik Wright' (Marshall *et al.* 1988: 60). In terms of internal (or criterion) validity, Wright's categories were too unreliable (especially with reference to reported autonomy) while Goldthorpe's categories seemed to measure what they were supposed to (namely, conditions and relations of employment). They also found that Wright's class categories were less robust in explaining patterns of social mobility, proletarianisation, class consciousness and class action. In terms of external (or construct) validity, Goldthorpe's categories made more sense of the variance of the data under investigation. They expressed serious 'reservations, therefore, in relation 'both to the construction of the class categories themselves and to the results of the analyses generated by them' (Marshall *et al.* 1988: 265). Goldthorpe's analysis of classes defined in terms of conditions and relations of employment was superior to Wright's conception of classes defined in relation to social relations of production.

Considerable prominence, therefore, was given to the methodological failings of Wright's class schema. However, Goldthorpe's operational procedures for allocating respondents to different social classes were subject to critical comment. His procedures for operationalising conditions and relations of employment, they argued, are never 'fully explained' in that he has never shown the 'available evidence' by which he locates different occupational categories into different classes (Marshall *et al.* 1988: 306). These brief comments still need to be considered further. The notion of conditions of employment, for example is supposed to capture levels of pay, prospects for promotion, and levels of job security. Rather than allocate people to class locations on the basis of this information, however, Goldthorpe (and the Essex team following his example) used occupational titles from the Registrar-General's OPCS classification of occupations as a 'proxy' indicator of these variables. Similarly, it could be argued that Goldthorpe does not operationalise the concept of relations of employment directly. The concept is supposed to capture a person's position in the division of labour of his or her workplace. It is operationalised through the 'proxy' indicator of employment status also devised by the Registrar General. The use of the OPCS classification of occupations is problematic however. Occupations are classified to each of the unit groups of the standard occupational classification on the basis of reported title. Goldthorpe then claims to group these occupational unit groups into classes according to shared conditions and relations of employment. However, it is not clear how Goldthorpe actually operationalises his class schema according to the theoretical rationale on which it was devised. Indeed, in their analysis, the

Essex team acknowledge this fact when they note that Wright's measures of class are a 'more obviously sociological approach than that pursued by John Goldthorpe, since the putative 'work situation' of respondents in the latter's class schema is determined by the official coding of employment status, and Goldthorpe's own perception of the authority and autonomy involved in these statuses' (Marshall *et al.* 1988: 93).

Once again, it might not be completely erroneous to presume that if greater attention were paid to direct information on conditions and relations of employment rather than indirect measures (occupational title and employment status) to allocate respondents to a class position, a somewhat different picture of the class structure might emerge. Again, such an exercise would demand that Goldthorpe's class categories are revised to capture the empirical reality of the class structure of post-industrial societies. After all, the class schema should be made to fit with empirical reality rather than vice versa (Scott 1996). Goldthorpe's class schema is a heuristic devise which should be constantly revised if it is to capture a fluid and ever-changing class structure. The criticism partially developed by the Essex team, in other words, could have radical implications since it raises serious questions about the operational procedures by which Goldthorpe has sought to allocate individuals to various social classes and the relationship of those procedures to the theoretical rationale which underpins his classificatory scheme.

Marshall *et al.*'s assessment of the two class schemas has been subject to considerable criticism. Pawson (1989; 1990) examined the Essex team's attempt to adjudicate between Wright and Goldthorpe's class schemas in detail. The exercise, he argued, amounted to no more than an empirical attempt to ground their preference for Goldthorpe's schema over Wright's schema. They used the discrepancies between the two schemas, for example, to highlight some of the anomalies of Wright's class schema rather than viewing them as '*joint* discrepancies'. Goldthorpe's schema was favoured, in other words, by examining the discrepancies 'from the perspective of one side of the class matrix' (Pawson 1990: 235). Furthermore, they selectively chose which categories to criticise as too heterogeneous. Marshall *et al.* happily unpacked Wright's category of semi-credentialed worker to highlight the strange bedfellows within this category but failed to do so with Goldthorpe's service class which might have thrown up equally 'odd couples'. Pawson (1990: 236) concluded, 'The only standards operating in these particular comparisons are notions like the 'integrity' and 'coherence' of categories, and these are, quite unavoidably, in the eye of the beholder'.

Pawson was highly sceptical of the Essex team's claim that it had established the robustness of Goldthorpe's class schema over Wright's class schema. He was also sharply critical of the way in which Goldthorpe's class schema was used more systematically in analysing the substantive topics of social mobility and proletarianisation than Wright's class schema which was employed on a more ad hoc basis (Pawson 1990: 236). Overall, Pawson was disappointed by the Essex method of evaluating the rival class schemas since the 'opportunity to formulate data in terms of rival conceptual frameworks' was never 'fully realised' (Pawson 1990: 236). A common empirical context was never established in which to evaluate the rival class schemas, and the content of both theories was never systematically put up to empirical test. The claim to establish the superiority of Goldthorpe's class schema over Wright's class schema, therefore, was based on prior theoretical persuasions rather than a genuine empirical adjudication of the rival class schemas (Pawson 1990: 239–40). Marshall and Rose (1990) contested Pawson's claim that they subjected Wright's schema to empirical interrogation unlike Goldthorpe's schema. However, even a cursory glance through the chapters of their monograph reveals that Goldthorpe's schema was employed more systematically than Wright's in their discussion of substantive topics like class consciousness and class politics. They did not evaluate the rival theories as impartially as they claimed.

Criticism of Marshall *et al.*'s research has also been made with reference to the limitations of quantitative research in class analysis. Savage *et al.* (1992) noted that the increasing dominance of cross-sectional survey research has meant that both conceptual and operational issues have been discussed at length. Considerable attention, for example, has been given to how social classes are defined and measured. However, operational issues about the boundaries of different social classes have come to dominate the research agenda and conceptual issues about the nature of class action, for instance, have been neglected. As a result, research has become 'focussed around narrow sets of issues to establish which class schema is the most statistically powerful as the effectiveness of class schemas is judged according to the respective power of statistical measures of association' (Savage *et al.* 1992: 223). Savage *et al.* also cite the Essex team's research as a prime example of this type of narrow class analysis which has got 'bogged down into questions of who fits into what class' (Savage *et al.* 1992: 223). Nor are they convinced that theories of class should be evaluated according to which correlates best with other social phenomena. Again, Marshall *et al.* are cited as the prime example of the limitations of appraising class theories on this basis. Doubt is therefore cast on Marshall *et al.*'s claim to have established the robustness of Goldthorpe's class schema over Wright's with reference to various statistical measures of association such as voting behaviour. Thus, Savage *et al.* (1992: 224) concluded, 'Statements such as 'Goldthorpe's theory certainly better explains class identifications and voting intentions than does that of Wright' (Marshall and Rose 1990: 265) conflates correlation with explanation. Goldthorpe's class schema may provide a better association with voting than does Wright's, but this does not demonstrate its explanatory superiority'.

Indeed, Savage *et al.* are highly critical of attempts to identify an objective structure of class positions. In this context, the similarity rather than the difference between Wright and Goldthorpe's approaches to identifying an objective class structure is noted. Both Wright and Goldthorpe, for example, have devoted considerable effort to defining economically distinct classes although the way in which they have defined the economic sphere has differed. They have embarked on very similar enterprises even though the results of their endeavour have differed. Both approaches share two major shortcomings. First, they assume that class places can be distinguished from the people (i.e. men and women) who occupy them. However, the sorts of people who fill class positions shape those class positions and vice versa. Second, they neglect historical change in an attempt to capture a class structure in a given point in time. The structure of class positions is taken as given so that issues of classes as ever-changing economic, social and political entities is neglected. The static nature of class schemas, in other words, is criticised once again. They disagree, therefore, with Goldthorpe's analytical distinction between class structure and class formation and the empirical enterprise which has flowed from it.

These criticisms have been repeated by Crompton (1993). She has also expressed her unease with Marshall *et al.*'s attempts to compare class schemas. Given their different theoretical underpinnings and empirical applications, she argued, it is not possible to identify one schema as superior to another. Schemas have to be judged on the basis of the uses to which they are put. In relation to the Essex team's evaluation of Wright's and Goldthorpe's schemas, Crompton (1993: 76) concluded, 'It is difficult, however, to see what is actually gained from this exercise, as the class schemas in question were devised for different purposes and on the basis of different (implicit and explicit) theoretical assumptions'. An empirical resolution of the issues is not possible, therefore, given the very different theoretical assumptions which underpin the two approaches to class analysis (Crompton 1993: 117). It is for this reason that Crompton has argued that disputes about which class schema is correct are actually 'pseudo-debates' which have contributed to the current disillusionment within class analysis more generally (Crompton 1993).

Crompton (1993) also expressed her long-standing misgivings about attempts to identify an objective structure of class positions and the tendency to treat issues of class structure and class consciousness as analytically separate within class analysis. This tendency has been exacerbated by the use of different research methods and techniques: namely, those interested in the issue of class structure have tended to conduct statistical analyses on large data sets while those interested in class consciousness have undertaken historical and case-study research (Crompton 1993: 12). She is highly critical of the way in which quantitative research has proceeded with huge effort being devoted to the development of increasingly elaborate class schemas with occupation used as one indicator of class position. The focus on occupational position does not capture other dimensions of inequality in terms of wealth and status, and ascriptive differences such as race and gender. Second, Crompton is unconvinced that Wright's and Goldthorpe's class schemas have theoretical value. They describe occupational inequal- ities but they do not explain class relations. The categories devised by Wright and Goldthorpe are economic aggregates but they are not classes with identifiable interests and the capacity to act (Crompton 1993: 114). Crompton concluded that employment based measures remain relevant in the study of structured social inequality but that the current interest in quantification and measurement should not be allowed to direct attention away from 'the significance of individual and collective human action within real social contexts' (Crompton 1993: 126).

Critics of Marshall *et al.*, therefore, are not all of one mind. Crompton (1993) is highly critical of the whole exercise of adjudicating between different theories because prior theoretical persuasions will always come to the fore. Pluralism is the order of the day. In contrast, Pawson argues that Marshall *et al.*'s prior theoretical persuasions shaped their final preference for Goldthorpe's class schema over Wright's because they did not genuinely adjudicate between the rival theories. Pawson (1989) has argued elsewhere for a set of standards for empirical data in sociological research (ie: a measure for measures). That is, it is possible to claim that one class schema is superior to another according to an agreed programme of adjudication. One way rival class schemas can be evaluated is according to the substantive problems which a commentator is researching and the empirical results his or her analysis produces. As we saw, the ways in which men and women are allocated to class locations influences the substantive findings on the shape of the class structure. It is from such analyses that plausible explanations of pleasing correlations emerge. This is not a conclusion from which Crompton or Savage *et al.* would demur. The task of clearly defining concepts of class, operationalising those concepts and evaluating different approaches is, therefore, an important task for sociologists within the sub- discipline. After all, critics of class analysis have drawn on atheoretical and poorly defined notions of class devised by market research organisations in predicting its demise (Goldthorpe and Marshall 1992). It is for these reasons that all approaches, concepts and heuristic devices like class schemas should be subject to critical evaluation described above.

It is hard to deny, however, that operational issues have come to dominate the research agenda as Savage and his associates have argued. Furthermore, the preoccupation with technical issues has contributed to the current disillusionment with class analysis as Crompton has suggested. The study of class action has been narrowed to an analysis of voting patterns and the opportunities which facilitate or the constraints which limit the propensity for a group of people to engage in a variety of different types of collective action have been neglected as a result. Now, this is not to suggest that this is an outcome which Wright, Goldthorpe and Marshall and his associates have sought. On the contrary, Wright and Goldthorpe repeatedly remark that the class structures which they outlined are of interest only in relation to substantive concerns. Erikson and Goldthorpe (1992a: 46), for example, have recently emphasised that their class schema 'is not be to regarded as an attempt at providing a definitive 'map' of the class structures of individual societies but essentially as an *instrument de travail*. Critics have sometimes forgotten that it is a heuristic device which 'must be judged by the value that it proves to have in enquiry and analysis'. Nevertheless, the huge amount of time and effort which has been put into refining the different class schemas by the authors themselves for quantitative research and the ensuing debate about the rival approaches has led to the neglect of class action.

It may be, as the critics have suggested, that such an outcome is the inevitable result of Goldthorpe's analytical distinction between class structure and class action. However, there are problems with abandoning such a distinction. To do so, for example, would be to deny that class divisions exist in periods when class conflict may be in abeyance. In this respect, the distinction should not be discarded. Marshall *et al.* have argued that sociological interest in the formation of classes as demographic entities should not be tied to the issue of classes as socio-political entities. As they showed in relation to the women and class debate, the topic of demographic class formation is of interest in itself. This argument can also be applied the other way round. The extent to which classes are socio-political entities should not be tied exclusively to whether classes constitute demographic entities. Otherwise, sociologists restrict themselves to issues of demographic class formation and equal attention is not given to issues over the extent to which classes are socio-political entities. After all, lots of factors intervene in the relationship between class structure and class action, and the processes by which a person's class location may or may not shape their party political choices, for example, should fall within the remit of class analysis. This argument implies that there should be room for both quantitative research and historical and case study research which address issues of class structure and class formation simultaneously.

CONCLUSION

This chapter has focused on sociological attempts to delineate the shape of the class structure of post-industrial societies. It has been seen that Wright's class schema identifies a large proletariat and a small bourgeoisie in America and Britain. Middle-class groupings which exist somewhere between the two main categories are also relatively small in both countries. In contrast, Goldthorpe's class schema identifies a relatively small working class and a relatively large range of middle classes. Wright's map is of a class structure which has remained unchanged for much of the twentieth century since any upgrading of the occupational order has been countered by proletarianisation. Goldthorpe's map captures the evolution of the class structure which has seen the decline of manual employment and the rise of nonmanual employment. Wright's and Goldthorpe's contrasting maps, in other words, have produced divergent explanations of the shape of the class structure in America and Britain in the second half of the twentieth century.

The inclusion of women in class analysis indicates that women tend to dominate the lower echelons of the class structure. Wright's class categories show that women are concentrated in the proletariat in both the US and Britain. However, Wright's class schema has been criticised for failing to capture the diversity of women's labour market experiences. By contrast, Goldthorpe's class schema does show this diversity by demonstrating that women tend to dominate the middle and bottom of the class structure although a case can be made for allocating more women in working-class positions than is currently the case. Unfortunately, there is no analysis of American women's class position using Goldthorpe's class categories. Evidence from research on women's employment in the labour market in America, however, suggests that women are concentrated into nonmanual work like their British counterparts (Reskin and Padavic 1994) although they are also dominant in low-level service work in the US economy (Jacobs 1993). Thus, American women share a similar range of class positions to their British equivalents in employment.

Finally, an evaluation of the two class schemas suggests that Goldthorpe's schema is superior to Wright's schema in terms of internal and external validity. Arguably, his schema offers a more plausible explanation of the development of the class structures of America and Britain in the second half of the twentieth century. That said, one of the major shortcomings of employing class schemas as heuristic devises is that they produce only snapshots of the class structures in question at any one point in time. It is appropriate, therefore, that attention now turns to the issue of class processes in America and Britain.

Chapter 3

Class Processes

The study of social mobility is about the movement of people between different social classes. It embraces research on the processes by which they are upwardly and downwardly mobile which may involve short and long-distance mobility across the class structure. It also includes the study of inter-generational mobility, which refers to mobility between a family of origin and a person's own class position, and the study of intra-generational mobility (or worklife mobility) which refers to mobility between a person's first job and their current job. Sociologists have sought to address two crucial issues in class analysis in the examination of patterns and trends of social mobility. Firstly, research on social mobility addresses issues of demographic class formation by identifying stable collectivities of people with similar life-chances. This has led researchers to examine absolute or overall *de facto* rates of mobility. Secondly, mobility researchers have addressed the degree of openness of a society by examining social fluidity. The focus of attention here has been on relative rates of mobility by comparing the mobility chances of different people or groups. The particular interest guiding mobility research, therefore, has shaped empirical work on the different aspects of social mobility. Invariably, however, researchers have commented on both issues of class formation and social fluidity and examined patterns and trends in absolute and relative social mobility within the confines of their research.

This chapter focuses on patterns and trends in social mobility in America and Britain with particular reference to the second half of the twentieth century. Special attention is also given to the role of education as a channel for social mobility in the two countries. The chapter is divided into three parts. First, attention focuses on social mobility in the US. The different mobility experiences of whites and ethnic minorities are considered in this context. The evidence suggests that structural change – the decline of farm occupations and the rise of nonmanual employment – facilitated considerable upward mobility from the 1940s to the 1970s. There was also a decline in the association between origins and destinations although more so for whites than ethnic minorities. The education system – that is, the growing number of people with college degrees – has played a major role in weakening this link. Rather than become increasingly rigid, therefore, America has become a more open society over the middle decades of the twentieth century. That said, research in the 1980s suggests that structural change is now slowing and, arguably, the decline in the link between origins and destinations has also slackened. The end of the long boom and the advent of variable economic growth rates and a political climate which has moved away from equalitarian reform to the dominance of market liberalism leaves future patterns and trends in social mobility unclear.

Second, patterns and trends of social mobility in Britain are examined. Specific reference is made to women's social mobility. Like America, the evidence suggests that structural change – the decline of manual employment and the rise of nonmanual employment – has facilitated a large amount of upward social mobility. Absolute rates of mobility, therefore, have increased although more so for men than women. However, the relative chances of gaining entry into the service class remains unequal since individuals of service-class origins have a better chance of remaining there than individuals of working-class origins entering the service class. There is still considerable social closure at the top of the class structure and a buffer zone operates between manual and nonmanual employment. Relative rates of mobility are unchanged. Britain, therefore, cannot be described as an entirely closed society though, equally, it is not an open society. Evidence from the onset of Britain's variable economic performance in 1970s and 1980s indicate that these patterns and trends remain unchanged. Thus, despite educational reform, class inequalities persist although debate continues over the relative importance of intelligence and education in the processes of mobility and immobility.

Third, a direct comparison of social mobility in America and Britain will be made. Comparative research provides the chance to consider whether the US is an exceptionally open society and whether Britain is an exceptionally closed society. The data indicate that neither nation fits the stereotypical view. The US has enjoyed high rates of absolute social mobility but they have not been exceptionally high in comparison to Australia and Sweden. Britain may have experienced lower levels of total social mobility than America but they have not been as low as Germany and Japan. The comparative research also indicates that America and Britain share a high degree of communality and consistency in their underlying patterns and trends in relative social mobility alongside other European nations. The US is rather like England and France and all three nations are similar in experiencing little direct political intervention to influence mobility patterns. That said, trends in relative mobility in the US indicate the possibility of greater fluidity over the middle decades of the twentieth century although the extent to which the trend may be described as substantial remains open to debate. Neither nation, therefore, is exceptional with reference to absolute and relative rates of social mobility.

AMERICAN SOCIAL MOBILITY

Some of the earliest observations of America were made about the seemingly high levels of social mobility in America. Marx, for example, noted that 'though classes already exist, they have not yet become fixed but continually change and interchange their elements in constant flux' (Marx quoted in Heath 1981: 15). Moreover, the opportunities for entrepreneurship explained the absence of organised labour in the US since the ruling class had effectively siphoned off potential leaders for any such organisation. Sombart (1906) also used these arguments to account for the failure of the working class to organise as an industrial and political force in the US. As we shall see, the extent to which the class structure has remained fluid or become more rigid over the twentieth century has dominated the research agenda on American social mobility.

The first substantial study of social mobility in the United States was conducted by Pitrim Sorokin (1927). He examined existing statistical data (including data collected in Minneapolis by himself and his students) and found evidence of considerable social mobility. Among the male respondents of his research, for example, he found that only 10.6% had the same occupations as their fathers. Sorokin did not believe, however, that the trends in social mobility which he identified were part of a broader trend towards increased social mobility. Canvassing a broader historical terrain, he argued there was no evidence of increased social mobility but merely a fluctuation in trends in mobility and immobility. Sorokin, therefore, was highly critical of unilinear theories of social mobility and distanced himself from evolutionary theories of the development of society. Periods of rigidity, where there is a poor fit between the most important occupations and the most talented individuals, lead to upheaval and increased social mobility where there is a closer fit between places and people until rigidity sets in again, and so the process continues indefinitely (Sorokin 1927: 152).

These findings were largely confirmed by Lipset and Bendix (1959). They conducted a secondary analysis of data collected in a labour market survey in Oakland, California. They also found considerable social mobility. The education system, they argued, was a major channel of mobility intervening in the relationship between origins and destinations. The seventeen-fold increase in the number of students attending university in the period between 1890 and 1950 indicated the increasing importance of higher education as an avenue of social mobility (Lipset and Bendix 1959: 85). However, they noted that upward mobility only amounted to short-range movement between groups of similar statuses. There was little long-range mobility across the manual/non-manual divide. Elite mobility was highly restricted, and its members shared very similar social backgrounds. Lipset and Bendix also conducted a comparative analysis of mobility, and argued that America did not have exceptionally high rates of social mobility in comparison to Britain and other industrialised nations. Their argument – that societies of similar economic development share similar patterns of social mobility – will be discussed more fully in due course.

The first nationally representative survey of social mobility – the 'Occupational Change in a Generation' (OCG) survey – was conducted by Blau and Duncan in 1962 and the results published in *The American Occupational Structure* in 1967. Blau and Duncan were the early exponents of the 'status attainment' research programme on social mobility. They viewed mobility in terms of mobility up or down a social hierarchy of status positions in which individuals could be ranked according to income and education. Their overriding interest was in individual attainment rather than mobility between classes and in the determinants of mobility rather than rates of social mobility (Heath 1981: 42). The focus of their attention, for example, was on the extent to which factors such as family background, ethnicity, gender and education influenced occupational success and failure. They were able to distinguish the effects, therefore, of ascribed and achieved status on occupational attainment. This shift in focus was partly the result of their methods: namely, the use of path analysis which allowed them to estimate the 'relative importance of different determinants of individuals' occupational attainment' (Heath 1981: 41). They were able to separate out the processes of occupational attainment and explore the factors which influenced an individual's experience of social mobility. It was these interests which guided their research.

Blau and Duncan found substantial opportunities for upward social mobility as a result of the changing occupational structure. Rather than increasing rigidity, the contraction of low-level jobs (especially farming occupations) and the expansion of high-level jobs (specifically managerial occupations) permitted both short and long-range mobility. As Table 3.1 shows, every occupational group recruited more than 10 per cent of its members from sons of farmers (as what was the biggest occupational group in 1940 declined rapidly thereafter). In contrast, the two occupations with the largest inflow of outsiders were retail salesmen and clerks (with recruitment levels of 97.1 per cent and 95.5 per cent respectively). The

Table 3.1. Mobility from father's occupation in 1962, for males 25 to 64 years old: inflow percentages

Father's occupation	Respondent's occupation in 1962																
	1	2	3	4	5	6	7	8	9	10	11	12	13	14	15	16	17
Professionals																	
1 Self-employed[1]	14.5	3.9	1.5	3.8	.8	.8	1.1	.3	.3	.6	.3	.3	.4	.2	.6	.5	.6
2 Salaried	7.0	9.5	4.9	5.8	2.1	3.8	3.4	1.6	1.9	.6	2.1	2.1	1.9	1.4	.4	.5	.3
3 Managers	8.7	7.9	8.7	7.0	4.0	4.4	2.6	2.7	2.6	2.2	1.4	1.2	1.0	1.8	.7	.3	.3
4 Salesmen, Other	5.6	3.4	5.2	8.1	2.6	1.7	4.4	.8	1.5	.8	1.0	1.0	.6	.0	.4	.4	.3
5 Proprietors	18.5	9.6	16.5	13.2	16.3	7.1	15.2	2.5	5.2	5.7	3.7	3.4	3.7	1.6	2.0	1.5	1.6
6 Clerical	4.9	7.3	4.4	5.9	2.3	4.5	2.6	2.9	3.1	1.2	1.2	1.9	3.2	1.5	1.3	.8	.0
7 Salesmen, Retail	.9	2.3	3.0	4.7	2.8	1.8	2.9	1.4	.8	1.1	1.5	1.1	1.4	.1	1.2	.7	.0
Craftsmen																	
8 Manufacturing	3.8	8.3	6.1	4.3	5.1	5.7	6.3	12.0	5.1	5.1	6.2	4.7	4.8	4.5	3.2	.5	.4
9 Other	4.0	7.0	7.4	7.9	6.0	8.0	6.1	6.9	11.0	5.8	5.3	7.8	5.4	3.8	4.1	1.2	1.2
10 Construction	3.0	3.2	4.4	4.1	5.8	6.2	2.6	6.9	5.5	13.7	3.6	3.9	4.6	2.6	4.9	.8	1.8
Operatives																	
11 Manufacturing	5.2	6.4	5.1	6.5	6.1	7.5	7.1	12.9	7.7	4.9	13.7	6.9	7.1	14.5	6.3	1.2	2.8
12 Other	2.8	7.5	4.2	5.4	6.2	6.7	6.0	6.5	8.6	6.6	6.9	10.9	7.1	6.5	6.4	1.2	4.4
13 Service	2.3	3.7	4.0	4.8	3.7	6.3	5.3	4.8	3.9	4.7	5.1	4.6	8.2	5.4	3.3	.8	.6
Labourers																	
14 Manufacturing	.0	1.0	1.2	.4	.8	1.3	.8	2.6	1.5	1.0	3.2	2.2	3.0	5.9	2.4	.6	.9
15 Other	1.0	2.0	1.9	3.3	2.1	6.0	4.7	4.5	4.8	4.8	5.3	5.9	6.2	6.7	9.6	.7	2.8
16 Farmers	11.2	10.8	13.3	10.1	24.3	18.3	17.6	20.1	24.4	30.4	26.6	29.4	22.8	29.5	32.6	82.0	59.7
17 Farm labourers	.3	.5	.9	.5	1.5	1.5	2.1	2.3	2.4	3.1	3.4	3.7	3.6	3.9	5.6	2.9	14.5
18 Total[2]	100.0	100.0	100.0	100.0	100.0	100.0	100.0	100.0	100.0	100.0	100.0	100.0	100.0	100.0	100.0	100.0	100.0

[1] The seventeen occupational groupings are defined in terms of median income and median education (years of schooling) in 1962.
[2] Columns as shown do not total 100.0 since men not reporting father's occupation are not shown separately.

Source: Blau and Duncan (1967), Table 2.8, p. 39. © 1967 by Peter M. Blau and Otis Dudley Duncan.

upward shift in the occupational structure, therefore, permitted substantial mobility. They also argued that America was an open society in that merit was the basis of mobility since, 'A man's social origins exert a considerable influence on his chances of occupational success, but his own training and early experience exert a more pronounced influence on his success chances' (Blau and Duncan 1967: 402). Path analysis, for example, showed that the zero-order correlations with occupational status were .54 for father's education, .40 for father's occupation, .60 for the individual's own education and .54 for their first jobs. These factors accounted for just under half of the 'variance in occupational achievement', the remaining half being accounted for in terms of subsequent career experiences (Blau and Duncan 1967: 402–3). It was in this respect that they spoke of America becoming a more 'universal' society.

Blau and Duncan also considered the effect of ethnic background on occupational success. Blacks did not have the same opportunities for occupational advancement as whites. They tended to have lower social origins, poorer education and started their careers at a lower level in the occupational structure than whites. The cumulative effect of these factors explained the 'handicaps Negroes encounter at every step in their lives that produce the serious inequalities of opportunities under which they suffer' (Blau and Duncan 1967: 238). They went on to suggest that, relatively speaking, unequal opportunities were more pronounced for the better educated black than the uneducated black. Educated black men had less return on their credentials than white men indicating discrimination at the highest levels of the occupational structure. These findings, they argued, had serious implications in that 'acquiring an education is simply not very profitable for Negroes' and that greater rewards were needed if Negroes were to be encouraged to improve their educational attainments (Blau and Duncan 1967: 239).

Overall, Blau and Duncan concluded that America exhibited 'a fundamental trend towards expanding universalism'. In all industrial societies, the drive towards efficiency heralded the decline of ascribed status (family background) and the rise of achieved status (educational attainment) for occupational success. It provided a legitimacy to the structure of opportunity which had not existed before and, thereby, decreased the possibility of class conflict in industrial societies. In other words, Blau and Duncan endorsed the liberal view of industrial societies as increasingly meritocratic and open. This view was confirmed when they considered their research in the context of other findings on comparative social mobility. They argued that the US had higher rates than most countries because of its 'advanced level of industrialisation and education' and the 'relative opportunities of underprivileged Americans with manual origins to move up into the top stratum are particularly good compared to those in other societies'. They concluded:

> It is the underprivileged class of manual sons that has exceptional chances for mobility into the elite in this country. There is a grain of truth in the Horatio Alger myth. The high level of popular education in the United States, perhaps reinforced by the lesser emphasis on formal distinctions of social status, had provided the disadvantaged lower strata with outstanding opportunities for long-distance social mobility. (1967: 435)

Blau and Duncan's research was well-received and generated a wide range of related and derivative studies in the status attainment tradition (Sewell *et al.* 1976; Jencks 1972; Treiman 1977). Jencks (1972), found that family background, IQ and schooling influenced educational attainment but less so occupational success. Rather, factors such as luck and job performance influenced socio-economic outcomes. That said, the status attainment tradition was not without it critics. Coser (1975), for example, accused the status attainment research tradition for being atheoretical in that its research agenda was driven only by methodological considerations. More recently, Knottnerus (1987: 113) has argued that underlying the status attainment research tradition was a functionalist image of society as 'fluid, stable, and becoming increasingly middle class due to technological progress, the rise of universalistic standards, and the growing importance of education'. Emphasis was placed on the role of individual factors in determining occupational success while the influence of structural factors on the attainment process was downplayed. As we shall see, the neglect of structural factors has been a recurring criticism of mobility research in the US.

Blau and Duncan's survey was subsequently replicated by Featherman and Hauser, and the main results of the 'Occupational Change in a Generation II' survey (OCGII) were published in *Opportunity and Change* in 1978. Unlike their predecessors, however, Featherman and Hauser's starting point was the relationship between origins and destinations as a way of exploring occupational inheritance, patterns of mobility between occupations, and figuring out the social distance between classes and their constituent occupations based on an analysis of mobility tables (Grusky 1994). They used Blau and Duncan's hierarchy of seventeen occupations (see Table 3.1) as strata ranked according to levels of education and income to measure trends in vertical mobility. They also aggregated the occupations into five broader occupation strata – upper nonmanual, lower nonmanual, upper manual, lower manual and farm – to facilitate their analysis of bivariate mobility tables. Like their predecessors, however, they

Table 3.2. US class distribution and class composition of men in the experienced civilian labour force aged 21–64, March 1962 and 1973

(a) Inflow to son's occupation from father's (or other family head's) occupation (row %)

Father's occupation	Son's current occupation					
	Upper nonmanual	Lower nonmanual	Upper manual	Lower manual	Farm	Total
1962 (N = 10,550)						
Upper non-manual	25.4	11.6	6.2	4.8	1.7	11.0
Lower non-manual	23.1	19.6	9.5	7.0	2.9	13.1
Upper manual	19.0	20.2	26.3	17.1	2.9	18.8
Lower manual	20.1	25.6	29.7	37.6	6.8	27.4
Farm	12.5	23.0	28.3	33.6	85.7	29.7
Total	100.0	100.0	100.0	100.0	100.0	100.0
1973 (N = 20,850)						
Upper non-manual	29.3	14.8	9.0	7.7	3.2	15.4
Lower non-manual	16.7	16.2	8.6	7.7	3.3	11.5
Upper manual	20.2	21.0	25.8	18.5	5.8	20.4
Lower manual	21.8	30.5	32.6	38.5	7.0	29.7
Farm	12.1	17.5	24.0	27.5	80.7	22.9
Total	100.0	100.0	100.0	100.0	100.0	100.0

(b) Outflow from father's (or other family head's occupation to son's current occupation) (column %)

Father's occupation	Son's current occupation					
	Upper nonmanual	Lower nonmanual	Upper manual	Lower manual	Farm	Total
1962 (N = 10,550)						
Upper non-manual	56.8	16.7	11.5	13.8	1.2	100.0
Lower non-manual	43.1	23.7	14.6	17.0	1.7	100.0
Upper manual	24.7	17.0	28.3	28.8	1.2	100.0
Lower manual	17.9	14.8	21.9	43.4	1.9	100.0
Farm	10.3	12.3	19.3	35.9	22.2	100.0
Total	24.5	15.9	20.2	31.7	7.7	100.0
1973 (N = 20,850)						
Upper non-manual	59.4	11.4	12.8	15.5	0.9	100.0
Lower non-manual	45.1	16.6	16.4	20.7	1.2	100.0
Upper manual	30.9	12.2	27.7	28.1	1.2	100.0
Lower manual	22.9	12.1	23.9	40.1	1.0	100.0
Farm	16.4	9.0	22.9	37.1	14.5	100.0
Total	31.2	11.8	21.9	31.0	4.1	100.0

Note: Broad occupation groups are upper non-manual: professional and kindred workers, managers and officials, and non-retail sales workers; lower non-manual: proprietors, clerical and kindred workers, and retail sales workers: upper manual: craftsmen, foremen and kindred workers: lower manual service workers, operatives and kindred workers, and labourers, except farm; farm: farmers and farm managers, farm labourers and foremen.

Source: Featherman and Hauser (1978), Tables 3.14 and 3.15, pp. 89–91.

addressed the on-going concern that opportunity was declining and that
the chances of social mobility were less than in the past (Featherman and
Hauser 1978: 2).

Featherman and Hauser found evidence of a continued upward shift
in the occupational structure. The farm strata (occupational categories
16–7) and the lower manual stratum (11–5) continued to decline while
the upper manual stratum (8–10) and low-level strata (5–7) and high-
level nonmanual strata (1–4) continued to grow (Featherman and Hauser
1978: 60). Moreover, upper nonmanual destinations were more common
and lower nonmanual destinations less common from 1962 to 1973
(Featherman and Hauser 1978: 90). This upward shift in the occupational
structure facilitated considerable occupational mobility, and upward mobility was more prevalent than downward mobility (37.3 per cent upwards
as against 22.8 per cent down in the first job) (Featherman and Hauser
1978: 135). More than half (60 per cent) of men entering their first jobs between 1930 and 1970, for example, moved out of their father's occupational
strata. Moreover, the trend was towards greater occupational mobility with,
for example, an increase in rates of intra-generational mobility between
1962 and 1973. Again, the changing distribution of occupational origins
and destinations as a result of structural change was seen as the major
source of social mobility. Thus, occupational mobility chances remained
stable in the period between the two surveys although the chances of career
mobility (movement between first to current job) had increased.

Featherman and Hauser also found a change in relative rates of mobility.
They found a 'moderate degree of correlation between occupational origins
and destinations both within and between generations'. However, they
found evidence of a declining correlation between father's occupations
(origins) and son's occupations (destinations) (Table 3.2). There were
small and consistent but significant differences between mobility chances
in 1962 and 1973. It led Featherman and Hauser to conclude that 'there ap-
parently were real changes in the relative chances of mobility from father's
occupation to son's current occupation' (Featherman and Hauser 1978:
137). Again, Featherman and Hauser attached considerable importance
to education as a channel for social mobility. Larger numbers of men in
each cohort, for example, were attending high schools and obtaining high
school qualifications, thereby raising the minimum educational level of their
sample. However, they also found that access to college remained unequal
in that 'matriculation in college remained the province of the offspring of
more advantaged families'. Thus, they concluded:

> In effect, the historic educational differentials by socio-economic
> background have not disappeared. Rather, they have shifted from

the precollege to college years. In as much as a minority of any
cohort attends college, greater equality of precollege education by
social background tends, in the aggregate, to mask the persistence
of unequal opportunity for a college education. (Featherman and
Hauser 1978: 309)

Overall, the value of educational credentials had not been downgraded in
that additional schooling, for example, influenced occupational success.
The beneficial returns on education remained clearly evident (Featherman
and Hauser 1978: 309–10).

Like Blau and Duncan, Featherman and Hauser also paid close attention
to the mobility experiences of ethnic minorities (generating additional
samples of blacks and Hispanics for a detailed analysis of mobility patterns).
On the one hand, they found that black families are increasingly able
to transfer their socio-economic advantages to sons to the extent that the
black population is more stratified by class than in the 1960s. Moreover,
they argued that the education system is an important channel for black
achievement. Young blacks especially are better educated than in the past
which has facilitated occupational success. On the other hand, there are
still considerable racial differences in terms of what advantages can be
gained from family resources and the returns on educational credentials.
Discrimination in the labour market prevails. Moreover, the likelihood of a
young black being in the labour market was less in 1973 than in 1962. Thus,
racial inequality persists in America. Featherman and Hauser concluded
that, 'In many instances, blacks have not yet achieved the statuses held by
whites in the early 1960s' (Featherman and Hauser 1978: 384).

Overall, Featherman and Hauser found 'two complementary trends:
declining status ascription and increasingly universalistic status allocation'.
The relationship between origins and destinations had weakened and the
role of education as a vehicle for social mobility increased. They stated:

> Taken together these trends imply no overall lessening of the
> opportunities for intergenerational social mobility among Ameri-
> can men in the labour force, If anything, the weight of evidence
> of change suggests that the acquisition of schooling, jobs and
> earnings has become less constrained by social background.
> (1978: 495)

Rather than provide unequivocal support for liberal theories of industrial
society like Blau and Duncan, Featherman and Hauser somewhat more
cautiously concluded that:

> The future course of social mobility in the United States is not

inevitable, our national ideology notwithstanding. It depends upon the job creation process, on demographic transformations, planned and unplanned actions by governments, public opinion and political action, and other factors even more dimly understood. (Featherman and Hauser 1978: 495)

Once again, Featherman and Hauser's research was well received although they were also criticised for failing to consider the structural factors which shape mobility processes (Abbott 1993; Baron 1994; 1995; Sorensen 1977; 1986). Sorensen, for example, has long been sceptical of the focus on the individual determinants (family background, ethnicity, education and so forth) of occupational success noting the parallels between status attainment research and human capital theory within economics. Instead, he has drawn on radical dual labour market theory and segmentation theory to account for social mobility. That is, positions in the primary or secondary labour market and within firms or organisations influence opportunities for advancement. It is not merely the lack of educational credentials which accounts for the poorer mobility chances of black men in comparison to white men, for example, but their position in secondary labour markets where pay is low and the possibilities for promotion are limited (Sorensen and Kalleberg 1981). Thus, Sorensen (1986; 1992) has called for more research on intergenerational mobility or worklife mobility to capture the effects on mobility of the industrial structure, the firm or organisation although the structuralist critique has been criticised by its own adherents for its overly economistic focus to the neglect of political initiatives on social mobility (Baron 1994).

Subsequent research in the 1980s and 1990s – including secondary analysis of the two OCG surveys – has confirmed many of Featherman and Hauser's conclusions. Michael Hout's work is a case in point. Hout (1984) examined the occupational mobility of black men between 1962 and 1973 to see if class cleavages within the black population had grown as Wilson (1978) argued. He found significant class effects (similar to those among whites) in intergenerational mobility which he argued had increased in importance between 1962 and 1973. He also found that the chances of upward mobility were greater for men from advantaged socio-economic backgrounds than those from disadvantaged origins in the decade in question. Thus, class divisions in the black population were increasingly evident. Interestingly, he also found that blacks in middle or high status jobs tended to be employed in the public sector implying that the state had facilitated black occupational mobility. That said, he also found that the public sector tended to recruit blacks from middle class and skilled manual backgrounds more than was the case in the private sector

(Hout 1984: 320-1). These findings were confirmed by Hout's (1986) subsequent comparison of blacks in the US with Catholics in Northern Ireland. He established, for example, that the residential segregation of the two minorities in each country had led to the creation of middle-class niches within an otherwise disadvantaged labour market. The middle-class employment that arises in these ecologies is distinct from the middle-class employment of majority groups. Employment is in various community service positions rather than jobs in, say, management. The middle-class American black, in other words, has been recruited into a narrow range of service-sector occupations in the public sector, primarily serving the needs of the black population rather than representing any form of integration into the labour force at large (Hout 1986: 222). The occupational mobility of black men, therefore, must be understood in this context.

Secondary analysis of the General Social Survey (GSS) has facilitated an examination of men and women's position in the american occupational structure in the 1980s. Hout's research (1988) shows that the composition of occupations is highly gendered and women's class destinations are heavily influenced by the sex segregation of the labour market which concentrates women into professional and managerial occupations, clerical work and service work (see Table 3.3). Hout (1988) confirmed that the influence of family origins on occupational destinations continues to decline and that education is playing an ever-important role in the mobility process. Between 1972–85, he found that the association between men's and women's socio-economic origins and destinations declined by nearly a third (30 per cent) overall (33 per cent for women and 28 per cent for men). This trend was accounted for with reference to the growing proportion of men and women who have college degrees 'whose graduation cancels the effect of background status'. The number of men with college degrees increased by 26 per cent while the number of women with college degrees increased by 39 per cent in the period in question. The growing number of college graduates in the labour market, in other words, has actually weakened the relationship between origin and destination in the labour force as a whole (Hout 1988: 384).

However, Hout argues that overall mobility patterns remain the same in the 1980s as they were in the 1970s as a result of the decline in structural mobility. That is, 'the force of structural mobility has declined because a growing proportion of the labour force is second-generation post-industrial: that is, more and more workers are the offspring of the first post-industrial generation' (Hout 1988: 1382) Upward mobility is still greater than downward mobility (especially for women) but the decline in structural mobility has offset the increased openness of the class structure (Hout 1988: 1389).

Table 3.3. Distribution of origins and destinations by sex and year: persons in the US labour force, 1972–85

	Male			Female			
	1972–75	1976–80	1982–85	1972–75	1976–80	1982–85	Total
Origin:							
Professionals, self-employed	1.7	2.2	2.7	1.8	2.7	1.8	2.2
Professionals, salaried	5.2	5.8	6.9	5.2	5.1	7.6	6.1
Managers/sales, non-retail	6.9	8.0	10.7	8.2	10.4	13.0	9.5
Proprietors	8.0	8.3	7.2	9.1	7.9	7.2	7.9
Clerical workers	3.3	3.3	4.2	3.6	3.0	3.7	3.6
Sales, retail	.7	.9	1.1	1.3	1.3	1.0	1.0
Crafts, manufacturing	7.1	9.2	8.3	8.1	7.5	8.1	8.1
Crafts, construction	6.7	4.9	7.1	5.3	5.3	7.2	6.2
Crafts, other	9.9	10.8	9.7	7.3	10.5	9.1	9.7
Service/operatives, other	13.3	11.8	12.2	13.9	13.3	13.1	12.8
Operatives, manufacturing	7.6	9.9	8.7	8.9	8.6	8.0	8.6
Labourers	6.3	5.7	6.0	5.7	5.6	6.5	6.0
Farmers	20.4	17.4	13.4	18.9	16.2	11.7	16.2
Labourers, farm	2.6	1.8	1.8	2.8	2.6	2.0	2.2
Destination:							
Professionals, self-employed	1.9	2.1	3.3	1.0	1.1	1.8	2.0
Professionals, salaried	15.6	17.3	15.6	18.0	19.3	20.7	17.6
Managers/sales, non-retail	15.5	15.1	14.3	6.9	9.2	10.7	12.5
Proprietors	4.5	4.4	5.6	2.3	2.3	2.8	3.9
Clerical workers	6.8	4.5	6.7	32.5	31.1	34.1	17.3
Sales, retail	.8	1.5	.8	2.4	4.2	2.9	1.9
Crafts, manufacturing	7.5	7.6	6.9	1.0	.6	.9	4.6
Crafts, construction	6.4	5.4	7.5	.1	.1	.3	3.8
Crafts, other	9.6	10.7	8.4	.4	1.4	1.6	6.0
Service/operatives, other	13.7	12.6	12.5	23.6	19.2	17.1	15.7
Operatives, manufacturing	8.6	9.8	10.1	10.5	10.6	5.4	9.1
Labourers	4.9	5.0	4.9	.8	.5	1.4	3.2
Farmers	3.5	3.2	2.8	.0	.2	.2	1.9
Labourers, farm	.6	.9	.6	.3	.2	.1	.5
Total number of cases	1,553	1,494	1,542	901	1,062	1,440	1,952
Dissimilarity between origins and destinations	24.5	21.6	17.4	54.2	53.2	49.4	

Source: Hout (1988), Table 2, pp. 1,370–1.

It was on this basis that Hout concluded that changes in the American occupational structure in the 1980s indicate 'more universalism (and) less structured mobility'. Hout also concluded that these findings undermine previous research which indicated that America and Britain have similar trends in social mobility arguing, 'Unless Britain has been changing along with the United States, these conclusions of fundamental similarity between the stratification systems of the two societies may be premature' (Hout 1988: 1390). This comparative issue will be addressed in the final section of the chapter.

Hout's findings have been partially confirmed by DiPrete and Grusky (1990) in their analysis of occupational attainment of American men and women between 1972 and 1987 from the General Social Survey (GSS). Despite the recurring predictions about increasing rigidity in the American class structure, they found little evidence of the re-emergence of ascriptive processes in status attainment. Contrary to Hout, however, they found some evidence of slowdown in the decline of ascriptive processes in the 1980s in comparison to the 1970s although the overall trend has not been reversed. They argue that the most notable decline in ascriptive process took place in the 1960s and 1970s when there was a strong political will to reduce discrimination, for example, against women and ethnic minorities. The slowdown in the trend of the declining significance of ascriptive processes in occupational attainment occurred in the 1980s when the commitment to the free market was the dominant political economy (DiPrete and Grusky 1990: 140). On this basis, DiPrete and Grusky (1990: 140) concluded that 'It follows that the historic decline in status inequality over the past 15 years may not continue into the future at the same pace'. The interpretation of trends and patterns of social mobility in the 1980s and beyond remained, therefore, open to debate.

Over thirty years of mobility research, therefore, has shown that structural change in the economy promoted considerable upward social mobility in the US in the middle decades of the twentieth century. Recent evidence suggests, however, that the end of the long boom in the early 1970s has witnessed a decline in the effects of structural change on social mobility as children of the first post-industrial generation secure their positions in high-level nonmanual occupations. Data from a variety of national sources also show that the relationship between origins and destinations has been declining – although more so for whites than ethnic minorities – and the acquisition of educational credentials has played a major part in the weakening of that relationship. New research, however, again shows a slowdown in this trend in the declining significance of ascriptive status and the growing importance of ascribed status in a changed political climate from the 1970s. Rather than become increasingly rigid, arguably, the US has become a more open society over time although whether this trend continues into the future remains open to serious doubt.

SOCIAL MOBILITY IN BRITAIN

The first national study of social mobility in Britain was conducted by Glass and his colleagues at the London School of Economics (LSE) in 1949. The findings of their survey of 10,000 men were published in *Social Mobility in Britain* in 1954. Glass discovered that Britain was far from being an open or meritocratic society. They found a considerable amount of short-range mobility (64.9 per cent) which had remained unchanged from the late eighteenth to the early nineteenth century. However, there was very little long-range mobility in that 'where there are changes in status between fathers and sons, the sons still tend to be fairly close to their father's level' (Glass and Hall 1954: 185). It was especially difficult to move from manual to non-manual occupations. As a consequence, they found a high degree of self-recruitment in the élite in that 'the highest rigidity is found in the professional and high administrative *cadres*' (Glass 1954: 19;). Finally, the LSE team noted that education was an important means of securing social mobility but social origins remained a significant factor in obtaining high social status. They concluded that, 'the general picture so far is of a rather stable social structure, and one in which social status has tended to operate, within so to speak, a close circuit. Social origins have conditioned educational level, and both have conditioned achieved social status' (Glass 1954: 21).

Glass's research was highly influential as a major pioneering study of its time in Britain and elsewhere (Heath 1981). An up-date of the survey was subsequently undertaken by the Oxford Social Mobility Group based at Nuffield College. Over 10,000 men aged between twenty and sixty living in England and Wales were interviewed in 1972 and a small sub-sample subsequently interviewed about their subjective experiences of social mobility in 1974. Some members of the Oxford Group – Halsey, Heath and Ridge – were especially concerned with the impact of educational reform on the processes of social selection. The results of their research are to be found in Halsey *et al.*, *Origins and Destinations* (1980). The overall findings on patterns and trends of social mobility by Goldthorpe and his collaborators, Llewellyn and Payne, were published in *Social Mobility and Class Structure in Modern Britain* at the same time and appeared as a second edition in 1987 (Goldthorpe 1987).

Before turning to the substantive findings, it should be noted that Goldthorpe promoted the view of social mobility as mobility between class positions. He pioneered the class structural tradition of social mobility research by arguing that 'the distribution of mobility chances within a society' are a 'basic source of class 'structuration' (Goldthorpe and Llewellyn 1977: 30). Social mobility, in other words, is crucial to the study of class formation. On this basis, Goldthorpe rejected the use of occupation as an indicator of socio-economic status or the notion that occupations could be ranked according to a status hierarchy as in the American status attainment tradition. Indeed, Goldthorpe was highly critical of the socio-economic scales used by Blau and Duncan (1967) because occupations of similar prestige were ranked alongside each other although they had very different structural locations. The socio-economic groups, in other words, were too heterogeneous for meaningful comparisons to be made. It was for this reason that Goldthorpe devised discrete class categories as outlined in the previous chapter. The overall assumption, therefore, of the class structural approach was that individuals occupy distinct social classes which shape their interests and social actions.

Against this background, Goldthorpe considered three contemporary theses on social mobility: namely, the closure thesis (argued by Parkin who claimed that the top positions are self-recruiting), the buffer-zone thesis (associated with Giddens who argued that most mobility occurs in the middle of the class structure) and the counter-balance thesis (promoted by Westergaard and Resler (1976) who argued that increased opportunities for upward inter-generational mobility have been cancelled out by reduced opportunities for upward intra-generational mobility). Firstly, Goldthorpe found little evidence of closure at the higher levels of the class structure. While he found nearly a quarter (25 per cent) of men in Class I were the sons of Class I fathers, the remaining three-quarters (75 per cent) came from the other six classes. Over a quarter (27 per cent) of the men in Class I were of working-class origin (16.4 per cent from class VI and 12.1 per cent from Class VII) (Goldthorpe 1987: 44). Secondly, Goldthorpe rejected the view that social mobility was confined to the middle of the class structure. He found little difference, for example, between men of skilled and unskilled working-class origin who had been mobile into other class positions (44 per cent and 43 per cent respectively). Similarly, he found that 7 per cent of the sons of working-class fathers appeared in Class I while a further 9 per cent appeared in Class II (Goldthorpe 1987: 48–50). Finally, Goldthorpe rejected the view that an increase in direct entry to the high social classes has been offset by a decline via indirect routes. Indirect routes (via work experience) into the service class had not been undermined by direct entry (via educational success) (Goldthorpe 1987: 56–58).

All three theses, Goldthorpe concluded, underestimated upward mobility in Britain. Proponents of the theses had failed to distinguish between absolute and relative rates of mobility. Moreover, they had failed to take

Table 3.4. Intergenerational class mobility among men in England and Wales (1972)

(a) Class composition by class of father at respondent's age 14
(% by column)

		I	II	III	IV	V	VI	VII	N	%
		Class of respondent								
	I	24	12	9	6	3	2	2	688	7
	II	13	12	8	4	5	3	2	554	6
	III	10	10	10	6	8	5	5	694	7
Class of father	IV	13	14	12	37	11	10	12	1,329	14
	V	12	14	13	9	16	11	9	1,082	12
	VI	16	21	25	19	29	39	30	2,594	28
	VII	13	18	24	19	29	29	39	2,493	26
	N	1,285	1,087	870	887	1,091	2,000	2,214	9,434	
	%	14	12	9	9	12	21	24		

(b) Class distribution of respondents by class of father at respondent's age 14
(% by row)

		I	II	III	IV	V	VI	VII	N	%
		Class of respondent								
	I	45	19	12	8	5	5	7	688	7
	II	29	23	12	7	10	11	9	554	6
	III	19	16	13	8	13	16	17	694	7
Class of father	IV	13	11	8	24	9	14	21	1,329	14
	V	14	14	10	8	16	21	18	1,082	12
	VI	8	9	8	7	12	30	26	2,594	28
	VII	7	8	8	7	13	24	35	2,493	26
	N	1,285	1,087	870	887	1,091	2,000	2,214	9,434	
	%	14	12	9	9	12	21	24		

Note: Percentages might not add up exactly because of rounding.
Source: Goldthorpe (1987), Tables 2.1–2.2, pp. 45–7.

sufficient account of the evolution of the occupational structure and its implications for the class structure. The shift from manual to nonmanual occupations could be seen in the marginal distributions of the mobility tables. While 14 per cent of fathers had occupied a service-class position, nearly twice as many sons (27 per cent) occupied the same positions. Conversely, while more than half of fathers (55 per cent) were in working-class positions, this proportion was 43 per cent among sons (Goldthorpe 1987: 59–60). The service class, in other words, had grown while the working class had contracted. The mobility data also showed that the class origins of the service class were heterogeneous while the class composition of the working class was markedly homogeneous. It indicated the formation of an inter-generationally unstable collectivity at the top and a stable collectivity at the bottom of the class structure. The findings on absolute mobility rates provided important evidence on issues of class formation.

Goldthorpe also examined relative rates of social mobility and their implications for questions of openness (see Table 3.4). He found that the percentage of sons of Class I origin reaching Class I destinations stood at 25 per cent even though they constituted only 8 per cent of the total sample while 14 per cent of sons of Class VII origins reached Class I destinations. In other words, self-recruitment into Class I positions was three times greater than if there had been perfect mobility while the inflow from Class VII was half what might have been expected (Goldthorpe 1987: 44–6) Similarly, he found that of the sons of Class VI and VII fathers, 16 per cent were found in Classes I and II compared with 60 per cent of sons who fathers were in Classes I and II. Sons with service-class fathers had a 4: 1 chance of gaining access to Class I and II positions over sons of working-class origin. The same chances applied in terms of sons of fathers of service-class origins being found in working-class positions compared with sons whose fathers were manual workers themselves (Goldthorpe 1987: 50). The findings on relative mobility, therefore, indicated that there are 'marked inequalities in mobility chances to the disadvantage of men of working-class background'. Goldthorpe judged that the social closure thesis and the buffer zone thesis were more applicable to relative rather than absolute rates of mobility.

Goldthorpe concluded, therefore, that Britain was not an open society. Even though there had been considerable upward mobility into the service class from the 1940s onwards, the relative chances of access to high-level positions were very unequal. He explained this apparent paradox with reference to the growth of the service class. Although 'more room at the top' had facilitated considerable upward mobility, it was still the case that children from advantaged social backgrounds had a better chance of advancement than children from disadvantaged homes. Their opportunities for advancement were still highly favourable because there was room in the service class for them and the socially mobile. This picture was confirmed by additional analyses of the 1983 British Election Studies (BES) which showed there had been an increase in both upward and downward mobility but there had been no change in social fluidity in the 1970s and 1980s (Goldthorpe 1987: 270-1). In the harsh economic climate of the 1970s and 1980s, however, the advantages of belonging to the service class and the disadvantages of belonging to the working class had heightened.

Overall, Goldthorpe found that the pattern of social fluidity had remained stable despite attempts to create a more open society through educational and social policies at a time of economic expansion. These findings, Goldthorpe argued, indicated the failure and limitations of social policies to reduce class inequalities. He concluded:

> What our results would suggest is that this strategy grossly misjudges the resistance that the class structure can offer to attempts to change it; or, to speak less figuratively, the flexibility and effectiveness with which the more powerful and advantaged groupings in society can use their resources at their disposal to preserve their privileged position. There is a serious underestimation of the forces maintaining the situation in which change is sought, relative to the force of the measures through which, it is supposed, change can be implemented. (Goldthorpe 1987: 328)

Indeed, the failure of egalitarian reform to bring about a more equal society was hidden by economic growth in the post-war period. This conclusion was confirmed by Halsey *et al.*'s findings on the limited effect of education reform on processes of social selection. In the context of educational expansions, the absolute chances of attending university, for example, increased while the relative chances of entry remained the same. Halsey and his associates concluded, 'that the Education Act brought England and Wales no nearer to the ideal of a meritocratic society' (Halsey *et al.* 1980: 210).

The central findings of the Oxford mobility studies were widely debated in academia and they received favourable attention in the media. In a more recent review, for example, Pawson (1993: 46–7) has suggested that Goldthorpe's work 'constitutes one of the finest achievements of British sociology'. Somewhat perversely, any criticisms of Goldthorpe's work focused on Goldthorpe's data and methods rather than his substantive findings on patterns and trends in social mobility. His class schema was (and continues to be) the source of much controversy. Similarly, the absence of women in the 1972 survey created much unease. His male-only sample, it was argued, offered only a partial understanding of class mobility (Abbott and Sapsford 1987). It led to the protracted debate on women and class and the appropriate unit of class analysis which was discussed in the previous chapter.

In response to the debate, Goldthorpe (1987) reported on an analysis of men's and women's mobility using the 1983 BES in the second edition of his monograph. He applied three approaches – the conventional, individual and dominance approaches – to the study of the social mobility of women. Comparing the employment experience of men with women's marital mobility (the conventional approach), he found that women experienced neither higher nor lower rates of social mobility than men. The absolute and relative rates of mobility of women and men were similar. Comparing men and women's employment experiences (the individual approach), he found that both sexes shared similar relative mobility patterns. However, he found differences in absolute rates of mobility in that men were more likely to be upwardly mobile into the service class while women were more often downwardly mobile into the intermediate classes. Finally, adopting the dominance approach (defining the head of household as the most dominant in the labour market whether male or female), he found similar rates of relative mobility between men and women and only slight differences in the absolute patterns of social mobility for both sexes. The conventional and dominance approaches indicated that focusing on the mobility experience of men had not produced a misleading account of class mobility (Goldthorpe 1987: 294–6).

Goldthorpe's empirical results arising from the individual approach were subsequently endorsed by Marshall and his colleagues (Marshall *et al.* 1988). They also found that women share the same patterns of relative mobility as men. Women of service-class origins have a greater chance of reaching service-class destinations than women of working-class origin. The Essex team also found women and men's absolute rates of mobility differed. Among men in service class positions, 74 per cent were mobile from other class destinations while the equivalent percentage was 60 per cent among women in service-class positions. Similarly, they found that of men from service-class backgrounds (Classes I and II), 60 per cent were in service-class positions compared with 49 per cent of comparable women. Looked at another way, only 8 per cent of men of service-class backgrounds had been downwardly mobile into routine nonmanual occupations compared with 40 per cent of women (Marshall *et al.* 1988: 75–7). The evidence pointed to 'the pronounced effects of sex upon patterns of social mobility'. The different mobility patterns were the product of sex segregation in the division of labour in work and at home.

Interestingly, Marshall and his associates looked at the relationship between educational attainment and occupational achievement to ascertain 'the extent to which occupational outcomes reflect meritocratic rather than discriminatory criteria'. They found that the relationship between qualifications and class was stronger for men than women with the former receiving 'a greater return on their credentials' than the later. The overwhelming majority (91 per cent) of men with high level qualifications, for example, are to be found in service class positions compared with 62 per cent of women. Put another way, nearly a third (32 per cent) of highly qualified women are to be found in routine nonmanual work in comparison to a

Table 3.5. Class composition by sex and class of chief childhood supporter at same age as respondent (Goldthorpe class categories)

| | | Males | | | | | | |
| | | Class of respondent | | | | | | |
		I	II	III	IV	V	VI	VII
	I	14.1	13.8	15.8	4.1	3.0	4.6	2.1
	II	12.0	19.3	5.3	8.2	1.5	6.4	3.4
Class of	III	8.7	6.4	0.0	2.7	4.5	9.2	1.4
chief	IV	14.1	12.8	13.2	35.6	13.6	9.2	9.0
childhood	V	17.4	19.3	13.2	11.0	22.7	13.8	21.4
supporter	VI	13.0	16.5	34.2	12.3	30.3	29.4	24.1
	VII	20.7	11.9	18.4	26.0	24.2	27.5	38.6
	Total	100.0	100.0	100.0	100.0	100.0	100.0	100.0
		(92)	(109)	(38)	(73)	(66)	(109)	(145)

(N = 632)

| | | Females | | | | | | |
| | | Class of respondent | | | | | | |
		I	II	III	IV	V	VI	VII
	I	20.0	8.9	8.6	4.3	0.0	0.0	2.1
	II	20.1	13.3	5.6	0.0	0.0	0.0	3.2
Class of	III	5.0	10.0	5.6	4.3	0.0	4.8	3.2
chief	IV	25.0	15.6	10.5	21.7	13.3	4.8	11.7
childhood	V	0.0	24.4	21.0	21.7	6.7	23.8	13.8
supporter	VI	20.0	18.9	30.2	13.0	40.0	42.9	24.5
	VII	10.0	8.9	18.5	34.8	40.0	23.8	41.5
	Total	100.0	100.0	100.0	100.0	100.0	100.0	100.0
		(20)	(90)	(162)	(23)	(15)	(21)	(94)

(N = 425)

Source: Marshall *et al.* (1988), Table 4.7, p. 76.

mere 2 per cent of men. More men than women obtained service-class positions irrespective of their educational attainment while many highly qualified women were stuck in routine nonmanual employment (Marshall *et al.* 1988: 80).

The Essex team concluded that gender segregation in the labour market explains variations in men and women's absolute mobility patterns. They argued:

The structure of occupational opportunities into which it is possible for women to be mobile is different from that available to men. In other words the sexually segregated social division of labour systematically disadvantages women in mobility terms. (Marshall *et al.* 1988: 83)

Like Goldthorpe, therefore, they found that gender segregation shapes patterns of social mobility of women and men. However, unlike Goldthorpe, they concluded that the gendered nature of employment opportunities falls within the remit of class analysis. The study of demographic class formation, they argued, should consider how the 'class structure is constituted through relations between the sexes'. The findings show that men have enjoyed more opportunities for advancement than women. The picture of more room at the top, in other words, need to be qualified with reference to women.

More recently, attention has turned to Goldthorpe's substantive findings on social mobility (Payne 1986; 1987; Saunders 1990b; 1995). Saunders, for example, has argued that Goldthorpe's focus on unchanging relative rates of mobility has deflected attention away from the high rates of upward and downward mobility in the British class structure. As a result, a considerable degree of fluidity has been overlooked. Moreover, the Oxford researchers had wrongly assumed that people have equal abilities and thereby systematically ignored differences of ability and effort among people. In contrast, Saunders (1995: 31) has asserted that differences in innate ability influence educational success and are one factor determining social mobility chances. Calculating the predicted class destination of children born to service class parents (service-class origins to service-class destination and service-class origins to working-class destinations) and working-class parents (working-class origins to service-class destinations and working-class origins to working-class destinations), Saunders (1995: 37) celebrated the 'extraordinarily high degree of fit' between his predictions and Goldthorpe's actual findings. He concluded that data on social mobility patterns in Britain are 'broadly consistent' with a meritocratic model and Britain, therefore, might be a meritocracy.

There have been some speedy responses to Saunders' argument (Heath *et al.* 1992; Payne; 1992; Marshall and Swift 1993; 1996). All the commentators are agreed that class origins effect class destinations even when controlling for educational attainment. Analysing data from the Essex class project, for example, Marshall and Swift (1993: 202) found that high levels of educational achievement facilitated equal chances of access for men into the service class. However, those of service-class origins with lower levels of educational attainment are able to circumvent downward mobility.

As Table 3.5 shows, 33 per cent of poorly qualified men from service-class families arrive at service-class destinations while 40 per cent are found in working-class destinations. In comparison, 11 per cent of poorly qualified men from working-class families arrived at service-class occupations while 64 per cent remained in working-class positions. The relationship between class origins and class destinations also applies for women although gender does have an effect. Among highly educated women, service from service class backgrounds have a better chance of securing service-class destinations than women of working-class origin. Remaining in the service class was achieved by 92 per cent of highly-qualified men but only 78 per cent of equivalent women. Women with lower level qualifications are invariably found in intermediate class positions because of their heavy concentration in routine nonmanual employment (Marshall and Swift 1993: 204).

Marshall and Swift concluded that class origins affect class destinations irrespective of educational achievements. This conclusion applies especially to those of service-class origins with middling educational achievements. It appears that parents in advantaged positions can circumvent the downward mobility of their less educationally successful children. In other words, Goldthorpe's (1987) findings on patterns of inter-generational fluidity are confirmed, the evidence showing that processes of social closure operate at the top of the class structure and a buffer zone exists between nonmanual and manual employment (as Goldthorpe argued). Saunders' (1996) subsequent secondary analysis of the National Children Development Study (NCDS) also indicates that less able members of the middle class fall only as far as low-level nonmanual work and avoid long-range downward mobility into manual employment. The findings have led him to qualify his more controversial argument that Britain might be a meritocracy although he still holds to the less controversial thesis that ability counts in the mobility process. The relative significance of ability in relation to other factors in the process of mobility has yet to be established however.

Overall, the evidence suggests that structural change in the economy facilitated a large amount of upward social mobility as manual occupations declined and nonmanual occupations grew in size in the mid-twentieth century. Absolute rates of mobility increased from the 1940s onwards although more so for men than women because of gender segregation in the labour market. Over the same period, however, relative rates of mobility stayed the same for men and women. People of service-class origins have a better chance of remaining in the service class than people of working-class entering it. Britain, therefore, is not entirely a closed and unchanging class society although it has not become a more open society over time either. The evidence suggests that these patterns and trends in social mobility have

Table 3.6. Inter-generational mobility trajectories and educational attainment (percentage)

Educational attainment			Male Destinations					Female Destinations					All Destinations			
			S	I	W			S	I	W			S	I	W	
High[1]	Origins	S	92	3	5	100	(38)	78	22	0	100	(27)	86	11	3	100
		I	90	5	5	100	(40)	63	35	2	100	(49)	75	21	3	100
		W	91	9	0	100	(32)	57	39	4	100	(23)	76	22	2	100
Medium	Origins	S	43	32	26	100	(47)	30	61	9	100	(23)	39	41	20	100
		I	31	41	29	100	(101)	22	63	16	100	(64)	27	49	24	100
		W	15	37	48	100	(110)	21	60	19	100	(78)	17	47	36	100
Low	Origins	S	33	27	40	100	(15)	0	57	43	100	(7)	23	36	41	100
		I	13	33	54	100	(92)	13	37	50	100	(46)	13	34	53	100
		W	11	25	64	100	(157)	2	43	56	100	(108)	7	33	60	100

[1] Low: holds no formal qualifications: CSE Grades 2–5; or job training (e.g. HGV driving licence) only.
Medium: holds CSE Grade 1; GCE O or A level or Scottish equivalents; Overseas School Leaving Certificate; ONC, OND, City and Guilds; HNC, HND, City and Guilds; RSA Clerical or commercial; or full apprenticeship qualification.
High: holds teacher training qualification; full nursing qualification; other technical or business qualification; professional qualification; degree or higher degree; or other vocational qualification equivalent to a degree.

Source: Marshall and Swift (1993), Table II, p. 203.

continued since the end of the long boom in the early 1970s although the advantages and disadvantages of occupying different class positions have polarised. The recent debate on meritocracy highlights the need for further research on the processes by which those in advantaged positions are able to mobilise their resources a consequence of which is the persistence of class in late twentieth century Britain.

AMERICA AND BRITAIN COMPARED

Finally, comparative research on social mobility offers the opportunity directly to examine whether America is an exceptionally open society and whether Britain is an exceptionally closed society (see Ganzeboom *et al.* 1989; 1991; Trieman and Ganzeboom 1990). Do the two nations, in other words, conform to popular stereotypes? It has long been presumed that the US has exceptionally high levels of upward mobility especially into top positions. However, Lipset and Zetterberg (1956) and Lipset and Bendix (1959) broke this consensus when they argued that mobility rates are similar in all Western industrialised societies (as a result of their level of economic development). The LZ hypothesis (as it became known) was subsequently criticised by Miller (1960) who argued that cultural and political diversity can produce variations in mobility rates and, indeed, in the occupational structure itself. Miller (1960) found considerable variation in élite mobility across the eighteen countries of his research and that élite mobility was high in America in comparison to other countries as Blau and Duncan (1967) later argued. Social mobility, it was argued, was easier in a 'new' nation like America than 'old' nations like Britain. However, the technical problems associated with comparative research have led to doubts about this view. Heath (1981: 198), for example, has argued that Blau and Duncan found high levels of long distance upward mobility in the US because they employed a very wide definition of the élite. High levels of upward mobility, therefore, were an artifact of the methods employed. It was not firmly established that America was an exceptionally open society.

The LZ hypothesis was then reformulated by Featherman, Jones and Hauser (1978). The FJH hypothesis posits that variations in mobility rates might derive from historical and cultural differences in occupational structures but not from differences in exchanges between occupations. This hypothesis implies that once variations in the distribution of origins and destinations are taken into account, mobility chances do not vary (or, to put it another way, absolute mobility rates may vary across countries but relatives rates of mobility do not). This thesis has found widespread support in relation to the US and Britain among other nations. Grusky and Hauser (1984), for example, found substantial similarity in mobility and immobility across the sixteen countries of their research including the US

and Britain. They found 'severe immobility at the two extremes of the
occupational hierarchy and considerable fluidity in the middle' (Grusky
and Hauser 1984: 35). Differences between societies were the result mostly
of variations in the marginal distributions of the mobility tables. The task
of comparative mobility researchers, they concluded, is to consider these
differences in marginal distributions and the economic and political factors
which may influence these factors (Grusky and Hauser 1984: 36).

The FJH hypothesis has also been reaffirmed in comparative research
focused on Britain and the US (Kerchoff and his colleagues 1985). Drawing
on data from the OCGII survey and the Oxford Study, Kerchoff *et al.* argued that the US does not exhibit higher levels of social fluidity than Britain.
There is more intergenerational and intra-generational mobility in the US
than in Britain. However, the differences between the two societies are the
result of shifts in the distribution of kinds of occupations. In the US, the most
important change has been the huge shift out of farming and the growth
of high-level white-collar occupations while the same processes have been
happening in Britain but on a much smaller scale. Britain has more manual
workers and fewer professional and managerial employees. It is for these
reasons that America has exhibited more intergenerational upward mobility
than Britain. However, in terms of patterns of fluidity, Kerchoff *et al.*
found little difference between the two countries once the differences in
marginal distributions had been taken into account. They concluded that,
'the United States and Britain have the same fluidity patterns and any
apparent differences between them are due to the particular shifts in the
societies' occupational distributions' (Kerchoff *et al.* 1985: 300).

The FJH hypothesis has also been largely confirmed by Erikson and
Goldthorpe (1992a) in their comparative research on twelve nations from
west and east Europe and including the US, Australia and Japan under
the auspices of the CASMIN (Comparative Analysis of Social Mobility in
Industrial Nations) project. To empirically evaluate the hypothesis, Erikson
and Goldthorpe proposed a model of 'core fluidity'. They found that
relative rates of mobility are not entirely identical (ie, they do vary) but,
at the same time, they share a high degree of commonality. Erikson and
Goldthorpe proposed that:

> within the modern world, relative mobility rates have a 'basic'
> cross-national similarity may be taken to mean that a particular
> pattern of such rates is identifiable, to which the patterns actually
> found in different national societies will all approximate even
> though any, or indeed all, of these societies may show some
> amount of deviation. (Erikson and Goldthorpe 1992a: 117)

To test this hypothesis, they defined a 'space' embodying a core (central position) and the parameters of variations in fluidity. England and France were found to occupy the central positions. By using this model, Erikson and Goldthorpe could explore if there is a 'common or core pattern of social fluidity that is generic to industrial societies although one on which particular national variations may occur' (Erikson and Goldthorpe 1992a: 139).

Erikson and Goldthorpe subsequently fit their model of core social fluidity to the intergenerational mobility tables of their nine European nations. They found a 'a sizeable commonality' in patterns of social fluidity confirming their model. They also found 'deviations from the core model that are real *and* that express features of national fluidity patterns that are of a persisting rather than a passing kind, (Erikson and Goldthorpe 1992a: 175). In seeking to explain these deviations, they recognised the 'specificities of historical events, conjuctures and processes'. More importantly, however, they emphasised the importance of political intervention, namely; the 'role of the *state* as an agency of intervention in, and against, the processes of 'civil society' through which inequalities of opportunity are 'spontaneously' generated and perpetuated' (Erikson and Goldthorpe 1992a: 179). England and France are the two central nations in the model because 'fluidity patterns have been allowed to operate within a minimum of intervention via the state' (Erikson and Goldthorpe 1992a: 180). Thus, Erikson and Goldthorpe refined the FJH hypothesis to take account of these factors while still holding to the core model of cross-national commonality.

Erikson and Goldthorpe also explored whether their conclusions applied to the US with reference to claims about American exceptionalism (see also Erikson and Goldthorpe 1985). The American data were the least satisfactory for comparative research. Nevertheless, they applied their model of 'core' social fluidity to intergenerational mobility tables. They found that American patterns of social fluidity do not differ substantially from the European nations although the patterns are distinctive. There is greater mobility between the service class and routine nonmanual employees and between the service class and non-skilled manual workers in both directions (Erikson and Goldthorpe 1992a: 319). Rather than confirm Blau and Duncan's claims, however, Erikson and Goldthorpe saw the findings as an artifact of heterogeneous occupational categories which tend to exaggerate mobility in to and out of the service class. In substantive terms, they concluded, 'the United States lies towards the 'more fluid' end of the European range'. If the data had been of a better standard, 'then the United States would have been found to stand rather close to England and France as in fact one of our 'central nations – in which, again, the processes of 'civil society' that shape fluidity patterns could be regarded as operating with a large measure of freedom from direct political intervention'

(Erikson and Goldthorpe 1992a: 321). Finally, their examination of trends in relative mobility rates indicated the possibilities of a shift towards greater overall fluidity in the mid-twentieth century. This finding confirmed Hout's (1988) view that there might have been a rising trend in fluidity in America during this period although Erikson and Goldthorpe remain sceptical as to whether the changes can be described as substantial or not.

Turning to absolute rates of mobility (of which they found considerable variation among the European nations), Erikson and Goldthorpe explored whether America had an exceptionally high level of observed mobility as a result of rapid economic expansion and related structural change. As we saw in Chapter 2 (Table 2.2), the US has a relatively high proportion of men in high and low-level nonmanual positions and a high proportion are of nonmanual origins as well. In this respect, the US can be described as 'being at the end of the post-industrial' end of the European range' (Erikson and Goldthorpe 1992a: 328). At the same time, however, the development of the American class structure has not differed from its European counter-parts and the differences between origins and destinations distributions is not unique either. The US, in other words, has not experienced exceptionally rapid structural change. That said, it is a nation characterised by relatively high mobility within the European range. The US was found to have a total mobility rate of seventy-three (the same as Sweden) which is higher than England's rate of sixty-five but lower than Hungary's rate of seventy-six although the incidence of upward over downward mobility was not at the higher end of the European scale. Thus, the US is not exceptional in terms of absolute rates of mobility.

Finally, turning to worklife mobility, Erikson and Goldthorpe found that the extent of opportunities for men to be mobile over the life-course is not exceptional in the US compared with European countries. As Table 3.6 shows, levels of entry into the service class and self-employment are high in the US but not exceptionally so. America has higher entry rates from skilled employment to service class positions (20 per cent compared with 16 per cent) although it is not as high as Sweden (22 per cent). The US has a much higher entry rates from small employment to the service class (7 per cent compared with 3 per cent) but again it is not as high as Sweden (8 per cent). The same findings applied when origins were taken into account; namely, America exhibits higher rates of entry than Britain but not as high as either Sweden or Australia. On this basis of all of this evidence, Erikson and Goldthorpe concluded that:

> No matter how distinctive the United States and Australia may
> be in the economic and social histories of their industrialisation
> or in their ideas, beliefs, and values concerning mobility that are

Table 3.7. Work-life outflow mobility rates between selected classes: men aged 35–64 (percentage)

Outflow	USA	AUS	ENG	FRA	HUN	IRL	NIR	POL	SCO	SWE
Entry in V+VI to 1+II	20	18	16	15	15	8	15	12	16	22
Entry in VIIa to I+II	15	19	11	13	11	5	6	9	11	16
Entry in IVc/VIIb to I+II	7	8	3	5	5	1	4	2	6	8
Entry in V+VI to IVa+b	11	19	10	15	5	16	13	3	7	13
Entry in VIIa to IVa+b	8	8	8	9	1	9	9	2	4	10
Origin and entry in V+VI/VIIa to I+II	15	16	12	12	14	7	7	12	11	20
Origin and entry in IVc/VIIb to I+II	6	7	3	3	4	1	3	2	5	6
Origin and entry in V+VI/VIIa to IVa+b	7	14	7	10	2	4	9	2	4	8

Source: Erikson and Goldthorpe (1992a), Table 9.5, p. 331.

> prevalent in their national cultures, it could not, on our evidence, be said that they differ more widely from European nations in their actual rates and patterns of mobility than do European nations among themselves. (Erikson and Goldthorpe 1992a: 337)

Overall, the comparative evidence indicates that America is not an exceptionally open society and Britain is not an exceptionally closed society. Rather than occupy opposite ends of the spectrum, the two nations share similar patterns of absolute and relative social mobility, and that similarity arises from the fact that both nations have been characterised by a minimum of state intervention to reduce class inequalities.

CONCLUSION

This chapter has examined patterns and trends in social mobility in America and Britain in the second half of the twentieth century. We have seen that the US enjoyed considerable absolute mobility as a result of structural change. There has also been a decline in the association between origins and destination, and education has undermined this link. These trends were enjoyed more by whites than ethnic minorities however. Rather than becoming increasingly rigid, therefore, America has become a more open society over the middle decades of the twentieth century. However, the evidence suggests that this trend towards openness may slowing or coming to an end as structural change has slackened and the pace of the decline in the link between origins and destinations has decreased. The somewhat more hostile economic and political climate in the 1970s and 1980s may be taking its toll on patterns and trends in social mobility.

Britain also enjoyed considerable amounts of absolute social mobility in the mid-twentieth century as a result of structural change. Again, men have enjoyed more opportunities for advancement than women. However, the chances of advancement are still heavily influenced by social origins. Children of advantaged backgrounds have a better chance of enjoying privileged positions in the class structure than children from disadvantaged backgrounds. Unlike America, therefore, there is no evidence of Britain becoming a more open society over time. The top of the class structure remains relatively closed and a buffer zone operates between nonmanual and manual occupations. A more hostile economic and political climate in the 1970s and 1980s does not appear to have altered these patterns and trends in social mobility although the advantages and disadvantages of belonging to different social classes have become more pronounced than in the past.

This evidence suggests that America and Britain confirm to the popular stereotypes of the two nations. However, a direct comparison of the two countries suggests that the opposite conclusion holds. Comparative research indicates that America is not an exceptionally open society and Britain is not an exceptionally closed society. Rather than occuping opposite ends of the spectrum, the two nations share similar patterns and trends of absolute and relative social mobility, and that similarity arises from the fact that both nations have been characterised by a minimum of state intervention to reduce class inequalities. This chapter has focused on the movement of people between different social classes identified in the previous chapter. The next chapter examines the extent to which these objectively defined demographic entities constitute socio-political entities in America and Britain.

Chapter 4

Class Consciousness

The study of class consciousness is about the extent to which classes are organised in pursuit of their interests. The central issue at stake revolves around whether members of a class have a shared sense of common interest which is mobilised by class organisations in pursuit of those interests. Whether or not classes are collective actors, therefore, raises organisational issues such as the degree to which the trade unions and political parties mobilise collective interests over sectional concerns. Research on class consciousness, however, has focused on the narrower issue of individual levels of class awareness including popular conceptions of the class structure, the extent to which people identify with classes, which social factors influence class identities and the implications of class identities on wider social and political attitudes and behaviour. The major debate on 'class consciousness' has centred on the extent to which class identities may or may not have declined in the second half of the twentieth century. More recently, attention has also focused on the extent to which other social identities such as race and gender have undermined class identification. The significance of other social identities, therefore, is interrelated with the debate on the decline or persistence of class identities in the twentieth century.

This chapter considers whether class identities have declined and other social identities have become more important over time. The extent to which class identities affect political proclivities is also explored. The chapter is divided into three parts. The first section focuses on the debates in America. The evidence suggests that class is a salient social identity in the US. Americans are willing and able to identify predominately with the middle class or the working class. Class also structures social attitudes about the nature of inequality in American society. Those who occupy middle-class positions take a more benign view of class while members of the working class are more critical of inequalities in the US. However, class attitudes cannot be described as polarised although they have become more so in the 1980s. There is a widespread commitment to equal opportunities even though they can produce large economic inequalities. There is also a widespread opposition to government intervention in terms of redistributive measures to create equality of outcomes. The ongoing debate on affirmative action policies is a case in point. These socio-political views are a reflection of American politics where the language of class is largely absent. Class issues, for example, have not been mobilised in any radical way by the Democratic Party which is largely committed to moderate liberalism. The political impact of class, therefore, is muted. The failure of the Democratic Party to mobilise class issues rather than the increased salience of racial identities explains low levels of class consciousness in the US.

The second section focuses on class consciousness in Britain. Overall, the evidence suggests that class is the most common and salient social identity in Britain and other social identities such as gender and race have not undermined an affiliation to class. Class also structures perceptions of and attitudes towards inequality. However, class attitudes are not highly polarised. Arguably, members of all classes think the distribution of wealth and income in Britain is unfair and share broadly similar views as to why it is unfair although members of the working class are notably more disillusioned than their middle-class counterparts about the effects of government on changing existing socio-economic arrangements. That said, a close relationship between class position, class identification and voting patterns persists in Britain and there is little evidence of class dealignment. Disillusionment and cynicism suggests that class organisations have failed to mobilise members of the working class behind collective rather than sectional interests. This argument implies that America and Britain may have similar levels of class consciousness although this issue demands a direct comparison between the two countries.

The third section directly compares class consciousness in American and Britain. The comparative evidence suggests that Americans are less class conscious than the British. They share similar levels of class identification and class awareness to their British counterparts. However, Americans are more liberal and Britons more radical in their social and political views. While attitudes are structured by class, Americans endorse policies for equal opportunities and are hostile to redistributive policies. The British, in contrast, support equal opportunities and redistributive policies to ensure equal outcome although, again, these views are shaped by class. A relationship between class and party persists in the US but the association is stronger in Britain. How far these differences will persist depends on political circumstances. In the face of heightened class consciousness in the 1980s when the political economy of the free market prevailed, it may be that Americans are becoming more like their British counterparts.

Similarly, the promotion of policies of equal opportunities rather than equal outcomes by a Labour Party desperate for electoral success suggests that the British may not be so unlike their American counterparts in the future either.

CLASS IDENTITIES IN AMERICA

An interest in the subjective dimension of social class can be found in the early American community studies (Lynd and Lynd 1929; 1937) The Lynds identified a business class and a working class in Middletown mostly preoccupied with earning a living and not especially class conscious. In their re-study, however, they found a growing rift between the two classes and they predicted 'the emergence of class consciousness and possible eventual conflict' (Lynd and Lynd 1937: 72). Warner also addressed issues of subjective class in 'Yankee City' although he discussed it interchangeably with issues of status. Using a prestige scale, Warner argued that 'class' distinctions were clear cut, and a 'class order' predominated (Warner and Lund 1941; Warner *et al.* 1949).

The first major study of subjective social class – a national representative survey of 1,100 white males conducted in 1945 – was conducted by Centers (1949). He was highly critical of a series of studies published by *Fortune* magazine in the early 1940s which had found that almost 80% of the population defined themselves as middle class. Dissatisfied with the choice of lower class, middle class and upper class presented to *Fortune*'s respondents, Centers added the option of 'working class' to his fixed-choice question. The result was that a majority of his sample identified with the working class (see Table 4.1). He also found that each class was associated with particular occupations and that there was a clear relationship between occupational strata and class identification. Business, professional and white-collar workers identified strongly with the middle class (74 per cent) while manual workers (79 per cent) overwhelmingly identified with the working class (Centers 1949: 85). Occupation, therefore, was the major criterion by which social classes were defined. Just under half of the sample (47 per cent) also defined class membership in terms of beliefs and attitudes confirming Centers' (1949: 106) view that classes are groups of people with shared interests and outlook.

Centers found that the middle class and the working class had different economic and political orientations. Members of the middle class were con-servative and individualistic while members of the working class were more radical and collectivistic on such issues as public verses private ownership, the treatment of working people, levels of pay and so forth. Similarly, the middle class was more optimistic about the opportunities for advancement and the factors determining success while working-class people were more

Table 4.1. Class identification of a national cross-section of white males
(July 1945 and February 1946)

	1946	%	1945
Upper class	3		4
Middle class	43		36
Working class	51		52
Lower class	1		5
Don't know	1		3
'Don't believe in classes'	1		—
Total	100		100
Number	1,097		1,337

Source: Centers (1949), Tables 18 and 19, p. 77.

pessimistic in their replies. The middle class and working class, in other
words, constituted two different 'ideological' camps. Centers concluded
that class conflict had reached a 'critical phase' since 'Americans have
become class conscious, and a part of them, calling themselves the working
class, have begun to have attitudes and beliefs at variance with traditional
acceptances and practices' (Centers 1949: 218). However, he noted that
working-class consciousness was restricted to a 'narrow politico-economic
compass'. Trade unionism was confined to the pursuit of immediate goals
while there was no political party which explicitly mobilised the interests
of the working class. Class consciousness, therefore, was evident although
it was extremely limited.

Centers's findings on working-class consciousness were the source of
considerable debate. Many commentators were critical of his methodology
and whether the inclusion of the category of 'working class' in his fixed-
choice question – really tapped working-class consciousness. Gordon
(1958), for example, argued that Centers' thesis was neither valid, nor
reliable and 'his concept of class was not particularly useful for the American
scene'. Subsequent research in the 1950s showed that the existence of
class was often denied and when acknowledged, identification with the
middle class was more popular than with the working class (Kahl and
Davis 1955) while research in the 1960s attributed high levels of middle-
class identification with higher standards of living at the time (Hodge and
Treiman 1968). High levels of working-class consciousness were dismissed
as an artefact of the methods used or assumed to have declined in the
post-war period of prosperity.

The prevailing view was confirmed by Coleman and Rainwater (1978) in the 1970s. Following in Warner's footsteps, they carried out two local surveys in the metropolitan areas of Boston and Kansas City. The majority (90 per cent) of their respondents felt that social class had declined in importance because social mobility was so commonplace. A rigid system in which people stayed in the same class as their parents had been supplanted by a fluid system in which family (and ethnic) background had declined. Hence, it was widely perceived that most Americans occupied the middle-income middle class which enjoyed a comfortable standard of living (Coleman and Rainwater 1978: 296). Not surprisingly, the abolition of remaining restrictions on social mobility was seen as the major way of changing the class structure. This view was supported by high and low status Americans alike since as the authors noted, 'No reduction in inequality of results is proposed, only a reduction in inequality of initial opportunity' (Coleman and Rainwater 1978: 302). Overall, Coleman and Rainwater concluded, 'In the final analysis, the deepest and broadest source of opposition to a major change in the American class system, and especially to the elimination of a lowest class, derives from devotion to the effortocratic ideal' (Coleman and Rainwater 1978: 304).

Coleman and Rainwater's findings – of a society perceived by its members as predominately open and middle class – was widely discussed and largely endorsed (Rothman 1993; Gilbert and Kahn 1993). However, their portrayal of respondents as predominately content with the class structure and the absence of any class conflict among them also met with criticism. Their treatment of social status, social class and social standing as synonymous was seen as problematic. It was not clear, for example, whether Coleman and Rainwater had tapped people's opinions on the decline of the status system rather than the demise of class divisions. Hochschild's (1981) intensive study of social justice, for example, also found little support for redistributive measures to achieve equality. However, her poor respondents saw some economic inequalities as unjust. She found plenty of scepticism about portrayals of American as a classless society in which people could advance through ability and effort. Thus, inequality was not merely accepted and endorsed along the lines implied by Coleman and Rainwater.

These findings were subsequently confirmed by a series of nationally representative studies in the 1980s. The first such study was Jackman's and Jackman's, *Class Awareness in the United States*, published in 1983. They conducted a national representative survey of nearly 2,000 respondents. Jackman and Jackman found that the overwhelming majority (97 per cent) of their respondents were prepared to identify with one of the five categories – upper class, upper middle class, middle class, working class, poor class – they provided. The distribution of the respondents to the class identification

Table 4.2. Distribution of 'responses to class-identification question' (per total sample, by race and class)

	Poor %	Work- ing	Middle	Upper- middle	Upper	Other[1]	No social classes	Don't know	Not ascer- tained	Total
Total sample	7.6	36.6	43.3	8.2	1.0	1.3	0.5	1.5	0.2	1,914
Whites	4.8	35.8	46.4	9.0	1.0	1.1	0.5	1.3	0.2	1,648
Blacks	27.7	41.5	22.1	1.5	1.5	2.6	0.5	2.6	0.0	195
Others[2]	14.1	39.1	32.8	7.8	0.0	1.6	0.0	3.1	1.6	64
Men	5.4	41.4	40.5	8.5	1.1	1.4	0.9	0.5	0.4	802
Women	9.2	33.1	45.2	8.0	0.9	1.2	0.2	2.2	0.1	1,112

[1] This category includes identification with two classes (e.g. 'poor and working', 'working and middle') and irrelevant responses.
[2] This category includes Orientals, Spanish, Americans and American Indians.
Source: Jackman and Jackman (1983), Table 2.1, p.18. © Mary Jackman and Robert Jackman 1983. Reprinted with the permission of the University of California Press.

question for the sample as a whole and by race and sex can be seen in Table 4.2. As in previous research, they found that only small numbers of respondents identified with the upper class and upper middle class but, in contrast to other research, they had a high level of identification with the poor class. The majority of their respondents identified either with the middle class or the working class (43 per cent and 37 per cent respectively). They concluded that the use of the nonodious category of 'poor class' rather than 'lower class' drew away from identification from the working class although roughly similar proportions identified with the middle class and working class as in past research. They also considered the criteria for class membership. They found that beliefs and feelings, style of life and occupation were considered very important criteria (40 per cent, 39 per cent and 37 per cent respectively). Confirming Center's earlier findings, they concluded that, 'These patterns imply that class is indeed popularly interpreted as a social as well as an economic phenomenon' (Jackman and Jackman 1983: 38). There was no evidence to suggest that the cognitive identification of class is no longer significant in the US.

Jackman and Jackman also found that social class has emotional signifi-cance. It is the basis of group identity, interpretations of group differences and in perceptions of class interests. Not surprisingly, they found that the effective and interpretative implications of class identification are felt most keenly by those in the lower classes. Well over a half (61 per cent) of poor respondents felt that class differences result from biased opportunities compared with a third of upper middle-class respondents (1983: 69). The perception of mutually opposed class interests was also more prevalent in the lower class indicating that ' class is more keenly felt by those who experience its deprivations than by those who enjoy its privileges' (Jackman and Jackman 1983: 69). Finally, in terms of group identity, they found that social class is at least as strong a factor as race although there was a strong identification among the black middle class with their race rather than class. They also found that occupation, education and income affect class identification and that respondents translate social standing into a class identification in a rational and consistent manner although, again, for high-status blacks, they found that 'their low racial status renders their socio-economic status relatively insignificant.' Class is a major source of group identity although class is interpreted differently by the black middle class whose low racial status is a source of grievance (Jackman & Jackman 1983: 69).

Finally, but most importantly, Jackman and Jackman considered the effect of social class on political orientations. Class differences were pronounced between those who were satisfied with the status quo as against those who supported more government intervention. The respondents' views on the role of federal government in social welfare activities, for example, varied with class. Less than a quarter of the upper middle class (24 per cent) felt that the government should be doing a lot more to guarantee full employment in comparison with nearly half of the poor (49 per cent) (Jackman and Jackman 1983: 203). Turning to egalitarian opinions, they found little support for income equality with only slight differences of opinions across the different classes. Each class justified inequality in terms of achievement indicating an endorsement of equal opportunities rather than equal outcomes. There was little support for more distributive forms of taxation across all classes and redistributive measures more generally. Overall, Jackman and Jackman concluded that the political impact of class was somewhat qualified.

Jackman and Jackman explained the weak link between class and politics with reference to the nature of American politics. That is, there is little debate on class and redistribution issues in the political domain. The reforms of the New Deal and Great Society envisaged a minimal role for government as a 'safety net' against poverty and deprivation. Political discourse, in other words, is focused on liberal preoccupations such as equal opportunities rather than the equal distribution of rewards. The absence of public discussion of these fundamental class issues is compounded by a weak party system comprising of various coalitions organised around a variety of different and often inconsistent policy goals. The American party system has failed 'to provide a clear electoral outlet for distinctive class views'. As they argued:

> Given all these factors, organised political life provides the elector-
> ate with only a sparse education on class issues. People are loosely
> familiar with the general parameters of social welfare issues, but
> they have not been educated in either the more fundamental issue
> of social inequality or in the specific redistributive implications of
> alternative economic policies. In all, the potential political impact
> of class remains limited because an established counter ideology
> from which people might readily draw is not available. (Jackman
> and Jackman 1983: 215)

Thus, while Jackman and Jackman rejected claims that the US is a classless
society, they acknowledged that the potential of class is unrealised in the
political sphere.

The second major study of class consciousness is Wright's study of class
structure and class consciousness in the US and Sweden already discussed in
Chapter Two. He also concluded that the low levels of class consciousness
in the US can be explained with reference to the weak class organisations
which have failed to mobilise collective class interests over individual
sectional concerns. Wright measured class consciousness by examining
the extent to which individuals have attitudes which are consistent with
working class or capitalist class interests. Using a class consciousness scale
to analyse responses to specific class attitudes, he found a direct relationship
between the class structure and class consciousness in the United States
and Sweden. As Table 4.3 demonstrates, proletarians endorse pro-working
class attitudes while the bourgeoisie endorse pro-capitalist attitudes. He
also found a similar pattern in working-class identification across the two
countries (Wright 1985: 263). However, the degree of polarisation in
attitudes between the two countries was very different (4.6 points in the
US compared with 2 points in Sweden). American workers, for example,
sought compromises on the outcome of strikes while Swedish workers
were more supportive of outright victory. Thus, Wright concluded that
30 per cent of the labour force in the US could be considered part of a
bourgeois coalition compared with only 10% in Sweden. The US, therefore,
has a smaller working-class base which is less polarised ideologically from
the bourgeoisie than in Sweden (Wright 1985: 265).

Overall, Wright concluded that the underlying nature of class relations
shapes the overall pattern of class consciousness. The level of working-
class consciousness in a society and the nature of class coalitions are
shaped by 'organisational and political practices'. The strong unionism and
class politics found in Sweden has reinforced class consciousness. Weak
unionism and the moderation of the Democratic Party in the US, in contrast,
has undermined class consciousness. The language of class is absent from

Table 4.3. Working-class identification and responses to individual items by class location

I. United States	Working Class I.D.	% who take the working class position on:					
		Individual items in consciousness scale[1]					
Class location		(1)	(2)	(3)	(4)	(5)	(6)
1 Proletarians (12)[2]	32	56	27	49	55	75	19
2 Semi-credentialled workers (9)	28	61	28	48	58	82	14
3 Uncredentialled supervisors (11)	31	56	24	56	44	87	16
4 Expert employees (6)	15	58	26	36	36	80	13
5 Semi-credentialled supervisors (8)	32	50	27	35	42	77	11
6 Uncredentialled managers (10)	28	55	15	28	46	76	13
7 Expert supervisors (5)	9	57	22	26	34	69	5
8 Semi-credentialled managers (7)	16	52	19	33	45	80	7
9 Expert managers (4)	8	33	24	27	22	60	9
10 Petty Bourgeoisie (3)	31	49	35	30	43	79	7
11 Small employers (2)	29	50	17	31	24	66	8
12 Bourgeoisie (1)	9	28	27	23	25	65	0
II. Sweden							
1 Proletarians (12)	57	70	48	51	81	81	58
2 Semi-credentialled workers (9)	51	72	52	59	82	82	63
3 Uncredentialled supervisors (11)	61	59	52	55	81	77	39
4 Expert employees (6)	21	62	39	44	71	64	32
5 Semi-credentialled supervisors (8)	40	57	27	35	78	68	30
6 Uncredentialled managers (10)	39	64	40	46	82	82	47
7 Expert supervisors (5)	19	36	26	19	84	67	20
8 Semi-credentialled managers (7)	36	68	47	35	77	66	30
9 Expert managers (4)	14	37	35	22	65	47	14
10 Petty Bourgeoisie (3)	43	38	31	40	65	60	22
11 Small employers (2)	31	31	20	34	50	54	15
12 Bourgeoisie (1)	25	13	13	25	25	50	13

[1] The items are as follows:
(1) Corporation benefit owners at the expense of workers and consumers;
(2) It is possible for a modern society to run effectively without the profit motive;
(3) If given the chance, the non-management employees at the place where you work could run things effectively without bosses;
(4) During a strike, management should be prohibited by law from hiring workers to take the place of strikers;
(5) Big corporations have far too much power in American (Swedish) society today;
(6) Imagine that workers in a major industry are out on strike over working conditions and wages. Which of the following outcomes would you like to see occur: (a) the workers win their most important demands: (b) the workers win some of their demands and make major concessions: (c) the workers win only a few of their demands and make major concessions; (d) the workers go back to work without winning any of their demands. (% who give response a).

[2] The numbers in parentheses correspond to the cells in Table 2.1.

Source: Wright (1985), Table 7.2, pp. 262.

political discourse, social conflicts are organised in non-class ways, unions are merely special interest groups, state welfare policies have heightened class divisions and there is little sense of alternative arrangements of property and power. It is for these reasons that class has less ideological salience in the US than in Sweden (Wright 1985: 280).

Finally, the third study on class, *The American Perception of Class*, was published by Vanneman and Cannon in 1987. Drawing on a secondary analysis of surveys including the General Social Survey and the National Election Studies, they also found a high level of class awareness – of classes with opposing interests which are rooted in the sphere of production, although radical views on class conflict were absent (Vanneman and Cannon 1987: 90). Their analysis showed that members of the middle class held an image of the class structure as a middle mass while members of the working class have an image of the class structure in terms of an élite power model. There were clear class differences, therefore, in perceptions of the class structure. There was no evidence of a declining awareness of class divisions over and above changes in the shape of the class structure. Class divisions – including a distinction between the middle class and the working class – are still widely perceived and largely understood (Vanneman and Cannon 1987: 90).

Vanneman and Cannon concluded American workers are class conscious in that 'they are amazingly clear on the shape of the American class system and their place within it' (1987: 283). The absence of strong class organisations in the US, therefore, cannot be explained with reference to low levels of class consciousness. Rather, their absence is best explained in relation to capitalist strength. The strength of capital rather than the weakness of labour explains the absence of class action in the US. Vanneman and Cannon's conclusions are open to dispute, however, since their argument is somewhat confusing. Indeed, it is questionable whether their findings indicate high levels of class consciousness or, more likely, high levels of class awareness and class identity. It is doubtful, therefore, whether a focus on capitalist strength would explain the absence of class organisations in the US. Rather, explanations for the low levels of class consciousness in the US lie in the realm of politics.

This argument has been recently been forcefully restated by Brooks (1994). Drawing on Wright's comparative data and a follow-up to the original survey for the US (not yet fully available), Brooks found class consciousness is lower among American than Swedish workers although there had been a slight increase in class consciousness in the US during the 1980s (3.26 in 1980 compared with 3.43 in 1991 on the class consciousness scale) (Brooks 1994: 183). Moreover, in contrast to Swedish workers, American workers fail to make connections between questions of class and questions of politics. Indeed, nearly two thirds (1973) of workers in the American National Election Studies feel alienated from politics (Brooks 1994: 190). Brooks concluded:

> In the absence of parties and movements which would inte-
> grate workers' interests into political platforms and institutional
> reforms what working-class consciousness there is in the con-
> temporary United States risks political impotence. The further
> development of American working-class consciousness thus faces
> not one but two obstacles. Not only is its quantity modest by
> comparative standards, but what class consciousness there is
> among American workers is largely unconnected to the fabric of
> contemporary political life. (Brooks 1994: 192–3)

Class identities, therefore, do not translate into socio-political attitudes and behaviour because of the nature of the political system in the US.

More recently, it has been argued that race has become a more salient social identity than class in the US, and that the salience of racial identities explains the low levels of class consciousness in the US. Jackman and Jackman's findings on the relative significance of race and class are of interest here. It will be recalled that blacks and other racial groups are more likely to identify with the working class and poor class than whites. Blacks also felt strongly about their class identification. Jackman and Jackman argued that in feelings of group identity, in the interpretation of group differences and in perceptions of groups' interests, class is as strong if not stronger than race as the basis of social identity. It is only among the black middle class that feelings of racial solidarity outweigh feelings of class solidarity. Like Wilson (1978), who argued that class divisions are becoming more important among the black population, Jackman and Jackman concluded that race does not undercut class identity, and class is the major source of group identity. The salience of racial identities does not explain the low levels of class consciousness in the US.

Subsequent research, however, has suggested that race is relatively more important than class. Kluegel and Smith (1986) conducted a survey of over 2000 respondents examining American's images of socio-economic inequality conducted in 1980. They also found a high level of support for the 'dominant ideology' of equal opportunities and unequal outcomes. However, they found variations among groups in beliefs that challenge this ideology in that, 'The largest and most consistent group disparities in expressed doubts about the workings of the American stratification order are those between blacks and whites'(Kleugel and Smith 1986: 289). Race surpassed both class and gender in structuring beliefs about inequality. They found, for example, that twice as many blacks as whites felt that they had not had a fair chance to make the most of themselves in life (50 per cent compared with 26 per cent). A strong group consciousness among blacks, therefore, prevails. They are the most 'class conscious' group in American society although they still subscribe to the ethos of equal opportunity and unequal outcomes. Kleugel and Smith (1986: 290) concluded that blacks do not constitute a threat to existing social arrangements and nor does the working class given the racial divisions within it.

Drawing on a secondary analysis of the Black Election Study, Sigelman and Welch (1991) examined black Americans' views of racial inequality and explored the heterogeneity of views. They found blacks and whites hold separate but overlapping world views. Different attitudes were also noted within the black community. High status blacks 'are less likely to perceive racial discrimination, more likely to emphasise black shortcomings in assessing the reasons for racial inequality, and less likely to favour government spending programmes for welfare and the poor' than low-status blacks (Sigelman and Welch 1991: 167). They found, however, that 'in most perceptions and opinions, better-off blacks have much more in common with lower-status blacks than they do with lower-status or better off whites. Although some socio-economic differences are obvious in blacks' racial perceptions, these tend to be fairly limited and inconsistent' (Sigelman and Welch 1991: 167). Thus, Sigelman and Welch acknowledged class divisions within the black population although they emphasised the overall importance of racial identity in attitudes to inequality.

Sigelman and Welch concluded that in the face of economic setbacks, disillusionment is setting in among black Americans. This theme is taken up by Hochschild (1995: 248) who argues that the black middle class is increasingly alienated 'from the American Dream as they come closer to achieve its promise'. Drawing on a wide range of survey data, she argues that success has only highlighted what middle-class African-Americans have been and what they are still denied. In the face of persistent discrimination, there is growing disaffection with the American Dream and a strengthening belief that society is inherently racist (Hochschild 1995: 255). The empirical evidence in support of this argument is strong. Nevertheless, it is doubtful whether the importance of racial identities can explain the low level of class consciousness in the US. A racial identity may be relatively stronger than a class identity among the small black middle class but, arguably, among the rest of the black and white population the strength of class over race prevails. The increasingly salience of race, therefore, cannot explain low level of class consciousness in the US.

Overall, the evidence suggests that class is a salient social identity in the US. Americans are willing and able to identify predominately with the middle class or the working class. Class also structures social attitudes about the nature of inequality in American society. Those who occupy middle-class positions take a more benign view of class while members of the working class are more critical of inequalities in the US. However, class attitudes cannot be described as polarised although they have become more so in the 1980s under the presidencies of Reagan and Bush. There is a widespread commitment to equal opportunities even though they can produce large economic inequalities. There is also a widespread opposition to government intervention in terms of redistributive measures to create equality of outcomes. The ongoing debate on affirmative action policies in a case in point. These socio-political views are a reflection of American politics where the language of class is largely absent. Class issues, for example, have not been mobilised in any radical way by the Democratic Party committed to moderate liberalism in search of electoral success (Przeworski 1980; Przeworski and Sprague 1986). The political impact of class, therefore, is muted since class does not translate into political action. The failure of the Democratic Party to mobilise class issues rather than the increased salience of racial identities explains low levels of class consciousness in the US.

CLASS IDENTITIES IN BRITAIN

The early community studies in Britain, as in America, touched upon issues of subjective class identity. Members of the 'traditional' working-class community (Dennis *et al.* 1956; Young and Willmott 1957; see also Bott 1957), for example, held a dichotomous view of the class structure distinguishing between capitalists (them) and workers (us). This division was seen as 'unbridgeable' in that people were born into one class or another, and there was little opportunity for upward mobility. The class structure, in other words, was perceived as closed and rigid (Goldthorpe *et al.* 1969: 118. See also Crow and Allan 1994; ch. 2). Moreover, a strong sense of class solidarity was the bedrock of unconditional support for the trade unions and the Labour party acting in pursuit of their interests. There was, therefore, a high level of class consciousness in Britain in the first half of the twentieth century.

The first major study of subjective attitudes to class inequalities, based on a nationally representative study of 1,415 men and women conducted in 1962, was published by W.G.Runciman in *Relative Deprivation and Social Justice* (1966). Runciman employed the concepts of 'relative deprivation' – the sense of deprivation when comparing oneself with others – and 'reference groups' – the person or group who are the basis of comparison – to understand the relationship between inequality and grievance. He found that class was an important reference group to which people easily assigned themselves and the basis on which they expressed relatively coherent views of their position in the social structure. He found, for example, that the overwhelming majority of his respondents were prepared to assign themselves to a class (83 per cent, rising to 99 per cent when prompted). Similar proportions of nonmanual workers defined themselves as middle class (51 per cent rising to 74 per cent) and manual workers defined themselves as working class (52 per cent rising to 66 per cent). While sizeable minorities of nonmanual workers assigned themselves with the working class (19 per cent) and manual workers with the middle class (22 per cent), the majority of respondents 'correctly' identified their class position. Classes were defined primarily in terms of occupation although other criteria such as income, life-styles, values and attitudes including expressions of approval and disapproval were also mentioned. Runciman concluded that his respondents had a definite picture of the class structure and their own position within it.

Runciman then examined the respondents' sense of relative deprivation over issues of income, consumption and state services. Focusing on attitudes to income differences, he found that over a sixth (17 per cent) of manual workers on the lowest income did not think there were other sorts of people doing better than themselves while a similar proportion (20 per cent) did not know (Table 4.4). Comparative reference groups were limited and demonstrated the 'considerable discrepancy between inequality and relative deprivation' (Runciman 1966: 193). Runciman also found that the respondents compared their income with people of similar income. Their focus for comparison, therefore, was with people close to their own social situation whose personal circumstances could be easily compared with their own (Runciman 1966: 195). Manual workers, for example, compared themselves with manual rather than nonmanual workers. Any resentments were narrow in scope. Where respondents were conscious of other people being better off than themselves, these differences were perceived in personal terms – such as stage in the family life-cycle – rather than in class terms (Runciman 1966: 196), indicating that a limited sense of relative deprivation even among those at the bottom of the hierarchy. The restricted use of reference groups as the basis for comparison diminished the sense of relative deprivation felt by manual workers, and explained why class inequalities were not resented more by those who experience the deprivations arising from a class society (Runciman 1966: 207–8).

Runciman found, therefore, that the relationship between social inequalities and feelings of relative deprivation are more 'complicated and variable' than might have been supposed. Runciman's work has been widely cited since its publication in the mid-1960s although a number of criticisms have been made of his argument. First, (as Runciman acknowledged)

Table 4.4. Perceptions of relative deprivation by income within occupational structure (percentage)

| | Nonmanual | | | Manual | | |
	High	Medium	Low	High	Medium	Low
Yes	59	66	62	51	56	63
No	31	25	21	39	32	17
Don't know	10	9	17	10	12	20
Total	100	100	100	100	100	100
Number	160	107	75	99	278	368

Source: Runciman (1966), Table 19, p. 193.

his argument suffers from the problem of dual causality: namely, is the choice of restricted reference groups by the underprivileged a case of their modest expectations or a consequence of them? The underprivileged, for example, may already have modest ambitions and choose other people who share their narrow concerns as their normative reference group (Parkin 1971: 61). Second, the concept of reference groups is not unproblematic in that we know little about the processes and circumstances in which they are selected. Moreover, people may have various reference groups for different spheres of their life which may influence them in different ways. The usefulness of the concept of reference groups, therefore, is not stated explicitly (Parkin 1971: 161).

Other interpretations of the 'acceptance' of class inequalities were proffered by Goldthorpe *et al.* (1969), Parkin (1971) and Mann (1970; 1973). Goldthorpe *et al.*'s argument that working-class support for trade unions and the Labour Party is instrumental rather than collectivist in nature will be explored more fully in Chapter Eight below. Parkin argued that how people interpret class inequalities will be influenced by the nature of the meaning system on which they draw. The working class, he argued, draw on a subordinate value system. That is, there is a recognition of class conflict and doubts about the 'morality of the distributive system and the persistent inequities it generates'. Nevertheless, Parkin emphasises that this subordinate value system is not class consciousness. Rather, it is a bulwark to class consciousness since it embraces accommodative or adaptive responses to the status quo. The defining feature of this meaning system is, he argued, 'its uneasy compromise between rejection and full endorsement of the dominant order'. He went on to argue, 'dominant values are not so much rejected or opposed as modified by the subordinate class as a result of their social circumstances and restricted opportunities (Parkin

1971: 92). The subordinate value system, therefore, is a stretched version
(Rodman 1963) of the dominant value system.

Mann's (1970; 1973) interpretation of the acceptance of class inequalities in not dissimilar to Parkin's account although he emphasised the
ambivalence rather than coherence of class attitudes. Drawing on American
and British data, he argued that the western working class is characterised
by their 'pragmatic acceptance' of inequalities. He stated that a mature class
consciousness is comprised of four elements: class identity (a feeling of
class), class opposition (to class enemies), class totality (the ability to analyse situations in class terms) and class alternatives (a conception of a better
society). These elements exist in different degrees and mixtures among the
working classes in the industrial West. A sense of class identity and class
opposition is often found but the totality of class and alternatives to class
are frequently absent. Thus, he found little evidence of an endorsement of
general values and beliefs but rather a pragmatic acceptance of concrete
and specific realities of everyday life. Class inequalities, therefore, do not
have moral legitimacy and the social order lacks a normative consensus
(Mann 1970). For both Parkin and Mann, therefore, 'class consciousness'
is highly ambivalent.

The second major national survey (and part of the international study
of class and class consciousness) was conducted by Marshall and his
colleagues (1988) also referred to in Chapter Two above. Against the
background of economic restructuring, one of the aims of the research was
to explore the extent to which class is a salient social identity or whether
other social identities are important in shaping socio-political perspectives.
The Essex team asked respondents to place themselves into a class. Over
half (60 per cent) placed themselves into a particular social class (rising
to 90 per cent when asked to do so). Occupation, employment, income
and status were the most popular criteria to assign themselves and others
to a class. Three quarters of the sample believed that people are born into
particular classes, that it is difficult to move from one class to another, and
that class is an inevitable feature of society. Finally, half (50 per cent) of
the respondents agreed that there is still a dominant class with economic
and political control and a subordinate class which lacks such control. In
contrast, less than a fifth (19 per cent) found it easy to identity with another
social grouping, the most frequently mentioned groups being business and
religious groups (27 per cent and 21 per cent respectively). The Essex team
concluded that social class is the most common and salient social identity
and other social identities have not undermined an affiliation to classes.

A high level of class identification, however, was not indicative of a radical
class consciousness. The majority (78 per cent) of respondents saw class
conflict as distribution of monetary rewards 'within current economic and

socio-political arrangements'. Among union members, for example, it was widely believed that unions should concentrate on raising pay levels. A majority of the sample (47 per cent) felt the distribution of income and wealth was unfair with 80 per cent of respondents wanting to redistribute wealth downwards. The Essex team also found that the majority of those who thought that the distribution of wealth was unfair believed that something could be done and suggested changes including increased taxes, increased welfare, income policies and so on. There was, therefore, a widespread concern for social justice and a conviction that it could be brought about. However, they also found considerable cynicism towards the organisations – the trade unions and the political parties – which might bring about social change. Nearly half (42 per cent) of their respondents, for example, felt that it made no difference which political party ran the country. An 'informed fatalism' prevailed. It is in this context, therefore, that attitudes to the distributive order have taken an instrumental form. As Marshall et al. argued:

> Class awareness and class identities, though well to the fore as sources of meaning that structure the world views of the majority, are held in check as sponsors of collective action, apparently by a realistic appraisal of the likely outcome of class actions undertaken through the medium of a political party or trade union, at least as they are presently constituted. (1988: 165)

Marshall et al. also replicated Wright's analysis of class consciousness, while establishing that attitudes are not always consistent – a feature which Wright ignored. They also constructed a scale like Wright's to measure class consciousness across a range of pro-capitalist and pro-working class attitudes. They found that attitudes are structured by social class. They established, for example, that support for taxes on company profits in order to create jobs was widely supported by working-class respondents and largely rejected by service-class respondents (63 per cent and 24 per cent respectively). However, they found that support for the general principle of distributional justice could be found across all classes. Virtually equal numbers in the service class and the working class, for example, agreed that the distribution of wealth was unfair (69 per cent and 71 per cent respectively). The reasons given as to why it was unfair were also similar across the classes (see Table 4.5). The Essex team, therefore, were struck 'by the degree of uniformity in the responses across the social classes' (Marshall et al. 1988: 187). Contrary to Wright, they suggested that people's class attitudes do not reflect a high level of class consciousness. They argued:

> It is true that class, rather than alternative sources of social

Table 4.5. Attitudes to distributional justice by Goldthorpe class

		Is distribution of wealth and income fair?	
		Yes	No
Class	I	31	69
	II	34	66
	III	28	72
	IV	44	56
	V	24	76
	VI	25	75
	VII	22	78
	All	29	71
		(368)	(914)

	Why not?[1]						
				Class			
	I	II	III	IV	V	VI	VII
Distribution favours those at top							
Gap between haves and have nots is too wide	57	59	63	64	55	63	63
Pay differentials too wide	21	19	19	19	26	21	19
Too much poverty, wages too low, too many reduced to welfare	13	17	20	16	13	17	18
Some people acquire wealth too easily (unearned income, etc.)	31	16	13	13	20	10	9
The higher paid are not taxed severely enough	9	15	11	9	12	20	16
Welfare benefits are too low	6	5	6	2	8	9	6
The lower-paid or working class are taxed too severely	2	3	3	5	3	0	2
Inequalities of opportunity (in education, for jobs, etc.)	2	2	2	0	0	1	2
Unequal regional distribution (of jobs, income, etc.)	4	3	3	0	2	1	2
Distribution favours those at the bottom							
There are too many scroungers around	6	2	12	9	15	8	10
Pay differences are too narrow	5	4	1	3	4	4	4
The higher paid are taxed too severely	4	2	3	8	3	3	3
Other reasons							
Inequality of wealth and income inevitable	1	4	4	2	7	2	2
Key groups of workers can hold the country to ransom	1	1	0	0	0	0	0
Other reasons							

[1] Percentages in the 'Why not?' columns are based on respondents. Valid cases = 899.

Source: Marshall *et al.* (1988), Table 7.10, p. 186.

cleavage, continues to structure ideological packages or at least those ideological packages that were investigated in this particular study. But these class structured ideological packages hardly amount to coherent class ideologies, either of a dominant kind among those in privileged class positions, or of a 'radical' alternative among the workers and their possible class allies. (Marshall *et al.* 1988: 191)

Marshall and his colleagues concluded, therefore, that class attitudes in Britain are not as polarised as Wright's analysis led them to expect.

Finally, Marshall *et al.* addressed the issue of class politics. They rejected the class dealignment thesis as an explanation for the Labour Party's electoral misfortunes in the 1980s. They found a close relationship between objective class position and voting patterns. The majority (50 per cent) of the middle class, for example, voted Conservative while the remaining middle-class voters split almost equally between Alliance and Labour (23 per cent and 21 per cent). The majority (57 per cent) of the working class voted Labour with the remaining voters aligning themselves with the Conservatives (22 per cent) and Alliance (15 per cent) (Marshall *et al.* 1988: 236–7). They also found that class identification had an important influence on party preferences. An identification with the working class greatly increased Labour voting in each class (36 per cent among the service class, 35 per cent among the intermediate class and 59 per cent among the working class) while an identification with the middle class increased Conservative voting (58 per cent among the service class, 53 per cent among the intermediate class and 34 per cent among the working class (Marshall *et al.* 1988: 247). The relationship between class attitudes and voting behaviour was even stronger again. Members of the working class who identified with the working class, believed that the class structure had not changed and saw class conflict as an important characteristic of British society were more likely to vote Labour than those who did not. The parties were also perceived in class terms (83 per cent for Labour and 45 per cent for Conservatives). Marshall *et al.* (1988: 248) concluded that 'classes have not withered away, and class identities exert a powerful influence on electoral choice'.

Overall, Marshall and his colleagues argued that Labour's electoral failures could not be explained with reference to shifts in the class structure and related changes in class identities and class cultures. Rather, they argued that voters have moved away from Labour for ephemeral political reasons – unpopular policies, lack of unity and so on – and instrumental reasons (though self-interest, they argued, is shaped by class awareness). The Labour Party has failed to mobilise class identities by reinforcing the formation of these collectivities or mobilise class attitudes by discussing issues in class terms. Labour voters, for example, are strongly committed to egalitarian principles on the one hand yet many of its working-class supporters feel it makes no differences which country runs the party on the other (Marshall *et al.* 1988: 255–6). Disillusionment and cynicism abound. On this basis, the Essex team concluded, 'Contemporary sectional struggles are testimony to the failure of national class organisations to mobilise members behind centrally organised initiatives on behalf of general rather than particular interests. But class background and class attitudes remain a powerful influence on electoral behaviour' (Marshall *et al.* 1988: 260). Not unlike American writers (Jackman and Jackman 1983; Wright 1985; see also Elster 1982), therefore, Marshall and his associates concluded that class consciousness in Britain is shaped by class organisations – especially in the political sphere – which have neither pursued class objectives nor contained sectional struggles.

The Essex team's findings on class identities were the source of immediate controversy. Critics, for example, cast doubt on the finding that class is a major social identity and other social identities are unimportant. Saunders (1989; 1990b) argued that the extent of class awareness was an artefact of the large number of questions on class asked of the respondents. Other social identities could not be so easily disregarded. Echoing these sentiments, Emmison and Western (1990) (members of the Australian team in the International Class project) found that when given a choice of social identities their respondents identified more readily with occupational groups, families and the nation than with class. In reply, Marshall and Rose (1989; 1990) claimed that their arguments had been misrepresented and nowhere did they suggest that other social identities are insignificant. Whether this reply amounted to a qualification of their earlier claims is open to debate. Nevertheless, they insisted that class remains crucial for understanding one particular context – the political arena of Thatcherite Britain. The fact that class identity shapes political action is highly significant. This conclusion was subsequently confirmed by more contextualised research (Devine 1992b) which found that people hold a range of social identities, and a national identity is a significant social identity as the Australian team found. However, class identities remain the major influence on party political affiliations, political attitudes and voting patterns. As Marshall and Rose argued, class continues to shape electoral behaviour in contemporary Britain.

The Essex team's findings on class consciousness were also subject to critical comment. Evans (1992b; see also 1993b) was highly critical of their six-item index failing to measure a unitary concept of class consciousness. Evans argued that the items such as identity, perceptions and attitudes were only poorly related, and the index inappropriately aggregated items with different meanings to respondents. In his re-analysis of their data, he found that class was not the only structuring influence on class consciousness since education, trade union membership, age and income affected levels of class consciousness. Thus, the Essex team's arguments about the pre-eminence of class as a structuring influence on identities and attitudes did not hold up against renewed empirical scrutiny (Evans 1992b: 241). Instead, Evans (1992b: 243–4) argued that it is important to distinguish between explicitly class-related identities and perceptions (where he found class dominated), attitudes towards redistributive polices which benefit members of the working class and attitudes towards redistributive policies which cost the working class (where class was not dominant and other factors like education and housing tenure were influential in shaping attitudes). Evans argued that class differences over redistributive issues reflected self-interested instrumental concerns rather than a commitment to egalitarian values amongst the working class. Overall, he concluded that the importance of class in structuring attitudes was overstated by the Essex team and Britain is less of a class-divided society than they claimed (Evans 1992b: 253).

Alternatively, it could be argued that the bluntness of their survey method prevented the Essex team from tapping into class-structured ideological packages. The uniformity of responses across all classes to the question 'is the distribution of wealth and income fair?' was hardly surprising given the abstract nature of the question. Class differences in attitudes to distributional issues would probably have been uncovered in a discussion of the importance of the redistribution of wealth relative to other goals which a government might pursue, what specific policies might be put into practice to make society more equitable and so on in the context of Thatcherite Britain. Indeed, their subsequent findings on the cumulative relationship between class identities, class attitudes and voting behaviour suggests that attitudes are highly structured by class. Parkin's concept of meaning systems, therefore, might still have something to offer in the study of class consciousness. However, if Britain is a more class-divided society than the Essex team portrayed, it is even more crucial to explain why social attitudes have not necessarily translated into political behaviour in the 1980s and 1990s. The failings of class organisations are important issues of consideration as acknowledged by the Essex team. However, so too are the economic, social and political constraints under which class organisations operate. The 1980s and 1990s have proved to be a harsh climate for the trade unions and the Labour Party in Britain, and the circumstances were not all of their own making. The difficulties of sustaining collective action at the individual level and organisational level are, after all, well known in the abstract as well as in situational contexts.

Finally, controversy surrounded the Essex team's findings on women's class identity and political proclivities. Briefly, Marshall *et al.* found that a woman's class identity, her social attitudes and political affiliations are strongly affected by her husband's class position. These findings can be seen most clearly in relation to cross-class families. Women in the inter-mediate class, for example, married to service class men tended to adopt a middle-class identity (55 per cent) while women married to working-class men were more likely to adopt a working-class identity (67 per cent). Attitudes and beliefs were also patterned in this way. Similarly, the relation-ship between a wife's class and her vote was disrupted by her husband's occupation. Intermediate-class women married to middle-class men had a high propensity to vote Conservative (62 per cent) while women married to working-class men had a high propensity to vote Labour (49 per cent) (Marshall *et al.* 1988: 131–3). The Essex team argued, therefore, that the socio-political attitudes and behaviour of men are more important than women within families and that 'partisanship clearly runs between rather than through families (Marshall *et al.* 1988: 72). However, they concluded that, 'A more complete understanding of socio-political class formation therefore demands that one allocates men and women to class positions according to their own employment' (Marshall *et al.* 1988: 183).

Critics, however, were unhappy with both the empirical findings (Hayes and Jones 1992a; 1992b; Mills 1994; De Graaf and Heath 1992) and the conclusions drawn from them (Erikson and Goldthorpe 1992b; Goldthorpe 1990; Mills 1994). Using Australian data, Hayes and Jones, for example, argued that married women do not derive their subjective class locations predominately from their spouse but their own characteristics – most notably education – have important effects on their subjective class identity. Mills' analysis of cross-class families using data from the Social Change and Economic Life Initiative (SCELI) found that a woman's characteristics are important influences on her party identification when she works full time but her spouse's characteristics are more important when she works part-time (Mills 1994: 654–5). A woman's economic status, therefore, seems significant although Mills argued that it is important to consider the influence of assortative mating in the marriage market as well. Similarly, De Graaf and Heath (1992) examined the relative impact of respondent's and spouse's class on voting behaviour from an analysis of the British Election Studies (BES). They also found that women tend to be more influenced by their partner's class position than men. However, when they looked more closely at each of the classes, their findings became more complicated. They found that women at the top (service classes) and bottom (working classes) of the class structure behave much like men in taking their own class into account rather than that of their partner. However, women in the

petty bourgeoisie and in the intermediate classes take relatively little account
of their own class positions but take their husband's class position into
account. They suggested that these findings illustrate the heterogeneity of
values and interests in the intermediate classes rather than male dominance
(De Graaf and Heath 1992). These are not conclusions from which
Marshall and his associates detract, and there is an element of participants
in the debate talking past each other. Almost everyone (bar Goldthorpe)
is agreed that men and women's class identities and political proclivities
should be included in an analysis of socio-political class formation.

Overall, the evidence suggests that class is the most common and salient
social identity in Britain and other social identities such as gender and race
have not undermined an affiliation to class. Class also structures perceptions of and attitudes towards inequality. However, class attitudes are not
highly polarised. Arguably, members of all classes think the distribution
of wealth and income in Britain is unfair and share broadly similar views
as to why it is unfair although members of the working class are notably
more disillusioned than their middle-class counterparts about the effects of
government on changing existing socio-economic arrangements. That said,
a close relationship between class position, class identification and voting
patterns persists in Britain and there is little evidence of class dealignment.
Disillusionment and cynicism suggests that class organisations have failed
to mobilise members of the working class behind collective rather than
sectional interests. This argument implies that America and Britain may
have similar levels of class consciousness although this issue demands a
direct comparison between the two countries.

AMERICA AND BRITAIN COMPARED

Comparative research provides the opportunity to directly examine levels
of class consciousness in America and Britain. Are Americans less class
conscious than the British and vice verse as popular stereotypes suppose?
Research in New Haven and London by Robinson and his associates found
that the British held a more dichotomous image of the class structure while
Americans distinguished between three or more classes. Money was the
most specified criterion of social class although Americans mentioned money twice as often as the British. Thus, Americans and Britons have broadly
similar perceptions of class inequalities although the different views reflect
the different histories and cultural beliefs about the two nations (Bell and
Robinson 1980; see also Robinson 1983). However, Robinson and Kelly
(1979) found that class position has a stronger impact on class identity and
class politics in Britain than in the US. Vanneman (1980) and Vanneman
and Cannon (1987) also found the relationship between objective position
and subjective position was as strong in the US as in Britain. However, there

were considerable differences in how subjective class affects political affiliations. Vanneman found that 'Britons affiliate with political parties and vote
in a far more 'class conscious' manner than do US citizens. The explanation
for this difference 'owes more to the structure of the party system itself
than to the consciousness of voters' (Vanneman 1980: 785; Vanneman
and Cannon 1987). That is, the political system in Britain provides more
opportunity for class voting than the American political system.

The ability to compare and contrast the US and Britain directly has
been facilitated more recently by a comparative project involving identical
questions being asked of respondents in the GSS Survey in the US and
the BSA surveys in Britain (known as the ISSP programme and including
a large number of other nation-states) (Davis 1986). Focusing on the
American-British comparison, Davis (1986: 111) also found that perceptions of the amount of inequality are similar with a mean national difference
of -2.7 per cent between the two countries. That said, there were some
differences in the mechanisms by which inequality is reproduced in that
British respondents were more likely to think that 'what you achieve in life
depends largely on your family background' than American respondents
(a+21 per cent difference). In terms of government policies to reduce
class inequalities, the Americans and British held very different opinions
(the mean national difference being +23.1 per cent). Despite a low sense
of political efficacy in Britain compared to that in the US, Britons were
more favourable to 'leveller' proposals such as reducing income differences
(+35 per cent) and supporting a progressive income tax (+19 per cent).
The only proposal on which Americans are keener on than Britons is
increased opportunities for young people to go to university (+13 per cent).
Thus, while levels of awareness of class inequalities were similar, there
were different political views about how class inequalities might be reduced
across the two countries.

Subsequent analysis of ISSP data (Smith 1989; Taylor-Gooby 1989; see
also Taylor-Gooby 1993) has confirmed that Americans express lower
levels of support for redistributive policies than is found in Britain.
Taylor-Gooby (1989: 40-1), for example, found that universal welfare
programmes such as health are more popular in Britain than the US
(86 per cent compared with 36 per cent) although assistance services for
specific groups such as the unemployed are even more unpopular among
Americans than Britons (45 per cent compared with 16 per cent). Smith
also found that Americans are far less supportive of 'levelling' policies,
Only a fifth (20 per cent) of Americans believe that governments should
provide everyone with a guaranteed basic income compared with nearly
three-fifths (59 per cent) of Britons. At the same time, however, nearly as
many Americans as Britons agree that the government should provide more

chances for children from poor families to go to university (75 per cent compared with 83 per cent). Smith argued that, 'Educational programmes are, *par excellence*, a means of promoting equality of *opportunity* rather than equality of *outcomes*'. The 'opportunity ideology', in other words, is as strong in the US as it was in the past (Huber and Form 1973).

Turning to issues of taxation and redistribution, Smith again found that equality is associated with equal opportunity and that attempts to reduce inequality are seen as inequitable. Americans are more preoccupied with the tax burden of the middle classes in comparison to Britain (68 per cent compared with 40 per cent). They support progressive taxation but remain hostile to government actions which might facilitate income redistribution. Less than a third of Americans (28 per cent) favour government action to reduce income differences compared with nearly two-thirds (63 per cent) of Britons who support such policies. Again, this is evidence of American hostility 'to government programmes designed to promote greater equality of outcomes' (Smith 1989: 65). Overall, Smith concluded that perceptions of social inequality are very similar but 'it is in the evaluation of inequality – how unfair it is felt to be and whether government is seen as an appropriate redistributive agent – that varies enormously between nations'. Smith (1989: 74) concluded, 'the lower levels of support among Americans for redistributive measures, and the relatively greater enthusiasm for measures that allow scope for individual opportunity suggest that an ideology of opportunity plays a key role'.

Finally, issues of class conflict and inequality have been directly addressed across the two nations using data from the third wave of the ISSP (Evans 1993a). Evans found that the association between objective and subjective class position was strong in Britain while class divisions appear to be more blurred in the US. Britain is also more divided by class than the US in relation to attitudes towards inequality. Americans and Britons of all classes attached importance to personal attributes over class-based factors for getting ahead although when asked about opportunities to improve their particular standard of living, Americans and Britons differed once again. That is, 'working-class Americans retain a strong belief in the American Dream along with the middle class (65 per cent and 73 per cent) while British respondents were highly divided along class lines on this issue (25 per cent in the working class compared with 53 per cent in the middle class). That is, working-class Americans perceive greater opportunities for improvement in their standard of living than do middle-class people in Britain!' (Evans 1993: 130-1). Evans also found that a functionalist justification of inequality of outcome was only endorsed by small proportions in the two countries although, again distinctively, the working class was as likely to endorse this view as the middle class in America. In a number of respects, therefore, Americans appear to be less class conscious than their British counterparts.

Evans also examined class and support for redistribution across the two nations. Employing a five-time scale (see Table 4.6), he found stronger support for redistribution among the British in comparison with Americans (a total mean score of 2.3 compared with 3.0). He also found a relationship between class position and support for redistribution in both Britain and the US. Members of the working class are more supportive of redistribution than the salariat in Britain (a mean score of 1.9 compared with 2.7). The same pattern was found in the US (a mean score of 2.7 among the working class compared with a mean score of 3.2 among the salariat). The evidence suggests, therefore, that the working class in America are as unenthusiastic for redistributive policies as the salariat in Britain (Evans 1993a: 133–4). Evans (1993a: 138) concludes that attitudes towards redistribution are influenced by political factors in both nations. There is a strong relationship between left-wing partisanship and support for redistribution, for example, in Britain and America although it is stronger in the former than the latter. High levels of support for redistribution in Britain and low levels of support for redistribution in America can only be explained with reference to the political histories and cultures of the two nations.

The comparative evidence suggests, therefore, that Americans are less class conscious than the British. They share similar levels of class identification and class awareness to their British counterparts. However, Americans are more liberal and Britons more radical in their social and political views. While attitudes are structured by class, Americans endorse policies for equal opportunities and are hostile to redistributive policies. The British, in contrast, support equal opportunities and redistributive policies to ensure equal outcome although, again, these views are shaped by class. A relationship between class and party persists in the US (Hout *et al.* 1995) but the association is stronger in Britain (Heath *et al.* 1985; 1991). How far these differences will persist depends on political circumstances. In the face of heightened class consciousness in the 1980s when the political economy of the free market prevailed, it may be that Americans are becoming more like their British counterparts. Similarly, the promotion of policies of equal opportunities rather than equal outcomes by a Labour Party desperate for electoral success suggests that the British may not be so unlike their American counterparts in the future either.

CONCLUSION

This chapter has focused on class consciousness in America and Britain. Contrary to predictions, a high level of class identification and class awareness prevails in both nations. Similarly, attitudes and beliefs are

Table 4.6. Class position and support for redistribution

Mean score[1] on the redistribution scale	Britain	USA	Australia	Austria	West Germany	Hungary	Netherlands	Switzerland
Total	2.3	3.0	2.9	2.4	2.3	2.0	2.5	2.7
Salariat	2.7	3.2	3.1	2.6	2.5	2.1	2.8	2.9
Routine non-manual	2.4	3.1	2.9	2.5	2.3	2.0	2.5	2.6
Petty bourgeoisie	2.6	3.3	3.1	2.3	2.4	2.0	2.6	2.8
Skilled manual	2.1	2.9	2.8	2.4	2.2	1.9	2.4	2.4
Working class	1.9	2.7	2.7	2.1	2.0	1.9	2.2	2.4
Agricultural labourers	—	—	—	—	—	1.9	—	—
Eta	.34	.25	.21	.26	.22	.11	.25	.22

[1] The higher the mean score, the *less* the enthusiasm for redistributive policies.

Source: Evans (1993a), p. 134.

structured by class to a greater or lesser degree in America and Britain. However, attitudes as a whole vary between the two countries. Americans strongly favour equal opportunity initiatives like the promotion of higher education and they remain hostile to redistributive measures to create economic outcomes. The British support equal opportunities as well and, to a greater or lesser degree, redistributive policies to ensure equal outcomes. Finally, as we saw, a relationship between class and party persists in the US but the association is stronger in Britain. These different attitudes and actions reflect the different political histories and political cultures of the two nations. America's weak trade union movement and the moderate Democratic Party have long failed to mobilise issues in class terms although the extent to which the trade unions and the Labour Party are currently able to do so in Britain is open to debate.

The interrelationship between class and other social identities – notably race and gender – was discussed at length in America and Britain respectively. The evidence suggests that race is a highly salient social identity in a nation heavily divided by ethnic divisions. However, the empirical evidence also shows that rather than undermine class identities, racial identities reinforce class identities. The salience of racial identity, therefore, does not explain low levels of class consciousness in the US. To repeat, political factors account for the lower levels of class consciousness in the US in comparison with Britain. These arguments can also be applied to debates about gender identities and class identities in Britain. Factors such as women's social origins, education and work histories affect their class identification and class attitudes although that does not mean that these factors undermine the socio-political proclivities of families and households. That said, debates about whether race is more significant than class or whether gender is more significant than class are somewhat sterile and the interrelationship between class, race and gender in America and Britain should prove more fruitful areas of research.

Once again, the evidence suggests that long-standing stereotypes of the two nations do not stand up to empirical scrutiny. In the narrowly defined sense of class identification and class awareness, Americans and Britons are similarly 'class conscious' . In the more broadly-defined sense of socio-political attitudes and behaviour, Americans are less 'class conscious' than their British counterparts. In other words, the two nations share similarities and differences according to how class consciousness is defined and measured. On the whole, however, American is not a classless society and Britain is not a class-divided society. This chapter concludes Part I of this book which focused on general debates embracing all social classes. Attention now turns, in Part II, to specific debates on each of the five classes which exist in the broadly similar class structures of America and Britain. The next chapter focuses on the upper class and the extent to which it enjoys a powerful position in the economic, social and political spheres of contemporary America and Britain.

Part II

Chapter 5

Social Power

The capitalist class is often overlooked in class analysis for a variety of theoretical and methodological reasons. First, changes in the ownership and control of capital have witnessed both the demise of family proprietors who existed at the end of the nineteenth century and the rise of corporate enterprises led by businessmen who are both owners and managers in the late twentieth century. This has led commentators to dismiss the idea of a capitalist class and to discuss an economic élite at the 'top' of the class structure. Second, the small number of company directors, business managers and so forth mean that they rarely feature in nationally representative surveys of the class structure. As a result, there is little empirical material on their terms and conditions of employment, patterns of social mobility and socio-political attitudes and behaviour. The capitalist class seems invisible and reinforces the widely held view that it is resilient to sociological investigation. Nevertheless, the capitalist class has been the source of considerable interest to sociologists and political scientists. The main debate has centred on whether the capitalist class has disintegrated over time or whether it is still possible to identify a capitalist class as a distinct economic, social and political entity. Furthermore, social scientists have been able to draw on a wide variety of empirical material ranging from historical research, contemporary case studies and official statistics to evaluate the controversy over the capitalist class.

This chapter, which has been divided into three parts, engages in this debate by drawing on the diverse empirical material available in America and Britain. The first part focuses on the issues of ownership and control. The evidence suggests that the rise of large corporations in America and Britain has witnessed a change in the nature of ownership and control although not in the ways predicted in the early twentieth century. The decline of family stake-holdings and the increasing importance of financial institutions as shareholders in non-financial and financial enterprises has led to a move from personal to impersonal ownership. Similarly, family control has declined but rather than be replaced by bank control, the dominant mode of control has become control through a constellation of interests. As a result of their different experiences of industrialisation, these trends began in America in the 1920s and accelerated quickly while Britain changed more gradually from the 1930s onwards. The presence of families in the corporate world has not disappeared, and the importance of families is more notable in Britain than America as a result of different historical social relations. Trends towards globalisation appear to reinforce the importance of financial institutions in the corporate world but there is little evidence of the emergence of a transnational capitalist class. Similarly, the recent privatisation of state-owned industries in Britain has not changed patterns in share ownership and business control. Far from disappearing, therefore, the capitalist class in America and Britain has reorganised over the twentieth century.

The second part focuses on patterns and trends in the distribution of wealth and income in the two nations. Official statistics show that the top 20 per cent of the population has become richer in terms of both wealth and income while the bottom 20 per cent have become poorer over the 1980s. Wealth and incomes is increasingly concentrated at the top especially among the top 1% of families. A number of factors have contributed to these trends including the rise in value of corporate stock, the increased pay of company directors, finance directors and so forth and decreased tax bills on high earners. Wealthy individuals and families, therefore, have far from disappeared. Such affluence sustains a privileged life-style among a small group of highly-interconnected people of equal social standing who socialise in various overlapping social circles. This exclusivity, bolstered by the private education system, gentleman's clubs and so forth, sustains the socio-cultural distinctiveness of the wealthy. However, the wealthy are not merely a leisure class for segments of it are active in sustaining their wealth in the corporate world. Within this business class, finance capitalists have become increasingly important as board members of the top businesses. It is not surprising to find, therefore, that there are close links between the business class and the wealthy upper class in America and Britain.

The third section focuses on the political power of the capitalist class. The exceptional power of the American capitalist class is considered in this context. The findings indicate that a disproportionate number of individuals of upper-class origins involved in the business world hold positions in the machinery of government in both the US and Britain. Moreover, their considerable resources and privileged access means corporate business is highly influential in the policy-making process. However, while corporate businessmen might share some broadly defined principles, they often disagree about substantive policies and practices. The different views of manufacturers and financiers is a case in point. Moreover, corporate business may enjoy considerable influence but it is not all powerful since it contends with other classes and interest groups in pursuit of its interests. What power they might enjoy is highly variable and subject to constant challenge. The varying accomplishments of the New Deal in the US in the 1940s and the Welfare State in Britain in the 1940s demonstrate these points. The reforms of the New Deal were modest in comparison to the Welfare State. However, the strength of capital and the weakness of labour cannot exclusively account for these different outcomes. State and party structures limited intervention in the economy and administrative reorganisation in the US. While US capitalists may have been strong relative to organised labour, it was not in an exceptionally powerful position. Thus, economic power does not simply translate into political power. Neither America or Britain can be said to be ruled by a capitalist class.

OWNERSHIP AND CONTROL

The debate about the separation of ownership and control within industrial enterprises followed the publication of *The Modern Corporation and Private Property* by Berle and Means in the US in 1932. They documented the decline of the privately-run family business (individual proprietorship) and the rise of large publicly-financed corporations (joint-stock companies). Briefly, they argued that company owners had facilitated the growth of their enterprises by issuing shares to individuals who provided investment by risking their money in return for a share of the profits. Noting the change in property rights with the advent of joint-stock ownership, Berle and Means argued, 'that parallel with the growth in the size of the industrial unit has come a dispersion of its ownership such that an important part of the wealth of individuals consists of interests in great enterprises of which no one individual owns a major part' (Berle and Means 1968: 64). The dispersal of share ownership meant that individual proprietors lost control of their companies. However, share-ownership was so widely dispersed that no individual or group had control instead. Rather, control passed to managers responsible for business operations whose power could not easily be overridden. Over half (58 per cent) of the top 200 companies, for example, were under management control in 1930. Changing property rights, therefore, had led to the separation of ownership and control within the modern corporation.

Berle and Means' account of the increasing concentration of business in large enterprises in America and Britain proved correct. Statistics show that the top 100 corporations accounted for 46 per cent of manufacturing assets in US and 41 per cent in Britain in the late 1970s (Hannah 1983;

Szymanski 1984). Large industrial enterprises, reinforced by numerous waves of company mergers and takeovers, dominate economic decision-making to the extent that America and Britain may be described as 'corporate economies' (Hannah 1983). Berle and Means' description of the separation of ownership and control – especially the growing importance of business managers – was widely endorsed by numerous American and British commentators in the post-war period (Burnham 1941; Dahrendorf 1959; Galbraith 1967). Indeed, Berle and Mean's work retains its popularity today as can be seen in the work of Herman (1981) who has argued that management control of large corporations is an 'established truth' even if control is not unfettered. The managerialism thesis still holds considerable sway not least in the business circles of the two nations.

However, Berle and Means' claims were also subject to considerable criticism. The American Marxist, Zeitlin (1974), pointed to the dominance of financial institutions in economic decision-making. He argued that large corporations are heavily dependent on external finance for investment (Zeitlin 1989: 30). Shares, as a result, are concentrated in the hands of financial institutions such as banks and insurance companies. Thus, non-financial and financial corporations are highly interconnected. In the US, he noted, 'Among the 200 largest non-financial corporations ranked by assets, the bigger the non-financial corporation, the more interlocks it has with the 50 largest financial corporations (32 banks and 18 insurance companies)' (Zeitlin 1989: 31). Financial intermediaries, therefore, enjoy control over large business organisations. However, he argued that the major banks and insurance companies are still under family control. Rather than the dispersal of ownership, there has been a transformation of family control via minority bank control within large corporations. Zeitlan concluded,

> Therefore, it may be hypothesised that the social and economic interweaving of once opposed financial and industrial interests, increased economic concentration, the fusion of formally separate large capitals, and the establishment of an effective organisational apparatus of interlocking directorates highlights the cohesiveness of the capitalist class and its capacity for common action and unified policies. (Zeitlin 1989: 41)

Indeed, the increasing importance of the banks only indicated a more cohesive economic class than had existed previously.

Zeitlin's article proved to be a seminal piece in the study of the large corporations and the capitalist class. A number of studies confirmed his theory of bank control (Kotz 1978: Mintz and Schwartz 1981; 1985). The study of networks of interlocking directorates, for example, has shown that commercial banks play a very important role within the system of corporate interaction although business is often organised on a regional basis. Mintz and Schwartz (1985) have argued that financial institutions dominate the non-financial institutions via the flow of capital and shape the circumstances in which firms operate. That is, financial institutions make decisions about the use of capital which affect the business decisions of corporate business. Control, therefore, is exercised through the decision-making process of financial institutions, and it shapes the nature of intercorporate relations (Mintz and Schwartz 1987: 252). Despite divisions within the corporate world, financial hegemony is maintained as well as the unity of intercorporate relations (Mintz and Schwartz 1987; 1990). More recently, McDermott (1991) has described the important strategic role which a range of financial institutions, top accountancy firms and law practices play alongside company directors and top managers. They determine company policy to ensure corporate growth and sustain profits. They make the investment decisions, decide shareholders' dividends and determine the overall level of profit. Echoing Zeitlan, McDermott (1991: 88) argued that the capitalist class is more united than it was in the past since competition between individual proprietors has been replaced by a harmonisation of interests between the different institutions working together.

In Britain, Zeitlin's ideas were developed most prominently by Scott in *Corporations, Classes and Capitalism* (1979; 1985). Scott argued that there has been a movement from personal to impersonal forms of ownership in America, Britain and other major capitalist economies. Individual proprietorship has not disappeared altogether in that individuals and families still own substantial personal share-holdings which allow them to exercise considerable control over large corporations. Nevertheless, the majority of stocks and shares are concentrated in the hands of corporate shareholders and financial institutions such as banks and insurance companies who administer mortgages, pension funds, insurance schemes and unit trusts. However, Scott rejected Zeitlin's thesis that banks enjoy minority control. They play an important intermediary role in the complex system of interlocking directorships but their role does not constitute a form of minority control (Scott 1979: 40). Rather, institutional shareholders with substantial share-holdings enjoy 'control though a constellation of interests'. The largest ten or twenty shareholders may own enough shares to have minority control but they do not necessarily act in concert. They might agree over the composition of the board although Scott emphasised, 'effective possession is an attribute of the major shareholders collectively, yet this constellation of ownership interests has no unity and little possibility of concerted action' (Scott 1979: 41). It is in this respect that personal ownership had been replaced by depersonalised possession.

Table 5.1. Corporate control in the USA: final classification (1980)

Mode of control	Personal	Corporate USA	Foreign	Mixed	Other	Totals
Exclusive majority	2	1	4	0	0	7
Shared majority	0	0	0	1	0	1
Secure minority	10	5	0	1	0	16
Limited minority	16	15	0	0	0	31
Shared minority	1	0	0	1	0	2
Unknown minority	3	1	0	0	0	4
Mutual	—	—	—	—	11	11
Constellation of interests	—	—	—	154	—	154
Not known	—	—	—	—	26	26
Totals	32	22	4	157	37	252

Note: Incomplete data meant that it was not meaningful to divide the 154 enterprises controlled by constellations according to the composition of their constellations. This question is, however, discussed in the text. The total of 154 includes 29 enterprises with dispersed ownership but for which lists of the 20 largest vote-holders were not available.

Source: Scott (1986), Table 6.2, p. 139.

Turning to the empirical evidence, Scott argued that Berle and Means had overstated the extent of managerial control in the US in the 1910s and 1920s since individuals and families still enjoyed majority control in large business operations. Between the 1930s and 1960s, however, family holdings began to dissolve and share ownership was increasingly concentrated among financial groups. Scott noted that ninety-three of the top 200 non-financial companies were in minority control (fifty-eight by families and fourteen by banks) while eighty companies were under management control or control though a constellation of interests in 1965 (Scott 1979: 57). Control moved from private majority ownership to control through a constellation of interests, rather than management control. He found little evidence of a straightforward separation of ownership and control in the US (Scott 1979: 60). In Britain, Scott also found a change in the balance between personal and corporate share ownership in the 1960s and 1970s. Personal holdings in British companies declined from 54 per cent in 1963 to 42 per cent in 1975 while financial interests increased their portfolio from 30 per cent to 40 per cent in the same period. Scott concluded that the transition from personal proprietorship to institutional share-ownership came somewhat later and developed at a slower pace than in the US although a trend in the same direction was discernible nonetheless (Scott 1979: 67).

Scott's (1986) subsequent comparative research on America, Britain and Japan highlighted similarities and differences between nations. There is an Anglo-American system of share ownership and business control. In the US, Scott found that most of the top 252 enterprises had no dominant interest. He found majority control in eight enterprises and minority control in fifty-three business organisations in 1980. In 1980, the dominant form of control was control through a constellation of interests among 165 of the 252 companies (Scott 1986: 138–9). However, while the Ford, Rockefeller, Du Pont and Mellon families are still important in the corporate world (and the American upper and middle classes remain wealthy enough to have significant investments (Marcus 1992)) personal control by individuals and families is less evident in the US than Britain (Scott 1986: 144). The phenomenal increase in the scale of production to cater for a large American market alone in the 1920s meant that family control weakened rapidly. As a result, financial institutions – especially banks including Bank America and Northwestern Bancorp involved in the management of pension fund capital – became the major sources of capital instead. Scott found that many of the largest enterprises had their own pension and saving schemes and these internal funds were the largest shareholders in their own companies. Other large pension funds, however, were managed by banks with full voting control over the shares (Scott 1986: 201). He also found that the mobilisation of capital was fragmented along regional lines with the New York national banks occupying a dominant position. Banks occupy a cental position although Scott insisted that control through a constellation of interests was the dominant form of control.

In Britain, Scott found a similar pattern of share ownership and business control although Britain lagged behind the US in the decline of family control and the growth of institutional control in the corporate world. A single controlling interest was found in just over half (142) of the top 250 enterprises. Personal control by individual and families, and foreign (predominantly American) corporations, were the dominant forms of controlling interest (46 and 43 companies respectively) (Scott 1986: 63). Eight out of ten large merchant banks, for example, were found to be family controlled in Britain. Thus, there was some form of impersonal possession in just under half (108) of the top 250 companies where no dominant interest could be identified. In terms of modes of control, Scott found that just under half (100) of the top 250 enterprises had no single controlling interest but control through the constellation of interests. That is, the top twenty shareholders – invariably financial institutions – held at least 10%

Table 5.2. Corporate control in Britain: final classification (1976)

	Type of controller							
	Corporate							
Mode of control	Personal	British	Foreign	Mixed	State	Mixed	Other	Totals
Public corps	—	—	—	—	13	—	—	13
Wholly owned	7	1	28	0	2	0	0	38
Majority	15	2	9	0	2	0	0	28
Shared majority	0	7	1	3	0	1	0	12
Secure minority	13	9	3	0	1	3	0	29
Limited minority	11	4	2	0	0	1	0	18
Shared minority	0	2	0	0	0	2	0	4
Mutual	—	—	—	—	—	—	8	8
Constellation of interests	—	—	—	—	—	100	—	100
Totals	46	25	43	3	18	107	8	250

Source: Scott (1986), Table 5.2, p. 64.

of all shares with the remaining shares being widely dissipated among individual share-owners. As in the US, companies have formed their own pensions schemes and there has also been an expansion of personal savings plans which has strengthened the position of financial institutions. Overall, however, the dispersal of shares militated against minority control but the concentration of institutional share-ownership – including the large number of bank directors sitting on company boards – did not allow for management control (Scott 1986). Again, therefore, the dominant form of control was through a constellation of interests.

Scott found differences and similarities, therefore, in patterns of financial power in the US and Britain. Differences between the two countries – the persistent importance of family influence in Britain for example – were the result of their different experiences of industrialisation and historical social relations. That said, recent evidence shows that Britain continues to follow the same path of American development. Over half (56.8 per cent) of the top 250 industrial and financial enterprises (i.e. 142 enterprises) were subject to the control of a dominant interest or a group of closely allied interests in 1976 but had fallen to 50 per cent (125 enterprises by 1988 (Scott 1988: 362). Within this category, the number of majority-owned (often family owned) industrial enterprises actually increased from thirty-four to forty-seven while the number of majority controlled industrial enterprises declined from thirty to fourteen indicating that families with less than complete ownership fared less well in the 1980s. The same trend was evident among financial enterprises. Similarly, while 40% (100 enterprises) were subject to control through a constellation of interests in 1978, the percentage figure had risen to 45.2 per cent (113 enterprises) in 1988 (Scott 1990: 367). As a result of the decline in family control, therefore, the balance between the different modes of control is gradually shifting in an American direction (although family control is still important). This trend has been highlighted somewhat exceptionally by the fate of Barings Bank which was a wholly-owned family merchant bank (Lisle-Williams 1985) until it collapsed in 1995 after rogue trading by Nick Leeson on the financial markets in Singapore. The restructuring of Britain's financial markets in the 1980s – especially the 'Big Bang' of 1986 also contributed to the decline in family share holdings and the growth of institutional share holdings.

The globalisation of the world economy (Waters 1995) has enhanced these patterns of capital mobilisation and business control. American and Britain have long been members of an international economy (Sklair 1991) although there has been a increase in the number of foreign subsidiaries in the manufacturing sectors of the American and British economies while American and British enterprises have expanded into foreign markets in the face of increased domestic competition in the 1980s and 1990s. On the one hand, for example, there has been a growing number of Japanese companies operating in the US (and of much concern) while, on the other hand, American fast food operators have been opening outlets abroad in the face of a saturated home market (Waters 1995: 70). Similarly, there has been significant Japanese investment in Britain in the 1980s although it was welcomed by successive Thatcher administrations committed to free trade principles. The Japanese were keen to invest in a European country and to get a toe-hold in the single European market in 1992. For the same reason, there has been an increase in the number of subsidiaries of European enterprises operating in Britain although the number of American subsidiaries has continued to increase (Scott 1990: 367). There has also been an internationalisation of financial institutions as 'Black Monday' stock market crash of October 1987 testified. Despite efforts by the Bank of England to coordinate a rescue package to starve off the total collapse of Barings in 1995, it was a Dutch bank which eventually bought the remaining assets of the merchant bank. The operation of multinational corporations in the international economy has seen financial institutions become even more important over time as larger units have required more and more capital. While globalisation is not an inevitable universal process since nations have different cultural practices and legal systems, similar patterns and trends in corporate development and business control are evident in the US and Britain (Scott 1990).

Globalisation has led to a debate on whether it is possible to identify a transnational capitalist class (van der Pijl 1989; Sklair 1991). Sklair (1991), for example, has argued that it is important to consider transnational relationships. He argues that the globalisation of practices operates at three levels: the economic dominated by the multinational corporation, the political sphere dominated by the transnational capitalist class and the cultural/ideological sphere dominated by the culture of consumerism (Sklair 1991: 7). However, critics doubt whether the owners and controllers of multinational corporations can be said to constitute a transnational capitalist class. Mintz (1989), for example, has argued that since capital accumulation is the driving force of multinational corporations, there has been little evidence of cooperation among capitalist countries. While US hegemony in the world economy has declined, Mintz predicts 'an autonomous economic US economic strategy rather than any form of cohesive action by members of multinational corporations across capitalist nations even in the face of economic dominance of nations in the Pacific Rim (Mintz 1989: 227–8). The danger of the concept is that it neglects the impersonal nature of ownership and control and the difficulties of concerted action as a consequence. Sklair's thesis, in other words, tend to 'reify a global capitalist class that effectively runs the planet on its own behalf' (Waters 1995: 66; see also Pakulski and Waters 1996).

Finally, there has been much speculation on the effects of privatisation of nationalised industries on patterns of share ownership in Britain (Saunders and Harris 1994). Rather than reverse the trend toward institutional dominance, however, privatisation has actually benefitted financial institutions as enterprises such as British Airways, British Gas and British Telecom fell under control through a constellation of interests. New, individual shareholders quickly sold their shares on the stock market to financial institutions. An analysis of the share registers of UK listed companies shows that the proportion of individually-owned shares dropped steadily from 54 per cent in 1963 to 18 per cent in 1993 with only a slight blip in the trend in 1990 following the privatisation of the electricity boards. The main beneficiaries of the process were investments by pension funds and insurance companies who owned over half of the total equity in 1993 (*Social Trends* 1995). The growth of individual share-ownership, therefore, was extremely short-lived and failed to undermine the long-term trend towards the concentration of share ownership into institutional hands.

Overall, the evidence suggests that the rise of large corporations in America and Britain has witnessed a change in the nature of ownership and control although not in the ways predicted in the early twentieth century.

The decline of family stake-holdings and the increasing importance of financial institutions as shareholders in non-financial and financial enterprises has led to a move from personal to impersonal ownership. Similarly, family control has declined but rather than be replaced by bank control, the dominant mode of control has become control through a constellation of interests. As a result of their different experiences of industrialisation, these trends began in America in the 1920s and accelerated quickly while Britain changed more gradually from the 1930s onwards. The presence of families in the corporate world has not disappeared, and the importance of families is more notable in Britain than America as a result of different historical social relations. Trends towards globalisation appear to reinforce the importance of financial institutions in the corporate world but there is little evidence of the emergence of a transnational capitalist class. Similarly, the recent privatisation of state-owned industries in Britain has not changed patterns in share ownership and business control. Far from disappearing, therefore, the capitalist class in America and Britain has reorganised over the twentieth century.

WEALTH AND PRIVILEGE

While the personal possession of large enterprises has declined, this is not to suggest that wealthy families have disappeared. Numerous families have retained substantial company holdings and, spread their wealth in other investments while new entrepreneurs have emerged. The existence of a wealthy upper class can be demonstrated by examining statistics on the distribution of wealth and income in America and Britain. All the evidence indicates that both wealth and income became increasingly unequal in the 1980s and 1990s (Fritzell 1993; Levy 1987; Nelson 1995; Phillips 1990; Wolff 1995). Both nations, in fact, witnessed a decline in the concentration of wealth held by the top 1 per cent from the 1920s until the 1970s. In the US, for example, the share of the top 1 per cent fell from 35 per cent to 19 per cent between 1929 and 1975 (Rubinstein 1986; Smith 1987: 80). Most of the decline took place during the Great Depression and the Second World War. It then remained stable for much of the post-war period until the 1970s when the value of corporate stock of top wealth owners declined (Atkinson 1983: 174; Smith 1987). Rubinstein (1986: 148) suggests that decline has been closely tied to economic and political events because, 'American wealth is held disproportionately in the form of share ownership and capital assets traded on a particularly volatile share market" Nevertheless, the overall trend was towards a reduction in inequality of wealth.

In the 1980s, this trend was reversed, and the accumulation of considerable personal wealth accelerated during the period of rising stock markets

Table 5.3. Percentage shares of total wealth and income by percentage group in 1983 and 1989 (USA)

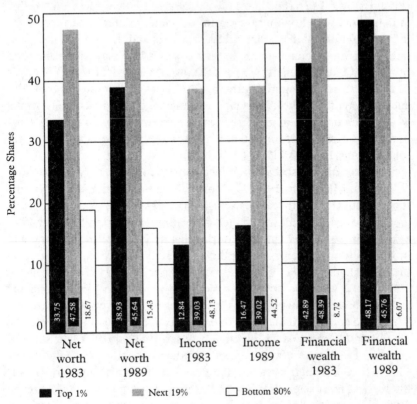

Source: Wolff (1995), Figure 3.3, p.11. © Edward N. Wolff. Reprinted with the permission of The Twentieth Century Fund, New York.

in the 1983–9 economic recovery. Table 5.3 draws on Wolff's most recent report on increasingly inequality of wealth in America. The Table shows that the share of marketable net worth held by the top 1 per cent rose from 34 per cent in 1983 to 39 per cent in 1989. At the same time, the share of wealth held by the bottom 80 per cent fell from 19 per cent to 15 per cent. In terms of financial net work, the top 1 per cent of families owned 48 per cent of total wealth and the top quintile owned 94 per cent of total financial wealth (Wolff 1995: 10-11). It was corporate business which enjoyed the extraordinary boost in affluence over this period. Billionaires such as Sam Walton (worth $8.2 billion), Warren Edward Buffett (worth $3.5 billion) and John Warner Kluge (worth $3.2 billion) saw their corporate share holdings soar in value in the early 1980s although Walton and others subsequently experienced large declines in their net worth following the stock market crash of October 1987 (Phillips 1990: 112). Indeed, there were fifty-one billionaires and over a million and a half millionaires in 1988 (Phillips 1990: 157). The late 1980s and early 1990s witnessed a decline in household wealth with the drop in the value of interest-earning assets in financial institutions, assets held in business and the professions. That said, 1991 Census data shows that net worth is still heavily concentrated by the top. The median net worth of the top 20 per cent of households was $123,166 dollars compared with $5,224 for the bottom 20 per cent. Put another way, the highest household quintile enjoyed 45 per cent of total wealth in comparison to just 7 per cent owned by the lowest quintile. Corporate business, therefore, benefitted out of the polarisation of American society in the 1980s (Phillips 1990: 158).

Statistics on the distribution of income in the US tell a very similar story (Mishel and Bernstein 1993). Income is highly skewed and has become more unequal over the 1980s and 1990s. There was a trend towards greater income inequality from the post-war period to approximately 1975 although it was still very unequal during that period. In terms of household income before tax, for example, the top quintile earned 46.4 per cent in the US while the bottom quintile earned 3.8 per cent in 1974 (Rubinstein 1986: 149). With the onset of world recession, the real incomes of the richest 20 per cent soared while the incomes of the lower 60% stagnated. This trend accelerated in the 1980s especially at the very top of the income distribution. Census data shows that between 1980 and 1988, the share of income of the upper 20 per cent of American rose from 41.6% to 44.0% (Table 5.4). The figures caught the attention of the media because it was the highest ratio since the Census Bureau began its official measures in 1949. Moreover, the share of the top 1 per cent rose from 9 per cent to 11 per cent indicating that those at the very top enjoyed most of the top quintile's advances (Phillips 1990: 12). Between 1977 and 1990, for example, the average income of the top 5 per cent of the population rose from approximately $142,000 to $206,000 while the average income of the top 1 per cent jumped from nearly $295,000 to $549,000 (Gilbert and Kahn 1993: 104). Again, the main beneficiaries were corporate chief executive officers. While they earned twenty-nine times as much as the average factory worker in 1979, they were earning ninety-three times as much as them by 1988 (Phillips 1990: 179–180). The richer, in other words, became richer as the poor became poorer throughout the decade.

There are various explanations for these trends in wealth and income (Harrison and Bluestone 1988; Levy 1987; Phillips 1990; Thurow 1984). The rising inequality in wealth was closely associated with the boom in investments and corporate share holdings in the 1980s. With reference to income, Harrison and Bluestone, for example, argued that corporate

Table 5.4. Growing income inequality in the USA, 1969–88

Year	Percentage of money income received by each quintile				
	Lowest	2nd	Middle	4th	Highest
1969	5.6	12.4	17.7	23.7	40.0
1974	5.5	12.0	17.5	24.0	41.0
1979	5.2	11.6	17.5	24.1	41.7
1980	5.1	11.6	17.5	24.3	41.6
1981	5.0	11.3	17.4	24.4	41.9
1982	4.7	11.2	17.1	24.3	42.7
1983	4.7	11.1	17.1	24.3	42.8
1984	4.7	11.0	17.0	24.4	42.9
1985	4.6	10.9	16.9	24.2	43.5
1986	4.6	10.8	16.8	24.0	43.7
1987	4.6	10.8	16.9	24.1	43.7
1988	4.6	10.7	16.7	24.0	44.0

Source: Phillips (1990), Chart 2, p. 13.

strategy in the face of increased competition was to introduce a new industrial regime characterised by low wages and low costs. Jobs with medium earnings disappeared (ie, the disappearing middle). The low-paid jobs were taken primarily by single parents and young people (Levy 1987). Finally, the federal government under the Reagan presidency deregulated industry and cut taxes for the wealthy while reducing welfare service for the poor. The 'net tax burden on rich Americans as a percentage of their total income *shrank* substantially because of the sweeping rate cuts' (Phillips 1990: 82). A range of socio-economic factors compounded by political measures, therefore, led to the increasing concentration of wealth and income in the US in the 1980s and 1990s.

The distribution of wealth in Britain is also highly concentrated and has become more so since the late 1970s. The share of the top 1 per cent of the population fell steadily from 61 per cent to 23 per cent between 1923 and 1980 (Shorrocks 1987: 33). That said, the share of the top 10 per cent dropped by less than the top 1 per cent from 89 per cent in 1923 to 58 per cent in 1980. Wealth, in other words, was being redistributed within the top 10-25 per cent of households rather than among the population as a whole. Changes in patterns of asset ownership among wealthy families was occurring rather than an equalisation of wealth (Shorrocks 1987: 33). However, the overwhelming evidence indicates that this trend halted in the late 1970s (Pond 1989). The share of marketable wealth owned by the top 1 per cent dropped from 21 per cent to 18 per cent between

Table 5.5. Distribution of wealth in the UK, 1976–92[1]

	1976	1981	1986	1991	1992
Marketable wealth					
Percentage of wealth owned by[2]					
Most wealthy 1%	21	18	18	17	18
Most wealthy 5%	38	36	36	34	37
Most wealthy 10%	50	50	50	46	49
Most wealthy 25%	71	73	73	70	72
Most wealthy 50%	92	92	90	92	92
Total marketable wealth (£ billion)	280	565	955	1,801	1,811
Marketable wealth less value of dwellings					
Percentage of wealth owned by[2]					
Most wealthy 1%	29	26	25	29	29
Most wealthy 5%	47	45	46	51	53
Most wealthy 10%	57	56	58	64	65
Most wealthy 25%	73	74	75	80	82
Most wealthy 50%	88	87	89	93	94

[1] Estimates for 1976, 1981 and 1986 are based on the estates of persons dying in those years. Estimates for 1991 and 1992 are based on estates notified for probate in 1991–92 and 1992–93 respectively. Estimates are not strictly comparable between 1991 onwards and earlier years.
[2] Applies to adult population aged 18 and over.

Source: *Social Trends* 25 (1995), Table 5.23, p. 96. Crown Copyright 1995. Reproduced by permission of the Controller of HMSO and the Office for National Statistics.

1976 and 1981 where it has remained since (Table 5.5). The Table also indicates that distribution of marketable wealth after the value of dwellings (net of mortgage debt) has been excluded is even more unequal. The richest 10 per cent, for example, own 49 per cent of marketable wealth and 65 per cent of marketable wealth less the value of dwellings (*Social Trends 1995: 76–7*). Again, these statistics indicate that while there has been some redistribution of wealth away from the top 1 per cent, it has been circulated among other wealthy families rather than the population as a whole. There is still an unequal distribution in wealth since it remains heavily concentrated among the top 10 per cent of the population. Inheritance remains the major mechanism by which wealth is transmitted from one generation to another although the wealthy are increasingly passing on their assets to their children during their life-time in the forms of trusts as a way of avoiding inheritance tax on their death (Harbury and Hitchens 1979). Beresford (1990), for example, found twelve billionaires in Britain in 1990 headed by the Queen who has a fortune worth over £6,700 million. A total of seventy-eight

Table 5.6. Shares of disposable household income in the UK, 1979–92 (percentage)[1]

	Quintile groups of individuals					
	Bottom fifth	Next fifth	Middle fifth	Next fifth	Top fifth	All individuals
Net income before housing costs						
1979	10	14	18	23	35	100
1981	10	14	18	23	36	100
1987	9	13	17	23	39	100
1988–1989	8	12	17	23	40	100
1991–1992	7	12	17	23	41	100
Net income after housing costs						
1979	10	14	18	23	35	100
1981	9	14	18	23	36	100
1987	8	12	17	23	40	100
1988–1989	7	12	17	23	41	100
1991–1992	6	11	17	23	43	100

[1] The unit of analysis is the individual and the income measure is net equivalised household income.

Source: Social Trends 25 (1995), Table 5.19, p. 94.

individuals were listed as super rich with fortunes of £100m+ including landowners such as Earl Cadogan and Viscount Portman and also new entrepreneurs such as Richard Branson and Anita and Gordon Roddick. Finally, Beresford also identified 118 very rich families with £50m+ and 192 rich families with £20m+ including landowners, industrialists, politicians and pop stars. There was, in other words, an increasing mix of people with some wealth.

The statistics on the distribution of income in Britain also indicate considerable inequality (Stark 1987). Before the Second World War, there was marked income inequality in that the top 1 per cent earned 17 per cent of all pre-tax income (Rubinstein 1986). In the post-war period, there was a decline in inequality of pre-tax and post-tax income during periods of Labour administration. The share of the top 1 per cent income before tax dropped from 11 per cent in 1949 to 6 per cent in 1974 (Rubinstein 1986: 80). After 1977, however, the trend towards equalisation was reversed. Evidence from the Family Expenditure Survey shows that the share of disposable household income taken by the top 20 per cent rose from 35 per cent in

1979 to 41 per cent in 1991–2 at a time when the share taken by the bottom 20 per cent fell from 10 per cent to 7 per cent. Indeed, when housing costs are taken into consideration the gap between the rich and the poor widens. The share of the top quintile group increased its share by 8 per cent while the share of the bottom 20 per cent fell by 4 per cent (*Social Trends 1995*: 94). Clearly, the 1980s was a decade of growing income inequality in Britain.

Again, there are a number of reasons why income inequalities have increased. One of the major reasons is change in the tax system since 1979. The higher income tax rates were reduced (especially in the 1980 and 1988 Budgets) from a maximum of 83 per cent on earned income to a single rate of 40 per cent. Of the £31.4m saved by changes in the tax system since 1978/9, nearly half of it (15.2 million) was saved by the top 10 per cent of tax payers (Oppenheim 1993: 178). In 1992–3, a new, lower rate of tax was introduced so that all taxpayers now pay a rate of 20 per cent on the first £2,500 of taxable income while the surcharge of up to 15 per cent on investment income has been abolished (*Social Trends 1994*: 73). The other major reason for the growing inequalities in wealth is the huge rise in the income of the high earners. In 1990, for example, Lord Hanson, director of the Hanson Trust, earned an annual salary of over £1 million (Scott 1991: 86). More recently, controversy has surrounded the increased earning of managing directors of newly privatised industries Top earners, in other words, have been earning more and being taxed less through the 1980s in Britain.

Wealth, of course, confers privilege. The wealthy enjoy superior life-styles which include numerous properties, art treasures and pursue exclusive leisure pursuits such as polo, hunting, breeding horses and yachting. They socialise with other wealthy individuals, and their social activities are reported in the gossip columns of magazines such as *Vanity Fair* and *Harper's and Queens*. This exclusive life-style suggests that they constitute a distinct socio-cultural entity. The social cohesiveness of this 'upper class' has been substantially documented by G. William Domhoff (1967; 1983). Despite the lack of an old, titled aristocracy, Domhoff argues that America has a wealthy upper class of interacting families who amount to 0.5% of the population. Their cultural identity is sustained through private schooling (Groton (Mass,), St. Pauls (New Hampshire), and St. Marks (Mass)) which facilitate entry into the top universities (such as Harvard, Yale, Princeton and Cornell) where the wealthy join the elite fraternities (such as the Cap and Gown, Tiger and Ivy). Similarly, exclusive clubs such as Links and Knickerbocker in New York, the Philadelphia and Rittenhouse in Philadelphia, and the Pacific Union and Bohemian in San Francisco have been important sites for sociability shared with a small group of other people of equal social standing. The stability of the upper class is reinforced through inter-marriage between members of wealthy families. He concluded that the upper class consists a complex network of overlapping social circles which are knit together by the members they have in common and by the numerous signs of social status that emerge from a similar life-style (Domhoff 1983: 50).

The importance of status in the reproduction of the upper class in Britain is well known. The landed aristocracy originally dominated High Society in which the Royal Family and the Court played a pivotal role, and it was integrated with the activities of the state. They participated in a year-long social calender of sporting activities, parties and balls. This exclusive life-style was confined to a set of intersecting social circles from which eligible marriage partners were found (Scott 1982). However, the declining fortunes of aristocratic families in the Edwardian period (Beard 1989; Beckett 1988; Cannadine 1990; Thompson 1994) led to their withdrawal from High Society and it declined with them. A similar range of activities are still pursued by young members of the landed aristocracy, new members to the Royal Family and various newcomers referred to as Sloan Rangers and Yuppies by the media in the late 1980s. These social circles are no longer as exclusive as they once were and their activities are certainly completely separate from state activities (Scott 1991: 108). Nevertheless, public schools (Eton, Harrow and Winchester usually followed by a higher education at Oxford and Cambridge) and the gentlemen's clubs (Whites, Jockey Club and the Garrick) continue to play a crucial role in reinforcing networks of kin and friends and the pro-capitalist values and attitudes of the upper class (Rubinstein 1993). Both sets of institutions facilitate sociability among the wealthy and sustain an old boys' network through which information on business and politics is passed (Scott 1982; 1991).

A socially cohesive upper class of wealthy families, therefore, has not disappeared. However, the upper class is not merely a 'leisure class' for it has proved remarkably successful in sustaining its wealth. Domhoff stressed that members of the upper class are 'working people' in that 'the American upper class is a business aristocracy, and business is its primary concern' (Domhoff 1967: 31). Members of the upper class are still involved in the world of business, especially on boards of directors of the large corporations, banks and insurance companies. He found, for example, that 62 per cent of banks' high-level personnel, 44 per cent of insurance directors and 54 per cent of the industrial business élite were of upper class origin. He concluded that, 'Interlocking directorships show beyond question that there is a national corporate economy that is run by the same group of several thousand men' (Domhoff 1967: 57). For Domhoff (1983: 77), therefore, the upper class are the 'corporate rich'.

Useem (1984) confirmed these findings in his comparative study

of American and British businessmen. The concentration of corporate
resources has led to the formation of an inner circle of directors and top
managers involved in a world of 'intercorporate networks through shared
ownership and directorships of large companies (Useem 1984: 3). Useem
noted that this inner circle has very close ties to the upper class in that 'when
scions of the upper class do enter business, they tend to reach the inner circle
more often and more rapidly then those of more modest origins' (Useem
1983: 66). There is a close alliance between the two in that the network of
family contacts and financial assets provide access for upper class business
men into the inner circle. Useem found, for example, that 15 per cent of
American business leaders who constituted the core of the inner circle had
received public schooling in comparison with 10 per cent outside the inner
circle (the equivalent figures in Britain being 14 per cent and 6 per cent
respectively) (Useem 1983: 68). In relation to financial assets, 37 per cent
of the single directorship managers held at least half a million dollars in
assets compared with 69 per cent of many-boarded directors who were
worth more than $500,000 (Useem 1983: 70). Members of the inner
circle are also leaders of the major business associations in America with
a notable presence on such organisations as the Business Roundtable, the
Business Council and the Council on Foreign Relations while in Britain they
are leaders in the Confederation of British Industry (CBI) and the British
Institute of Managers (BIM) (Useem 1984: 72)

In Britain, Scott (1982) has identified an active business class which is
small in number in comparison to the top 1 per cent referred to in statistics
on wealth and income. The core of the business class who strategically
control the major enterprises consists of less than 0.1 per cent of the
population and no more than 0.2 per cent (Scott 1982: 124). He divides the
economically active core of the business class into three parts. They are:

1. Entrepreneurial capitalists who have a considerable ownership stake in
   the enterprise in which they are associated.
2. Internal capitalists who have a business interest within a particular
   company without having a large share-holding in the company.
3. Finance capitalists who have primary and additional interests in number
   of major enterprises. (Scott 1982: 125)

The members of this core are the business leaders in the top 1,000 monopo-
lies, dominating the markets in which they do business. The interplay of
the three groups on the boards of directors shape the corporate strategies
of the large enterprises. Scott argues that changes in the structure of capital
ownership have seen the growing importance of the finance capitalist who
increasingly sit on the boards of the top business companies (Scott 1982:
140). As multiple directors, they are crucial members of an intercorporate

network who sustain the corporate system as a whole. This small group of approximately 300 businessmen are, therefore, the most important part of the business class. They are the business leaders 'in a system of class-controlled large enterprises' who sustain the 'privileges of the wider business class' (Scott 1982: 146).

Research in Britain demonstrates that there are close links between the business class and the upper class. Somewhat dated evidence shows that a high proportion of company directors and company chairmen have upper-class social origins, have been educated at Eton and elsewhere, attended Oxford and Cambridge and belong to various exclusive London clubs (Whitley 1974). Stanworth and Giddens (1974: 82), for example, found that 74 per cent of chairmen of banks and 100 per cent of chairmen of merchant banks had upper-class origins. It is a background which they share with members of the higher civil service, the top of the judiciary and so on. Again, the evidence suggests that the business class occupies an another exclusive social circle where private education and club membership sustain a 'common culture'. Stanworth and Giddens (1974: 219) concluded that while the number of business leaders from families with substantial wealth has declined a high proportion of them still come from the upper middle class who dominate the old professions. Changes in patterns of recruitment into the business class, therefore, are more apparent than real. There are problems with this evidence from both the US and Britain however. A disproportionate number of the business class have upper-class origins and belong to distinct status groups within the upper class. However, there are also a large number of business people who do not come from these privileged backgrounds, and they are certainly neglected in the work of Domhoff and Useem. The social exclusiveness of the business class, therefore, and it's significance has been overstated.

Overall, the evidence indicates that there is a wealthy upper class to be found in both America and Britain. They have become relatively more wealthy in terms of both wealth and income over time, and they form a disproportionate number of the business class active in the corporate world. It has been argued that this business class has a great deal of political power in that it has considerable resources and access to government officials who also share their upper-class background. Its influence on policy-making and especially government economic policy has meant that its economic interests have never been threatened by the state. The extent to which the upper class constitutes a ruling class or power élite will now be discussed.

A RULING CLASS?

Whether the economically dominant capitalist class also has political power and thereby constitutes a ruling class has long been the source of debate among élite theorists, pluralists and Marxists in the US and Britain. The most famous exponent of élite theory was C. Wright Mills (1956) who argued that power in America resided in an élite which consisted of three interrelated parts: the economic, the political and the military domains (Mills 1956: 9). Mills believed that the rise of the large corporation heralded the 'reorganisation of the propertied class' and, consequently, 'the narrow industrial and profit interests of specific firms and industries and families have been translated into the broader economic and political interests of a more genuinely class type' (Mills 1956: 148). The corporate rich had consolidated their economic power and had also enhanced their political power with contributions to campaign funds and close contact with key politicians. Mills also emphasised the shared social backgrounds of the élite and the networks between personnel. Indeed, he identified the major corporations as the key organisation in this networking process since 'on the boards of directors we find a heavy overlapping among the members of several élites' (Mills 1956: 283). He argued, 'Nowhere in America is there as great a 'class consciousness' as among the élite: nowhere is it organised as effectively as among the power élite' (Mills 1956: 283).

Mills' argument 'created waves in the larger academic community and even spilled onto the pages of popular magazines and political journals' (Domhoff: 1980: 8). The major critic of Mills' view of an essentially closed society was Dahl who came to represent the pluralist view of power in the US. Dahl (1961a) argued that Mills' theory was impossible to disprove, not least since a suitable test of the theory has not been devised. In his study of local decision-making in New Haven, Connecticut, he found an economic élite which was not all powerful. It was influential in some areas although not in others. Rather, there were a number of distinct élites competing with either other. In other words, Dahl argued that American society was an open and democratic society in which power was dispersed. There was no all powerful ruling élite (Dahl 1961b).

Mills' thesis found support in the work of Domhoff (1967; 1983) who argued that the upper class is a governing class in that 'it contributes a disproportionate number of its members to the controlling institutions and key decision-making groups of the country' (Domhoff 1967: 5). The federal government is dominated by leaders of the upper class or former employees of institutions controlled by members of the upper class. They are highly influential, in terms of defining debate and decision making, on such bodies as charitable foundations, the élite universities and associations such as the Council on Foreign Relations, the Foreign Policy Association, the Business Advisory Council and the National Advertising Council (Domhoff 1967: 83). They control the executive branch of federal govern-ment through the financing of parties (especially the Republican party by the upper class) and especially presidential nominations (including again, Republicans such as Goldwater and Rockefeller). They are also highly influential on the legislative branch of the federal government (Congress), most state governments and most city governments through campaign finances, lobbying and the control of regulatory agencies (Domhoff 1983: 135). More recently, the upper class, through its corporate businessmen, is involved in the candidate selection process, in special interests groups which lobby government and in the policy-making network which influence Congress and the White House. The advent of Political Action Committees (PACS) in the 1970s, for example, has witnessed huge company donations to political campaigns influencing 'who enters politics with any hope of running a nomination' (Domhoff 1983: 126; see also Clawson *et al.* 1986; Mizruchi and Koenig 1986). These developments, Domhoff argues, have brought the 'power élite into direct and very often successful involvement in government' (Domhoff 1983: 219). It is through these mechanisms that the upper class 'wins more than its loses' on a wide range of issues from taxes to consumer protection.

The expansion of corporate political activities has also been documented by Useem (1984: 4). He found that members of the inner circle intervene in politics on behalf of the business community in a number of ways. Firstly, they are active through its advisory service to the national government. He found 'that the number of corporate directorships that business leaders held was a reliable predictor of whether they were called to public service on advisory committees'. In 1975–6, single directors outside the inner circle held only 9 per cent of possible appointments to the federal advisory committee compared with 25 per cent of many-boarded members of the inner circle. Only 3 per cent of single directors were appointed to British public boards in 1978–9 compared with 12 per cent of many-board directors (Useem 1984: 78). Secondly, members of the inner circle were on the governing bodies of non-profit organisations such as foundations, universities and so forth. Thirdly, the inner circle is politically active in its support for political parties and candidates through PACS as Domhoff also documented. Finally, the inner circle, with its enormous financial resources, is able to appeal to the public through the mass media. Useem concluded that, 'The inner circle has thus become the leading edge of business political activity, a special leadership cadre' (1984: 115). The rise of institutional capitalism in both America and Britain, therefore, has witnessed the parallel rise of class-wide politics.

Domhoff's and Useem's work, however, has been criticised by political scientists and sociologists alike. Pluralists and neo-pluralists such as Lindblom (1977) and Vogel (1990) have argued that business enjoys exceptional resources and access to government. It is in a strong negotiating

position with government because government depends on economic success for political success. Business makes important decisions over which
the government has no control (Lindblom 1977: 175). It is recognised
that business has become more organised than it was in the past and has
increasingly influenced economic policy-making. Nevertheless, business is
not all powerful. The political organisation of business, for example, was
a response to the increasing voice of consumers and environmentalists in
the 1970s and 1980s (Vogel 1989). Business, in other words, has had
to compete with other groups in seeking to influence decision-making,
and it has not always won. It may be very influential but it is not all
powerful.

There has also been an ongoing debate between Skocpol (1981; Skocpol
and Finegold 1982; Skocpol and Ikenberry 1983; Skocpol and Amenta
1985), Domhoff (1991) and others (Quadagno 1984; 1985) over the New
Deal. Skocpol (1981) was critical of Domhoff's instrumentalist 'corporate
liberal' perspective on increasing state intervention in the US economy in
the twentieth century. The notion that enlightened capitalists recognised
that an extension of the state's role would serve their long-term interests
amounts to a crude view of the New Deal 'as a set of clever capitalist
strategies to stabilise and revitalise a US economy dominated by large
corporations' (Skocpol 1980: 336). On the contrary, there was considerable
capitalist opposition to the New Deal especially over labour concessions
(which the state pushed for) in the form of the 1935 Social Security Act.
Nevertheless, Skocpol acknowledged that the accomplishments of the New
Deal were limited although the state and party organisations, rather than
capitalists, explained the piecemeal nature of the reforms. Thus, Skocpol
(1980: 362) argued that Domhoff had overstated the power of a 'far-sighted
capitalist ruling class' and neglected the importance of state structures and
party organisations in shaping political conflicts and outcomes.

In reply, Domhoff (1991) argued that Skocpol had misrepresented his
work by identifying it as representative of a 'corporate liberal' perspective.
He reasserted his view that a class based theory of power was more
useful than a state autonomy theory for understanding the New Deal. He
acknowledged that there was considerable political conflict over various
initiatives such as the Agricultural Adjustment Administration, the National
Recovery Administration, the Social Security Act and the 1935 National
Labor Relations (Wagner) Act. Nevertheless, corporate businessmen
dominated the debates. The 1935 Social Security Act was a case in point
since key political experts worked closely with business leaders (Domhoff
1991: 445). Domhoff (1991: 462) concluded that 'America is relatively
unique in being a completely capitalist society with a powerful capitalist
class, and these factors are embedded in the nature and actions of its state'

and 'In the face of a massive depression and growing militancy, a power élite rooted in large income-producing property was able to play the major role in creating or shaping four of the most important initiatives taken by the state during the New Deal'. The New Deal – and the role of political officials during the period in question -can be understood from this class perspective.

It is not easy to adjudicate between the rival theories of the New Deal since participants in the debate have marshalled considerable historical material in support of their claims. Both Skocpol and Domhoff make important points. Skocpol (1980: 362), for example, rightly argues that 'capitalism in general has no politics, only (extremely flexible) outer limits for the kinds of supports for property ownership and controls of the labor force that it can tolerate'. Similarly, Domhoff (1991: 448) correctly asserts that not all businessmen have the same beliefs and that some of them supported the New Deal legislation. These points are not contradictory since broadly defined interests can translate into a variety of political practices. It could be argued, therefore, that Skocpol and Domhoff have argued past each other and the differences between them are a matter of degree. What the debate also highlights is the difficulties of employing adequate empirical material – especially in relation to the socio-political attitudes and beliefs of the different arms of business – as a suitable test of competing theories of class and power. The activities of businessmen in politics in the US is hard to deny. The 1980s and 1990s has seen corporate businessmen Ross Perot and Steve Forbes put themselves forward as presidential candidates after all. Reducing the role of big government and reducing federal taxes dominated each candidate's political programme. Nevertheless, corporate business is one only of many players in the political world and an understanding of business influence has to be placed in this context.

Parallel debate about whether the capitalist class is a ruling class can also be found in Britain and Europe (Miliband 1969; Poutlantzas 1975; (Urry 1981). In the 1970s, Giddens was critical of Mills' view of a 'unified, conspiratorial élite' and argued that there are numerous élites defined in terms of positions of formal authority. The most powerful élites, however, include those who hold the top positions in economic, legal and political institutions such as the top businesses, the judiciary and the House of Commons (Stanworth and Giddens 1974). Numerous contributors (Guttsman 1974; Hewitt 1974; Whitley 1974; Stanworth and Giddens 1974) showed how top industrialists and government personnel make close links with the upper class. Heath (1981: 88) also examined trends in élite recruitment and noted that élite occupations such as high level politicians, the civil service and top judges shared wealthy and privileged backgrounds. Power, in other words, can only be understood in the context of class relations.

More recently, Scott (1991: 5) has argued that Britain is ruled by a ruling class since power is rooted in class relations (Scott 1991: 4). In seeking to establish whether the capitalist class is a ruling class, Scott argues it is necessary to distinguish between a power bloc, a state élite, a political élite and a power élite. A power bloc, Scott (1991: 32) argues, refers to a particular alignment of social groups (such as the capitalist class, the service class and the entrepreneurial middle class) who occupy the leading positions in society. A state élite refers to positions of formal authority in the state (such as the government, Houses of Parliament, civil service, military and judiciary). The personnel who occupy those positions comprise a political élite. Scott argues that where the political élite is 'strongly rooted in a power bloc', the political élite takes the form of a power élite (Scott 1991: 37). On this basis, he argues, 'A capitalist class may be regarded as forming a ruling class when its economic dominance is sustained by the operations of the state and when, alone or through a wider power bloc, it is disproportionately represented in the power élite which rules the state apparatus (Scott 1991: 38). The capitalist class is a ruling class, therefore, where, firstly, it dominates the power élite and secondly, where the state protects and enhances the economic interests of the capitalist class. The existence of a power élite, for example can be demonstrated by the fact that upper-class businessmen continue 'to dominate recruitment to the state élite' (Scott 1991: 130). Mrs Thatcher headed the 1990 Cabinet but she was one of only two of the twenty-three members who had not attended a fee-paying school. She was one of the overwhelming majority (sixteen) of cabinet members who had been to Oxbridge (Scott 1991: 134). Thus, people of similar social origins, educational experiences and work histories 'are to be found in the state élite in far greater number than would be expected if positions were allocated more equitably' (Scott 1991: 137). The business class holds a dominant position within the power bloc, and it is from this power bloc that a power élite has emerged (Scott 1991: 139).

Scott went on to argue that the capitalist class is politically and ideologically dominant in reproducing its economic advantages since the state protects private property and private profit to the material advantage of the capitalist class over all other classes (Scott 1991: 140-1; see also Abercrombie *et al.* 1980; 1986; 1990). Members of the power élite also shape the nature of political rule through their privileged (formal and informal) access to government. As organised special interest groups, they have drawn on considerable resources to employ lawyers, advertising agencies, and have exploited their network of formal and informal contacts (aided by the circulation of personnel between the worlds of business and politics) in pursuit of their interests (Scott 1991: 146). Moreover, members of the business class are frequently appointed as experts to various advisory bodies, enquiries, and commissions which influence the policy-making process. Finally, business has long offered financial support to the Conservative Party as a means of influencing politics and donors have enjoyed the disproportionate award of titles and honours from Conservative Governments in the 1980s and 1990s (Scott 1991: 147–8). The knighthood offered to Graham Kirkham, for charitable services, in the 1996 New Year's Honours List, caused much controversy since he is believed to have given the Conservative Party a £4 million bridging loan (*The Guardian* 30.12.1995). The services of one of the richest men in Britain, it seems, did not go unrewarded.

Scott provides a novel theoretical model which acknowledges the role of the service class and entrepreneurial middle class in the status apparatus and the benefits accrued from their participation. Nevertheless, there are several shortcomings with the empirical evidence employed in support of this arguments. First, there is plenty of current evidence to confirm the exclusive social background of Conservative MPs (Borthwick *et al.* 1991; Baker 1995; Baker *et al.* 1992a; 1992b; 1995). However, the shared social background of Conservative MPs cannot be taken as an indicator of shared political values and behaviour. They may well share certain abstract principles but disagree over substantive policies and practices. The opposing views about the European Community within the Conservative Party is a case in point. Second, there is plenty of evidence collected by political scientists which shows that business has unparalleled access to government (Grant 1985; 1987; Grant and Marsh 1977; Ingham 1984; Jordan and Richardson 1987; Moran 1984). However, there are important divisions within business such as the different views of financial institutions and manufacturing industry over interests rates. Again, business is but one of many voices claiming to be heard alongside other pressure groups, organised labour, public opinion and so on and it does not always win. Finally, the evidence demonstrates that donations to the Conservative Party invariably derive from big business and that company directors donating funds have enjoyed various honours in the 1980s (Walker and Walker 1987). Yet, it is also the case that 'corporate political donations are the exception rather than the rule' in that only 242 (6 per cent) of the top 4,000 companies made relatively modest political donations in 1991/2 (Fisher 1994a). While company chairmen might hope to enhance their business interests, it does not mean they get what they want, and while a title may bring some prestige to an individual, it is of little economic consequence to the corporation and its shareholders (Fisher 1994b; 1995).

Thus, Scott's assertion that Britain is governed by a ruling class is unconvincing. While it enjoys privileged access to government, its power is not unfettered. Business/government relations are often troubled. Most importantly, it is also in constant contention with other groups to get its voice heard in the din of the political arena in Britain. Not all government policies and practices favour the interests of capital even in the long run. Business is not the victor in all circumstances, and the success of other groups, like organised labour, cannot be dismissed as trifling concession. Scott's claim that, 'The Labour Party has *governed* but it has not *ruled*' (Scott 1991: 139) suffers from the same problems of interpretation as Domhoff's views of the New Deal in the US. That is, the 1945 Labour electoral victory and the subsequent establishment of the Welfare State cannot be dismissed as inconsequential (especially in comparison to the New Deal). It was an important victory for members of the working class from which they benefitted. This is not to suggest that there is no place for a class perspective on British politics. However, a class perspective needs to acknowledge that economic power does not simply translate into political power, nor should it ignore the complex political relationships, struggles and the nature of power which are evident in contemporary Britain.

CONCLUSION

This chapter has focused on the extent to which the capitalist class has disappeared or survived as a distinct economic, social and political entity over the twentieth century in America and Britain. It has been argued that the capitalist class still exists as an economic entity in both nations. That said, there have been important changes with the demise of personal forms of ownership and the rise of impersonal ownership in the form of large corporations. Similarly, the nature of control has moved away from families to institutions who enjoy influence though a constellation of interests. It has also been argued that the capitalist class in America and Britain has a distinct socio-cultural identity. The increasing wealth and income of its members facilitates a privileged and exclusive life-style from which others are excluded. It is assumed that this milieux sustains a distinct outlook on the rest of society and their place within it although it must be said that there is not enough evidence of the social attitudes on the wealthy to empirically substantiate this finding.

Whether the capitalist class has a distinct political entity has proved even more difficult to substantiate. The business class – and especially finance capitalists within it – have privileged access to the state. They employ considerable resources to lobby government over economic policy through the normal channels of protest although, of course, they can exploit networks of personal relations whom they are often heavily inter-connected. Nevertheless, business is not all powerful. Other classes have resources which they can mobilise such as mass support which is far from inconsequential for electoral success. Government, therefore, does not bow to the interest of capital and the involvement of other classes and interests in the political process makes political decision-making and political outcomes highly variable. It is for these reasons that it is difficult to argue that the capitalist class rules in either America or Britain.

Chapter 6

Social Closure

The rise of modern corporations characterised by bureaucratic forms of organisation has seen the phenomenal growth of high-level nonmanual employment in America and Britain over the twentieth century. Not surprisingly, this upward shift in the shape of the occupational structure of the two nations has captured the attention of sociologists. Interest has focused on the rise of the middle class – or what is sometimes referred to as the service class – and there are a variety of competing explanations for its emergence. There has also been considerable debate as to whether there is one middle class or two or more middle classes. Various forms of differentiation within the middle class, in other words, have raised doubts as to whether it is possible to identify a distinct economic, social and political entity. The demand for highly qualified professionals and managers has facilitated a substantial amount of upward social mobility as was noted in Chapter Three above. However, sociologists have looked closely at the extent to which the middle class is 'open' to men and women irrespective of their ethnic origin or whether processes of social closure bar groups of people from positions of privilege and power. Finally, there has been much controversy over the socio-political proclivities of the 'new' middle class. The extent to which it constitutes a conservative force in support of the status quo or is a radical force for socio-economic change is considered of paramount importance to the future direction of post-industrial societies.

This chapter is divided into three parts. The first part examines the growth of the middle class and lines of cleavage within the middle class in America and Britain. Both nations have witnessed the growth of high-level nonmanual jobs although professional and managerial jobs began to grow in the late nineteenth and early twentieth centuries in America while middle-class jobs started to increase after the Second World War in Britain. While a process of professionalisation of high-level nonmanual work was evident in America, the position of professional occupations in Britain was sponsored by the state. That said, the size of the middle class within each country is now remarkably similar. The huge growth of high-level nonmanual jobs has led commentators to distinguish between the 'old' entrepreneurial middle class and the 'new' salaried middle class or between managers and professionals although the importance of these lines of differentiation for the shape of the class structure – whether there is more than one middle class – remains open to dispute. Finally, there has been much interest in the slowdown in the growth of professional and managerial jobs and the implications for the middle class. To date, however, it is too early to say whether the upward shift in the occupational structure has come to an end or that the security of the middle class has been undermined in a period of slow economic growth and recurring recessions.

The second part of the chapter focuses on the extent to which opportunities for advancement into the middle class have been available to ethnic groups and women in the two nations. The evidence suggests that a small number of blacks and women have entered high-level professional occupations, and, to a lesser degree, managerial jobs in the last thirty years. The fortuitous combination of economic prosperity and political liberalism, for example, facilitated the growth of the black middle class in the US. The political impact of feminism also facilitated women's entry into high-level nonmanual jobs in the 1970s and 1980s in Britain. For blacks and women, the acquisition of education credentials has been crucial to their entry into middle-class positions and, as a result, those from relatively privileged backgrounds who enjoyed a good education, have been the main beneficiaries of social change. That said, neither group has received the return on their credentials to the same extent as their white equivalents. Moreover, neither blacks nor women have entered the world of top management to any noticeable degree so they remain excluded from positions of power. Finally, the changed economic and political climate has led to a slowdown in the growth of the black middle class in America but it does not appear, as yet, to have forestalled women's progress in the occupational structure. The extent to which the position of blacks and women will solidify and they, in turn, will be able to transfer their resources on to the next generation remains an empirical question. Sections of the middle class, therefore, remain closed to blacks and women.

The third part examines the politics of the middle class in America and Britain. Debate has centred around the extent to which the middle class constitutes a conservative force which upholds the status quo or is a radical force for change. The evidence from America suggests that, on the whole, members of the middle class support the Republicans rather than the Democrats on a range of economic issues. However, there is a segment of the middle class – namely, public-sector welfare professions – who can be described as liberal on social issues ranging from environmentalism to feminism. Indeed, they are the most active members of new social movements. A remarkably similar picture also emerges in Britain. The middle class as a whole support the Conservative Party. That said, members of the welfare and creative professions tend to be more liberal on social rather than economic issues and transfer their political allegiances to the Liberal Democrats or Labour. The evidence suggests that prior political orientations from a family of origin shape job choices which are then compatible with a person's world views. Overall, therefore, the middle class in America and Britain may be characterised as largely conservative in inclination although sections of it adopt liberal attitudes on various social issues. The socio-political identity of the middle class, however, is contingent on political circumstances so its political character remains an open question.

GROWTH AND DIFFERENTIATION

The growth of the service class in the twentieth century is the product of a phenomenal increase in professional, managerial and administrative occupations in the US, Britain and other advanced capitalist countries in Europe. America experienced a rapid growth in these occupations from the mid-nineteenth century while Britain had a somewhat slower and more modest rate of growth over the twentieth century. By the 1990s, however, census data indicates that the size of the middle class is remarkably similar in both nations (40% and 37% respectively). In the US, professionals constituted the largest occupational category (17%) with managers a short way behind on 13 per cent in 1990 (Gilbert and Kahn 1993: 71). In Britain, professionals and managers comprised 17 per cent and 10 per cent of the workforce respectively in 1991 (*1991 Census Report for GB (Part 2)*). The rise of the middle class has, of course, facilitated large amounts of upward social mobility discussed in Chapter Three above. The growth of professional and managerial occupations has more than offset the decline in the numbers of self-employed (petty bourgeoisie) which arguably has dropped in both countries (Dale 1986; Linder and Houghton 1990; Steinmetz and Wright 1989; 1990). The growth of salaried occupations, as we shall see, has generated considerable interest in the middle class or what some commentators refer to as the middle classes in contemporary society.

The growth of high-level occupations has been tied to the rise of large corporations in the US. The economic historian, A.D. Chandler (1977), for example, argued that the emergence of large corporations in the early twentieth century led to a rise in professional managers. In order to keep their edge over smaller firms in a competitive market, a variety of functions such as research and development, marketing and finance were kept in-house. Large organisations, therefore embraced a variety of functions undertaken by various semi-autonomous units. They were characterised by a management hierarchy and the role of managers was to co-ordinate activities previously left to the market. Management careers were established and quickly professionalised in that graduates were recruited to managerial posts and enjoyed promotion up the bureaucratic ladder of the internal labour market on the basis of merit (Chandler 1977). In a not dissimilar vein, DiPrete (1989) emphasised the professionalisation of high-level white-collar work as the division of labour of nonmanual work became more complex within bureaucracies. In contrast, John Urry and his colleagues (Abercrombie and Urry 1983; Lash and Urry 1987), attached greater importance to the implementation of Scientific Management (embodied in the principles of Taylorism) prior to the First World War. They argued that Scientific Management necessitated the rapid growth of managers and administrators involved in 'the coordination of *written* work orders' (Lash and Urry 1987: 171). The large number of technical specialists, mostly engineers, were quickly professionalised and fully integrated into the management of large corporations. The development of increasingly complex occupational hierarchies occurred in both manufacturing and services, and were accompanied by the rapid growth of higher education from the 1880s. Thus, there is some debate over the importance of the professionalisation of administration and the implementation of Scientific Management in the growth of high-level occupations but, nevertheless, the growth of professional and managerial jobs is not in dispute.

For C. Wright Mills, the growth of nonmanual employment heralded the demise of property as the major 'axis of stratification' and the growing significance of occupation in a complex division of labour. In *White Collar* (Mills 1951), he distinguished between an 'old' middle class (of small entrepreneurs, self employed professionals and so on) and a 'new' middle class (of salaried professionals and managers as well as lower-level office workers). The 'old' middle class was in decline since small entrepreneurs were unable to compete with large corporations. These large corporations, in contrast, employed increasing numbers of salaried employees engaged in management, accountancy, design and marketing. This trend was also evident in bureaucracies in the state sector. Bell also noted the growing importance of high-level nonmanual employees – especially knowledge workers – in *The Coming of Post-Industrial Society* (Bell 1973). Given their role within the production process, he argued that the intelligentsia would be a pre-eminent social group in shaping the future direction of society. However, he argued that there was a growing split between the technical intelligentsia who are preoccupied with 'functional rationality and technocratic modes of operation' and the literary intelligentsia who are resistant

Table 6.1. The old and new middle classes in the USA, 1870–1940

	%	
	1870	1940
Old middle class	85	44
Farmers	62	23
Businessmen	21	19
Free Professionals	2	2
New middle class	15	56
Managers	2	6
Salaried professionals	4	14
Salespeople	7	14
Office workers	2	22
Total	100	100

Source: Mills (1951), p. 65.

to the dominance of science and bureaucratic forms of organisation. It was these types of conflicts between fractions of the middle class which would characterise post-industrial society (Bell 1973: 214–5). Thus, both Mills and Bell identified a growing middle class – although it was a class which was increasingly internally differentiated – of sociological and political importance.

Indeed, the socio-political significance of the expansion of the middle class, especially professional employees, increasingly preoccupied writers in the 1960s and 1970s. The involvement of members of the professional middle class in the 'new politics' of that period led various commentators to identify a 'new class' (Ehrenreich and Ehrenreich 1979; Gouldner 1979; Kristol 1972; Ladd 1978; Moyihan 1972). Marxists such as Ehrenreich and Ehrenreich (1979), for example, noted the growth of a 'professional-managerial class' (PMC) under monopoly capitalism. They argued the PMC play an important role in the reproduction of classes in that their main functions is one of social control. In this respect, their interests are in opposition to the working class. Ehrenreich and Ehrenreich also argued, however, that the PMC is also opposed to the capitalist class over issues of ownership and control. It is neither aligned with the working class nor the capitalist class but is an independent 'reservoir of radicalism'. Similarly, non-Marxists such as Gouldner (1979) argued that intellectuals within the middle class have an increasingly important role within a 'knowledge society'. While not denying that the intelligentsia have individual aspirations of its own, he argued that its distinctive 'culture of critical discourse' meant that it acted in pursuit of collective interests. The intelligentsia, in particular, is critical of all forms of economic power and political domination. Gouldner was also hopeful, therefore, that this new class of intellectuals would become a 'universal class' ready to challenge the prevailing order. Other commentators (Kristol 1972; Moynihan 1979) held somewhat less optimistic views of the new class which they saw as a frustrated group in search of power and status in its own interests. Nevertheless, there was a convergence from writers from different positions in the political spectrum who subscribed to the theory of the 'new class' (Brint 1984).

These accounts of the rising importance of the middle class, however, were the subject of criticism (Bell 1979; Bruce-Briggs 1979). Bell, for example, was highly critical of the links which commentators drew between the emergence of a 'new class' and the rise of 'new politics' in the 1960s and 1970s. He argued that the rise of liberalism among high-level white-collar workers could not be seen in terms of antagonism with the capitalist class. Bell believed that professionals were not a class with a shared set of economic and political interests for they were also divided by occupation and employing organisations. Only a small minority of professionals, after all, were involved in new political groupings. More importantly, Bell argued that liberalism was not confined to the educated young but infused the whole of society. Anti-institutional and anti-conservative attitudes were indicative of cultural change in post-industrial society. He was highly critical, therefore, of explanations of 'new politics' which sought to account for the distinctive structural location of political activists. In any event, the rise of conservatism in the 1970s and the 1980s undermined the 'new class' thesis although the characterisation of the middle class as a radical force for change has remained popular among Marxist thinkers (Burris 1986; Wright 1985).

In the 1980s and 1990s, attention has turned to the slowdown in the growth of high-level occupations, and the impact of technological and organisational change on the middle classes. Economic restructuring and the downsizing of organisations (Harrison and Bluestone 1988) have undermined bureaucratic careers and witnessed the growth of white-collar unemployment and downward mobility (Ehrenreich 1989; Newman 1988; 1991; 1993; Phillips 1993; Strobel 1993). The seemingly secure position of the middle classes are under threat. In this economic context, commentators have focused less on the potential radicalism of the middle class or middle classes but on an increasing conservatism in the 1980s and 1990s instead. Newman (1991: 115), for example, has discussed the cultural costs of downward mobility which is evident, she argued:

in our fears for the country's economic future and our frustrations

over the impact of change on our standard of living, a resurgent
conservatism over the responsibilities of the fortunate toward the
fate of the poor, a heightened sense of competition between and
within generations for the resources need to raise a family or retire
in comfort, and increasing worries over the long-term impact of
inner-city decay and minority poverty. (Newman 1991: 115)

To date, however, Newman's claim that a Wall street financier 'is nearly as
vulnerable to downward mobility as the steel worker on Chicago's South
Side' exaggerates the level of middle-class job insecurity in comparison to
the insecurity of working-class jobs. The social and political implications
of downward mobility read as over-statements of, as yet, disputable trends
about the slowdown in the growth of high-level nonmanual jobs.

In Britain, historical and sociological accounts of the middle class
emphasised its slow growth over the twentieth century, and its importance
only since the Second World War (Abercrombie and Urry 1983; Lash
and Urry 1987; Savage *et al.* 1992). Lash and Urry (1987), for example,
argued that the separation of ownership and control occurred very gradually
as family firms remained important. The professions remained under the
sway of the landed aristocratic class and held a genteel status rather than
an occupational professional status. The slow implementation of Scientific
Management practices meant that the demand for managers was low, and
there was little push for professional status. The majority of managers in
British industry, therefore, were without educational credentials not least
since the system of higher education remained small. All these factors
hindered the growth of non-productive white-collar in Britain in the first
half of the twentieth century (Lash and Urry 1987: 184). The service class
only emerged in Britain in the 1960s with the growth of the welfare state. It
was the new expressive professional, employed in the health and education
services provided by the state who became dominant. The British service
class, therefore, was 'state sponsored and occurred during the period in
which British political culture was peculiarly 'progressivist' and when the
long post-war boom ensured fairly high levels of welfare expenditure (Lash
and Urry 1987: 146).

As in America, the growth of the middle class commanded early sociological attention. In *Class and Class Conflict in Industrial Societies* (1959),
Dahrendorf argued that the 'authority structure' in large organisations
was now 'the structural determinant of class formation and class action'
(Dahrendorf 1959: 136). The separation of ownership and control in
corporations and the emergence of managers with high levels of authority
in bureaucratic hierarchies heralded new forms of institutionalised class
conflict (Dahrendorf 1959: 55). Dahrendorf drew on the work of Karl

Renner, an Austrian Marxist, who argued that high-level bureaucrats constituted a 'service class'. They served their employers by controlling and regulating the process of production. Dahrendorf emphasised that bureaucrats exercised 'delegated authority' not on behalf of capitalists *per se* but on behalf of the bureaucracy. That is, their power lay in providing the bridge between the rulers and the ruled. They were primarily responsible for the administration of laws within bureaucratic organisations and were committed to them even though they had not made them. Dahrendorf (1961: 145), therefore, saw the service class as largely conformist in character. Dahrendorf's work, however, was criticised by Giddens (1980: 187) for failing 'to deal adequately with the problem of the heterogeneity of services offered by those in the diversity of occupations'. He argued that managers and administrators are part of an authority system which oversees the production process while professionals are frequently autonomous within the division of labour (Giddens 1980: 187). Thus, Giddens was highly sceptical of Dahrendorf's characterisation of a unitary service class, emphasising differentiation within the middle classes instead.

However, Dahrendorf's work found support from Goldthorpe who developed the concept of the service class from his mobility studies. Like Renner, he emphasised that its members enjoy a high degree of autonomy from a relationship of trust with their employers (Goldthorpe 1982: 167). It is a distinctive characteristic of their work situation which managers and professionals share (Goldthorpe 1982: 170). Goldthorpe noted that the service class was very homogenous in character but he emphasised its increasingly solidity as well. That is, considerable upward mobility sat alongside evidence of a density of mobility (Goldthorpe 1987: 48–9). The intergenerational stability of the service class would cement over time as careers in the service class were secured early though education rather than slowly through work experience. Goldthorpe went on to predict that the service class would be a conservative force. Occupying privileged employment positions with favourable intrinsic and extrinsic rewards, members of the service class have a stake in preserving the prevailing order. He argued:

> that these employees will in the main act in the way that is characteristic of privileged stata; that is that they will seek to use the superior resources that they possess in order to *preserve* their positions of relative social power and advantage, for themselves and their children. (Goldthorpe 1982: 180)

Goldthorpe's position, was subsequently challenged by Lash and Urry (1987) and Savage *et al*. 1992. Lash and Urry (1987) who argued that since the service class was closely associated with the rise of the welfare state, professional employees of the state would be concerned with enhancing welfare services as well as other political activities on the left of the political spectrum (CND, environmental groups, feminist groups and so forth). The service class, therefore, is politically fragmented but includes a radical group of professionals. This argument was subsequently developed by Savage *et al.* (1992). Following Wright, they argued that the possession, storage and transmission of three assets, property (associated with the petty bourgeoisie), bureaucracy (associated with managers) and culture (associated with professionals) are the 'axes of exploitation' around which middle-class formation has taken place in Britain. The professional middle class has been able to exploit its cultural assets through the state while the managerial middle class has been increasingly unable to exploit its organisational assets in the face of economic restructuring and organisational change. There is evidence, therefore, of a growing divide between the professional middle class and a managerial middle class in the late twentieth century (Savage *et al.* 1992).

Savage and his colleagues demonstrated the existence of middle classes with reference to social mobility and politics. Drawing on the Longitudinal Study (LS), linking census records of 1% of the population between 1971 and 1981, they examined intra-class mobility by focusing on worklife mobility between groups within the service class. They found that the professional middle class, who rely on cultural assets (and property assets) are more secure in the middle class than the managerial middle class relying on organisational assets. Male professionals enjoyed the best survival rates while the managerial middle class were far less secure (56% compared with 34%) (Savage *et al.* 1992: 140-1). A similar pattern was evident among women professionals (predominately nurses and teachers) and managers (47% compared with 17%). The findings indicated that the professional middle class is a stable collectivity while the managerial middle class is far less secure in comparison. Secondary analysis of the 1987 British Election Study by Savage *et al.* found a political cleavage between managers and professionals. High levels of Conservative voting were found among large employers (63%) and managers of large and small establishments (69 per cent and 58 per cent respectively) while professionals (whether self-employed or employees) supported the Conservatives to a lesser extent (50 per cent and 52 per cent) while nearly over a third voted Alliance (39 per cent and 36 per cent respectively) (Savage *et al.* 1992: 194). Savage *et al.* argued that support for the Conservatives had dropped among the professional middle class as successive Conservative governments had undermined the state which previously protected their cultural assets. They found, for example, Conservative Party support was low among managers and professionals employed in the public sector (40 per cent and 38 per cent respectively). The Alliance enjoyed similar levels of support among each occupational group (35 per cent and 36 per cent) but there was also some strong evidence of voting for the Labour Party amongst both groups (26 per cent and 27 per cent) (Savage *et al.* 1992: 196–7). The split between professionals and managers implies that the politics of the middle class is 'fractured' and that the professional middle class has a potentially radical role to play in British politics.

Savage and his associates research, however, is open to criticism. Arguably, it is the managerial middle class which has grown in the 1980s and 1990s to the detriment of the professional middle class in the advent of the new managerialism which has undermined professional autonomy in state services (Dent 1993; Flynn 1992). It is equally plausible to argue that the managerial middle class is now less subordinate to the professional middle class than it may have been in the past (which may also account for managerial allegiance to the Conservatives and declining support among beleaguered professionals). Goldthorpe (1995) also remains unconvinced by Savage *et al.*'s arguments. Erikson and Goldthorpe's (1992a) refor-mulation of the basis of class differentiation in terms of employment relations and employee relationships (noted in Chapter Two above) has implications for his definition of the service class. He no longer attaches importance to the service relationship but to the compensation enjoyed in terms of salary and incremental increases, job security and pension rights and well-defined career opportunities (Goldthorpe 1995: 315). These rewards remain important even if members of the service class enjoy continuity of employability if not continuity of employment (Goldthorpe 1995: 325). Definitional issues aside, Goldthorpe criticises Savage *et al.*'s exaggeration of differences in intra-generational mobility when professional and managerial careers become increasingly similar over time (Mills 1995). Moreover, their observation that managers and professionals are often married to each other undermines their argument (Goldthorpe 1995: 321). Finally, it should be added that Savage *et al.*'s analysis of distinctive cultural patterns among managers and professionals is limited without information on patterns of association in work and play.

As in America, there is an increasing interest in the implications of economic restructuring and organisational change (Clegg 1990) for the middle class, the arguement being that it is proving increasingly difficult for members to secure advantages for themselves and their children in the future. Economic restructuring, for example, has forced the middle class to mobilise their cultural resources to facilitate job opportunities in 'new' ways (Brown 1995; Brown and Scase 1994). Similarly, the threat to middle-class security has fostered a 'new' individualism in which families come first (Jordan *et al.* 1994). As yet, these claims have to be substantiated over a longer time-span, and the evidence suggests that the bureaucratic career is

Table 6.2. Men's and women's work-life mobility, 1971–81

(a) *Men*

1971 SEG	1981 SEG									
	1.1	1.2	2.2	3	4	5.1	All SC	PB	Others ¹	N =
1.1	3.7	9.3	13.0	3.7	—	5.6	35.2	25.1	15.5	54
1.2	0.0	32.6	17.6	4.2	3.4	3.8	52.7	3.1	18.1	5,008
2.2	0.0	13.6	34.4	0.5	1.8	2.8	53.2	9.8	21.6	6,790
3	—	1.0	3.0	55.5	12.6	4.5	76.6	3.7	2.7	1,118
4	0.0	9.3	8.6	5.6	40.0	11.1	74.4	2.0	13.3	5,497
5.1	—	10.9	4.4	0.4	8.6	41.6	65.9	2.1	16.9	6,373
All SC	0.0	15.2	16.2	4.1	12.8	14.8	63.1	4.5	16.9	24,849
PB	0.0	0.7	6.2	0.3	0.3	1.6	9.3	50.2	22.7	10,671
PWC	0.0	7.7	9.5	0.3	3.0	4.9	25.4	4.2	50.6	17,062
PBC	0.0	1.5	2.3	0.0	0.9	1.7	6.5	4.7	69.8	69,170
UE	—	1.0	2.6	0.3	1.1	2.2	7.3	6.5	62.3	4,528
Total LM	0.0	5.0	6.3	0.9	3.5	4.7	20.4	8.5	61.1	126,277

(b) *Women*

1971 SEG	1981 SEG									
	1.1	1.2	2.2	3	4	5.1	All SC	PB	Others ¹	N =
1.1	—	—	—	—	—	—	—	—	33.3	3
1.2	—	17.4	8.3	—	0.8	8.0	34.6	1.3	19.3	827
2.2	—	4.1	16.0	0.1	0.4	4.7	25.4	4.3	25.5	1,607
3	—	1.0	3.3	37.0	14.1	7.6	63.0	4.3	7.6	92
4	—	3.3	7.0	3.8	18.4	16.6	49.1	1.7	16.7	603
5.1	—	3.3	1.3	0.0	1.3	47.1	52.9	1.1	11.4	7,566
All SC	—	4.5	4.4	0.6	2.2	35.6	47.2	1.7	14.4	10,698
PB	0.0	0.6	3.5	0.0	—	2.5	6.7	23.9	21.6	2,845
PWC	0.0	1.3	2.0	0.0	0.1	2.6	6.1	1.6	47.7	39,100
PBC	—	0.3	2.0	0.0	0.1	1.6	2.7	1.1	47.8	21,666
UE	—	0.7	1.4	0.0	0.3	6.1	8.5	1.7	36.1	2,477
Total LM	0.0	1.4	1.9	0.1	0.4	6.4	10.6	2.3	40.5	76,696

¹ Others in different labour market groupings (PWC, PBC, UE).

Notes: (a) For a 1% sample of men and women in England and Wales who were in the labour
market in 1971.

(b) Percentages do not match to 100%, since the balance have left the labour market
between 1971 and 1981 (usually through retirement).

(c) Classification 1.1   = Large employers
1.2   = Managers, large establishments
2.2   = Managers, small establishments
3   = Self-employed professionals
4   = Professional employees
5.1   = Ancillary workers
All SC = All service class
PB   = Petit bourgeoisie (SEGs 2.1, 11, 13)
PWC = White-collar proletariat (SEGs 5.2, 6, 7)
PBC = Manual working class
UE   = Unemployed
Total LM = Total labour market

Source: Savage *et al.* (1992), Tables 7.1 and 7.2, pp. 140–2.

changing but not disappearing (Halford and Savage 1995a; Halford and Savage 1995b). Overall, the evidence is that America and Britain have witnessed the growth of the middle classes over the twentieth century which is characterised by a number of cleavages (the importance of which remains open to dispute). There may be signs of a slowdown in the pace of growth in high-level nonmanual occupations, but there is no clear evidence as yet that the privileged position of members of the middle class has been seriously undermined in either nation.

PROFESSIONS AND SOCIAL CLOSURE

Despite the phenomenal growth of the middle class, not all high-level nonmanual occupations have been 'open' to everyone. It has long been established, for example, that the professions are relatively 'closed' occupations (Abbott 1988). Work by Larson (1977) and Friedson (1986), for example, has shown how professions have organised and controlled knowledge, and this 'cognitive base' has been the source of a professional's autonomy and independence from organisations and employers. Moreover, professional associations have been crucial in protecting and enhancing the strong position of professionals within the labour market by controlling the number, selection and training of new recruits, managing the standards of work through, for example, codes of practice and, as noted above, organising and controlling knowledge. In these ways, the professions have become associated with high levels of formal education and financial renumeration (Abbott 1988; Larson 1977). In both the US and Britain, these privileged positions within the labour market have been dominated, for the most part, by white men. US data, for example, demonstrates that black men and women are under-represented in managerial and professional positions in comparison to their white counterparts. While 13.2 per cent of whites occupied managerial positions and 13.8 per cent occupied professional positions in 1989, the equivalent percentages for blacks were 7.6 per cent and 8.6 per cent respectively (Gilbert and Kahn 1993: 77).

The extent to which it is possible to identify a black middle class has long been the source of debate in the US (Frazier 1957; see Lester 1971 for the writings of Dubois; see also Small 1994 for a good summary of the material). In *The Declining Significance of Race* (1978), for example, W.J. Wilson argued that the shape of the black class structure has changed over the twentieth century. The small black middle class of the early twentieth century, comprising many small businesses, suffered in the Depression of the 1930s. The New Deal policies of Roosevelt, however, had an important effect on the black community as the state employed black professionals for the first time (Wilson 1978: 127). The greatest opportunities for advancement, however, arose with the expansion of the corporate and government

Social Class in America and Britain

sectors in the 1950s and 1960s. It was during this period that barriers to employment were removed and affirmative action programmes implemented. These programmes were most effective in occupations which required training and education, and where supply rarely exceeded demand. As a result, it was talented and educated blacks who moved into high-level nonmanual jobs and benefitted most from affirmative action programmes (Wilson 1978: 100-1). Simultaneously, the growth of the government sector, especially the continued expansion of bureaucracies to administer welfare programmes for unemployed and poor blacks, facilitated the growth of high-level jobs which educated blacks entered. The post-war period represented the 'first time the national professional-managerial job market was open to blacks' (Wilson 1978: 102).

A fortuitous combination of economic and political factors, therefore, led to the growth of a highly-educated black middle class. Wilson argued that the growth of the black middle-class continued in the 1970s although the pace of growth slackened. He also noted that the 1970s was characterised by increasing class divisions within the black population as one section enjoyed relatively privileged positions while another section was confronted increasingly by unemployment and poverty (Wilson 1978: 132). The growing polarisation of the black class structure had created, for example, greater income inequality among black families than among white families. Wilson (1978: 134) concluded, pessimistically, that there 'are clear indications that the economic gap between the black underclass (close to a third of the black population) and the higher-income blacks will very likely widen and solidify'. Nevertheless, Wilson was charged with being a 'black conservative' for his optimistic account of the effect of affirmative action policies on the position of the black community and for seemingly downplaying the significance of race in shaping life-chances. His account of the rise of the black middle class was seen as overly confident when it was highly educated blacks from relatively privileged backgrounds who benefitted from the fortuitous circumstances. Black professionals, in other words, had not entered the well-renumerated high-level occupations of the private sector which was still dominated by whites. This was a charge subsequently rejected by Wilson (1980) who argued that he, unlike his critics, had considered the growth of the black middle class in the context of the changing class structure as a whole. His main interest, he maintained, was with the growing black underclass (which will be considered more fully in Chapter Nine).

Subsequent research has confirmed the existence of a black middle class (Boston 1988; Hochschild 1995; Landry 1987; O'Hare *et al.* 1991; Farley and Allen 1989; Farley and Frey 1994). Drawing on a survey of black and white middle-class families in the 1970s, Landry identified a 'new' middle

Table 6.3. Distribution of middle-class black and white workers by strata in 1950 and 1976 as percentage of total black and white labour forces

	1950	%	1976
Black			
Professionals	3.4		10.1
Managers	2.0		3.5
Clerical-sales	4.8		17.8
White			
Professionals	8.6		16.2
Managers	9.8		11.5
Clerical-sales	21.5		24.9

Source: Landry (1987), Figure 6, p. 110.

class not confined exclusively to serving its own community but one which had made some progress into the mainstream. However, Landry found 'the experience of today's black middle class remains separate and substantially different from that of the white middle class' (Landry 1987: 94). Strong parental aspirations and a college education were especially important for black mobility yet these resources were not automatically translated into occupational success. Landry noted that blacks had difficulty entering the labour market at a level appropriate to their educational credentials, and career progression was slow as a result of racial discrimination in the workplace. He also noted that, 'The degree to which the new black middle class lags behind in the managerial-entrepreneurial stratum is particularly significant since it is here that the middle class finds its greatest opportunities for the accumulation of wealth and the exercise of power and authority' (Landry 1987: 109). Not surprisingly, Landry found a considerable income gap between black and white middle-class men and women as a result of their concentration in low-paying jobs in the public sector and racial discrimination which meant that blacks did not enjoy the same returns on their education, experience and seniority as their white counterparts. Thus, black middle-class standards of living were not as high as their white equivalents and, yet, black middle-class life-styles depended on the joint income of husbands and wives. Thus, by the mid 1970s, 'even with two incomes middle-class blacks as a group had not reached the living standard attained by whites with primarily one income' (Landry 1987: 175).

Contrary to Wilson, Landry (1987) argued that the positions of middle-class blacks deteriorated in the 1970s as the pace of growth slacken and their concentration in certain occupations increased. This trend was also evident in the early 1980s because of 'blacks greater vulnerability to economic slowdowns' (Landry 1987: 195). Greater competition for jobs and persistent discrimination in the workplace meant that middle-class blacks were especially vulnerable and, as a result, the gap between the proportion of blacks and whites in middle-class positions remains. Furthermore, Landry (1987: 206–7) noted the decline in the number of male black high school graduates (which dropped by 8.3 per cent between 1980-2) as a result of cuts in college grants. The income gap between the black and white middle classes has also increased. Against this background, Landry predicted that the black middle class would increase to 48.6 per cent and the white middle class to 59.5 per cent by 1990 (Landry 1987: 219). The unfavourable economic climate of the 1970s, therefore, had undermined the growth of the black middle class. In subsequent commentary, Landry (1991) emphasised the changed political climate on the fortunes of the black middle class. The struggle for civil rights which characterised the Johnson administrations in the 1960s were replaced by challenges to busing, affirmative action and increasing concern with 'reverse discrimination' in the Reagan and Bush eras. He conceded that his prediction for the black middle class was overly optimistic in that it stood at 45 per cent although his projection for a white middle class of 59.5 per cent was largely accurate in 1990 (Landry 1991: 205). Landry (1991: 200) concluded that, 'From the very beginning, the class system in America has been a color-conscious class system', and race remains an deeply ingrained source of structured inequality within American society. The changed political climate in the 1980s and 1990s has made vulnerable the position of blacks in high-level positions within organisations which are dependent on affirmative action programmes (Collins 1993) and heightened racial conflict in the political sphere (Wilson 1990).

In Britain, the increasing representation of ethnic minorities within the middle class has only just reached the research agenda. There has been a growing interest, for example, in the number of Indians gaining educational credentials and entering the professions (Jones 1993; Robinson 1988; 1990) although, as in the US, there is a debate over whether members of ethnic minorities have obtained genuine middle-class positions (Daye 1994; Phillips and Sarre 1995; Sarre 1989; Small 1994). Rather, it is the under-representation of women in the service class which has attracted attention (Crompton 1995; Dex 1985; 1987; Walby 1986). Women constitute 42 per cent of all professionals and 32 per cent of all managers and administrators (*Social Focus on Women 1995*). It is their under-representation in high-level nonmanual jobs that explains the limited presence in the highest echelons of the service class in comparison to men (17.9 per cent compared with 82.1 per cent). Women's over-representation in teaching and nursing accounts for their stronger presence in the lower echelons of the service class alongside men (43.8 per cent and 56.2 per cent respectively) (Marshall *et al.* 1988: 74). Thus, just as the middle class is 'racialised', so is it 'gendered'. As we shall see, educational credentials and state policy facilitated women's entry into the service class in Britain in a similar manner to ethnic minorities in America.

Research on women's under-representation in the service class has drawn on the sociology of the professions to explain how regulatory bodies excluded women by the way in which they controlled the numbers, selection and training of new recruits, managed the standards of work and controlled knowledge on which their expertise rests. Witz (1992), for example, in a historical case study of gender segregation within medicine (namely; doctors, midwives, nurses and radiographers) drew on Parkin's (1979) classic account of social closure. Parkin (1979: 44) defined social closure as 'the process by which social collectivities seek to maximise rewards by restricting access to resources and opportunities to a limited circle of eligibles' and which 'determine the general character of the distribution system'. He distinguished between two types of social closure: exclusionary practices associated with the dominant group and practices of upsurption whereby the subordinate group challenge closure with their own standards of distributional justice. He also distinguished between different forms of social closure: namely; those relating to property and those relating to credentials. He was particularly interested in credentialism and the ways in which professional associations used credentials to restrict access to rewards by monitoring entry to key positions. Professional associations play a crucial role in limiting supply by demanding high levels of education in order to practice, thereby perpetuating the scarcity of educated labour which, in turn, strengthens their market position. The professions are a highly effective interest group in protecting privilege within the labour market.

Witz showed how gender interacted with class to produce hierarchies of power and prestige in professional work. She drew on the concept of patriarchy to illustrate how men limited and controlled women's access to professional work and thereby maintained their position of domination in the professions. That said, she stressed that women did not acquiesce in this process but were also engaged in strategies of social closure (Witz 1992: 36–7). Women, for example, were excluded from medical education and examinations which would have allowed them to register as required under the 1858 Medical (Registration) Act. In response, women also adopted credentalist tactics – by enrolling on medical courses and presenting themselves for examination where they could – and legalistic tactics such as campaigning for the amendment of the Medical (Registration) Act which was finally achieved in the 1876 Medical (Qualification) Act. Nevertheless, the 'citadel of male monopoly did not collapse, but crumbled very slowly' as a result of various educational institutions' 'dogged pursuit of gendered credentialist tactics' which the General Medical Council (GMC) did not challenge (Witz 1992: 97). Credentialism proved to be an effective form of institutionalised male power over the medium term at least. Thus, Witz argued that the formation of the service class was 'gendered' since the 'formation of professional, managerial and administrative hierarchies in nineteenth-century Britain ... depended upon the maintenance of gendered exclusion and the manipulation of occupational boundaries by means of gendered demarcation in the labour market' (1992: 206). Male domination of the service class, in other words, can be explained with reference to gendered strategies of social closure.

However, the credentalist strategy has its limitations as Parkin was well aware and which Witz demonstrated in her research. Contemporary research indicates that women have made inroads into the established professions (Allen 1988; Crompton and Sanderson 1990; Greed 1991). Crompton and Sanderson's research, for example, showed that women are entering the professions (like accountancy and pharmacy) as they have acquired high-level educational qualifications. They argued that 'education may be assuming an important role in breaking down occupational segregation for a growing number of women' (Crompton and Sanderson 1990: 558). Professional practices of social closure, therefore, have been undermined by the 'liberal feminist' strategy of pulling the 'qualifications lever'. Moreover, in a climate in which feminism has been influential, it is no longer possible to exclude women from professional occupations by formal practices. Equal opportunities policies, for example, ensure that men and women with the appropriate 'human capital' are treated equally in recruitment procedures. As a result, the sex composition of occupations has changed which has required 'neither disruptions of the labour supply nor restructuring of the labour process' (Crompton and Sanderson 1990: 558). However, Crompton and Sanderson also noted that women's entry into high-level jobs has been accompanied by the growth of a secondary labour market of women practitioners who remain in the lower echelons of the professions. That is, women still face barriers – such as the demand for continuous work experiences and geographical mobility – in their progress through the internal labour markets of organisations (Crompton and Sanderson 1990: 70-1). Occupational segregation may be breaking down in some respects but more complex and subtle forms of closure are being remade at the same time.

Although Crompton and Sanderson's optimistic account of the decline of gender segregation is tempered with a notion of caution, the trends do not necessarily auger well for women. As their own research on women accountants demonstrates, the percentage increase in women entering the profession might be impressive but the actual numbers indicate the low base

Table 6.4. Membership of the Institute of Chartered Accountants in England and Wales, selected years.

Year	1945	1955*	1965	1975	1980	1986
Total membership	13,332	18,772	40,759	61,718	71,677	84,543
Women members	105	182	464	1,413	2,971	6,479

* Part of the increase from this date is due to the merger of ICAEW with the Society of Incorporated Accountants from 1958 onwards, which added 10,076 members, 36 former members, and 3,321 students.

Source: Crompton and Sanderson (1990), Table 5.2, p. 96.

from which progress is being made. There were 105 women among 13,332 members of the Institute for Chartered Accountants in England and Wales in 1945 and there were 6,479 women among a total membership of 84,543 in 1986 (Crompton and Sanderson 1990: 96). Moreover, other high-levels occupations like the technical professions – the fastest growing and often the most well renumerated of jobs – are still dominated by men. The percentage increase (331 per cent) of women in the technical professions between 1978 and 1990 was substantial, but, nevertheless, there were still only just over 5,000 women engineers, scientists and technologists in 1990 in comparison to over 90,000 men (Devine 1992b: 561). The gendered nature of subject choices – where women shun maths, physics and chemistry at school – has been identified as a major impediment to change. It is also the case, however, that women who enter the engineering profession still face discrimination in that men remain suspicious of their long-term career plans, continue to sponsor men over women for promotion and block women's access to particular jobs which would provide them with the necessary experience for high-level management. The limitations of equal opportunities policies – especially in the process of translating process into practices – are readily apparent in existing research (Aikenhead and Liff 1991; Cockburn 1991; Coyle and Skinner 1988). There are a variety of processes within organisations, therefore, which continue to impede women's progress into top professional positions.

The under-representation of women in high-level management positions – especially in the private sector of the economy – is stark. A survey by the Hansard Society (1990) found that the overwhelming majority (80 per cent) of top companies had no women on the main boards and indeed, the majority (58 per cent) had no women on main and subsidiary boards either. Of the 799 executive directors, only four were women (representing 0.5 per cent) while twenty-six out of a total of 668 non-executive directors were women (representing 3.9 per cent). The evidence suggests that women rarely occupy positions in which they exercise power and authority. There are a variety of explanations for women's exclusion from top jobs over and above the difficulties of pursuing a career with family commitments, notably male prejudice exemplified in the reluctance of senior male managers to place women in positions of authority over men, and the operation of the internal labour market within organisations (Crompton and Le Feuvre 1992; Devine 1992c; Witz and Savage 1992). Savage's (1992: 135) analysis of the Longitudinal Study showed that 18 per cent of men in professional occupations and 15 per cent of men in ancillary work (primarily teaching and nursing) moved into managerial jobs compared with only 10 per cent and 5 per cent of women professionals and ancillary workers between 1971–81. Women rarely progress up bureaucratic hierarchy into managerial work (Savage 1992: 137). Even where women have entered managerial jobs – as in the banking and finance industry in the 1980s – the restructuring of management suggests that progress is more apparent than real. They have not been promoted to high-level positions where managerial discretion is significant, and nor have they been promoted to top positions in specific sectors. Overall, Savage (1992: 148) concluded that 'women are gaining access to the middle classes for the first time, but the middle and upper classes themselves are undergoing transformation'.

Finally, it should be noted that women who have entered high-level occupations tend to come from middle-class backgrounds. As we saw in Chapter Three, women share the same relative chances of upward mobility as men (Marshall *et al.* 1988). They also marry men in professional and managerial positions (Savage *et al.* 1992) although they tend not to have children and to adopt surrogate male careers (Crompton 1995). The growth of women's high-level employment has been accompanied by the increase in dual career families (Gregson and Lowe 1994; 995) which has, in turn, heightened life-style inequalities between middle-class and working-class families (Bonney 1988a; 1988b). Inequalities between women and between households, therefore, are grown in tandem with the small but growing number of women entering middle-class occupations. The growth of the middle class in Britain, then, has also seen the entry of relatively privileged women into professional and managerial jobs. As with blacks in America, however, even they remain considerably under-represented in high-level nonmanual positions of power and authority. To date, there has been little comment on how the cutback on state services affects the position of women professionals although the privileged position of some professions which women have entered – such as medicine and higher education – have declined notably (Allen 1988; Halsey 1995). The evidence suggests, therefore, that the opportunities for advancement into the middle class since the Second World War have not been 'open' to social groups without power and privilege. Sections of the middle class are blocked for ethnic minorities and women through various strategies of social closure even during periods of considerable social change.

MIDDLE-CLASS POLITICS

The politics of the middle class – whether it is a conservative or radical force for change – has long interested sociologists in America and Britain. In the 1960s and 1970s, for example, political scientists and sociologists focused their attention on middle-class involvement in the civil rights movement, the feminist movement, demonstrations against the Vietnam War and so forth. The political scientist, Ingelhart (1977; 1990), charted the rise of affluent young people preoccupied with post-materialist concerns of a non-class kind – peace, the environment and life-styles – rather than materialistic concerns such as economic redistribution of a class-based kind. He anticipated a major change, therefore, in the nature of politics in the post-war period. However, there has been considerable scepticism regarding claims about the radical pretensions of the new middle class (Bazelon 1979; Bell 1979; Brint 1984; 1985; Bruce-Briggs 1979). Analysing data from the General Social Survey (GSS) from 1974–80, Brint (1984) found no evidence that the new class were in conflict with the capitalist class. Only 14 per cent of respondents defined in terms of Gouldner's new class thesis, for example, did not have any confidence in business leaders in comparison to 6 per cent of high income business. Nor, for that matter, did they favour a reduction in income differentials. Conservative attitudes, therefore, prevailed among high-level white-collar employees. That said, Brint found that salaried professionals were left of centre over issues such as full racial integration (supported by 62 per cent of new-class respondents compared with 40 per cent of high-income business) (Brint 1984: 41). Re-formist (rather than radical) views were concentrated among young, highly educated people employed in social science and arts related occupations in the public sector in the late 1970s. This evidence, he argued, highlighted the cumulative effect of a number of social trends including the growth of higher education, the coming of age of a liberal cohort and historical circumstances in which dissatisfaction with conservatism prevailed rather than the emergence of a new class. Thus, Brint dismissed some of the exaggerated claims of new-class theorists in support of a more qualified argument that a strata within the middle class – notably, highly-educated professionals – had become more radical over time (Brint 1984: 58; 1985). Lamont (1987; see also 1992), in reply, argued that the new class theory 'should not be rejected but modified, with a focus on the opposition of relatively autonomous cultural capital workers to business-class interests

Table 6.5. Percentage dissenting in four new-class aggregations

	Favours reduction of income differentials between rich and poor	Hardly any confidence in business leaders	Less than full confidence in business leaders	Voted for McGovern in 1972 Presidential Election	Strong support for federal spending on social programs	Favours full racial integration	Intellectual orientation	Non-restrictive on moral and sexual issues	Oriented to self-fulfilment at work	Not strongly oriented to high income as job characteristic
Total sample	28 (2,170)	15 (8,851)	60 (8,851)	39 (3,591)	37 (8,971)	29 (5,611)	16 (4,978)	19 (8,820)	50 (5,819)	57 (5,819)
High-income business	14 (35)	6 (186)	45 (186)	18 (121)	26 (165)	40 (114)	20 (104)	21 (183)	62 (109)	51 (109)
Kristol's new class	13 (39)	15* (149)	78* (149)	52* (84)	49* (150)	67* (91)	43* (70)	50* (144)	86* (105)	68* (105)
Gouldner's new class	13 (66)	14* (217)	60* (217)	40 (116)	43* (218)	62* (130)	39* (102)	52* (211)	79* (152)	59 (152)
Ladd's new class	19 (242)	12* (898)	71* (898)	42* (881)	43* (902)	53* (577)	28 (473)	37* (881)	78* (612)	66* (612)
Ehrenreichs' professional-managerial class	20 (297)	11* (1,066)	67* (1,066)	38* (559)	40* (1,075)	48* (704)	25 (568)	32* (1,055)	71* (717)	64* (717)
Blue-collar wage workers	34* (764)	17* (3,125)	64* (3,125)	46* (1,204)	37* (3,179)	18** (1,772)	12** (1,772)	14** (3,134)	37 (2,088)	40** (2,088)

Note: Numbers in parentheses are *N*'s for each particular cell; *N*'s vary because not all questions were asked in all years.

* Significantly more likely to be in positive range as compared with business owners and executives at $P < .05$.

** Significantly less likely to be in positive range as compared with business owners and executives at $P < .05$.

Source: Brint (1984), Table 2, p. 41.

but Brint (1987) argued that the nature of political and cultural conflict needs to be explained within a more sophisticated class framework.

Recent case studies of new social movements (NSMs) (Eder 1993; McAdams 1988; Fendrich 1993) have confirmed much of Brint's analysis although the emphasis has been less on loose references to education and more on specific formative experiences in shaping reformist values and subsequent job choices. The study of these processes accounts for the prevalence of left-wing views among public-sector professionals left unexplained by Brint. McAdam (1988), for example, conducted a case study of a group of Freedom Summer (FS) volunteers who worked in the southern black communities in the 1960s. They were invariably well-educated middle-class young people who were engaged in a variety of public-spirited activities. Their radicalising experiences – coming face to face with racial discrimination against blacks and the hostility and racism of the local white population – strongly influenced their socio-political values. Moreover, McAdam found that a high proportion of these volunteers later entered the public sector liberal professions. They were not inclined towards the corporate world of business and finance since they attached little importance to monetary success. Rather, their reformist views predisposed them towards the liberal professions so their jobs were congruent with their world views. Their employment reinforced their values not least since they became integrated into networks of like-minded people. A number of circumstances, therefore, had a cumulative effect by reinforcing their socio-political views. Not surprisingly, and as others – for example, Herring (1989) – have found, McAdam noted that this cohort of radicals felt very alienated in the hostile political climate of the 1980s under Reagan.

A similar picture is drawn by Fendrich's (1993) study. He followed up cohorts of black and white civil rights activists into the 1980s. He found that the black respondents were far more active in demonstrations than their white counterparts (70 per cent compared with 20 per cent). The black activists came from 'striving working-class' backgrounds and their political activism was supported by family and friends (Fendrich 1993: 52). They subsequently enjoyed upward social mobility by becoming teachers, social workers and administrators in the public service. Thus, Fendrich also found that values affected job choices. The white activists, in comparison, came from middle-class families who were hostile to their political activism. Interestingly, Fendrich's research also embraced conservatives who grew up in the 1960s, and who subsequently supported Nixon and Ford in the 1970s and Reagan and Bush in the 1980s. His research goes some way to undermine arguments charting the emergence in middle-class individualism (Bellah et al. 1985; Gans 1988; Newman 1993) in the 1980s and 1990s since individualism has long been associated with the middle class. Overall, his research confirmed that there are important political cleavages within the middle class.

Survey research has also case doubt on claims regarding new politics and the new class while also acknowledging the importance of political cleavages within the middle class. Brooks and Manza (1994), for example, rejected Inglehart's post-materialism thesis. They found his distinction between materialist and post-materialist values unhelpful for 'grasping the nature of value structure and value change' (Brooks and Manza 1994: 560). Value pluralism prevailed instead, and they found that citizens with post-materialist values believed in state intervention to achieve political outcomes. Similarly, Hout *et al.* (1996) recently demonstrated that there has been no consistent long-term tendency for the net association between class and vote to decline. The middle class are still more likely to vote Republican than members of the working class who tend to vote Democrat. However, a disaggregation of the data showed that professionals have different political orientations to managers within the middle class. They were more likely to vote Democrat than managers in US presidential elections since 1972. The evidence showed that support for the Democrats was associated with 'social liberalism' on a range of issues including abortion, gender equality and civil rights. Thus, the middle class as a whole has a conservative socio-political identity especially in comparison to the working class. However, professionals within the middle class constitute a distinct stratum. Disaggregating the data, therefore, suggests that the middle class does not constitute a coherent socio-political entity. The interpretation of the findings depends on whether the focus of comparison is with other classes or with other stratum within the middle class.

In Britain, not dissimilar debates about the socio-political proclivities of the middle class and segments within it have taken place. Goldthorpe, as was noted earlier, argued that the middle class would increasingly adopt a conservative socio-political identity in that, once established, its members would be keen to protect and enhance their privileged position. In contrast, Lash and Urry (1987) argued that the middle class would be a radical force for social change in disorganised capitalist societies. It has long been known that professionals are more liberal than other members of the middle class. Parkin's (1968) classic study of the Campaign for Nuclear Disarmament (CND) in the 1960s found a high level of activism among members of the middle class working in the public-sector caring and creative professions. Rather than argue that middle-class radicalism resulted from political alienation, however, Parkin stressed that political values, invariably derived from family socialisation, influenced activism. They also explained support for and involvement in a range of other campaigning groups. Finally, political orientations shaped job choices which explained why so

many activists were public-sector professionals. Subsequent research has
confirmed that this groups of people are activists in other social movements
(Bryne 1988; Eckersley 1989). Recent research has also shown that they
increasingly dominate centre (Rudig *et al*. 1991) and left political parties
(Seyd and Whitely 1992). The literature, however, has been criticised for
failing to unpack the relationship between the professional middle class and
new social movements and for neglecting the important insights of Parkin's
casual account of the relationship between them (Bagguley 1991; 1995).

Survey research on social attitudes and voting behaviour has produced
similar findings on the political attitudes of professionals in the middle
class (Heath *et al*. 1985; Heath et al 1991; Heath *et al*. 1995; Heath and
Evans 1988. Marshall *et al*. 1988). Despite claims of class dealignment,
the association between class and vote has not declined. The middle class
are more likely to vote Conservative than the working class. Nevertheless,
cleavages within the middle class have grown in importance in the 1980s.
In the 1987 General Election, for example, those employed in the welfare
and creative professions divided their vote between the three major parties
almost equally (32 per cent for the Conservatives, 33 per cent for the
Alliance and 34 per cent for Labour) (Heath *et al*. 1991: 93). This political
cleavage resulted from Labour having taken over from the Liberals as
the party of equal opportunities, civil rights and so forth, and ideological
changes between Labour and the Conservatives which led voters to change
their behaviour (Heath *et al*. 1991: 99). Further research on social attitudes
showed that members of the middle class adopt left-wing positions on
new agenda, non economic issues such as women's rights, gay rights
and so forth. Conservative and Labour voters within the middle class,
however, have contrasting views on both non-economic and economic
issues. The majority (65 per cent) of middle-class Labour voters took a
left-wing position on nuclear defence compared with a tiny minority of
Conservative middle-class voters (7 per cent). A similar pattern could be
seen over the issue of inequality of wealth in that 88 per cent of Labour and
32 per cent of Conservative voters took a left-wing position (Heath and
Evans 1988: 58–9). Middle-class support for the Labour Party, therefore,
can be explained with reference to their social liberalism on new agenda
non-economic issues.

Secondary analysis of the 1987 British Election Study by Savage *et al*.
found a political cleavage between managers and professionals. High levels
of Conservative voting were found among large employers (63%) and
managers of large and small establishments (69 per cent and 58 per cent
respectively) while professionals (whether self-employed or employees)
supported the Conservatives to a lesser extent (50 per cent and 52 per cent)
while nearly over a third voted Alliance (39 per cent and 36 per cent

Table 6.6. Attitudes within the salaried on new-agenda social items and old-agenda economic items

New-agenda social items			
	Conservative	Alliance	Labour
Percentage adopting 'left-wing' position on:			
Nuclear defence	7%	27%	65%
Sex discrimination law	70%	85%	93%
Right to protest	62%	83%	85%
Cultural diversity in schools	31%	44%	69%
Homosexuality	9%	29%	43%
Death penalty	12%	36%	58%

Old-agenda economic items			
	Conservative	Alliance	Labour
Percentage adopting 'left-wing' position on:			
Inequality of wealth	32%	64%	88%
Unemployment v. inflation	47%	77%	89%
Trade union power	1%	12%	37%
Tax cuts v. social spending	34%	72%	80%
Welfare v. self-help	30%	66%	71%

Source: Heath and Evans (1988), pp. 58–9.

respectively) (Savage *et al.* 1992: 194). Savage *et al.* argued that support for the Conservatives has dropped among the professional middle class as successive governments have undermined the state which previously protected and enhanced professionals cultural assets. They found, for example, Conservative Party support was low among managers and professionals employed in the public sector (40 per cent and 38 per cent respectively). The Alliance enjoyed similar levels of support among each occupational group (35 per cent and 36 per cent) but there was also some strong evidence of voting for the Labour Party amongst both groups (26 per cent and 27 per cent) (Savage *et al.* 1992: 196–7). Professionals have grown increasingly radical on the issues of state welfare and educational provision since the Thatcherite policy of undermining the role of the state has 'evoked a set of interests that could be mobilised against the social democratic consensus, and hence *against middle-class interests enmeshed in the state*' (Savage *et al.* 1992: 205). The split between professionals and managers implies that the politics of the middle class is 'fractured' and that the professional middle class has a potentially radical role to play in British politics.

Finally, Heath and Savage (1994; 1995) joined forces to explore the nature of middle-class politics using the British Social Attitudes survey data. Examining the party identification of people in various middle-class occupations, they found three significant left leaning groups – social workers, higher education lecturers and junior civil servants who identified with the Labour Party (45 per cent, 41 per cent and 40 per cent respectively) – and two significant right-leaning groups – the security forces and large employers who identified with the Conservative Party (91 per cent and 84 per cent respectively) (Heath and Savage 1994: 70). The majority of occupational groups cluster around the middle-class norm of identifying with the Conservatives. Even those occupational groups which leaned to the left did not have majorities in support of Labour. The evidence vindicated Goldthorpe's claim that there are 'no systematic sources of division' within the middle class. They emphasised, however, that Conservative identification (55 per cent) across the middle class is not especially high which implies that 'the growth of the middle class may not guarantee the continuing success of conservatism in Britain (Heath and Savage 1994: 73). This analysis was subsequently extended to consider change over time (Heath and Savage 1995). Comparing their findings with data from the Nuffield Mobility survey, they found little evidence of changing allegiances. Conservative Party identification as a whole was largely stable (46.8 per cent in 1972 compared with 49.6 per cent in the 1980s). However, there was considerable movement away from the Conservatives among particular occupational groups like doctors and dentists as a response possibly to the government's National Heath Service policy. However, right-leaning groups also shifted to the right. Overall, Heath and Savage (1995: 291) concluded that the middle class has not become more fragmented over time (Heath and Savage 1995: 292).

There has been a slight shift in Heath and Savage's argument to acknowledge the conservative character of the middle class as a whole and to downplay the alleged radicalism of the professions within it. As in America, therefore, exaggerated claims about middle-class politics have been modified and the differences between groups within the middle class have been set along with important similarities as well. Not surprisingly, these conclusions have been endorsed by Goldthorpe (1995). He remains committed to the view that the middle class is conservative in character and support for centre-left leaning derives from personal characteristics – working-class origins and prior Labour support – rather than structural divisions within the middle class (see also De Graaf and Heath 1992; Weakleim 1989 on the effects of social mobility on political identification). He also concedes, however, that the socio-political identity of the middle class is fluid and that changes in the political positions of the parties – the more centrist position of the Labour Party and the more right-wing position of the Conservative Party – might lead to party dealignment so that middle-

class support for centre-left parties will increase. The socio-political identity
of the middle class, therefore, is contingent upon political considerations
of this kind. The middle class is largely conservative in character but its
future socio-political identity remains an open question.

CONCLUSION

This chapter has charted the growth of high-level nonmanual jobs in
America and Britain over the twentieth century. The increase of professional and managerial jobs has led to the growth of the middle class to the
extent that it now constitutes approximately 30 per cent and 27 per cent of
the population in America and Britain respectively. Various forms of differentiation exist within the middle class such as that between old and new,
professional and managers, private sector and public sector employees.
higher-level and lower-level non-manual workers. However, the extent to
which these cleavages undermine the middle class as a demographic entity
remains subject to unresolved debate. The divisions within the middle class
cannot be denied but whether intra-class patterns of differentiation are
more important than inter-class differences remains the key question to be
addressed.

The extent to which middle-class positions have been open to previous
disadvantaged groups or whether processes of social closure have barred
ethnic groups and women from positions of privilege and power was
also considered. The evidence suggests that small numbers of (relatively
advantaged) ethnic minorities and women have entered the professional
middle class in recent decades. However, they have not made progress
into managerial positions of power. Within organisations, it seems, blacks
and women are still without the necessary power to advance their own
careers and those of other blacks and women. Despite its rapid increase,
therefore, members of ethnic groups and women remain substantially
under-represented in the middle classes in both nations.

Finally, attention focused on the socio-political identity of the middle
class, and whether it might be described as a conservative or radical force
in post-industrial America and Britain. The evidence from both nations
suggests that the middle class as a whole is conservative in inclination rather
than liberal or socialist. Members of the middle class have protected rather
than undermined their privileged economic positions in class structure.
That said, there are sections of the middle class – most notably welfare
and creative professionals employed in the public sector – who may be
described as liberal on a range of social issues. Their active involvement in
new social movements has, arguably, challenged the status quo. However,
the extent to which any social class has a political identity is dependent on
contingent factors and the issue remains open to empirical investigation.

The next chapter turns to the growth of low-level non-manual work in America and Britain. The rise of the modern corporation characterised by bureaucratic forms of organisation also witnessed the phenomenal growth of routine clerical work increasingly performed by women. The extent to which nonmanual workers have joined the working class, whether they have been subject to a process of degradation and deskilling, and the socio-political proclivities of women clerical workers are the issues to which we now turn.

Chapter 7

Degradation

America and Britain have both witnessed the growth of low-level non-manual work – namely, routine clerical work invariably performed by women – over the twentieth century. This trend has challenged sociologists to account for the position of what is popularly referred to as the lower middle class in the class structure of post-industrial societies. The major debate surrounding the clerical workforce has centred on whether it has been proletarianised and is, as a consequence, no longer distinguishable from the mass of manual workers. In other words, should clerical workers be seen as members of the middle class or the working class? The controversy has taken three forms. First, debate has focused on changes in the occupational structure as a whole and the implications of changes in occupations on the relative size of the middle and working classes. The mobility experiences of men and women clerical workers have been considered here thereby embracing both the class structure and people's position within it. Second, attention has centred on the extent to which routine nonmanual jobs have suffered from degradation and deskilling and the implications for clerical worker's terms and conditions of employment. The focus here has been on the labour process within employing organisations. Finally, the socio-political attitudes and behaviour of clerical workers has been examined to explore whether they align themselves with the middle class or the working class. The class identity and voting behaviour of women clerical workers and the extent to which they are influenced by their partner's socio-political proclivities arises, once again, in this context.

This chapter considers all three debates in order to evaluate the position of clerical workers in the class structure in America and Britain. The chapter is divided into three sections. The first section examines the growth of low-level nonmanual employment and its implications for the class structure. The proletarianisation thesis will be considered with reference to the relative sizes of classes in the class structure and the mobility trajectories of individuals within them. It will be argued that the growth of low-level nonmanual work has not swelled the ranks and increased the size of the working class. There has been a continued rise in the growth of both high and low-level nonmanual work as the manufacturing sector has declined and the service sector has increased. These jobs have also increased as a result of intra-industrial shifts in both nations following technological and organisational change. Similarly, the mobility data shows there is no evidence of experiences of proletarianisation as a result of blocked mobility chances for men. It is true that women are concentrated into routine clerical work but this is a result of the sex segregation of the labour market and the sex-typing of jobs rather than proletarianisation. Finally, contrary to Braverman's thesis, there is some evidence of a decline in clerical jobs but as a result of continuing technical and organisational change instead of degradation and deskilling.

The second section examines historical research, case-studies and survey data on the deskilling of clerical work. The interconnected issue of the feminisation of clerical work is also considered here. The American evidence suggests that the growth of female dominated low-level nonmanual work was more complex than Braverman supposed. The division of labour within white-collar work evolved not as a result of the implementation of Scientific Management but as the product of the professionalisation of high-level administrative work and the redefinition of boundaries between white-collar jobs. Moreover, women had entered clerical work prior to the evolution of the division of labour rather than being attracted to clerical work after it had been deskilled. Thus, the processes by which routine white-collar work emerged and was performed predominately by women in the modern office were rather different to those described by Braverman. Similarly, the American and British evidence shows little evidence of deskilling even in a period of rapid technological change. On the contrary, a process of up-skilling is occurring especially in routine nonmanual work where advanced technology is used. The terms and conditions of employment of some low-level nonmanual workers, therefore, still compares favourably with those of manual workers.

The third section concentrates on socio-political proletarianisation, and the debate on gender and class consciousness is considered again. There is little evidence in America or Britain to show that women clerical workers have organised collectively in the industrial sphere on a national scale in the 1980s and 1990s. In terms of class identification, women clerical workers are as likely (if not more likely) to identify with the middle class than with the working class, and their class identity is influenced by a range of factors including their social origins, their education, their partner's social origins and current class position and their own class position. Similarly, these factors shape the extent to which they align themselves with political parties on the right or left of the political spectrum. Overall, therefore, clerical workers do not share the socio-political proclivities of members of the working class and, indeed, the intermediate class cannot be said to have a distinctive socio-political identity in either America or Britain.

GROWTH AND DEGRADATION

Low-level nonmanual work has grown over the twentieth century in both America and Britain. It is estimated that clerical workers constituted approximately 16 per cent in both nations in the early 1990s (Gilbert and Kahn 1993; 70-1; *1991 Census Report for GB; Part 2*). The growth of low-level nonmanual work has been associated, once again, with the rise of the modern bureaucracy which led to a growth in clerical work from the mid to late nineteenth century onwards. In both nations, the growth of clerical work has been closely associated with the increasing participation of women in the labour market. Clerical work is the largest occupational grouping of all working women. In America, for example, over a quarter (27.8 per cent) of working women are in clerical occupations (Gilbert and Kahn 1993: 74–5). The equivalent figure in Britain is 28 per cent (*1991 Census Report for GB; Part 2*). A previously male-dominated occupation, therefore, became increasingly feminised over the twentieth century in both nations. It is not surprising, then, that issues of gender have come to occupy centre stage in sociological debates about the position of clerical workers in the class structure.

Early interest in the lower middle class focused on its decline in social status (Mills 1951). Previously, Mills noted, white-collar workers enjoyed high levels of prestige. They performed mental tasks, and the demands of literacy and numeracy meant that a certain amount of education was required. They worked closely with their employers. They were rewarded with relatively high levels of pay which facilitated a comfortable life-style. Clerical workers were, in other words, distinct from manual workers. However, the sheer growth of white-collar employment undermined this special status. The nature of work in expanding bureaucracies changed, contact with employers declined, education expanded and, arguably, the experience of work was closer to that of the manual worker. Indeed, the wage gap between white-collar and blue-collar workers started to decline. Mills found that the average annual income of white-collar workers was nearly twice that of manual workers in 1890. By the late 1940s, however, their income was only 1.2 times that of manual workers (Mills 1951: 72–3). The division between nonmanual and manual work was blurred and, as a consequence, the lower middle class was indistinguishable from the working class.

The degradation of work and its implications for the class structure was subsequently taken up by the American Marxist, Harry Braverman, whose book, *Labour and Monopoly Capital*, proved to be highly influential when it was first published in 1974. A restatement of his views can be found in Braverman (1994). Braverman argued that the degradation of work was an inherent feature of capitalist societies. The logic of capitalism demanded the fragmentation of tasks according to the principles of Scientific Management (or Taylorism) so that managers could maintain control over labour and employers could sustain their profits. The aspect of Braverman's argument which attracted most attention was the notion that as the clerical workforce grew in size and importance, its power had to be curtailed. He argued that tighter managerial control was achieved by subdividing the work leading to the degradation of work tasks and the loss of the previously favourable work situation of nonmanual workers. As a result of mechanisation and computerisation, they were divided into groups performing a small range of monotonous tasks to the extent that the 'all round clerical worker' had been replaced by the 'subdivided detail worker' (Braverman 1974: 315). The 'labour process' in the modern office was controlled in a similar way to that of the factory floor. Coupled with a declining market situation as pay fell below manual workers and a diminishing status (thereby attracting men and women of working-class origin), the degradation of work accounted for the increasing propensity of non-manual workers to engage in collective action through trade unions. That is, since the position of clerical workers was no longer dissimilar from that of manual workers, it was not surprising to find that they adopted the attitudes and behaviour of manual workers as well.

The degradation of clerical work, therefore, had far reaching consequences for the shape of the class structure. Rather than the growth of non-manual occupations, Braverman pointed to an enlarged working class when he described:

> the polarisation of office employment and the growth of one pole of an immense mass of *wage workers*. The apparent trend to a large non-proletarian 'middle class' has resolved itself into the creation of a large proletariat in a new form. In its conditions of employment this working population has lost all former superiorities over workers in industry, and in its scales of pay it has sunk almost to the very bottom. (Braverman 1974: 353)

It was on this basis that Braverman estimated that two-thirds of the American population belonged to the working class, including variously titled managerial jobs which were no more than routine white-collar jobs either. Large-scale downward mobility of this kind had important implications, therefore, for the whole of the structure of employment. Braverman's account of the changing class structure confirmed Marx's portrayal of the polarisation of two classes in conflict with each other in capitalist society.

Braverman's work spawned a huge debate on the labour process within industrial sociology in America and Britain. Research was re-orientated around the ways in which employers and managers control the labour process – including the degradation of work -to ensure profit. Subsequent research, for example, looked at strategies of management control neglected by Braverman's emphasis on Scientific Management as the sole strategy by which capitalists control the labour process. Edwards (1979) examined the different ways of organising work – simple control, technical control and bureaucratic control – in the 'entrepreneurial firm' in the US. He subsequently linked the different types of control with the segmentation of three labour markets: a secondary labour market, a subordinate primary market and an independent primary market (Gordon *et al.* 1982). Other researchers (Buroway 1979; 1985) examined how control over the labour process is organised through various 'factory regimes'. Buroway also explored worker resistance to management control through the adoption of production processes via various 'games' which had been neglected by Braverman. However, he argued that management tolerance of such games actually meant that worker consent and cooperation was secured. Various writers, in other words, were broadly sympathetic to Braverman's work while adding a more complex picture of different types of management control of the labour process in the US.

Braverman's argument regarding the changing class structure was also endorsed by Wright. Wright and Singelmann (1982) argued that the growing numbers of professionals, managers and administrators in the American workforce was the result of the growth of industries where high-level white-collar work had long been dominant. However, behind these inter-industry shifts, the degradation of labour was continuing apace in offices and factories. The organisation of production was changing in the opposite direction to the structure of employment. Analysing Census data for the 1960s, they concluded that such a trend was in evidence, and they predicted that proletarianisation would become more apparent in the period of recession in the 1970s. However, both authors subsequently changed their minds about the seeming inevitability of proletarianisation. Singlemann and Tienda (1985), for example, examined the industrial location of occupational change in the 1970s. Despite the slowdown in the US economy in the mid 1970s, they found a continued growth of high-level nonmanual work although the pace of the trend had slackened. In the 1970-5 period, there was a substantial decline in low-level manual employment. In the 1975–80 period, there was an upward shift of occupational structures – especially an increase in managers – within industries. Intra-industrial

Table 7.1. Occupational structure of US employment, 1960–80

Occupation	Per cent in 1960	Per cent in 1970		Per cent in 1975		Per cent in 1980
	PUS	PUS	CPS	CPS	CPS	PUS
Professional	10.2	12.8	12.3	12.9	13.4	14.6
Technical	1.6	2.0	2.0	2.3	2.5	2.8
Farmer	4.1	1.8	2.2	1.8	1.5	1.3
Manager	8.7	8.3	10.5	10.5	11.1	10.9
Clerical	15.2	17.8	17.4	17.8	18.7	19.1
Sales	7.6	7.3	6.2	6.6	6.4	6.5
Craft	14.2	13.7	12.6	12.5	12.7	12.1
Operative	19.4	17.6	17.7	14.8	14.2	14.8
Service	11.7	13.0	13.0	14.6	13.9	12.6
Labourer	5.0	4.6	4.5	4.8	4.5	4.2
Farm labourer	2.4	1.2	1.6	1.4	1.1	0.9
Total	100.1	100.1	100.0	100.0	100.0	99.8

PUS=Public Use Samples, Population Censuses, 1960–80.
CPS=Current Population Surveys, 1970–80.
Source: Singlemann and Tienda (1985), Table 2.2, p. 55.

occupational change was the 'primary source of change' during the late 1970s. Thus, predictions about the downgrading of work proved incorrect (Singlemann and Tienda 1985: 64). Indeed, the evidence indicated that economic recession had led to the decline of work opportunities altogether – as witnessed in higher levels of unemployment – rather than the degradation of work. The fate of some workers, therefore, was harsher than Braverman had predicted. The importance of intra-industry shifts indicated that occupational upgrading would continue after industrial transformation from manufacturing to services had been completed.

Similarly, Wright and Martin (1987) undermined earlier predictions about increasing proletarianisation. Employing Wright's new conceptualisation of the class structure, they found a decline in working-class occupations and an increase in managerial occupations in all sectors of the economy in the 1970s. They conceded, therefore, that post-industrial theory rather than the thesis of intensive proletarianisation accounted for changes in the occupational structure of advantaged capitalist societies. However, rather than dismiss the proletarianisation thesis altogether, Wright and Martin argued that the findings were the product of the internationalisation of American class relations in the 1970s which has seen 'capital flight' to industrialising countries where proletarian positions have expanded.

Technical and organisational changes in production which have witnessed the growth of managerial positions, therefore, must be considered in this international context (Wright and Martin 1987: 14–5). Despite the weight of empirical evidence against him, Wright remained in sympathy with the proletarianisation thesis as an account of the changing class structure in the US.

In Britain, early research also considered the changing position of clerical workers in the class structure. Lockwood (1958) argued that the market and work situation of clerical workers remained favourable in comparison to manual workers (Lockwood 1989: 67–8). Bureaucratisation and mechanisation were evident, for example, but the 'personal and particular relationships' had not been undermined by the rationalising tendencies of modern office administration' (Lockwood 1989: 95). Finally, he argued that a clerk's

> original claim to middle-class status has been slowly undermined during the rise of the modern office. The growth of universal literacy, the recruitment of clerks from lower social strata, the gradual transformation of office work into predominately 'women's work' and the increased emphasis laid on productive contribution, have all adversely affected the prestige of blackcoated work. And yet we are forced to recognise that not being middle class is not identical with being working class. In certain socially relevant respects the clerk continues to be distinguished from the manual wage-earner. (Lockwood 1989: 132–33)

Lockwood argued that the rise of white-collar trade unionism was the result of changes in clerks' work situation. Where personal relationships had given way to bureaucratic rules, occupational mobility had been thwarted and work tasks had been standardised, white-collar unionism had grown. However, Lockwood noted that clerks and manual workers still remained hostile to each other because of their social and physical distance and the close proximity of clerks to 'the general organisation of discipline and authority' (Lockwood 1989: 207). Hence, white-collar unionism was distinct from blue-collar unionism as well.

As in the US, Braverman's work generated a huge amount of work on the labour process in the 1970s – including the annual labour process conference – within industrial sociology (Brown 1992; Salaman 1986; Thompson 1989). Of greater interest here, Braverman's account of structural change and proletarianisation met with considerable criticism. Goldthorpe (1987), for example, argued that the thesis contradicted the structural changes which had occurred in America and Britain; namely, the growth of nonmanual jobs and the decline of manual occupations

over the twentieth century. He argued that the evolution of the occupational structure and its implications for class distributions, rather than
the organisation of production account for the overall shape of the class
structure. For Goldthorpe, the degradation of jobs has few implications for
class relationships (Goldthorpe 1987: 270-1). Reiterating Singelmann and
Tienda's argument, he emphasised that the growth of high-level nonmanual
occupations was the product of inter-industry and intra-industry changes
in the context of technological and organisational change (Gershuny 1983;
Penn 1983; 1986). The overall effect of these changes was to increase skills
levels and the *the proportion of the workforce in salaried or 'bureaucratic'
conditions of employment'* (Goldthorpe 1987; 194). Indeed, he noted some
evidence of a dwindling in demand for routine white-collar work as
productivity has increased as a result of computerisation (Gershuny 1983).
Goldthorpe went on to argue that the levels of mobility and fluidity among
the groupings which he called the intermediate classes needs to be taken
into account. The 'middle mass' is in a high state of 'flux' since a sizeable
number of male workers enjoy relatively high rates of work-life mobility
often across the long range. The majority (85%) of men of service-class
origin, for example, begin their career in low-level clerical work and through
promotion return to the service class where they stay (Goldthorpe 1987:
124). The high levels of mobility to be found here are the product of
'their *marginality* in relation to the two main organisational principles or
forms which underlie the occupational division of labour; namely, those
of bureaucracy and market' (Goldthorpe 1987: 141). Thus, given the
broad based recruitment to and from the intermediate class, the notion of
proletarianisation, Goldthorpe concluded, was misleading.

Research focusing specifically on male clerks came to similar conclusions.
Stewart *et al.* (1980), for example, addressed both Lockwood's and
Braverman's contrasting claims about the position of clerks in the class
structure. They also examined the mobility experiences of the clerical
workers of their survey. They argued, 'Whether or not there has been
a 'degradation' of clerical work, clerical workers as a whole have not
suffered proletarianisation' (Stewart *et al.* 1980: 93). Their research showed
that clerical workers were invariably young men who would enter high-
level nonmanual employment in the future or they were older men, in
the 'twilight' of their working years who had been mobile from manual
occupations (Stewart *et al.* 1980: 139). Stewart *et al.* were highly sceptical, therefore, of the proletarianisation thesis. They were also critical of
Lockwood argument that clerks do not have a particular class location
although they concurred with his account of the growth of white-collar trade
unionism (Stewart *et al.* 1980: 133). They found that changes in the work
situation of clerical workers, principally the bureaucratic organisation of

Table 7.2. Class distribution of respondents by sex and class of chief childhood supporter at same age as respondent (Goldthorpe class categories)

		Males Class of respondent								
		I	II	III	IV	V	VI	VII	Total	
	I	27.7	31.9	12.8	6.4	4.3	10.6	6.4	100.0	(47)
	II	20.8	39.6	3.8	11.3	1.9	13.2	9.4	100.0	(53)
Class of	III	25.0	21.9	0.0	6.3	9.4	31.3	6.3	100.0	(32)
chief	IV	14.4	15.6	5.6	28.9	10.0	11.1	14.4	100.0	(90)
childhood	V	14.4	18.9	4.5	7.2	13.5	13.5	27.9	100.0	(111)
supporter	VI	8.0	12.4	9.5	6.6	14.6	23.4	25.5	100.0	(139)
	VII	11.9	8.1	4.4	11.9	10.0	18.8	35.0	100.0	(160)

(N = 632)

		Females Class of respondent								
		I	II	III	IV	V	VI	VII	Total	
	I	13.8	27.6	48.3	3.4	0.0	0.0	6.9	100.0	(29)
	II	14.3	42.9	32.1	0.0	0.0	0.0	10.7	100.0	(28)
Class of	III	4.2	37.5	37.5	4.2	0.0	4.2	12.5	100.0	(24)
chief	IV	9.1	25.5	30.9	9.1	3.6	1.8	20.0	100.0	(55)
childhood	V	0.0	27.5	42.5	6.3	1.3	6.3	16.3	100.0	(80)
supporter	VI	3.6	15.3	44.1	2.7	5.4	8.1	20.7	100.0	(111)
	VII	2.0	8.2	30.6	8.2	6.1	5.1	39.8	100.0	(98)

(N = 425)

Source: Marshall *et al.* (1988), Table 4.8, p. 77.

office work within large establishments which often blocked or tightened the chances of occupational mobility, facilitated the growth of a shared identity and propensity to engage in industrial action to resolve grievances (Prandy *et al.* 1983). Clerical workers, in other words, joined trade unions to protect their threatened positions at work.

Recent research on the mobility patterns of both men and women have also undermined the proletarianisation thesis (Marshall *et al.* 1988). The Essex team looked at changes in the shape of the class structure by comparing the distribution of origins and destinations of their respondents. They found that the intermediate class (including clerical workers and personal service workers) increased from 5.3 per cent to 18.9 per cent confirming the growth of low-level nonmanual employment in the occupational structure at large. Disaggregating the data by sex shows the percentage of male members of the intermediate class grew by a modest 0.9 per cent (from 5.1 per cent to 6.0) while the percentage of women members of the intermediate class increased by a striking 32.5 per cent (from 5.6 per cent to 38.1 per cent) (Marshall *et al.* 1988: 102). The data demonstrate the fact that the growing number of intermediate class positions have been filled primarily by women. The data confirm the wider finding that a large proportion of all women arrive at intermediate class destinations - predominately clerical work – while men are spread across service-class and working-class destinations. However, this is not to suggest that women are uniformly proletarianised since women of service-class origins are more likely to arrive at service-class destinations than their counterparts of working-class origin. As we saw in Chapter Three above, women's relative mobility chances, in other words, are similar to those of men.

Turning to absolute mobility, however, the evidence shows that women of all origins tend to enter the intermediate class indicating that men and women have different patterns of inter-generational mobility and there is a greater dissimilarity between origins and destination for women than for men. Marshall and his associates, for example, found that the majority of women from each of Goldthorpe's three classes enter the labour market as clerical workers or personal service workers (52 per cent, 60 per cent and 53 per cent among women of service-class, intermediate-class and working-class origin respectively). Moreover, the majority of these women remained in the intermediate class (52 per cent, 59 per cent and 52 per cent). Women of service-class or intermediate-class origins were more likely to be upwardly mobile out of intermediate-class jobs into service class jobs (33 per cent and 24 per cent) while women of working-class origins were more likely to be downwardly mobile out of intermediate-class jobs into working-class jobs (37 per cent) (Marshall *et al.* 1988: 109). The 'bunching up' of women of all social origins in intermediate-class positions is not, however, the result of proletarianisation but 'results from a sex segregation in employment which persists to the general disadvantage of women' (Marshall *et al.* 1988: 111). Thus, an examination of the proportionate size of the different classes and an analysis of mobility experiences fail to uphold the proletarianisation thesis in either America or Britain. Both nations have experienced the growth of low-level nonmanual work and these 'pink-collar jobs' have become increasingly associated with women over time. The feminisation of clerical work is considered further in case studies of deskilling and degradation.

DESKILLING AND DEGRADATION

Research has focused on the proletarianisation of particular low-level white-collar occupations. Braverman (1974) argued that managerial con-

deskilling

trol over clerical workers was tightened to curtail their potential power. Control was achieved by applying the principles of Scientific Management to the office including the subdivision of work into narrowly-defined tasks. The degradation of work skills undermined the conditions of clerical employment and its status to the extent that clerical work became increasingly attractive to women and men of working-class rather than middle-class backgrounds. A number of historical and contemporary case studies have focused on Braverman's account of the evolving labour process in the modern office. There is now a body of research on specific occupations which both supports and undermines Braverman's thesis (Baran 1988; De Kadt 1979; DiPrete 1988; Glenn and Feldberg 1979; 1995; Zimbalist 1979). This has led some commentators (Form 1987; DiPrete 1987; 1988) to argue that it is difficult to adjudicate between the competing claims for and against Braverman's work, and that case study research has not proved an appropriate means of evaluating the proletarianisation thesis. At the very least, however, the research has demonstrated that while a process of deskilling may have occurred in some occupations, it is far from being an inevitable trend within capitalist society. In this respect, far more complex processes of change in the shaping of low-level nonmanual work occurred than those described by Braverman.

feminised

Research on low-level white-collar work has centred, in particular, on the interconnections between proletarianisation and the feminisation of clerical work. In an analysis sympathetic to Braverman, Glenn and Feldberg (1979; 1995: 263) argued that while 'clerical workers as a group have become a large and important part of the economy . . . their jobs and status have become less desirable'. The growth of nonmanual occupations witnessed the emergence of a new stratum of office managers who were predominately men and a large mass of clerical workers who were women. The size and importance of clerical work for basic production activity, however, gave women clerical workers a lot of potential power. As a result, male managers were keen to bring office work under tighter managerial control. Applying the principles of Scientific Management, they subdivided work into a range of narrow tasks which could be performed by largely unskilled workers. The process was facilitated by mechanisation which dictated the pace of work rather than the clerical workers themselves (Glenn and Feldberg 1995: 270-1). While these changes in the office were uneven at first, the drive for managerial control saw the rise of large offices where pools of typists and clerks became the norm. Again, new technology such as the advent of micro-processors routinised clerical work still further. More recently, further savings have been made by reducing the number of permanent clerical staff employed by organisations and subcontracting clerical work

Table 7.3. Median yearly wage or salary income for year-round, full-time clerical workers and operatives by sex, 1939–90

Workers/Operatives	1939	1949	1960	1970	1980	1990
Clerical workers, women	$1,072	$2,235	$3,586	$5,539	$10,997	$18,475
Clerical workers, men	1,564	3,136	5,247	8,652	18,247	26,192
Operatives, women	742	1,920	2,970	4,465	9,440	14,606
Operatives, men	1,268	2,924	4,977	7,644	15,702	21,988
Women clerical workers Wages as percentage of men operatives' wages	84%	76%	72%	72%	70%	84%
Women clerical workers Wages as percentage of women operatives' wage	144%	116%	121%	124%	116%	126%

Sources: For 1949: U.S. Bureau of the Census, *1950 Census of the Population of the United States: Special Reports*, Vol. 4, P-E no. IB, Table 20. For all other years: U.S. Bureau of the Census, *Current Population Reports*, Series P-60, no. 69, Table A 10 (for 1939 and 1960), no. 80, Table 55 (for 1970), no. 132, Table 55 (for 1980), and no. 174, Table 32 (for 1990). The figures given for all years except 1949 are for year-round full-time workers. Those for 1949 are for all year-round workers.

Source: Glenn and Feldberg (1995), Table 4, p. 269.

out to other agencies (Glenn and Feldberg 1995: 273). In sum, clerical work has been deskilled, first, by a reduction in the variety of skills required and second, in the downgrading of the level of skills expected of clerical workers (Glenn and Feldberg 1995: 275).

Drawing on intensive interviews with clerical workers, Glenn and Feldberg (1995) found that many of the women's experiences of clerical work were poor. There were considerable variations in levels of pay even among women doing similar kinds of work. Conditions of employment such as entitlements to fringe benefits were not good. They quickly found themselves at the top of career ladders with no opportunities to enter professional or managerial jobs within their organisations. Job insecurity was an increasing problem. In terms of work tasks, many of the women were overeducated and overskilled for the work for which they were responsible. One interviewee commented, for example that, 'The things on the job description any sixth grader could do' (Glenn and Feldberg 1979: 275). They experienced less control over the work as new technology allowed managers to track the number of documents completed or listened to calls to customers. Control had, therefore, become increasingly impersonal. As a result, the women found their jobs more and more stressful and reported stress-related illnesses. Despite these alienating experiences, however, the women did find satisfaction from their work. They enjoyed social contact with other women and they took pleasure from being engaged in useful activity which structured their day. Finally, work was an important source of independent identity for married women outside their family roles (Glenn and Feldberg 1995: 278). In sum, however, Glenn and Feldberg concluded that women clerical workers had experienced deskilling and degradation in their working lives.

Yet, other historical case studies have provided a somewhat more complex account of the growth of clerical work in the US (Davies 1979; Fine 1990; Kocko 1980; Rostella 1981; Strom 1992). Fine, for example, cast doubt on Braverman's emphasis on the application of Scientific Management to enhance efficiency and profits in the modern office, and the subsequent feminisation of clerical work. Rather, she argued that predominately middle-class women entered clerical work from the 1880s onwards, and they always experienced different levels of pay and opportunities for promotion to men as a result of patriarchical relations (Fine 1990: 96). The rationalisation and mechanisation of clerical work occurred once women had entered the office and, again, the gendered nature of the increasing division of labour is best explained with reference to the patriarchical sex-tying of jobs. Similarly, Strom (1992) argued that while the division of labour became increasingly complex in the modern office, many low-level nonmanual jobs were left untouched by rationalisation and mechanisation. Trends varied according to the size of the establishment and the nature of white-collar work. It was only in the large office that the principles of Scientific Management were applied and, even then, not until the 1920s. There was an increasing division of labour within clerical work as some jobs became more skilled while other jobs became less skilled. However, the process was neither uniform, nor inevitable and the circumstances by which low-level white-collar work was feminised was more complicated than Braverman supposed (Strom 1992: 184).

The increasingly complex division of labour within white-collar work has also been documented by DiPrete (1987; 1988; 1989) in his research on clerical workers in the federal government. Interestingly, he argued that case studies supporting the deskilling thesis 'have typically been insensitive to the internal heterogeneity found within occupations, and to the fact that the boundary between adjacent occupations located in the same functional hierarchy can shift over time' (DiPrete 1988: 725). Contrary to the deskilling thesis, he found a process of status redefinition occurred as part of a wider process of professionalisation. Increasing bureaucratisation (before the advent of Scientific Management) led to the redefinition of top white-collar jobs as professional (and concerned with policy-making) and low white-collar jobs as nonprofessional (confined to structured work with some low-level supervisory functions) (DiPrete 1988: 739). The creation of this boundary between managerial and administrative work and clerical work was the basis on which office work was reorganised and not fully crystallised until the Second World War. DiPrete argued:

> In short, whereas in the ninetieth century, there was only one route to lower-and middle-management jobs, namely the clerical route, in the middle twentieth century, there were two routes to these positions, with the college route becoming increasingly dominant. This change has affected the process of mobility, and no doubt has had implications for the self-image of modern-day clerical workers as well. (DiPrete 1988: 743)

Thus, any 'downgrading' which may have been occurring has to be understood in the context of the changing boundaries of administrative and clerical work within bureaucratic labour markets. By implication, the various processes – including the professionalisation of high-level administrative work noted in Chapter Six – which contribute to occupational transformation over time should be taken into account (DiPrete 1988: 744; 1989).

Overall, there is little doubt that the division of labour within nonmanual work has become more complex, but considerable scepticism about Braverman's account of the deskilling of low-level clerical work persists. A concern with deskilling and degradation remains, however, as computer rationalisation continues to transform the nature of clerical work (Albin and Applebaum 1988; Applebaum 1988; Applebaum and Albin 1989; Hartmann 1986). Albin and Applebaum (1988: 14), for example, have argued that there are a range of potential outcomes over the reorganisation of work resulting from computer rationalisation, and the choice of management strategies, the extent of knowledge required, and the entry and mobility requirements of clerical work will determine the implications for worker's skills. While there are signs of Taylorist forms of work organisation being implemented, there is also evidence of other strategies which involve the integration of tasks and the decentralisation of control and decision-making (see also Piore and Sabel 1984).

Technical and organisational change, therefore, may see the emergence of a streamlined workforce of highly skilled workers. Again, the evidence suggests that deskilling is far from inevitable, and indeed, the greatest threat facing women clerical workers is job loss, temporary casual work or reduced job opportunities rather than degradation (Albin and Applebaum 1988).

In Britain, attention also focused on the deskilling of low-level nonmanual workers (Abercrombie and Urry 1983). Crompton and Jones (1984) in *White-Collar Proletariat* argued that women rather than men have experienced the brunt of deskilling. Their case study of three bureaucratic organisations (a bank, an insurance company and a local government authority) found that work tasks were 'largely routine and unskilled or semi-skilled'. The majority (90%) of the employees felt that they had little scope to exercise discretion or job autonomy. Clerical work was also being further downgraded as a result of computerisation, stratifying a labour force already subdivided by earlier trends in mechanisation. They also noted men and women's different experiences of career mobility. The majority of women (82 per cent) were in clerical grades compared with under a third (30 per cent) of the men, 12 per cent were in supervisory grades in comparison to 36 per cent of men and only 1 per cent were in managerial positions while 34 per cent of men were in such occupations (Crompton and Jones 1984: 138). In other words, men escaped the impact of deskilling to more favourable jobs while women remained confined to less favourable jobs. Crompton and Jones (1984: 210) concluded, 'In a very real sense, therefore, our research findings provide concrete evidence to support the 'Bravermanesque' thesis that clerical work has been proletarianised'. They also argued that lower administrative jobs, many of which are dominated by women, differ little from the unskilled clerk. The proletarianisation thesis applied, therefore, to those higher up the bureaucratic hierarchy as well (Crompton and Jones 1984: 225). Finally, Crompton and Jones (1984: 208) stated that clerical workers' declining work situation explained why they had turned to trade unions in the 1970s.

Crompton and Jones' findings were endorsed by other case studies of clerical work (West 1984; Liff 1986). Others (Bird 1980; Daniel 1987; Kelly 1980; Lane 1988; McNally 1979; Webster 1990), however, were sceptical of their claims. Lane (1988: 72) argued that the impact of technology across industrial sectors remains very uneven, and is mediated by factors such as manager's organisational strategy, the actual process of implementation and wider economic and social factors. There is no inevitable trend towards proletarianisation. These arguments were well illustrated by Webster's (1990) case study of the impact of word processors on the work of secretaries and typists. She found that office automation had not had 'a single impact such as deskilling' since the WP was invariably 'assimilated into existing structures' in the office (Webster 1990: 126). Since the impact of new technology has been uneven and variable, to talk of women's office work as having undergone proletarianisation is, Webster (1990: 123) concluded, 'misleading'. Indeed, evidence suggests that rather than their work situation deteriorating, some office workers (i.e. personal secretaries) are being upgraded as they acquire skills in using new technology.

Similar conclusions were also reached in the recent study by Marshall and his colleagues (1988). Examining skill in terms of 'job technique', they found that 68 per cent of men and 66 per cent of women routine non-manual workers felt they required more skill in their jobs than previously. However, they also found that female nonmanual workers have less favourable work situations than their male counterparts. Men enjoy more autonomy and are more involved in decision making than women although men and women share equal amounts of supervisory responsibilities (Marshall *et al.* 1988: 78). It was found that men can design and plan important aspects of their work more than women (41 per cent compared with 30 per cent), use their own initiative (72 per cent compared with 51 per cent), decide on the amount and pace of work (82% compared with 73 per cent), decide on start and quit terms (50 per cent compared with 33 per cent), reduce work pace (77 per cent compared with 59 per cent) and initiate new tasks (52 per cent compared with 44 per cent). Only in terms of deciding on day to day tasks are women nearly equal with men (51 per cent compared with 46 per cent) (Marshall *et al.* 1988: 118–20). While these statistics do not give us a coherent picture of the ways in which women are disadvantaged in their work situation in comparison to men, nevertheless, on various indices, their inferior position is discernable. Secondary analysis of the Essex data by Rose and Birkelund (1991: 10) showed that women's inferior work situation may be a result of their greater propensity to work in larger organisations employing more than a hundred employees. That is, the circumstances in which they work are likely to be the most rationalised and mechanised. Women occupy inferior positions to men in the clerical world although it is the result of gender segregation and the sex-typing of jobs (Cohn 1985; Lowe 1987) rather than a process of deskilling and degradation.

Finally, recent research under the Social Change and Economic Life Initiative (SCELI) – which involved interviews with six thousand respondents across six contrasting labour markets in Britain – found no evidence of a general process of deskilling. Job skills are undergoing complex changes with the majority of existing jobs witnessing an increase in skill (of both a substantial and modest kind), deskilling occurring in a small number of jobs although many newly created jobs require little or no skills at all (Rose *et al.* 1994: 9). The majority of lower nonmanual employees reported an increase rather than a decrease in skill (55 per cent compared with 7 per cent) and responsibilities (60 per cent compared with 8 per cent) (Gallie 1994: 52–3). Those in lower nonmanual work using advanced technology were more likely to have experienced increases in skill and responsibility (66 per cent and 68 per cent respectively) than lower nonmanual jobs not using advanced technology (41 per cent and 50 per cent respectively)

Table 7.4. Advanced technology and skill change by class (percentage)

	Lower Service	Supervisory/ non-manual	Skilled technical	Non-skilled manual	manual
		USING ADVANCED TECHNOLOGY			
Experiencing increases in:					
Skill	74	66	66	66	53
Responsibility	78	68	88	71	59
		NOT USING ADVANCED TECHNOLOGY			
Experiencing increases in:					
Skill	57	41	48	44	27
Responsibility	65	50	65	53	37

Source: Gallie (1994), Table 2.8, p. 66.

(Gallie 1994: 66). Examining the increases in skill and responsibility among men and women, Gallie found that male and female nonmanual workers report similar increases in skill (56 per cent and 55 per cent respectively) although male clerical workers were more likely to have experienced an increase in responsibility than women clerical workers (66 per cent and 58 per cent respectively) (Gallie 1994: 69). There is no evidence, therefore, of deskilling among either men or women low-level nonmanual workers, and, indeed, the evidence suggests that they may both be experiencing increases in skill in work using advanced technology (although men are more likely than women to be in jobs using the latest machinery).

Overall, therefore, there is little evidence in support of the deskilling of clerical work for either men or women. Interestingly, Lockwood (1989) recently argued that the preoccupation with deskilling has drawn attention away from other important dimensions of clerks' employment relations. The social organisation of the office, for example, has been ignored in that little attention had been given to the fact that clerical workers are still dispersed across small offices, relations between management and employees – like those between a boss and his personal secretary – are often highly personalised and clerical work frequently involves dealing with the public which adds to the variety of work tasks which they perform. The 'atmosphere' of the office, in other words, remains distinct and arguably better than that of the factory floor. Most importantly, the social relationships in which clerical workers are enmeshed – whether with fellow clerical workers, their bosses or the public – are gendered. The effects of these social relations between men and women on work experiences, the nature of power and authority and identification with management and fellow workers have been surprisingly under-researched with few exceptions (Pringle 1989; see also Jackman 1994 for gender relations more generally). In other words, a preoccupation with the labour process has directed attention away from the study of employment relations which remain crucial to any understanding of women's clerical worker's class position in comparison to female (and, for that matter, male) manual workers working on the factory floor. This comment suggests that the conditions and relations of employment of female low-level nonmanual employment are more favourable than those of female (and, in some respects, male) manual employment in America and Britain.

SOCIO-POLITICAL PROLETARIANISATION

Finally, the subjective dimension of proletarianisation needs to be considered. That is, to what extent do low-level white-collar workers within the labour force identify themselves with the working class and support working-class organisations – trade unions and left political parties – in pursuit of their interests? Braverman, as we have seen, predicted that clerical workers would increasingly engage in collective action alongside manual workers. However, there is little contemporary material in support of Braverman's prediction. In the US, for example, trade unionism had fallen to 16 per cent of the non-agricultural workforce by 1990 which is the lowest point since the 1930s (Gilbert and Kahn 1993: 260). Women have always been less likely to join trade unions than men for a variety of reasons, and there is little evidence to suggest this pattern of trade union membership is changing. While they subscribe to the proletarianisation thesis, Glenn and Feldberg (1995: 280), for example, argued that the diverse educational and class backgrounds of clerical workers militates against collective action. Their diversity is also underlined by the fact that they are married to men of a variety of social backgrounds including managers and professionals with whom they would be in conflict. Glenn and Feldberg (1995: 283) reported on some cases of collective action by clerical workers, and they predicted, 'When clerical women organise widely, they will become one of the largest groups within the union movement. They may well alter the issues and concerns addressed by organised labour'. To date, however, there is little evidence of a growth of union activism among women clerical workers across the US.

Instead, attention has turned to women's class identification and voting behaviour in the debate on gender and class consciousness. As we saw earlier in Chapter Four, there has been a long running debate on the influences on women's class identity and vote in the US and Britain. A variety of researchers, for example, have argued that a women's class identity is influenced more by her husband's class position than her own (Felson and Knoke 1974; Hammond 1987; Hodge and Treiman 1968; Jackman and Jackman 1983; Rossi *et al*. 1974). Jackman and Jackman found that while a husband's class identity is unaffected by his wife's occupational position, a wife derives her class identification from her husband's occupational position rather than her own employment position. That said, the Jackmans found that a wife's employment does have a modest effect on the way she derives her class identification. Non-working married women were found to be sensitive to their husband's education in their class identification while working married women considered their own education in their class identification. Education, however, is a background factor linked to a women's family or origin rather than her current family position. The influence of a husband's class position on a wife's voting behaviour explains why women who occupy the lower echelons of the class structure – lower middle class and working-class position – do not exhibit higher levels of working-class identification. Jackman and Jackman, however, were careful to dismiss the view that women are 'falsely conscious' or 'status seekers'. They argued,

> Both the husband and wife are trapped by general sex-role norms into discounting the wife's contribution to family status, regardless of whether her contribution might result in a lower or higher class identification. In other words, even when the wife is employed, entrenched cultural norms dictate that she continues to be seen by her family and herself as primarily a housewife'. (Jackman and Jackman 1983: 148)

Other research, however, has indicated that women's increasing participation in the labour market has important implications for their socio-political perspectives (Davis and Robinson 1988; Hiller and Philliber 1978; Ritter and Hargens 1975; Simpson *et al*. 1988; Van Velson and Beeghley 1979). Ritter and Hargens (1975: 939), for example, found that over two-thirds of women in clerical and sales who identified with the middle class were married to men in professional, technical and managerial positions (69 per cent), compared with less than a third (27 per cent) who were married to men who were operatives, labourers or in other low-level service occupations. However, they also found middle-class identification drops among women as their occupational rank declines. They concluded that women and men's occupation are almost equal in their influence on a women's class placement. Davis and Robinson (1988) reached broadly similar conclusions. They drew on data from the General Social Survey to analyse the class identification of men and women in the 1970s and 1980s. In both decades, they found that married men exhibit an: independence

Table 7.5. Class identification of married men and women, aged 18–50/64, by employment status of spouse

Class identification	Men		Women	
	1974–8	1980–5	1974–8	1980–5
Only husband employed				
Upper	2%	5%	3%	3%
Middle	44	41	51	47
Working	52	53	43	46
Lower	2	2	3	5
Total	100%	100%	100%	101%
N of cases	(590)	(363)	(750)	(373)
Both spouses employed				
Upper	3%	3%	2%	2%
Middle	45	44	45	44
Working	51	51	52	53
Lower	1	2	1	1
Total	100%	100%	100%	100%
N of cases	(565)	(652)	(647)	(738)

Source: Davis and Robinson (1988), Table 1, p. 106.

model' in which only their own characteristics affected class identification irrespective of whether the wife worked outside the home or not. In the 1970s, they found that women, irrespective of whether they were employed or not, attached more significance to their husband's characteristics rather than their own characteristics. In other words, they exhibited a 'borrowing model'. In the 1980s, however, employed women moved towards a 'sharing model' where they take account of their own and their husband's characteristics in class identification. They concluded,

> Thus, women's class identity may be changing in the 1980s, not only because there are more women with direct connections to the relations of production, but also because the meaning of such a connection has taken on more salience for female identity. (Davis and Robinson 1988: 110)

In the light of such contradictory findings, it has proved difficult to adjudicate between the different theories of gender and class consciousness. The difficulty is compounded by the fact that men with high-level jobs tend to be married to women with high-level jobs. The majority of men in white-collar jobs are married to women in white-collar jobs. Although a high proportion of men in blue-collar jobs are married to women in white-collar jobs, it has been suggested that 'it is likely that such women are concentrated in the lowest sorts of clerical or sales positions. The data entry operator and the sales clerk at Woolworth's comes to mind' (Gilbert and Kahn 1993: 238). That is, it is not clear whether white-collar women workers married to working-class men identify with the working class because of their family position or their employment experience. Of course, it is likely that both factors work in tandem. Similarly, other research has indicated that women's attitudes towards gender roles affect class identification. Beeghley and Cochran (1988) found that working wives with traditional views about gender roles borrow the class identity of their husbands while those with equalitarian views share their own and their husband's class position in assigning themselves to a class. This analysis, however, brings other influences into account in the analysis of class identification which have never been denied by those holding the conventional view. As Sorensen (1994: 35) recently concluded, 'The main impression left by studies of subjective class identification is that married women's employment does make a difference, but this difference is small although possibly increasing'.

Unfortunately, the available empirical evidence on women's class identification in the US does not show whether the aggregate trends apply equally to women of all social classes. Without such disaggregation, it is not possible to examine women clerical worker's class identification and vote in detail. However, the aggregate patterns and trends suggest there is no support for Braverman's thesis of socio-political proletarianisation. The data indicate that women who occupy intermediate positions in the class structure do not have a distinct socio-political entity. There is considerable variation in their class identification and voting behaviour which appears to be correlated to their husband's class position to some degree. There is no evidence to demonstrate, therefore, that clerical women workers have become class conscious as a result of their experiences of deskilling and degradation.

In Britain, debates about the growth of white-collar unionism lost momentum in the face of a decline in overall union membership in the 1980s (see Winchester 1988). Again, it has long since been the case that women are less likely to belong to trade unions for a variety of reasons. Findings from the Essex survey show that the majority of clerical workers do not belong to unions. Just under half (48 per cent) of male clerical workers were union members while only just over a third (36 per cent) of women clerical workers belonged to a union. Among current non-members, nearly three-fifths (61 per cent) of men had not belonged to a union while nearly three quarters (72 per cent) of all women had no previous experience of membership. Indeed, women in low-level nonmanual jobs were less likely to be current members or to have belonged to a union in the past than their female service-class or working-class colleagues (Marshall *et al.* 1988: 129–30). There was no evidence, therefore, of increased levels of industrial activism among low-level non-manual women workers organising collectively as predicted by Braverman.

In contrast to America, the socio-political proclivities of women occupying intermediate-class positions in the class structure – especially those in cross-class families – has been central to the debate on gender and class consciousness. In terms of class identity, the Essex team found that men in clerical positions are more likely to identify with the middle class than the working class (59 per cent compared with 41 per cent). Women in equivalent positions, however, are slightly more likely to identify with the working class than with the middle class (53 per cent compared with 47 per cent) (Marshall *et al.* 1988; 130) These findings come as no surprise with respect to either men or women. Given that many men in low-level clerical positions are making their way up to positions in high-level managerial and administrative positions, it is hardly surprising that they are more likely to identify with the middle class than the working class. Similarly, given that women do not enjoy upward mobility into high-level nonmanual employment, it is not surprising that their level of middle-class identification is lower than their male counterparts. Moreover, since women clerical workers include women from middle-class origins who have been downwardly mobile and women from working-class origins who have been upwardly mobile, it is not surprising to find equally high levels of middle class and working-class identification. It comes as no shock to discover, therefore, that men and women clerical workers are more likely to support the Conservative Party (38 per cent and 43 per cent respectively) although sizeable minorities support the Labour Party (28 per cent and 25 per cent respectively) and the (then) Alliance Party (26 per cent and 20 per cent respectively) (Marshall *et al.* 1988: 130). Neither men, nor women are 'obviously proletarian by political preference'.

However, the picture is not as simple as it seems. Marshall and his colleagues turned to the question of cross-class families since 'the crucial question is whether or not couples having one partner in working-class and one in intermediate-class employment are noticeably different from those where both partners are in one class location or the other' (Marshall *et al.* 1988: 130). They found that class-homogeneous families and class heterogeneous families are different, and that a man's class has a significant effect on women clerical workers socio-political attitudes and behaviour. Wives in clerical employment married to working-class husbands were more likely to see themselves as working class than middle class (67 per cent compared with 33 per cent). They were also more likely to vote Labour than either Conservative or Alliance (49 per cent, 26 per cent and 15 per cent respectively). Women in clerical jobs married to service-class husbands were also more likely to see themselves as working class but less so (55 per cent compared with 45 per cent). However, they were more likely to vote Conservative than Labour or Alliance and by a large majority (86 per cent, 18 per cent and 18 per cent respectively) (Marshall *et al.* 1988: 131–33). Again, the evidence shows that intermediate-class women were more likely to vote Conservative or Labour depending on whether their partners were middle class or working class. There was no evidence, therefore, to suggest that women employed in routine clerical work have been 'subject to some universal process of socio-political proletarianisation' (Marshall *et al.* 1988; 135). They concluded:

> It is not the punitively deskilled nature of (routine and sales) work which best explains the voting intentions of those women who undertake it: it is, rather, the class situation of their husbands. Or, more generally, we can say that our results contain no evidence to support the thesis that routine clerical and sales workers are proletarian by temperament. (Marshall *et al.* 1988: 136)

Marshall *et al.*'s dismissal of socio-political proletarianisation received far less critical attention than their argument that a husband's class has a more important influence on a wife's socio-political proclivities than her own class position. As we saw, there was considerable controversy over the different influences on women's socio-political attitudes and behaviour (Abbott and Sapsford 1987; Charles 1990; Hayes and Jones 1992; 1992b; Payne and Abbott 1990; see also the debate between McRae and Dex in Clarke *et al.* 1990). In reply, other researchers confirmed Marshall *et al.*'s conclusions (De Graaf and Heath 1992; Erikson and Goldthorpe 1992). De Graaf and Heath (1992), for example, examined the relative impact of respondent's and spouse's class on voting behaviour from an analysis of the British Election Studies (BES). They also found that women tend to be more influenced by their partner's class position than men. Interestingly, they looked more closely at each of the classes, and their findings became more complicated. They found that women at the top (service classes) and bottom (working classes) of the class structure behave much like men in taking their own class into account rather than that of their partner. However, women in the petty bourgeoisie and in the intermediate classes take less account of their own class positions but take their husband's class position into account. They suggested that these findings illustrate the heterogeneity of values and interests in the intermediate classes between clerks (who are invariably men) and secretaries and typists (who are usually women). They concluded, that, 'The routine nonmanual class thus may

Table 7.6. Conservative voting by occupational class of the respondent and occupational class of his/her spouse[1]

Spouse's class	Respondent's class					
	1 Higher service	2 Lower service	3 Self- employed	4 Routine non-manual	5 Manual	Average Total
1	.5676	.5429	.4286	.6129	.5143	.5682
	37	105	7	124	35	308
2	.6143	.5225	.9032	.5930	.4403	.5533
	70	222	31	172	134	629
3	.6000	.5517	.7692	.7013	.4051	.6278
	20	29	104	77	79	309
4	.6239	.4915	.7033	.5766	.3541	.4879
	109	177	91	137	353	867
5	.6222	.4276	.5432	.3780	.2823	.3370
	45	152	81	381	1077	1736
	.6121	.4978	.6975	.5107	.3206	.4482
Total	281	685	314	891	1678	3849

[1] The Erikson, Goldthorpe and Portocarero (1979) classes have been collapsed into five categories: (1) the higher service class (I. Large proprietors, higher professionals and managers); (2) The lower service class (II. Lower professionals and managers); (3) The petty bourgeoisie (IVa. Small proprietors with and IVb. without employees; IVc. Self-employed farmers and farm managers); (4) Routine non-manual workers (IIIa and IIIb); (5) The working class (V. Lower grade technicians and manual supervisors; VI. Skilled manual workers; VIIa. Unskilled and semi-skilled manual workers; VIIb. Agricultural workers).

Source: De Graaf and Heath (1992), Table 1, p. 316.

exist at a lower degree of normative cohesion than the other classes' (De Graaf and Heath 1992: 320). It might also reflect the fact, of course, that occupying an intermediate-class position does not facilitate a clear class identity in the way that professional and managerial jobs are associated with the middle class and factory work and labouring work are associated with the working class. Since clerical workers are neither clearly middle class, nor working class, it is not surprising that employment does not provide them with an unambiguous class identity or influence their political affiliations (Saunders 1990a).

Marshall and his associates have recently returned to issues of class and gender and the effects of (and relationship between) class processes and household composition on women's socio-political attitudes and behaviour (Roberts and Marshall 1995; Marshall *et al.* 1995). They reject Payne and Abbott's (1990) claim that a women's class background accounts for her socio-political proclivities. Payne and Abbott argued that women clerical workers of middle-class origins are more likely to vote Conservative than women clerical workers of working-class origin. It is women's class origins rather than the class position of their partners which explains their party affiliations and, indeed, class origins affect the choice of marriage partner anyway. Roberts and Marshall, however, refuted this conclusion. Drawing on pooled data from the 1991 British Social Justice Survey (BSJS), and the 1987 and 1992 British Election Studies (BES), they confirmed their findings on the class identification and voting behaviour of intermediate-class women. They found that class background influences the choice of marital partner. Half of all women of middle-class origin were married to middle-class men for example. They also found that women's class background affects their class identity although not as much as expected according to Payne and Abbott's thesis. Women of middle-class origins married to working class men are only slightly more likely to see themselves as middle class as women of working-class origins married to working-class men (25 per cent compared with 17 per cent). The same pattern was in evidence in relation to voting. They concluded that class of origin has only a limited impact on class identification and voting behaviour. The findings applied to non-working and working women (either full-time or part-time) alike. While there is evidence of some effect, they concluded that 'controlling for women's classes of origin detracts little from the importance of the male partners' class positions, at least with regard to female class identities and voting behaviour' (Roberts and Marshall 1995: 55).

In subsequent comparative research, Marshall and his associates (1995) found that there is a close association between a men's class position and their socio-political proclivities but the association does not hold so strongly for women. Drawing on data from America, Britain and other European countries (including former communist countries), they found that a husband's class has a stronger effect on a women's class identity and political affiliation in western nations including Britain and America in comparison to postcommunist societies like E. Germany and Estonia. They found that men take their partner's employment into account when making judgements about their own class identity. This pattern was slightly more evident in Britain than in the US and elsewhere. They also found that an employed women's identity is more strongly related to her partner's class than her own class in only Britain and America while in the former West Germany and post-communist societies, the association between the women's class identities and their own jobs was stronger than that between their class identities and their partner's jobs (Marshall *et al.* 1995: 8–9). Thus, there was no evidence of a clear asymmetry in patterns of socio-political formation across the nations of the research. Turning to voting behaviour, they found that British women are more likely to vote according to the class of their partner's job than their own. Although there was a small association between man's class and his vote in the US, there was no association between a women's vote and her class. Marshall and his colleagues concluded that the process of socio-political formation has been different in the West and East. Women appear to be more independent of their partners in choosing their class identity in countries such as Poland and East Germany than in countries such as Britain and the US. The communist ideology of sexual egalitarianism may well have had this effect (Marshall *et al.* 1995: 11).

The empirical research by Marshall and his colleagues throws further light on women's class identities and political behaviour although it would have been useful to see the observed patterns in each of the different classes. However, the research also highlights the limitations of quantitative research in unpacking the multi-faceted processes at work. It is not surprising, after all, that class origins do not have a big effect on women's class identification and voting behaviour because they do not have a big effect on men's socio-political proclivities either. Men's current class position is more important than their origins. What Marshall *et al.* do not explore (and which Dr Graaf and Heath elude to) are women's experiences in the labour market, and the heterogeneity of clerical work springs to mind here. That is, it is not unreasonable to speculate that women of middle-class origins tend to occupy skilled clerical jobs while women of working-class origins occupy unskilled clerical work. It might not be surprising, therefore, that women of middle-class origins, married to middle-class men, and in skilled clerical jobs vote Conservative while women of working-class origins married to working-class men and in unskilled clerical work vote Labour. This point, of course, poses problems for the concept of cross-class families. That issue aside, a reallocation of women in semi-skilled and unskilled clerical work into the working class would avoid the spurious findings resulting from the heterogeneity of Goldthorpe's intermediate classes. This is not to support the proletarianisation thesis. It is difficult to deny that the conditions and relations of employment in some clerical work is akin to manual work, and should be re-classified accordingly. This is a quite separate point from Braverman's thesis that clerical work as a whole has been deskilled and degraded according to the logic of capitalist development. Furthermore, the absence of a clear socio-political identity among clerical workers undermines the notion of socio-political proletarianisation. Neither in America nor Britain is there data to suggest that women clerical workers increasing identify with the working class or have supported working-class organisations in pursuit of working-class interests.

CONCLUSION

It has been argued in this chapter that the growth of low-level non-manual work has not been accompanied by deskilling and degradation as described by Braverman. The class position of routine clerical workers remains distinct from that of manual workers so it cannot be said that the ranks of the working class have been swelled by low-level white-collar workers in either the US or Britain. Similarly, while there are plenty of routine clerical jobs which are dominated by women in both nations, the development of such occupations cannot be explained with references to the logic of capitalism in general or the assertion of management control in particular. Rather, the emergence of routine nonmanual – and its feminisation – needs to be understood in the context of the evolution of a more complex division of labour of white-collar work within bureaucratic organisations since the mid-nineteenth century in America and the early twentieth century in Britain. On this basis, Braverman's account of the deskilling of clerical work is found wanting and, indeed, contemporary evidence suggests that a process of upskilling is in evidence in the advent of technological change. Not surprisingly, therefore, there is little evidence to show that clerical workers have increasingly identified with the working class in the spheres of work and politics.

Chapters Six and Seven have dealt with the growth of high-level and low-level nonmanual work associated with the emergence of bureaucratic organisations in America and Britain. In the following chapter, our attention turns to skilled, semi and unskilled manual work which increased in the early twentieth century before starting to decline from the 1950s and 1960s in America and Britain. The implication, therefore, is that the working class has declined in size. Chapter Eight examines the decline in manual employment and the consequences for collective action via the trade union movement in the late twentieth century. It also considers the extent to which working-class life-styles remain distinctive. Finally, the extent to which the working class has its own socio-political identity will also be considered.

Chapter 8

Incorporation

The working class has been central to class analysis in America and Britain albeit in somewhat different ways. In the US, the absence of industrial collectivism has been used to confirm the American exceptionalism thesis. The low level of trade union membership, for example, has been cited as a clear example of how America is qualitatively different from Britain and other Eurpoean nations. The American working class has always been very different to that described by Marx. In Britain, where trade union membership has been high, debate has focused on whether the working class would fulfil the heroic role described by Marx. As an important collective force in the industrial sphere, would members of the working class be a major radical force for change? However, the decline in trade union membership in the 1980s and 1990s has meant that controversy now surrounds the issue of whether the working class exists as a collective entity in both countries. Commentators have focused on changes in three aspects of working-class life: namely, the industrial sphere, the cultural sphere and the political sphere. Firstly, in the world of work, it is argued that members are no longer prepared to act collectively in pursuit of working-class interests. Secondly, it is argued that the working class no longer possesses a distinctive socio-cultural identity. It has been, in other words, successfully incorporated into a consumerist capitalist society. Finally, there is a debate on the decline of the working class as a political force. Commentators have argued, for example, that members of the working class no longer align themselves with the political party which is supposed to represent their interests. Predictions about the working class, therefore, now centre around its demise in both nations.

This chapter examines all three debates with reference to America and Britain. The first section looks at the decline of manual work and associated decrease in trade union membership. It will be seen that America has always had a lower level of trade union membership than Britain for a variety of different reasons. It was certainly the case that the unions had to face strong anti-union sentiments from employers and forceful tactics to undermine collective action in comparison to Britain. That said, American unions were a powerful force in the 1920s and 1930s leading some commentators to argue that the US has become exceptional over time rather than always being different from Britain and other European countries. Nevertheless, both nations have experienced remarkably similar trends in trade union membership including a period of stability in the 1950s and 1960s and a substantial growth in public-sector white-collar unionism in the 1960s and 1970s. Similarly, trade unions in both countries were severely hit by economic restructuring and reccession in the early 1980s. They also experienced a hostile climate under Reagan and Thatcher. By the beginning of the 1990s, therefore, both countries are characterised by a relatively low level of trade unionism in comparison to earlier in the century. As a result, questions remain about the future of trade unionism in particular and industrial collectivism in general in both nations.

The second part examines the extent to which the working class retains a distinctive socio-cultural identity in late twentieth-century America and Britain. The embourgeoisement thesis which charted the disappearance of working-class life-styles was very popular in the post-war period of prosperity in both nations. Indeed, it retains its popularity today, especially in the US. However, the evidence suggests that members of the working class have not adopted middle-class patterns of association or leisure. On the contrary, the daily lives of blue-collar workers are governed by paid work and, increasingly, the threat of redundancy and unemployment associated with low-level manual work. Those experiences govern their daily lives including patterns of sociability and leisure. It also influences manual workers aspirations and images of the class structure and their position within it. Thus, the working class has far from disappeared as a distinct entity for the experience of work and leisure continue to generate a sense of identity and solidarity among the American and British working classes.

The third part examines the politics of the working class in the two nations. Does the working class retain a distinct political identity in either nations? Research shows that working-class identification does not necessarily shape political attitudes and behaviour in the US. As a consequence, centrist rather than left-wing political views prevail among American workers. In Britain, by contrast, working-class identification does shape political attitudes and behaviour which tend to be on the left of the political spectrum. In this respect, class has less of an impact on politics in the US than Britain, and the American working class does not have as strong a political identity as the British working class. That said, neither nation is experiencing a process of class dealignment. Members of the American working class still have a propensity to vote Democrat while members of the British working class still tend to vote Labour (albeit to different degrees). What is also evident in both nations, nevertheless, is considerable disillusionment with the political parties in particular and national politics in general. A shared sense of disillusionment prevails among the working class of both nations even though Democrats won the election in 1992 and 1996 while the Labour party has yet to be elected into office in the 1990s.

DECLINE AND CONSEQUENCES

America and Britain have witnessed both the growth and decline of manual work and, by implication, the size of the working class over the twentieth century. Again, the extent and nature of these trends has been influenced by the two nations' different experiences of industrialisation. In America, during a period of late but rapid industrialisation from the mid-nineteenth century, the number of manual workers and the size of the working class began to grow and rose to a peak in the 1950s. The industrial shift from manufacturing to services then saw a decline in the number of manual workers although there was a rise in low-level service workers. By 1990, therefore, the working class stood at approximately 24 per cent of the workforce (Gilbert and Kahn 1993: 71). Britain, in contrast, had a large manual workforce earlier in the nineteenth century which only began to decline in the 1970s as a result of the shift from manufacturing to services. By 1990, therefore, the working class stood at approximately 36 per cent of the workforce (*1991 Census Report; Part 2*). To a greater or lesser degree, therefore, both nations have witnessed a decline in the size and character of the working class (Esping Anderson 1993). Both nations have also experienced a decline in trade union membership (closely associated with manual work) in the second half of the twentieth century. In America, trade unionism reached a peak of 39 per cent membership in 1945 and has declined ever since (Brody 1993; Milkman 1991). By 1990, only 16 per cent of the non-agricultural labour force were unionised (Gilbert and Kahn 1993). In Britain, meanwhile, trade unionism reached a peak of 57 per cent in 1979 and then declined rapidly in the 1980s and 1990s (Winchester 1988). By 1992, trade union membership accounted for 36 per cent of the civilian labour force in employment (*Social Trends 1995*). America, therefore, has always had a much lower level of trade union membership among its workforce than in Britain.

Why manual workers have failed to organise collectively in the industrial sphere has long been at the heart of debate on the American working class. So too has the question of why trade unions sought relatively limited goals – legitimacy, security, wage rises and so on – and never embraced socialist alternatives of a different economic and political order (Brody

1993; Greenstone 1977). Commentators have stressed that American trade unions were not always weak or necessarily moderate. The 'new' social history, for example, has documented the radicalism of various unions and the Committtee for Industrial Organisation (CIO) in the first half of the twentieth century (Hirsch 1978; Katznelson and Zolberg 1986; Kimeldorf 1988; McNally *et al.* 1991; Zeitlan 1983). During the period of rapid industrialisation, there was considerable national industrial unrest over the working and living conditions of the industrial masses. Most notably, industrial disputes in the 1910s and 1920s were very violent, and the extent to which the capitalist class were prepared to break strikes in particular and their strong resistant to unions in general has been cited as one of the major impediments to trade unionism in the US. So too have divisions between different ethnic groups within the working class which employers exploited to weaken collective action during this period. The early twentieth century, therefore, was a time in which trade unions tried to win legitimacy as a vehicle for working-class interests.

The fight for trade union rights experienced setbacks during the Great Depression and it was not until the 1930s that the trade union movement obtained recognition. That is, it was in the more favourable political climate of the New Deal that industrial relations were transformed with the right to union representation (monitored by the National Labor Relations Board (NLRB) established in the 1938 National Labour Relations Act (Wagner Act) already discussed in Chapter 6 above. In a climate relatively friendly towards labour, the activities of employers interfering with the right to organise was curtailed. It was also in the 1930s that the unions broke out of the confines of the primary industries and established themselves in the newly-emerging mass production industries producing cars, electrical goods and so forth. Blacks were also incorporated into and played an important role in the trade union movement (Leggett 1968; Kornblum 1974). Trade union members continued to increase their membership, and by the end of the Second World War, 35 per cent of the non-agricultural workforce was unionised (Brody 1993).

After the Second World War, the 1947 Taft Hatley Act made it easier for employers to resist union organisation and the anti-communist witchhunts of the McCarthy period robbed the union movement of important political leaders. Nevertheless, during the postwar period of prosperity, the social contract between employers and unions prevailed and a period of industrial peace ensued. Trade union membership among blue-collar workers held steady and, in the political climate of the 1960s, increasing number of public sector white-collar workers joined trade unions. The period was also one in which links between trade unions and the Democrats were strengthened (Greenstone 1977). Commentators (Brody 1993; Rubin 1986) also noted, however, that class conflict was effectively institutionalised and contained to a narrow range of issues. The unions were preoccupied with wage negotiations and job security and there was little debate about worker participation. Managers retained their right to manage and were prepared to pay money to hold onto their power in the workplace. However, the political events of the mid to late 1960s gradually undermined the position of unions in the economic and political spheres of American life. The Vietnam War was highly divisive and undermined the momentum behind Johnson's Great Society Initiative. The position of the unions was subsequently undermined in the 1970s following the oil shock of 1973, the slowdown in economic growth, increased competition, rising inflation, less favourable relations with the Democrats and a less favourable political climate under Nixon and Ford. Trade union membership began to decline in manufacturing especially in the private sector and was only offset by the strength of public-sector unionism. Reviewing the period, Brody argued 'In the years since the Great Society, organised labour has been pressed inexorably into the mould of an interest group' (Brody 1993: 223).

It was against this background of declining membership that the unions entered the 1980s. The recession of 1982–3 had a major effect on the manufacturing sector of the American economy and saw mass redundancies among blue-collar workers – namely, in the sector where trade unionism was strongest (Harrison and Bluestone 1988). Over the 1980s, one in three jobs from heavy industry disappeared (Berman quoted in Gilbert and Kahn 1993). Structural economic change, therefore, witnessed the further decline of trade union membership. The political climate of the 1980s also proved to be especially hostile to the trade unions. Big business joined forces against labour in Congress to defeat the Labour Reform Bill in 1978 which would have restored the effectiveness of the Wagner Act. Worse, however, was to come with the election of the strongly anti-union president – Ronald Reagan – in 1980. The firing of several thousand striking air traffic controllers in the early 1980s was a 'defining moment' for the union movement (Fantasia 1995). The decade was subsequently characterised by a 'new' industrial relations in which business returned to an aggressive anti-union stance (Milkman 1991). The 'new' industrial relations has been greatly influenced by Japanese styles of work organisation including various worker participation schemes in quality circles and other employee involvement initiatives (Milkman 1991). The evidence seems to suggest, therefore, that the trade unions are a spent force. On the other hand, there is also evidence that workers remain highly sceptical of worker participation schemes. In her study of the highly automated Linden General Motors assembly plant, Milkman (1991: 147) found considerable dissatisfaction surrounding the failure of the various schemes to deliver

Table 8.1. Comparison of union membership in the USA and the UK as a percentage of non-agricultural employees, 1955–84

Year	United States	United Kingdom
1955	34[1]	46
1960	32[1]	45
1965	29[1]	45
1970	31	52
1975	29	54
1976	29	56
1977	n/a	58
1978	27	59
1979	25	58
1980	25	57
1981	n/a	56
1982	n/a	55
1983	20	55
1984	19	53

[1] Excludes members of employee associations.

Source: Goldfield (1987), Table 3, p. 16. © M. Goldfield, 1987. Reprinted with the permission of University of Chicago Press.

genuine employee involvement. Aspirations for industrial justice, therefore, have not disappeared and suggest that the trade union movement is far from redundant even in the US (Brody 1995).

Other micro-sociological studies of the workplace suggest that industrial conflict and industrial action is far from dead. The workplace continues to generate 'cultures of solidarity' (Fantasia 1988). Fantasia, for example, conducted three case studies of foundry workers (which allowed him to examine the microprocesses of worker solidarity), women hospital workers (where he observed workplace mobilisation), and corn mill workers (where a strike embraced a whole community). Interestingly, Fantasia documented women hospital workers' difficulties in forming a union in the face of management strategies of paternalism and repression. They experienced delaying tactics which posed difficulties in sustaining collective solidarity and which required results. He found that the women were forced to organise independently of formal structures of organisation although the process of mobilisation generated new values, action and bonds which sustained a new identity, of perceived interests and rejection of authority and hierarchy. Fantasia, argued, therefore, that collective action in the industrial sphere has far from disappeared but, rather, still challenges the individualism of American capitalist society. He concluded, 'While it is only a relatively small part of their reality, and while the forces that oppose them can be overwhelming, American workers are not as 'exceptionally' or as intrinsically averse to solidarity and collective action as we are sometimes led to believe' (Fantasia 1988: 243). Other studies (Delgrado 1993; Dudley 1994; Wellman 1995; see Fantasia 1995) have also emphasised that industrial conflict is far from absent in different sectors of the economy and involves different groups of workers. The workplace, therefore, remains an important site in which workers mobilise despite the decline of trade unionism in the US.

The trade unions established themselves in the late nineteenth and early twentieth century in Britain. As in America, membership dropped during the depression of the 1930s although it rose substantially up to the 1940s. By 1948, for example, trade union density stood at 45% (Winchester 1988: 498). It remained at this level throughout the 1950s and 1960s. British commentators also noted the narrowness of trade union demands – wage demands rather than more worker control – during this period. It was argued, for example, that changes in the workplace – especially the advent of new technology – were seen to undermine the group solidarity of the workplace, and, by implication, the industrial collectivism of the trade unions by promoting greater identification with employers (Woodwood 1958). This optimistic view of worker integration, however, was under-mined by Goldthorpe and his colleagues (1968a; 1969) in *The Affluent Worker* series. They rejected the importance attached to technology in sha-ping industrial attitudes and behaviour. Rather, they argued that workers held an instrumental orientation to work – viewed solely as a means of making money – which was fuelled by their non-work aspirations to sustain 'their relatively prosperous and rising standard of living' (Goldthorpe *et al.* 1968a: 150). This instrumentalism explained how workers tolerated boring and monotonous work tasks rather than become alienated by them. It also explained the limited relations between workers and their work groups. Finally, it accounted for collective support for the trade unions which was directed towards 'immediate 'bread and butter' issues.' Instrumental collectivism – 'directed to the achievement of individuals' private goals outside the workplace' – was the order of the day (Goldthorpe *et al.* 1968a: 106).

Goldthorpe *et al.*'s findings on orientations to work and trade unionism were the source of much debate (Daniel (1969; 1971; Goldthorpe (1970; 1972) and further research among industrial sociologists in the 1970s (see Brown 1992 for a full summary). Numerous commentators, for example, argued that the experiences of boring and monotonous work were the source of instrumentalism as well (Argyris 1972; Brown 1973; MacKinnon 1980; Whelan 1976). Subsequent research on orientations to work also found that workers attached greater importance to extrinsic rewards over the intrinsic rewards of work although few researchers could actually find a clearly and coherently expressed instrumentalism amongst other groups of workers (Beynon and Blackburn 1972; Blackburn and Mann 1979; Brown 1973). Blackburn and Mann (1979), for example, argued forcefully that workers were not as single-minded or as narrowly focused in the pursuit of economic rewards as the Luton team implied. Brown and his colleagues (Brown *et al.* 1983) concluded that instrumentalism was the predominant attitude towards paid work, especially when searching for a job, but that other intrinsic concerns were not prohibited by instrumental attitudes. Survey research has also confirmed that members of the working class are more instrumental towards paid work than their middle-class counterparts because primarily because of the uneven distribution of intrinsic rewards across the occupational structure. However, workers still enjoy some rewards from paid work like developing work skills and socialising with fellow workers (Marshall 1988: 208–10). Members of the working class, therefore, are largely instrumental in their orientation towards paid work although it is not as singular or as all-inclusive as the Luton team suggested (Marshall *et al.* 1988: 207).

The 1970s, however, was a period of rapid growth in trade unionism especially among white-collar workers in the public sector. That is, trade union membership rose to a peak of 13,447 by 1979 amounting to 55 per cent of the workforce (Bain and Price 1983). Bain and Price (1983) argued that public-sector unionism grew in a political climate which was favourable to increased membership. They also argued that the increased militancy of the 1970s could be explained by the inflation of the period which threatened prices and money incomes. In a not dissimilar vein, Goldthorpe (1987) accounted for the militancy of the period with reference to the decline of the status order, the realisation of industrial citizenship and the willingness of a mature working class to exploit their market position to the full (Goldthorpe 1978). The period of industrial militancy, however, was abruptly terminated by the election to power of Margaret Thatcher and the Conservative Party on a wave of anti-union sentiment following the 'winter of discontent' in 1978–9 when various public sector unions called their members out on strike and the special relationship between the Labour Party and the trade unions was seemingly in disarray.

The early 1980s, of course, was a period of massive job loss from the manufacturing sector of the economy. Trade union membership, there-fore, fell dramatically to less than eleven million and union membership dropped to 42 per cent of the workforce by 1986 (Winchester 1988). The political climate was also extremely hostile to the trade unions. The Thatcher administrations introduced a series of laws curtailing the power of trade unions to engage in collective action thereby undermining their

legitimacy (Marsh 1992). The one major example of industrial militancy
in the 1980s was the miners strike of 1984/5 (Beynon 1985; Warwick and
Littlejohn 1992). The strike was called in response to plans for a the closure
of a series of pits deemed uneconomic by the government (the mining
industry having been nationalised in the 1940s). The strike, in other words,
was about the preservation of jobs and communities during that period.
The strike lasted nearly twelve months. It was characterised by a number
of distinctive features. The policing of the strike, for example, was very
high profile with various incidents of violence on the picket lines (Green
1990), and there was a great deal of commentary on the solidarity of the
communities involved, the role of women in sustaining those communities
and its effects on the community generally (Waddington *et al.* 1991;
Winterton and Winterton 1989). There was much internal conflict within
the union with early pressure to ballot members of the strike which the leader
of the NUM, Arthur Scargill, resisted but which many saw as undermining
the legitimacy of the strike. Indeed, there was a split between the NUM
and miners in the Nottinghamshire Areas who formed the breakaway
Union of Democratic Miners and went back to work. The strike was also
characterised by a government under Thatcher determined to break the
unions and a management under McGregor determined to break the strike
using such tactics as importing coal from abroad, building up stocks of coal
and so forth (Lane 1996). The strike failed and the miners were forced to
return to work a year later. It was an heroic failure as a result of various
factor including government determination to break the strike but also bad
tactics by the union. Nevertheless, the predictions about pit closures did
come true and the miners unions have shrunk to as low a membership as
thirty-three thousand miners. Whether the mining industry would have
shrunk as much or more if the miners strike had not happened remains
unknown. Although there was much hostility to the strike at the time, the
residue of feeling against additional pit closures fed the 1990s in the form
of demonstrations against them by a wide group of people.

   The decline in trade union membership has led to debate about the
nature of trade union allegiance and the implications of recent trends for
the trade unions in the future (Gallie 1989; 1996). The major debate has
centred on whether individuals have turned away from the trade unions or
whether the decline in membership is a result of structural changes in the
economy, though evidence suggests that it is primarily structural factors
which account for this decline, at least, in the 1980s. There is, however, little
evidence of a decline in commitment to trade unionism. That is, members
remain convinced of its advantages. It was also found that the most important influence over trade union membership was the structural context
in which members were employed rather than their views about the trade

Table 8.2. Most important reasons for being a trade union member at present by class

	Service	Lower non-manual	Tech-nicians/ Super-visors	Skilled manual	Non-skilled manual	Total
Condition of job	11	15	21	23	22	17
Way of creating a more just society/solidarity	19	17	11	15	14	16
Higher pay and better conditions	17	20	27	25	23	21
Everyone else is a member	1	4	5	2	6	3
Protection if problems come up in the future	51	44	3 5	33	34	41
Other	1	1	1	1	1	1
Number	569	258	113	289	504	1733

Source: Gallie (1989), Table 3, p. 32.

unions. That is, the most important factor affecting union membership was whether or not employers accepted trade unions. A factor of secondary importance was whether members of the workforce were to be found in the private sector or the public sector of the economy. This picture was confirmed by an examination of why former members had left their unions. Again, the overwhelming reasons were structural in nature rather than any hostile attitude towards the trade unions. The major reason for lapsed membership was exit out of the labour market or unemployment. For those who remained in employment, their union membership mainly expired because of a move to another job where there was no union to join. There was little evidence of political disenchantment. The data imply therefore, that trade unions are not inevitably on the wain as a result of economic, social and political change. Rather, it seems that 'the future pattern of trade union membership . . . will depend upon the organisational skills of trade unions and the longer-term development of government policies' (Gallie 1989: 27).

Overall, therefore, America is characterised by a much lower level of trade unionism than Britain. In the 1990s, trade unionism in America stands at less than half that in Britain. That said, both nations have experienced remarkably similar trends in trade union growth and decline since the Second World War. Membership was steady in both countries over the 1950s and 1960s. Both countries experienced a growth in public sector white-collar trade unionism although this occurred in the 1960s in America and the 1970s in Britain. However, what is distinctive about America is that it did begin to experience a dramatic fall in trade unionism in manufacturing in the private sector in the 1970s. Both countries, however, experienced a sudden decline in the 1980s as a result of structural economic change and a political climate hostile to trade unionism. Despite its current fragility in both nations, however, there is no reason, as yet, to assume that trade unionism will disappear altogether. The future strength of the trade unions is contingent on economic, political and organisation factors which remain open for empirical investigation in the future.

CHANGING LIFE-STYLES

In the early twentieth century the working and living conditions of manual workers in the urban cities of American and Britain were extremely poor. After the Second World War, however, a period of sustained affluence saw working-class standards of living increase substantially. For the first time, manual workers and their families could afford to buy their own homes and equip them with the range of domestic goods bought from the newly-emerging mass consumer markets. These social changes led to debate on the extent to which working-class life-styles were changing and, most importantly, if they were now indistinguishable from middle-class life-styles (Handel and Rainwater 1964; Mayer 1963; Ogburn 1955; Wilensky 1966). It was argued that all aspects of working-class life-styles were changing. The importance of work in workers' lives was declining as the significance of their non-work lives was increasing (Blauner 1964; Chinoy 1955; Dubin 1956). The separateness of men and womens' lives within blue-collar marriages was being replaced by closer relations between couples (Komarsovsky 1962). Finally, working-class leisure patterns were increasingly similar to middle-class leisure pursuits (Gans 1967). These changes were seen to undermine the distinctive solidarism which had previously characterised community life and which had sustained an identification with the working class (Coleman and Rainwater 1978; Hodge and Treiman 1968). In the 1950s and 1960s, therefore, it was widely believed that America was becoming a middle-class society.

Other commentators, however, cast a sceptical eye over the various guises of the embourgeoisement thesis (Berger 1968; Kornblum 1974; LeMasters 1975; MacKenzie 1973; Rubin 1976). Berger (1968) studied the relocation of Ford car workers from an old suburb (Richmond) to a new suburb (Milpilas) in California. He found a distinctive working-class community persisted in the new suburbs which were segregated along class lines. That is, workers lived and socialised alongside fellow workers and spent their leisure time with them. It shaped their limited aspirations in that they did not seek more over and above their daily lives, and it sustained a strong identification with the working class. Similarly, MacKenzie's (1973) study of skilled manual workers in Providence, Rhode Island, found little evidence of overlap across working-class and middle-class social worlds (although he did find a convergence in life-styles between his labour aristocrats and members of the lower middle class). The majority of skilled craftsmen, for instance, drew their friends from among relatives, neighbours and workmates with whom they socialised on an informal basis. Like Berger, MacKenzie found a high level of working-class identification and strong allegiance to the Democrats as the party representing the interests of the 'common man'. Finally, LeMasters (1975) and Rubin (1976) dismissed the notion that blue-collar marriages were indistinguishable from middle-class marriages. LeMasters (1975) participant observation study of a blue-collar tavern (The Oasis) in Lakeside found that men and women had very different experiences and views about marriage. In a similar vein, Rubin (1976) found that blue-collar men and women's lives were still largely separate. Their lives were dominated by financial strains and the daily grind of work which left neither husbands nor wives with much energy or time for leisure. In their 'worlds of pain', circumstances dictated there was little space or inclination to develop more rewarding relationships. Overall, therefore, it was widely argued that a distinct working-class life-style had not disappeared.

Subsequent research emphasised both the continuities and changes in working-class life-styles. Halle (1984), for example, studied the work and non-work lives of home-owning blue-collar workers at a chemical plant in New Jersey. Contrary to Berger, he found that life outside work did not sustain a strong class identity. Although his informants were part of long-established networks of family and friends, they lived in occupationally mixed areas. Halle's interviewees attached considerable importance to home ownership and the residential area in which they lived. What they could afford and where they could afford to buy was dictated by income levels rather than occupation. Of paramount importance was that the residential area in which they lived was predominately white and not black or hispanic. Thus, it was race rather than class which was the major residential cleavage. This racial cleavage restricted an identification with poor or unemployed ethnic groups at the bottom of the class structure. Halle found that leisure patterns were highly segregated by gender and stage of the marital cycle. These factors rather than class, therefore, shaped the nature of leisure (Halle 1984: 75). Thus, he emphasised the similarities of leisure activities and marriage relations with other Americans. Overall, Halle argued that the non-work lives of blue collar workers were shaped by race, gender, stage in the marital cycle, income levels and consumption levels. It did not sustain a strong working-class identity. On the contrary, Halle's interviewees saw themselves as middle class or lower middle class

Table 8.3. Ethnic origin and housing details of Imperium workers

Ethnic or racial origins of Imperium workers % (N = 126)	
Eastern European[1]	58
German	13
Irish	9
Italian	8
English	5
Scottish	2
Hispanic	2
Black	2
Jewish	1

Place of birth of Imperium workers % (N = 93)	
Within two miles of Imperium	65
Elsewhere in New Jersey or Staten Island	5
Elsewhere in United States	24
Abroad	6

Distance from Imperium by size of lots on which Imperium workers' houses stand

	Average width of lot (feet)	Average length of lot (feet)
Within two miles[2]	41 (30– 50)[4]	112 (100–125)[4]
Two to four miles	43 (35– 50)	120 (199–150)
Over four miles[3]	68 (50–100)	122 (100–150)

Distance from Imperium by average value of their homes and average age of owners (1980)

	Average value of homes (dollars)	Average age of owners
Within two miles	51,738	51
Two to four miles	51,995	46
Over four miles	68,368	39

[1] Includes Poles (numerically the largest group of Eastern Europeans at Imperium). Austrians, Hungarians, Czechoslovakians, Romanians and Russians.
[2] Mostly the pre-war suburbs of Elizabeth and Linden.
[3] Mostly areas developed after World War II.
[4] The range within which at least three-quarters of the cases fall.

Source: Halle (1984), Tables A1–A4, pp. 303–4. © D. Halle, 1984.
Reprinted with the permission of University of Chicago Press.

(who enjoyed their position as a result of individual effort) and their image of the class structure was one of 'having some fluidity in its middle range' (Halle 1984: 77).

In the world of work, Halle found industrial workers faced with largely uninteresting jobs, with little chance of promotion into more rewarding work who spent much of their time wrestling control from managers to reduce their work and enjoy some autonomy. These experiences, Halle argued, generated a 'class consciousness' revolving around the notion of a 'common man'. That is, the informants distinguished between blue-collar workers and the rest of the class structure. He found a hostility to big business and other occupational groups. It sustained a concern 'with a politics surrounding the workplace, work-related issues, and the union, (Halle 1984: 219). However, he argued that this 'class consciousness' was limited because it also upheld a tacit racism, a tacit sexism, and there was little sense of an alternative economic and political system. He argued that the concept of the working man embodied a belief that, 'Those who perform the really productive work do not receive a fair reward compared with the reward of those who are related to production indirectly or not at all. But this is not accompanied by a view that capitalism itself should be replaced' (Halle 1984: 218). A class identity was sustained in the world of work but it was still limited. It led the majority of blue-collar workers, for example, to identify with the Democrats although they did not always vote for them especially when issues in their non-work lives – safer neighbourhoods, better schools and so forth – were high on the political agenda. Class was not always salient, therefore, in shaping their political attitudes and behaviour. Finally, Halle argued that these two identities – that of belonging to the middle/lower middle class and associating with the 'common man' – were joined by a national America identity which also shaped his interviewees' world views. Overall, therefore, Halle argued that class is not an important social identity among the American working class.

Halle's research was widely reviewed and well received as a 'realistic account' of blue-collar life in America. His thesis, of course, echoes the earlier arguments of Hirsch (1978) and Katnelson (1981; see also Rieder 1985) of a separation between the politics of the workplace and the politics of the community in America. It also draws on long-standing arguments which emphasise the ways in which race and other cleavages fragment the working class (see also Form 1985). However, this thesis about the special experience of class in the US begs as many questions as its seeks to answer. Halle's argument fails to explain why a class identity sustained in the workplace does not inform blue-collar worker's non-work lives when the extent to which they can participate in comsumer society is different to that of their middle-class counterparts. He does not consider the ways in which racial identities may reinforce rather than undercut class identification. Nor does he explain why issues about safer neighbourhoods and better schools were not perceived as class issues leading the interviewees to vote for the Democrats. What is missing, in other words, is an account of the role of the trade unions or the Democrats informing (or failing to inform) the views of American blue-collar workers. It may also be that his focus on seemingly very secure high-technology workers (interviewed in the 1970s) led Halle to effectively restate the embourgeoisement thesis in a new form.

Attention in the 1980s and 1990s, however, has turned to how working-class communities have coped with mass redundancies, high rates of unemployment and continuing job insecurity. Bensman and Lynch's (1988) study of a steel community in Chicago's South-east Side documented how the closure of a major steel works 'set out an avalanche of economy dislocation' as small businesses collapsed and the local job structure crumbled. They charted the mass redundancies which followed and the effects on the lives of the men and their families in the community. For families, it meant the loss of income, a decline in what had been regarded as lower middle-class standards of living and, in some instances, being forced to live on welfare. Bensman and Lynch (1988) found much despair, a loss of confidence and little optimism among the steel workers and their families about their future job prospects or standards of living. It had, in other words, undermined their faith in the American Dream and had led to disenchantment with the federal government, local politicians and the unions. At the same time, they also found that, 'The dense layering of social experiences and the bonds of trust and familiarity that grow in strong communities' had not been wiped out, and there was evidence of solidarity and community action in the face of adversity as well (Bensman and Lynch 1988: 126). Rosen's (1987) study of working-class women in Milltown, a New England industrial city, made redundant from the light manufacturing industry also showed the impact of unemployment, job security and new jobs in the poorly-paid service sector had on the daily lives of working-class families. They experienced a reduction in their standards of living and their hopes and aspirations were curtailed by the mundane reality of their material existence. At the same time, Rosen demonstrated how the women found ways of coping and working to sustain their family lives especially in the context of male unemployment. These studies show, in other words, the way in which the position of blue-collar men and women in the labour market – most notably the job insecurity with which they live – shapes their life-styles, aspirations and wider social and political attitudes and behaviour. The working class has shrunk but it has not disappeared from American life.

In Britain, debate about the socio-cultural distinctiveness of the working class also focused on changing life-styles. Embourgeoisement theorists (Klein 1965; Mogey 1956; Young and Willmott 1957; Zweig 1961) argued that affluence led members of the working class to adopt middle-class life-styles. Goldthorpe and his colleagues (1969) research among manual workers in Luton, however, found little evidence of the adoption of middle-class patterns of sociability and leisure activities. On the contrary, their respondents lived privatised life-styles. The search for highly-paid work, fuelled by economic motivations and an instrumental orientation to work led their respondents to move away from long-standing companions. As a consequence of geographical mobility, patterns of sociability and leisure were restricted to the immediate family in the home. Furthermore, demanding shift work and overtime to secure good wages militated against the development of new networks of friends. A privatised life-style centred around the immediate family in the home, therefore, was compatible with their aspirations for increased standards of living (Goldthorpe *et al.* 1969: 101–2). Working-class life-styles had shifted away 'from a community-orientated form of social life towards recognition of the conjugal family and its fortunes as concerns of overriding importance'. Rather than embourgeoisement, however, these changes amounted to a process of 'normative convergence' between manual and non-manual groups. Against the backdrop of this measured account of social change, Goldthorpe and his colleagues concluded that their respondents were 'prototypical' in being more representative of the future than the (then) working class.

The Luton team's account of changing working-class life-styles was certainly preferred over the embourgeoisement thesis although numerous writers (Allcorn and Marsh 1975; Crewe 1973; Davis and Cousins 1975; Westergaard 1965) cast doubt on the Luton team's characterisation of the 'traditional' working class. Their portrayal of it relied uncritically upon a small number of community studies (Dennis *et al.* 1956 and Stacey 1960) which were not necessarily representative of the working class of the first half of the twentieth century (Kent 1981: 137). They never systematically evaluated the extent to which the 'traditional working class led communal life-styles. As Franklin (1989) has subsequently argued, the 'traditional working class has rarely 'stood up to empirical scrutiny'. At the every least, the extent of working-class solidarism has been exaggerated in that working-class solidarity existed in specific conditions, like the isolated and sometimes dangerous workplaces in the primary or heavy manufacturing industries of fishing, mining and steel production. As Hill (1976) later showed in his study of London dockers, the 'traditional' worker was also instrumental and privatised. The confusion arose because it was never clear whether Lockwood's (1975) portrayal of the 'traditional' proletarian worker was an

historical figure or a hypothetical ideal type. Although Lockwood claimed
the concept was a heuristic device yet the traditional worker was also
portrayed as a figure of the past. The concept was, therefore, remarkably
slippery (Benson 1978: 156). It led critics like Moorhouse (1976) to
wonder if the Luton team, like embourgeoisement theorists before them,
had exaggerated the extent of change in working-class life-styles in the
post-war period of prosperity.

Nevertheless, the concept of privatism proved popular in the 1980s
for describing working-class life-styles in a period of economic recession.
Pahl (1984), for example, conducted a study of working-class life-styles
on the Isle of Sheppey in Kent. Pahl argued that men's and women's
daily lives have long been dominated by the work tasks and responsibilities
associated with supporting the household. In the context of rising levels
of male unemployment, Pahl found extensive 'self-provisioning' among
his working-class households. They were engaged in various forms of
formal and informal work in servicing their own needs (Pahl 1984: 100-
1). A busy home and family-centred existence were especially evident
amongst those households with two or more incomes from the formal
economy while those dependent on low incomes – usually state benefit
to relieve the hardship of unemployment – were less able to provide
for themselves. He argued that relatively affluent 'core' households were
joining the comfortable middle mass while impoverished households
were being marginalised (Pahl 1984: 313). Pahl also emphasised that
people's aspirations and values derive from the sphere of consumption
rather than production (Pahl 1984: 323). The values of domesticity and
individualism, choice and innovation are what Pahl describes as a form
of 'dynamic conservatism' subscribed to by both the middle and working
classes. In other words, domesticity and familism have long shaped
working-class aspirations and values and assumptions about the 'traditional' working class retreating from collective politics into the individual
home and family should be rejected once and for all. Privatism has long
prevailed.

However, the notion of working-class privatism has not gone uncontested
(Crow and Allan 1990; Franklin 1989; Proctor 1990). In her study of
the role of family networks in shaping employment chances in the steel
town of Corby, Grieco (1987) stumbled across people who had been
recruited to Luton by the Vauxhall car company which was one of the
major employers in the town from which Goldthorpe and his colleagues
drew their sample. It appeared that Vauxhall actively recruited workers
from Scotland and the North East in the 1960s and 1960s where
peripheral sections of the economy were in decline and unemployment
was higher than the national average. It was in these uncertain economic

Table 8.4. The Luton interviewees and their geographical origins

Interviewees' region of upbringing	
Region of origin[1]	Interviewees
Luton area[2]	32
London and the South-East	11
Northern Ireland and Eire	9
Abroad	5
Other parts of Britain	5
Total	62

Lutonians and their parents' geographical origins		
	Father	Mother
Kim Dodd	North	Surrey
Anthony Dodd	North	North
Bridget Underwood	Eire	Eire
Stephen Underwood	Poland	London
Rita Aziz	India	India
Uma Kasim	India	India
Ashok Kasim	India	India
Lisa Smith	London	Luton
Matthew Smith	Wales	Wales
Jane Bennett	Luton	Luton
Andrew Bennett	London	London
Colin Burgess	West Indies	West Indies
Alison Clark	North	North
Michael Clark	Scotland	Scotland
Teresa Mills	Luton	Luton
Gerald Mills	Wales	Wales
Angela Stone	Lincolnshire	Luton
George Stone	Lancashire	Suffolk
Irene Cass	Eire	Eire
Edward Cass	Wales	Wales
Anita Palmer	Luton	Luton
Roy Mayes	Eire	Eire
Robert Edwards	Wales	Cambridgeshire
Judith Hayward	London	London
Geoffrey Hayward	Hampshire	London
Christine Merrick	Eire	Eire
Heather Jackson	North	Luton
Kevin Jackson	Luton	Luton
Pauline Graves	Luton	Luton
Richard Graves	Luton	Luron
Dorothy Atkinson	Luton	Luton
Jack Foulds	Luton	Luton

Table 8.4 (cont.)

Interviewees from London and the south east

Interviewees	Region of origin
Shiela Ibbotson	London
Peter Ibbotson	London
Sandra Davis	London
Trevor Davis	London
Timothy Merrick	London
Brenda Richards	London
Brian Richards	London
Maria Knight	London
Daniel Knight	London
Frances Hills	St Albans
John Hills	St Albans

Irish members of the sample

Irish interviewees	Region of origin
Marion Capel	Eire
Catherine Mayes	Eire
Rachel Edwards	Eire
Julia Farrell	Eire
Martin Farrell	Northern Ireland
Margaret Kent	Eire
Leslie Kent	Eire
Karen Osborne	Eire
David Osborne	Eire

Interviewees from abroad

Interviewees	Country of origin
Malik Aziz	Kenya
Delia Burgess	West Indies
Neil Palmer	West Indies
Simon Sawyer	Jamaica
Carol Sawyer	Jamaica

Migrants from other parts of Britain

Interviewees	Region of origin
Elisabeth Adams	Tyne and Wear
Bruce Capel	Yorkshire
Barbara Wright	East Anglia
Lawrence Atkinson	Cambridgeshire
Daphne Foulds	West Midlands

[1] In keeping with the Luton team's definition of upbringing, the term refers to the locale in which the interviewees grew up.
[2] The Luton area is defined as the town and all land within a ten-mile radius of the town's boundaries.

Source: Devine (1992a), Tables 3.5–10, pp. 43–9.

circumstances that workers and their families moved to Luton. It was not an instrumental orientation to work which led them to forgo family and friends in search of jobs. More importantly, she was unconvinced of the Luton team's portrayal of a privatised working class. Information on kin from the Luton study, for example, was limited as was information on sociability between kin in the workplace. Her own research on chain migration over a long distance highlighted the importance of family and friends for information on job opportunities and housing facilities, and she documented the re-grouping of families over time. Her research led her to consider whether the 'disrupted and attenuated kin and community ties' found in Luton were permanent or merely transitional changes as a result of recent migration. Research by Harris and his associates (1987), who examined the impact of large redundancies from the steel industry in South Wales in the early 1980s, also highlighted the importance of kin and family networks in finding new employment. The notion of a privatised working-class, therefore, has been subject to considerable scepticism.

A qualitative re-study (Devine 1992a) of the *Affluent Worker* series conducted in the 1980s also cast doubt on Goldthorpe *et al.*'s portrayal of a privatised working class and Pahl's picture of highly insulated working-class households. Many of the Vauxhall car workers and their families who were interviewed had moved to Luton from depressed parts of Britain in search of employment or had moved away from London in search of affordable housing. The interviewees, in other words, exploited the opportunities for advancement in the post-war period although whether their actions could be described as singularly instrumental is a moot point. The push and pull factors which shaped the interviewees' motives for moving were more complex than the Luton team supposed. Furthermore, the majority of the interviewees and their families followed, or were followed by kin and friends to Luton. They invariably facilitated mobility by providing information on job opportunities and the availability of housing in the town as well as being an important source of companionship. Individual families, therefore, rarely moved alone but 're-grouped' as Grieco (1987) also found. There was plenty of evidence of solidarity in the process of mobility. Turning to the interviewees' life-styles, it was found that they were neither exclusively family centred, nor entirely family centred. There was plenty of sociability with extended kin, neighbours, colleagues from work and other friends. Similarly, the interviewees enjoyed leisure activities beyond the home in the company of other people. That said, their life-styles could not be described as solidaristic. Patterns of sociability and leisure were constrained by the demands of formal and informal work to sustain the well-being of the household. Moreover, the way in which work shaped the opportunities and constraints on sociability in the informants non-work lives varied between the husbands and wives of the families according to their stage in the family life-course. Working-class life-styles, therefore, were neither family centred, nor home centred.

The Luton re-study also cast doubt on Pahl's portrayal of working-class families as preoccupied only with themselves and not with others. Against the backdrop of redundancies, the interviewees were fearful about their jobs and especially the job prospects of their children. Job insecurity and all the implications of job loss hung over their daily lives. They did not look to national economic advancement as a collective means by which their lives would improve as in the 1960s. Instead, they expected modest improvements in the standards of living as they moved though the family life-course. Nevertheless, the interviewees' consumer aspirations centred around the economic, social and psychological well-being of their families. They attached considerable importance to owning their own homes (noted by Saunders 1990) and to equipping it with an array of basic and luxury items (Crow 1991). They also attached great significance to having money over and above household expenses for leisure activities for themselves and their children including holidays abroad. The ability to rise above the grind of their material existence, however, was enjoyed late in the family-course when the demands of raising children had been met. Yet, when the interviewees spoke of their hopes and plans for improving their standard of living, they did not speak of their aspirations in singular terms. Rather, they identified with other 'ordinary working people' and 'respectable families' seeking to 'better themselves'. They spoke, in other words, of a collective identity and collective advancement. They aligned themselves with the working class which they defined as the majority of people who had to work for a living. They were distinct from the rich and the poor and although there were different standards of living among the mass of working people, the overriding consideration was that they worked for a living. Aspirations for individual and family well-being did not, then, undermine collective class identification since the experiences of working-class life shaped those aspirations. There was little evidence, therefore, that members of the working class led an existence which necessarily undermined solidarity and promoted individualism. The interviewees's daily lives shaped their aspirations and class imagery in distinctive ways. Thus, even though it has shrunk in size, the working class still exists as a distinctive socio-cultural entity in America and Britain.

THE DEMOCRATIC CLASS STRUGGLE

In America, it has long been known that class influences voting behaviour (Manza *et al.* 1995). The American National Election Study (ANES), which has been carried out biannually since 1948, has established this fact. There have been various theories of the relationship between class and voting such as the rational choice model of material interests (Lipset 1954; Downs 1957), the emphasis on class networks, social organisations and the effects of common experiences of key historical moments (Berelson *et al.* 1954) and the Michigan School approach which has demonstrated the initial effect which class has on people's socio-psychological attributes which subsequently shapes voting behaviour (Campbell *et al.* 1960; Converse 1964). Nevertheless, it has also long been argued that the influence of class on voting has declined over time (Clark and Lipset 1991; Clarke *et al.* 1993; Nie *et al.* 1981; Piven 1992) and that America exhibits one of the lowest levels of class voting among western industrial nations (Franklin *et al.* 1992). Using the Alford Index of class voting, for example, Clark and Lipset (1991) showed that class voting declined from a high of 45 per cent in 1950 to approximately 10 per cent in 1984 (compared with Britain which stood at approximately 40 per cent in 1952 and has fallen to approximately 20 per cent in 1983). Using more sophisticated multiple regression techniques, Franklin and his associates (1992) also showed that class explains a reduced proportion of the variance in recent elections in both America and Britain. More recently, it has been argued that other social cleavages – most notably race – now shape political attitudes and behaviour. The racial cleavage was exploited to the full by the Republicans and explains their success in Presidential elections in the 1980s (Edsall and Edsall 1991; Huckfeldt and Kohnfeld 1989; Piven 1992; Pomper 1993). Class, therefore, has declined in relative importance while race has increased in relative significance over the last decade.

Proponents of the class dealignment thesis have paid particular attention to the defection of the working class from the Democrats in the 1980s. It has been argued that the core constituency of ethnic minorities, the working class and the lower middle class established in the New Deal era had fractured as the more affluent whites voted for Reagan and Bush leaving only the more disadvantaged (invariably ethnic minorities) in the working class and the poor supporting Mondale and Dukakis in 1984 and 1988 (Pomper 1988; 1993). This political version of the embourgeoisement thesis retains its popularity in America. Drawing on data from the ANES, for example, Halle and Romo (1991: 155) argued, 'The current disaffection of blue-collar workers, especially of the skilled and better-paid blue-collar workers, from the Democratic party represents one of the

Table 8.5. Party identification of skilled blue-collar workers, 1952–88

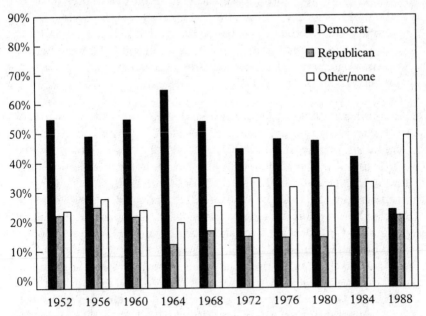

Source: Halle and Romo (1991), Table 8.16, p.163. © Alan Wolfe, 1991.
Reprinted with the permission of the University of California Press.

major changes in American politics'. They found that skilled blue-collar workers increasingly voted Republican throughout the 1980s or did not vote at all (Halle and Romo 1991: 158). They also found that party identification among blue-collar workers has changed in that the proportion of blue-collar voters identifying with the Democrats has declined. Whereas 50 per cent of skilled blue-collar workers identified with the Democrats in the 1950s and 1960s, only 23 per cent did so in 1988. The proportion of skilled workers with no party identification has also risen (Halle and Romo 1991: 164–5). Thus, the affluent home-owning skilled working class have become increasingly disillusioned with the Democrats and have voted Republican or not at all. While ANES data shows that working-class identification remains high (80 per cent in 1952 compared with 75 per cent in 1988), Halle and Romo insisted that election surveys failed to tap the different identities which blue collar-workers hold. Reiterating Halle's earlier argument, therefore, they argued that the data fail to tap a middle/lower middle class identity which blue-collar workers derive from their non-work lives (Halle and Romo 1991: 171–3). Overall, Halle and Romo concluded:

It is this fading of party loyalty and, perhaps, the declining
tendency of blue-collar workers to vote at all, that is probably
the most distinctive feature of the later decades of the twentieth
century. If class solidarity for blue-collar Americans means voting
for Democratic presidential candidates and identifying with the
Democratic party, then class solidarity is definitely on the wane.
(Halle and Romo 1991: 177)

This argument has been somewhat undermined, at least for the present
time, by the election of Bill Clinton as President in 1992 and 1996.

A different picture of working-class politics, however, is found in the
work of Brooks (1984) referred to only briefly in Chapter Four above.
Drawing on data from Wright's study (Wright *et al.* 1980) and a new survey
of class structure and class consciousness (Hout *et al.* 1991), Brooks (1994:
169) sought to explore 'whether working-class consciousness provides a
foundation for political activism and social change in the contemporary
United States'. His analysis, however, drew on a more restricted definition
of the working class than Wright – including manual workers but excluding
low-level non-manual workers. In the 1980 US survey, the working class
constituted 24 per cent of the sample according to this definition rather than
40 per cent under Wright's definition (Brooks 1994: 181). The indicators
of class consciousness were responses to questions on worker's control over
economic life. In both Sweden and the US, Brooks found that worker's class
consciousness can be seen as a coherent package of beliefs (i.e. pro-worker
on a number of items about control over one's economic life) while the rest
of the population has various unrelated attitudes on these issues. Brooks also
examined whether American workers' class consciousness changed over
the 1980s by comparing the results from the two surveys. On a seven-point
scale (0 equalling the pro-capitalist position and 6 the pro-worker position),
he found that American workers show a slight movement away from the
centre to a more pro-worker position (from 3.26 in 1980 to 3.46 in 1991).
Despite this slight shift, however, American workers remained centrist in
comparison to the Swedes whose score of 4.3 in 1981 was higher than that
of the Americans in 1991. Brooks also found that the majority (53 per cent)
of American workers had intermediate scores of 3 and 4 on the scale while
the majority (54 per cent) of Sweden workers had scores of 5 or 6 in 1980.
There are, therefore, more left-wing working-class Swedes than Americans.
Brooks concluded that American working-class consciousness has neither
fragmented nor declined in the 1980s. At the same time, the evidence shows
that 'American workers' class consciousness continues to have an essentially
equivocal character' in that they are neither committed to equalitarianism
nor inegalitarianism. Thus, 'American workers' . . . economic attitudes can

be characterised as occupying a centrist position somewhere between the poles of ideological left and ideological right' (Brooks 1994: 184). That said, Brooks also found the same trend among non-workers (although American workers in 1991 were still more 'right-wing' in comparison to Swedish non-workers in 1980).

Turning to the critical relationship between working-class consciousness and political attitudes, Brooks found that, in contrast to the Swedes, American workers' class consciousness is independent of their political attitudes and behaviour confirming the argument that societies like the US 'which lack national organisations to channel workers' interests and attitudes – tend to give rise to patterns of politically unorganised class consciousness' (Brooks 1994: 186). Brooks found that class consciousness was not a good predictor of Democratic party identification, the likelihood of participating in a protest or views about worker control. This evidence suggests that even if American workers were more class conscious, they would not necessarily be more left wing in their political attitudes and behaviour. Brooks noted that the prevailing view of politics among American workers is that of alienation. Thus, 'while class clearly has a place – and an undeniably important one at that – in American workers' lives, its effects on political attitudes are limited. The converse is also true' (Brooks 1994: 190). Overall, class consciousness is not highly developed in that American workers take centrist stands on items of workers control and it is largely unrelated to their political attitudes. This is not to suggest that American workers lack class consciousness or that class dealignment has occurred however (Manza *et al.* 1995; Hout *et al.* 1996). Hout *et al.* (1996), for example, have argued that the alleged decline of the effects of class on politics is an artefact of the nonmanual/manual division which disappears when a more refined set of class categories is used. Nor are other social cleavages like race replacing class in importance. The class/race trade off has not reduced the overall effect of class since decreases in Northern white working-class support for the Democrats have been offset by a falling regional effect as the American South behaves more like the rest of the country (Hout *et al.* 1996). The changing nature of party appeals to the electorate also needs to be considered in the debate on class voting. Clinton won in 1992 because he successfully appealed not just to the working class but also to the middle class disillusioned with the economic and politics of Bush (Edsall 1984). Despite electoral success, however, the low level of voting in the national election, especially among those in working-class positions, is indicative of political disillusionment with the Democrats in particular and American politics in general.

In Britain, the relationship between class and party has also generated much controversy in the field of election studies. One of the most trenchant debates in the 1980s centred on class dealignment. Proponents of the thesis like Crewe (Crewe 1986; Sarlvik and Crewe 1983; see also Franklin 1985) argued that the overall level of class voting between 1945 and 1983 dropped from 62 per cent to 47 per cent. The Conservative Party's share of the middle-class vote fell from 63 per cent to 55 per cent while the Labour Party's share of working-class support fell from 62% to 42% (Crewe 1986: 620). Crewe focused on the increasing reluctance of members of the working class to vote Labour. He argued that the decline in the size of the working class (with the loss of manual employment) accounted for half of Labour's electoral misfortunes between 1964 and 1979 (Crewe 1989: 13). More importantly, he stressed that the character of the working class had changed. Increased social mobility, the growth in cross-class families, the decline in trade union membership and so on had undermined the traditional working-class community (Crewe 1989: 24–5). The working class had lost its cohesiveness in that subjective class awareness had declined, and collectivism had been replaced by the pursuit of economic self interest. Members of the working class voted for the political party on the basis of issues which best served their economic interests. Hence, the declining segment of the working class – of the council estates in the industrial North – remained loyal to Labour while the increasing segment of the working class – of the new private housing estates in the South – placed their votes elsewhere (Crewe 1987: 83). Successive electoral defeats in the 1980s demonstrated that working-class support for the Labour Party was on the wane.

The fragmentation of the working class was discussed more explicitly by proponents of the 'new structuralism' (Dunleavy 1980a; 1980b; Dunleavy and Husbands 1985; Edgell and Duke 1991; Saunders 1980a, 1980b; see Devine 1996a for a review of this literature). Dunleavy (1990a; 1990b), for example, argued that class had been replaced by new structural cleavages – which divide voters in terms of whether they produce or consume in the private or public sectors – in shaping voting behaviour. Thus, in their analysis of the 1983 election, Dunleavy and Husbands (1985) argued that those members of the working class who owned their own homes and cars were likely to see their interests as best served by the Conservative Party while council tenants reliant on public transport aligned themselves with the Labour Party. Edgell and Duke (1991: 223) also found that production and consumption cleavages divided the working class in the 1980s. They argued that 'attitudinal and behaviourial opposition to and, to a less extent, support for Thatcherism in Britain in the 1980s were characterised by structured fragmentation'. These new cleavages, therefore, explained Labour's electoral failures and the Conservative's successes. Finally, focusing on what he saw as the most important consumption cleavage dividing the electorate, Saunders (1990a) explored the effect of home ownership on political attitudes and behaviour. He argued that the association between tenure and voting is so strong 'because owners and tenants have different interests which can lead them to support different political parties and to develop different sets of political opinions and values (Saunders 1990s: 261). The fragmentation of the working class, in other words, meant that more affluent members of the working class (the majority) had deserted Labour while more deprived members (the minority) remained faithful to them.

Both of these thesis, however, were undermined by findings from British Election Studies in the 1980s (Heath *et al.* 1985; Heath *et al.* 1991; see also Marshall *et al.* 1988). Heath and his colleagues agreed that the decline in the size of the working class had electoral consequences for Labour although they found that working-class identification had remained largely constant between 1964 and 1987 (82 per cent compared with 80 per cent) (Heath *et al.* 1991: 75–6). Turning to voting patterns, they agreed that the proportion of the electorate who voted for their natural class party had dropped from 64 per cent in 1964 to 52 per cent in 1987 (Heath *et al.* 1991: 65). However, they argued that the relative strength of the parties in each social class remained unchanged. The picture was one of 'trendless fluctuation'. Labour support is strongest among manual workers and foreman and technicians while the Conservatives are strongest in the petty bourgeoisie and salariat. They found a low level in relative class voting in the 1970 election which they attributed to the extension of the franchise to eighteen years of age and the increasing number of Liberal candidates. In the 1980s, however, they found that Labour enjoyed its strongest support from members of the working class but it performed badly in every class (except the petty bourgeoisie) while the Liberals gained in each class in these elections. There was no evidence, therefore, of the working class deserting the Labour Party in the 1980s (Heath *et al.* 1991: 72). Heath and his associates rejected the use of 'additional sociological factors' to explain Labour's decline in the 1980s and emphasised the importance of political factors instead. The breakdown of the social contract between Labour and the trade unions in the late 1970s, the ensuing 'winter of discontent' of 1978–9 and the subsequent in-fighting and disunity in opposition in the early 1980s undermined voter's confidence in Labour (see also Devine 1992a).

The election team also rejected arguments about the growing fragmentation of the working class. They found, for example, that the difference between public sector and private sector workers in voting patterns was not that great. In 1987, the majority voted Labour rather than Conservative or Alliance in each case (54 per cent and 47 per cent respectively) (Heath

Table 8.6. Housing tenure and vote in the working class, 1964 and 1987

	Conservative	Liberal	Labour	Other		N
1964						
Owner	35	10	56	0	101%	(220)
Other	26	4	70	0	100%	(191)
L.A. tenant	17	6	76	1	100%	(280)
1987						
Owner	37	23	39	1	100%	(574)
Other	41	15	45	0	101%	(74)
L.A. tenant	20	18	61	2	101%	(377)

Source: Heath *et al.* (1991), Tables 7.4 and 7.5, p.106.

et al. 1991: 104–5). Similarly, Heath and his associates found no evidence that the spread of home ownership undermined working-class support for the Labour Party. They found big differences in the propensity to vote Labour among local authority tenants and home owners in the working class (61 per cent compared with 39 per cent) but that cleavage existed in the 1964 as well (75 per cent compared with 56 per cent) (Heath *et al.* 1991: 106–7). Housing, therefore, has long divided the working class. There was some evidence to show that working-class voters who bought their council houses had a propensity to vote Conservative although they may have been more inclined to do so in the first place. Overall, Heath *et al.* concluded:

> It is simply not the case that the old working class of tenants remained faithful to Labour while the new working class of home owners defected. The major factors which lost Labour votes in the working class, whatever they were, affected local authority tenants as well as home owners. (Heath *et al.* 1991: 107–8)

Indeed, despite the importance which Saunders attached to home owner-ship, his empirical findings also demonstrated that it does not undermine working-class support for Labour. Results from his three towns survey showed that while 59 per cent of tenants voted Labour, nearly half (47 per cent) of home owners voted Labour as well. Saunders (1990a: 233) conceded that 'unskilled and (to a lesser extent) semi-skilled manual working-class households remain solidly supportive of the Labour Party even if they own a house'. Fragmentation within the working class, therefore, did not explain Labour's misfortunes in the 1980s.

Labour's fourth successive defeat in 1992 'showed the slowness of the progress back into contention since 1983' (Heath *et al*. 1994: 4). The recovery in Labour's vote in 1992 saw a rise in absolute class voting (56 per cent in 1992 compared with 52 per cent in 1987). In terms of relative class voting, the results in 1992 were unchanged from 1987 confirming the picture of 'trendless fluctuation' (Heath *et al*. 1994: 282). The evidence suggests, however, that Labour 'lost (and never regained) (the) emotional loyalty of a significant section of the electorate'. Among those who voted in 1992, for example, only 34 per cent had a Labour party identification compared with 42 per cent of Conservative identifiers. The events of the late 1970s and early 1980s, therefore, 'broke the long-term bond for many voters that formerly linked them to the party'. The Policy Review between 1987 and 1992 – designed to rid Labour of some of its most unpopular policies – had only a small effect on voting behaviour (Heath and Jowell 1994). The election of Tony Blair has had a significant effect on Labour's popularity but public perceptions of leaders are volatile and do not secure electoral success (Crewe and King 1996). The Conservative Party has experienced a series of crises under John Major's leadership, and it is increasingly perceived as divided and extreme. Labour is seen as more united and more moderate in comparison although it has suffered from crises as well. Under Blair's leadership, Labour has embarked on the strategy of appealing to the electorate as a competent managerialist party of the centre as a means of attracting both middle class and working-class support. Its class appeal – such as on issues regarding the redistribution of wealth and income – has been muted. Taking this course, the Labour Party has to 'inspire the confidence of a sceptical electorate that it has the economic as well as the social formula to succeed in office' (Heath *et al*. 1994: 294). The long term implications of this strategy – of convincing the electorate of its competence – on class politics have yet to be seen.

Overall, the evidence suggests that levels of class consciousness differ in America and Britain. Members of the American working class have a high level of class awareness although it does not necessarily shape political attitudes and behaviour. As a result, centrist rather than left-wing political views prevail among the working class in the US. In Britain, high levels of working-class identification also prevail. Class identities, however, also influence working-class political attitudes and behaviour which are to the left of the political spectrum. American and British working-class politics are different, therefore, in these respects. However, in neither country is a process of class dealignment occurring. Members of the American working class still have a propensity to vote Democrat and members of the British working class still have a high propensity to vote Labour (albeit to different degrees). In both countries, nevertheless, there is considerable disillusionment with the political parties in particular and national politics in general. Political alienation prevails, therefore, among the working classes of both nations. American and British working-class politics are similar, therefore, with regard to these issues. Interestingly, political alienation persists in America despite the election of a Democrat president in 1992 and 1996 while the Labour party has yet to win power in the 1990s.

CONCLUSION

This chapter has outlined debates about the working class in America and Britain. As was noted earlier, the low level of trade unionism in the United States has frequently been cited as proof of American exceptionalism. It makes America qualitatively and not just quantitatively different from Britain and other European nations. The American working class, in other words, is very different to that described by Marx. In Britain, however, where trade union membership has been high, sociological debate has focused on whether the working class would fulfil the heroic role described by Marx. As an important collective force in the industrial sphere, would members of the working class be a major radical force for change? Since the 1980s, however, trade unionism has fallen in Britain although it has not fallen as low as American union rates. Nevertheless, the debate in both countries now surrounds the issue of whether the working class exists as a collective entity either economically, socially or politically speaking.

Both nations have experienced the decline of manual work and an associated decrease in trade union membership. The United States has always had a lower level of trade union membership than Britain for a variety of different reasons. It was certainly the case that the unions had to face strong anti-union setiments from employers and forceful tactics to undermine collective action in comparison to Britain. That said, American unions were a powerful force in the 1920s and 1930s leading some commentators to argue that the US has become historically exceptional in this respect rather than always being inherently culturally different from Britain and other European countries. Nevertheless, both nations have experienced remarkably similar trends in trade union membership including a period of stability in the 1950s and the 1960s and a substantial growth in public-sector white-collar unionism in the 1960s and 1970s. Similarly, trade unions in both countries were severely hit by economic restructuring and reccession in the early 1980s. They also experienced a hostile climate under Reagan and Thatcher. By the beginning of the 1990s, therefore, both counties are characterised by a relatively low level of trade unionism in comparison to earlier in the century. As a result, questions remain about trade unionism in particular and industrial collectivism in particular in both nations. Overall, the evidence suggests that the US is quantatively rather than qualitatively different from other European nations in terms of levels of trade unions memberships.

Members of the working class in America and Britain enjoyed a new-found affluence in the post-war period of prosperity as they bought their own homes, cars and an array of domestic products for the first time. This affluence was noted by proponents of the embourgeoisement thesis. However, the argument that the members of the working class had adopted middle-class life-styles as a result of this affluence was dismissed. Despite its enduring popularity, the embourgeoisement thesis does not stand up to empirical scrutiny today either. On the contrary, the daily lives of blue-collar workers are governed by paid work and, increasingly, the threat of redundancy and unemployment associated with low-level manual work. These experiences shape patterns of sociability, leisure, aspirations, perceptions and feelings about class and political attitudes and behaviour. Thus, the working class has far from disappeared as a distinct entity. Their life chances – the opportunities which they enjoy and the constraints which they face – and the quality of their lives which flow from these opportunities and constraints continue to generate a sense of identity and solidarity among the American and British working classes. The threat of redundancy, unem-ployment and subemployment, to repeat, are an important constraint which maembers of the working class increasingly face in the 1980s and 1990s. The consequences of these constraints are discussed in the next chapter.

Finally, it was argued that members of the working class retain a distinctive political identity in both nations (although neither working class is the type of political actor envisaged by Marx). The evidence shows that the working-class identification does not necessarily shape political attitudes and behaviour in the US. Centrist rather than left-wing political views prevail among American workers. In Britain, by contrast, working-class identification does shape political attitudes and behaviour which tend to be on the left of the political spectrum although, arguably, the Labour Party is becoming increasingly a political party of the centre rather than the left which will impact on voters views. In this respect, class has less of an impact on politics in the US than Britain, and the American working class does not have as strong a political identity as the British working class. That said, neither nation is experiencing a process of class dealignment. Members of the American working class still have a propensity to vote Democrat while members of the British working class still tend to vote Labour. What is also evident in both nations is considerable disillusionment with political parties in particular and national politics in general. A shared sense of disillusionment prevails among the working class of the two nations even though the Democrats won the election in 1992 and 1996 while the Labour party has yet to be elected into office in the 1990s.

Chapter 9

Social Exclusion

The slowdown in the growth rates of industrialised nations like America and Britain in the early 1970s, the trend towards the increasing concentration of wealth and income from the mid-1970s and the substantial growth of unemployment in the early 1980s while those in power were committed to the free operation of the market, all contributed to the growth of poverty in this period. The persistence of poverty in affluent societies and its increasing visibility in terms of homelessness and destitution in the 1980s and 1990s generated a renewed interest in the poor and their position in the changing class structure of the two nations. It fuelled a debate on the extent to which an underclass of permanently poor people has emerged, and whether they are the perpetrators or victims of their own predicament. The debate has focused particularly on ethnic minorities (especially young black men) and women (single mothers be they white or black) as the main recipients of welfare assistance for the poor. The potential policy implications of the debate has meant that the underclass thesis has become the source of much political controversy as well. The debate on poverty and the underclass, therefore, is currently one of the most contentious issues within class analysis and raises important issues about the nature of social citizenship, social inclusion and exclusion and social order in late twentieth-century America and Britain.

This chapter examines whether a distinct underclass is evident in America and Britain. The chapter is divided into three parts. First, it focuses on the sociological debate on the underclass in the US. The evidence suggests that a sizeable minority (between 13.3 per cent and 19.5 per cent) of the population are poor. The numbers of poor, moreover, have increased in size and they have grown poorer over the last twenty years. The poor are disproportionately black and single-headed families dependent on welfare payments who are isolated in inner-city ghettos where overall poverty levels are high. Whether the poor constitute an underclass who are permanently poor and whose attitudes and behaviour contribute to their poverty, however, is debatable. Research indicates that a very small proportion of the poor are trapped in poverty over a long time span and whether or not the poor have a distinctive culture, it is not the cause of poverty. Rather, the poor are principally the victims of economic restructuring which has seen large swathes of the working class lose their jobs in the 1980s and they are poor because the American welfare state does not adequately provide for the needy in society. Single mothers are poor because they cannot find jobs which would provide them with a living wage on which to raise their children and they do not have childcare support to fully participate in the labour market anyway. The poor (be they young men or single mothers) are disproportionately black because they are also socially isolated in the ghettos of cities and their isolation compounds their difficulties. The ghetto poor, therefore, are an important indication of the persistence of class in post-industrial America.

Second, attention turns to the debate on the underclass in Britain. The evidence also suggests that a sizeable minority (between 8 per cent and 22 per cent) of the population are poor. Similarly, the numbers of poor have increased in size and they have grown poorer over the last twenty years. Again, the poor are disproportionably black and/or single parents who are the victims of multiple deprivations. The focus of attention, however, in Britain has been on poverty and unemployment. Again, the question of whether the poor constitute an underclass who are permanently poor and whose attitudes and behaviour contribute to their poverty has generated much controversy. The evidence suggests that the unemployed (including the long-term unemployed) do not constitute an underclass in that they remain eager to find work and live independently of the state. Dependency on the state is not a choice which the unemployed have made so they are not responsible for their predicament. Neither is their social isolation in networks in which kin and friends are also unemployed a choice which they have made. The concept of the underclass, therefore, has not proved a useful instrument for understanding the position of the poor in the class structure. Rather, the poor are primarily members of the working class (especially the unskilled working class) whose position in the labour market has become increasingly characterised by job insecurity in the harsh economic climate of the 1980s and 1990s. The class character of labour market insecurity is lost in the concept of the underclass.

Third, direct comparison is made of patterns and trends in poverty and inequality in America and Britain. Research indicates that both America and Britain exhibited exceptional trends towards polarisation in the 1980s in comparison to other nations. However, America has a greater level of wealth inequality and income inequality than Britain and other European nations. On this basis, America is a more unequal society than Britain. The depth of poverty – whether it is measured in terms of distance from the poverty line or the poor's share of income – is also greater in the US than the UK. The evidence shows that poverty is high among two-parent families with children and single-parent families with children while in Britain it is high among single-parent families and the elderly. This evidence has led to much concern about child poverty in the US. The lack of a universal income maintenance programme, especially for children in two-parent families, explains the high poverty rates in the US in comparison to the UK and other advanced industrialised nations.

THE AMERICAN UNDERCLASS

According to official measures of poverty, the poor constituted 13.5 per cent (33.6 million) of the American population in 1990. This figure is established by considering the cost of a minimum nutritious diet for a typical family of four and the proportion of income (including inflation on prices) that the average family spends on food. Other measures of poverty, however, indicate that poor are a much larger proportion of the American population. A relative standard of poverty which defines it in terms of half the median income indicates that 19.3 per cent (48.0 million) of Americans are poor. This higher percentage suggest that poverty levels have remained the same since the 1960s. However, the official statistics suggest that the poverty rate began to fall in the period of prosperity after the Second World War. There was a marked decline in poverty in the 1960s during the Johnson Administrations and the War on Poverty programmes although the extent to which poverty fell as a result of political initiatives or economic conditions is open to debate. Poverty flattened out at approximately 12 per cent for most of the 1970s but it started to rise steeply in the late 1970s and early 1980s. Poverty started to rise, therefore, during the Carter Administration and continued into the Reagan and Bush eras rising to 15 per cent before dipping to 13 per cent in 1990 (Gilbert and Kahn 1993: 278). Thus, more than 10 per cent of Americans are poor and as many as 20 per cent could be said to be living in poverty in the 1990s.

The majority of the poor are white who constitute 66.3% (22.3 million) of those in poverty compared with 29.1% (9.8 million) of blacks and 17.8 per cent (6.0 million) of hispanics. Most (49.1 per cent or 16.5 million) of the poor are of working age (18–64) although a large minority (39.8 per cent or 13.4 million) of children under eighteen are also poor while only a minority (11.0 per cent or 3.7 million) of the poor are elderly (over sixty-five). Most of the poor live in cities (42.5 per cent or 14.3 million) but, again, sizable minorities lives in suburbia or rural areas (30.6 per cent (14.3 million) and 27.0 per cent (9.1 million respectively)). Finally, the poor divide almost equally between those in dual-headed families and female-headed families (37.7 per cent (12.7 million) and 12.6 per cent (37.5 per cent) respectively). The poor, in other words, do not match the typical stereotypes (Gilbert and Kahn 1993: 279). However, turning the figures around to examine the incidence of poverty within different social groups produces a different picture. The incidence of poverty among blacks is twice that among whites (see Table 9.1). Poverty is highest among children under eighteen compared with other age groups, while the rate of poverty among blacks of this age is three time higher than that of whites. Finally, the rate of poverty among black and hispanic female-headed households is twice that of white female-headed families (Gilbert and Kahn 1993: 281). It is by looking at the risk of poverty among different groups that the stereotypes of the black female-headed family is confirmed. Indeed, the poor have become more likely to be blacks and hispanics living in the decaying inner cities over time. It is the growth of (predominately black) female-headed families and children in poverty which has been greatest, over the last thirty years (Jencks and Peterson 1991). There has also been growing interest among the homeless poor (Caton 1989; Rossi 1989) The composition of the poor, therefore, has changed as the rate of poverty has increased.

The rise in poverty in the 1980s generated a lively debate on the emergence of an underclass permanently trapped in poverty in the US (see Katz 1989 for a full review). The concept of the underclass was made popular by the journalist Ken Auletta (1982) and was subsequently employed by social scientists from the right and left of the political spectrum (Gilder 1982; Mead 1986; Murray 1984; Wilson 1987). That said, commentators from the right proffered cultural explanations for the persistence of poverty while those from the left promulgated structural accounts of the rise of the underclass. The numerous contributions to the debate cannot be individually evaluated here. Rather, attention will focus on the work of Charles Murray (1984) and Wilson Julius Wilson (1987) since their different arguments capture the main tenants of cultural and structural explanations for the rise of the underclass. Writing from a neo-conservative perspective, Murray's main argument is to be found in his book, *Losing Ground*, which was published in 1984. He sought to address the question of why poverty stood at 13 per cent in 1980 as it had done in 1968 while expenditure on social welfare had quadrupled over the twelve-year period (Murray 1984: 8). What, in other words, had costly social policies bought? Welfare policy, he argued, had largely failed in alleviating poverty as a result of strategic errors. Employing a rational choice theory of action, he argued:

> The most compelling explanation for the marked shift in the fortunes of the poor is that they continued to respond, as they

Table 9.1. Distribution of poverty and risk of poverty for selected groups: USA, 1990

(a) Persons in poverty (%)	
All	13.5
White	66.3
Black	29.1
Hispanic[1]	17.8
Under 18	39.8
18–64	49.1
Over 65	11.0
Central City	42.5
Suburban	30.6
Smaller urban/rural[2]	27.0
In dual-head family[3]	37.7
In female-head family	37.5
Unrelated individuals[4]	22.0

(b) Risk for selected groups (%)	
All	13.5
White	10.7
Black	31.9
Hispanic	28.1
Under 18	20.5
18–64	10.7
Over 65	12.2
White, under 19	15.6
Black, under 18	44.7
Hispanic, under 18	38.2
All families	10.7
White, dual head	5.1
Black, dual head	12.6
Hispanic, dual head	17.5
White, female head	26.8
Black, female head	48.1
Hispanic, female head	48.3

[1] Hispanic may be any race.
[2] Outside metropolitan areas. Generally under 100,000 population.
[3] Includes small number of members of male-headed families.
[4] Living alone or with non-relatives.

Source: US census 1996, quoted in Gilbert and Kahn (1993), Figures 10.2–10.3, pp. 279–81. © D. Gilbert and J Kahn, 1993. Reprinted with the permission of Wadsworth Publishing Co.

always had, to the world as they found it, but that we – meaning the not-poor and un-disadvantaged – had changed the rules of their world. Not of our world, just of theirs. The first effect of the new rules was to make it profitable for the poor to behave in the short term in ways that were destructive in the long term. Their second effect was to mask these long term losses – to subsidize irretrievable mistakes. We tried to provide more for the poor and produced more poor instead. We tried to remove the barriers to escape from poverty, and inadvertently built a trap. (Murray 1984: 9)

In setting 'the rules of the game', social policy had changed the stakes, risks, pay-offs, rewards and satisfactions which governed people's actions.

Examining the impact of social policies on the working-aged poor which he identified as predominantly black, Murray found little evidence of economic and social improvement but high levels of unemployment, illegitimate births, divorce and crime (Murray 1984: 55). He argued, for example, that the labour force participation of young black males had fallen because they had welfare (such as the Negative Income Tax (NIT) scheme) to fall back on as well as crime (Murray 1984: 119). Of greater interest to Murray (1984: 126), however, was the increasing number of teenage black women having illegitimate children which had risen from 17 per cent in 1950 to 48 per cent in 1980 (compared with 2 per cent in 1950 and 11 per cent in 1980 among the white population). Their behaviour, he argued, was the product of the allowances provided under the auspices of Adult Families with Dependent Children (AFDC) initially introduced as part of the New Deal package to help widows with small children but increasingly associated with 'welfare mothers' who had large families at the government's expense (Murray 1984: 17–9). It acted, then, as a disincentive on young men and women to get married by giving women financial security which potential husbands, legally responsible for their children, could not provide. In other words, it undermined work and family life and that of subsequent generations because 'poor, uneducated single teenaged mothers are in a bad position to raise children, however much they may love them' (Murray 1984: 127). Murray concluded that AFDC allowances induced dependency among the 'least industrious, least responsible poor' who cared little for their futures. That is, it induced 'dysfunctional values and behaviours' (Murray 1984: 220). It was for this reason that Murray (1984: 227) called for the 'scrapping of the entire welfare and income support structure for working-aged persons'. Without recourse to the welfare state, the labour behaviour of the underclass would change and this would, in turn, reaffirm family life.

Murray's account of the underclass, his emphasis on the culture of dependency (with echoes of Lewis's (1969) earlier culture of poverty thesis) induced by welfare benefits as the key source of the persistence of poverty and his radical policy prescriptions to scrap public assistance to the poor generated considerable controversy (George and Howards 1991; Katz 1989; Neckerman *et al.* 1988). It was acknowledged that spending on social welfare programmes increased throughout the 1960s and 1970s although it was social security benefits rather than AFDC which had increased the most over the period in question. Moreover, the value of AFDC benefits declined in the 1970s while the number of single-parent families were growing. There was little evidence, therefore, to suggest a causal relationship between the growth of AFDC and the increase in female-headed households (Corcoran *et al.* 1985). Ellwood (1988: 148–50) also found that single mothers used AFDC benefits for a short period of time and only a small proportion had been dependent on AFDC for over ten years. Similarly, drawing on the Panel Study of Income Dynamics (PSID), Duncan *et al.* 1984: 41–2) found that only a quarter of American families were poor for more than a year while 3 per cent of all families (13 per cent of poor families) were in poverty for more than eight years. There was little evidence, therefore, of a permanent underclass emerging in the US for, at most, only 8 per cent of the poor (i.e. 8 per cent of 13 per cent of American families) are locked into long-term poverty from which they cannot escape. Thus, a close scrutiny of empirical research showed little evidence in support of Murray's thesis that welfare benefits had generated a culture of dependency among a growing underclass in the US.

A somewhat different account of the underclass was proposed by W.J.Wilson whose work on the changing black class structure was discussed in Chapter Six above. In his early work on race and class, Wilson noted the growing polarisation between increasingly affluent blacks in professional and managerial jobs living in the comfortable suburbs and those increasingly impoverished blacks faced only with the prospect of unemployment in the decaying inner cities of America. In the context of deteriorating economic and social conditions in the 1980s, Wilson turned his attention to a black underclass increasingly marginalised and isolated in inner-city ghettoes. His book, *The Truly Disadvantaged*, was published in 1987. Wilson focused on economic recession and re-structuring in the 1970s and 1980s as the major cause of the underclass, arguing that changes in the economy led to very high levels of black joblessness. While unemployment among the white population stood at 6.5 per cent in 1984, for example, the rate of unemployment among black and other ethnic groups was more than double that at 14.4 per cent (Wilson 1987: 31). Against the background of the mobility of the black middle class and respectable working class out of

Table 9.2. Unemployment rates, by race, selected years, 1948–84

| | Unemployment Rate | | |
Year	Black and Other Races	White	Black-White Unemployment Ratio
1948	5.9	3.5	1.7
1951	5.3	3.1	1.7
1954	9.0	5.0	2.0
1957	7.9	3.8	2.1
1960	10.2	4.9	2.1
1963	10.8	5.0	2.2
1966	7.3	3.3	2.2
1969	6.4	3.2	2.1
1972	10.0	5.1	2.0
1975	13.8	7.8	1.8
1979	11.9	5.2	2.3
1981	14.2	6.7	2.1
1984	14.4	6.5	2.2

Sources: U.S. Department of Labor, *Employment and Training Report of the President* (Washington, D.C.: Government Printing Office, 1982), and idem, *Employment and Earnings* 32 (Washington, D.C.: Government Printing Office, January 1985).

Notes: The unemployment rate is the percentage of the civilian labor force aged sixteen and over that is unemployed. "Black and other races" is a U.S. Census Bureau designation and is used in those cases where data are not available solely for blacks. However, because about 90 percent of the population so designated is black, statistics reported for this category generally reflect the condition of the black population. The black-white unemployment ratio is the percentage of blacks who are unemployed divided by the percentage of whites who are unemployed.

Source: Wilson (1987), Table 2.4, p. 31. © Wilson, 1987. Reprinted with the permission of University of Chicago Press.

the inner cities, such high levels of unemployment witnessed an increasing concentration of a predominately young disadvantaged population in the ghettoes of so-called 'frostbelt' cities most affected by the decline in manufacturing in the North and West such as New York, Chicago, Detroit and Philidelphia. Wilson went on to argue that such high levels of unemployment had exacerbated social problems in the ghettoes such as violent crime, illegitimate births and female-headed families. There has been, for example, a 41 per cent increase in the number of black children growing up in fatherless families in the 1970s, headed by mothers who have never married and who are trapped in poverty for long periods of time. That is, the decline in stable employment and the poor labour market

status of black men explained the disintegration of poor black families. He
argued:

> the black delay in marriage and the lower rate of remarriage, each
> of which is associated with high percentages of out-of-wedlock
> births and female-headed households, can be directly tied to the
> labor-market status of black males. As we have documented, black
> women, especially young black women, are facing a shrinking
> pool of "marriageable" (i.e. economically stable) men. (Wilson
> 1987: 91)

It is black joblessness rather than welfare payments which accounted for
changes in family structure among black families.

Not surprisingly, Wilson's structuralist account of the rise of the
underclass led to radically different policy prescriptions to those of Murray.
Wilson recommended a 'comprehensive public policy agenda' to improve
the life-chances of disadvantaged groups with a commitment to full
employment to address the problem of joblessness. However, drawing on
the findings of his earlier work, he argued against race-specific policies
because it is the more advantaged families who do well out of initiatives
such as affirmative action rather than the 'truly disadvantaged'. Moreover,
general economic reform is more likely to have the support of the white
population rather than engender hostility. He concluded, 'Accordingly, the
hidden agenda for liberal policy makers is to improve the life-chances of
truly disadvantaged groups such as the ghetto underclass by emphasising
programs to which the more advantaged of all races and class backgrounds
can positively relate (Wilson 1987: 154– 5). Wilson concluded that policy-
makers have to think strategically about building coalitions around major
economic reform which would have advantages for all. The policy implications of his findings, and more generally, the need to build a new political
strategy in the 1990s to combat racial inequality has continued to interest
him (Wilson 1990; 1993).

Wilson's research enjoyed the considerable attention of the media, social
and political commentators and the academic community. He (1989)
subsequently edited a special edition of the ANNALS of the American
Academy of Political and Social Science in which contributors endorsed
his underclass thesis. Drawing on research on blacks who live in Chicago's
ghetto neighbourhoods, Wacquant and Wilson (1989) emphasised the
structural reasons (economic re-structuring) for the rise of the underclass
and the spatial dimension (hyperghettoisation) of joblessness and economic
exclusion in the US. Kasarda (1989) also noted the spatial dimension of
change in that low-level jobs requiring little education have grown in the
suburbs which undereducated blacks in the inner cities have been unable

to exploit without transport. Similarly, Tienda (1989) showed that declining employment opportunities in jobs where Puerto Ricans traditionally worked and the concentration of Puerto Ricans in areas experiencing the brunt of economic re-structuring demonstrated the effects of both economic and social factors on the urban underclass. Other researchers also endorsed Wilson's findings. Sawhill (1989), for example, argued that a strictly-defined underclass was to be found in neighbourhoods with high levels of unemployment, welfare dependency, single parents and school dropouts, the majority of whom were either black or hispanic. It was widely agreed, therefore, that a group of people suffering from multiple deprivations exists in the US.

A somewhat more critical collection of essays on poverty and the underclass was published by Jencks and Peterson (1991), in which Jargowsky and Bane (1991), for example, emphasised that ghetto poverty (defined as census tracts where more than 40 per cent of the population are poor) occurred predominately in the Midwest and Northeast while other parts of the nation witnessed declines in ghetto poverty. In the same collection Kirschenman and Neckerman (1991) noted the importance of racial discrimination against minorities in the workplace neglected in Wilson's research while Jencks (1991: 93–4) cast a critical eye over the usefulness of the concept of the underclass. He argued that the social problems associated with the underclass – unemployment, single parenthood, welfare dependency, drug addition, violent crime and so on – were not necessarily related. Moreover, male joblessness and female single parenthood had got worse but the dropout rate from school had improved while welfare dependency and violent crime had stabilised. Jencks concluded:

> To understand what is happening to those at the bottom of American society, we need to examine their problems one at a time, asking how each has changed and what has caused the change. Instead of assuming that the problems are closely linked to one another, we need to treat their interrelationships as a matter of empirical investigation. When we do that, the relationships are seldom as strong as our class stereotypes would have led us to expect. As a result some problems can become more common while other become less so. (Jencks 1991: 97)

The implication of this argument was that 'we all surely need to change our institutions and attitudes in hundreds of small ways, not one big way' (Jencks 1991: 98). In reply, Wilson (1991: 474) rejected what he saw as Jencks' atheoretical critique of the underclass thesis as a means of capturing 'dual problem of economic position and social location in highly concentrated poverty areas'. Like Gans (1990), however, Wilson (1991: 475) expressed his unease about the way the concept had deflected attention away from important theoretical and empirical issues. More recently, he has preferred the term 'ghetto poor' to link 'a disadvantaged group's position in the labour market and its social environment' (Wilson 1991: 476).

The debate on the underclass has now been usurped by the controversy surrounding Murray's new research on intelligence and class. It is of interest here because the issue of the causes of poverty have been raised once again. In *The Bell Curve* (1994), Herrnstein and Murray argued that those at the top of the class structure have high cognitive abilities (as measured by IQ) while those at the bottom of the class structure are deficient in these endowments and abilities. Moreover, those with high cognitive abilities are associated with socially desirable behaviour while those of low cognitive ability are associated with socially undesirable behaviour (Herrnstein and Murray 1994: 117). That is, those of low intelligence, (independent of economic, social and ethnic background) are the source of America's social problems including poor education, unemployment and idleness, single parenthood, welfare dependency and crime. Focusing specifically on poverty, for example, Herrnstein and Murray argued that it is low intelligence rather than low socio-economic background which is the primary cause of poverty. Analysing data from the National Longitudinal Survey of Youth (NLYS), they found that only 3 per cent of white children born of parents in high class positions were in poverty compared with 24 per cent of white children born of parents in very low classes. Focusing on cognitive classes, they found that only 2 per cent of white children born to very bright parents were found in poverty compared with 30 per cent of white children born to very dull parents. Thus, the evidence showed that, 'Poverty is associated with socio-economic disadvantage and even more strongly with cognitive disadvantage' (Herrnstein and Murray 1994: 132). They then conducted a regression analysis to assess the relative importance of socio-economic status (SES) and intelligence. They found that a person with a high IQ of 130 has only a 2 per cent chance of being in poverty while someone with a low IQ of 70 has a 26 per cent chance of finding themselves in poverty. The effect of parental SES on poverty, however, was not nearly as pronounced which led Hernstein and Murray (1994: 135) to conclude 'Cognitive ability is more important than parental SES in determining poverty'.

The most controversial part of their argument, however, is the thesis that intelligence levels differ among ethnic groups. Herrnstein and Murray argued that there are ethnic differences in cognitive abilities and genetic differences, which differentiate whites, blacks, asians and latinos. The average white person, for example, tests higher than approximately 84 per cent of the black population while the average black person tests higher than only 16 per cent of the white population (Herrnstein and Murray 1994: 269). They argued these differences in ethnic ability go some way to explain the relationship between social problems and IQ. They found, for example, that after controlling for IQ a larger number of blacks than whites graduate from college and enter the professions. Similarly, the differences between blacks and whites diminishes considerably when IQ is taken into account (Herrnstein and Murray 1994: 317). Herrnstein and Murray found that the black-white gap of people in poverty narrowed after controlling for IQ although they had to acknowledge that the probability of being in poverty was still nearly twice as likely for blacks than whites. There were similar findings in relation to male unemployment, marriage rates, illegitimacy, and welfare rates (see Table 9.3). Thus, they found that controlling for IQ reduces the differences between whites and blacks – so that ethnic disparities look less grave – but it does not eradicate the differences completely (Herrnstein and Murray 1994: 326–7). Although these findings somewhat undermined their central thesis, they concluded, 'the evidence presented here should give everyone who writes and talks about ethnic inequalities reason to avoid flamboyant rhetoric about ethnic oppression. Racial and ethnic differences in this country are seen in a new light when cognitive ability is added to the picture' (Herrnstein and Murray 1994: 340),

Finally, turning to the policy implications of their findings, Herrnstein and Murray argued that programmes – like Headstart – aimed at improving the educational performance of the disadvantaged should be scraped in favour of programmes for the gifted. Affirmative action programmes in higher education and the workplace should also be abolished. Overall, they concluded that American society is becoming increasingly polarised as the cognitive elite are largely isolated from the rest of society while those at the bottom of the class structure face a deteriorating quality of life. Herrnstein and Murray predicted the rise of a white underclass as young white women of low intelligence tend to bear children (causing dysgenic pressure in American society) while the position of blacks of low cognitive ability in the inner cities would worsen (Herrnstein and Murray 1994: 522). Thus, an even more spatially concentrated underclass would have to be controlled by an increasingly custodial state. Herrnstein and Murray called for a rejection of equality and a return to individualism to allow people to find their valued places in society while the activities of the federal government should be reallocated to the neighbourhood to make it easier for people to make a living and live a virtuous life. Trying to reduce inequality has been a disaster, they concluded, because inequality of endowments is a reality, and, thus, 'it is time for America once again to try living with inequality' (Herrnstein and Murray 1994: 551).

Table 9.3. Ethnic differences on indicators of social problems

	%	
	Before controlling for IQ	After controlling for IQ
a. The probability of being in poverty		
Whites	7	6
Blacks	26	11
Latinos	18	9
b. The probability of being unemployed for a month or more		
Whites	10	11
Blacks	21	15
Latinos	14	11
c. The probability of having married by age 30		
Whites	78	79
Blacks	54	58
Latinos	76	75
d. The probability that women bear their children out of wedlock		
Whites	12	10
Blacks	62	51
Latinos	23	17
e. The probability that a woman has ever been on welfare		
Whites	13	12
Blacks	49	30
Latinos	30	15

Source: Herrnstein and Murray (1994), pp. 326–32. © 1994 by Richard J. Herrnstein and Charles Murray.

Herrnstein and Murray's work generated a huge media storm. Fraser (1994: 1), for example, described it as 'clearly the most incendiary piece of social science to appear in the last decade or more'. Commentators were highly critical of the empirical findings regarding intelligence (controversially measured by IQ test scores) and class (Sowell 1994; Gardner 1994) arguing that the evidence on the relationship between genetic inheritance, IQ and social class was too weak to predict educational and occupational success or failure. Casting a sceptical eye over the cognitive elite, for example, Wolfe (1994: 116) argued that there was no evidence to suggest that an economic class structure had been superseded by a cognitive class structure. However, it was Herrnstein and Murray's explosive findings on differences in intelligence between blacks and whites and their interpretation of the data suggesting that blacks' low level of intelligence was the cause of their poverty which attracted the most attention. Again, the empirical findings of the research were found seriously wanting (Nisbett 1994). Gould (1994: 19), for example, noted that the authors failed to examine the form and the strength of the relationship between IQ, socio-economic status, poverty and associated undesirable behaviours. As a result, they ignored the variation in social factors explained by IQ and socio-economic status. Moreover, the relationships which they found were weak. The probability of blacks being in poverty was still nearly twice as great as that of whites after controlling for IQ (11 per cent compared with 6 per cent). The empirical evidence, therefore, did not support their argument. More generally, Herrnstein and Murray's work was seen as a form of eugenics claiming to substantiate the inferiority of black people and, in doing so, blaming them for all of America's social problems (Gates 1994). Fraser (1994: 4) argued that, 'At a time when most social indices recording expanding inequalities in American life – not only in income and wealth distribution, but in public and private schooling, in matters of health care, even in our varying capacities to rear the newborn – *The Bell Curve* naturalises those phenomena, turns them into inescapable symptoms of a biological class fate'. In a period of growing inequalities of class and race, in other words, the book had directed criticism away from the powerful, blaming the powerless in society.

Overall the evidence suggests that a significant minority of the American population are poor. The numbers of poor, moveover, have increased in size and they have grown poorer over the last twenty years. The poor are disproportionably black and single-headed families dependent on welfare payments who are isolated in inner-city ghettos where overall poverty levels are high. Whether the poor constitute an underclass who are permanently poor and whose attitudes and behaviour contribute to their poverty, however, is debatable. Research indicates that a very small proportion of the poor are trapped in poverty over a long time span and whether or not the poor have a distinctive culture, it is not the primary cause of poverty. Nor do (controversially measured) low levels of IQ explain why blacks are twice as likely to be poor than their white counterparts. Rather, the poor are principally the victims of economic restructuring which has seen large swathes of both the white and black working class lose their jobs and of an economic system which does not provide jobs for women on which they could raise their children out of poverty. Moreover, they are poor because the American welfare state does not adequately provide for the needy in society. The poor are disproportionately black because they are socially isolated in the ghettos of cities and their isolation compounds their difficulties. The ghetto poor, therefore, is an important indication of the persistence of class in post-industrial America.

THE BRITISH UNDERCLASS

There are two pictures of the poverty rate in Britain. First, examining people living below the income support level (ie: the level of welfare payment for those on income support is a proxy for poverty) indicates that the poor constitute 8 per cent (4.3 million) of the population in 1989. The equivalent figure was 6 per cent in 1979. However, if the poor include those living on as well as below the income support level, the percentage of the population in poverty shoots up to 20 per cent (11.3 million). In 1979, 14 per cent of the equivalent population were poor. Second, when poverty is defined in terms of 50 per cent of average income after housing costs, 22 per cent (12 million) of the population are poor. In 1979, the equivalent percentage was 9 per cent (Oppenheim 1993: 29). A not dissimilar picture emerges, therefore, when poverty is defined in terms of those living on or below the poverty line or in terms of 50 per cent of average income after housing costs (20 per cent and 22 per cent respectively). Moreover, the greatest percentage rise between 1979 and 1989 was in the relative measure of poverty which shows how those with low levels of income compared in relation to the average (which is arguably the best measure of poverty in advanced industrial societies (Townsend 1979)). As in America, the evidence shows that poverty fell in the favourable economic climate of the 1950s and 1960s when the trends towards the equalisation of wealth and income were still apparent. From the mid 1970s, however, poverty started to increase and did so rapidly from the late 1970s and in the 1980s (Pond 1989; Townsend 1979; Walker and Walker 1987). The major reason for the growth in poverty is the growth of unemployment which peaked at over three million people in the early 1980s and which has hovered around the one million mark ever since. While unemployment has grown, however, the value of welfare benefits have declined or been cut so that job loss is closely associated with financial deprivation (Bradshaw and Holmes 1989; Lister 1991; Mack and Lansley 1993; Richie 1990; Townsend and Gordon 1989) The statistics, therefore, indicate growing poverty and inequality in Britain.

Who are the poor? Examining the composition of the poor by family status, the evidence shows that couples with children constituted the largest group in poverty in 1989. In terms of economic status, it is the retired (where the head/spouse is aged 60 or over) who are the group of people living in poverty. However, looking at the risk of poverty by family status and economic status provides a different picture. In terms of family status,

Table 9.4. Unemployment rates by ethnic group, age and sex, 1989–90

%

	Age 16–59/64			Age 16–24			Age 25–44			Age 45–59/64		
	All	M	F	All	M	F	All	M	F	All	M	F
All origins	8	8	7	11	12	10	7	6	7	7	7	5
White	7	8	7	10	11	9	7	6	7	6	7	5
Total ethnic minority	13	14	12	19	20	19	11	11	11	12	13	10
Afro-Caribbean	14	16	13	23	24	23	12	11	12	11	15	6
African Asian	9	8	10	12	9	15	7	6	8	13	11	17
Indian	11	11	12	16	18	13	10	9	11	11	11	13
Pakistani	22	22	25	30	31	30	18	18	18	22	21	—[1]
Bangladeshi	24	24	—	19	15	—	23	26	—	33	33	—
Chinese	7	9	4	7	—	—	9	12	4	2	2	—
African	14	15	13	27	28	26	10	13	7	11	7	—
Other/Mixed	10	9	12	13	14	11	10	8	14	6	5	7

[1] Sample size too small.   *Source:* Jones (1993), Table 5.1, p. 124.

it is lone parents who are at the greatest risk of poverty (50 per cent). In terms of economic status, it is the unemployed and their families who experience the greatest risk of poverty (Oppenheim 1993: 43). Also, the poor have become more likely to be single parents and/or unemployed over time. The overwhelming majority (90 per cent) of lone parents are, of course, women (Glendinning and Millar 1992). Afro-Caribbean women are a large proportion of single parents but they have a high level of employment in the labour market (Bartholomew 1992; Jones 1993). The brunt of unemployment has been born by white men but a disproportionate number of ethnic minorities – notable Pakistani and Bangladeshi men – have experienced unemployment (as Table 3.4 shows) (Brown 1984; Jones 1993; Ward and Cross 1991). Finally, poverty and unemployment is highest in Northern Ireland, Scotland, the North and Wales and in the inner cities such as London, Liverpool and Manchester (MacGregor and Pimlott 1990; Willmott and Hutchinson 1992). Effectively, therefore, those who experience the greatest risk of unemployment are a very similar group of people isolated in the inner cities of America and Britain.

The growth of poverty in the early 1980s led to increasing controversy over 'the creation of a permanent underclass of the poor' (Pond 1989: 76; Brown and Scase 1991). The concept of the underclass was not entirely new to Britain (see Katz 1989 and Morris 1994 for full historical reviews). Giddens (1973;1980) defined a growing underclass, dominated by women and ethnic minorities, concentrated in a secondary labour market of low-paid jobs, subemployment and unemployment (Giddens 1980: 112). He predicted the rise of conflict especially ethnic confrontation, given that ethnic minorities were denied access to the exercise of 'citizenship rights' on a par with white workers in the economic and political sphere' (Giddens 1980: 218). Similarly, Rex and Tomlinson (1979), in their survey of Handsworth in Birmingham, documented the multiple disadvantages of a predominately black underclass in the education, labour and housing markets in comparison to the white working class. They also found evidence of increased radicalism – disaffection with society and conflict with the police (Rex and Tomlinson 1979: 224) and events in the 1980s – notably, the riots in Toxteth (in Liverpool) and Moss Side (in Manchester) – appeared to confirm their predictions of increased ethnic conflict (Rex 1986; 1988 and see his earlier predictions of 'urban riots' Rex and Moore 1967). However, Gallie (1988) cast a sceptical eye over these arguments. While not denying the multiple disadvantages which ethnic minorities face, Gallie concluded that there is a high degree of internal differentiation in patterns of employment and unemployment among ethnic minorities which has militated against collective action and, on the whole, ethnic minorities have been integrated into working-class organisations such as the trade unions and the Labour Party (Gallie 1987: 468; see Jones 1993). Distinct cultural and socio-political community groups have not led to national collective organisations which have usurped other forms of political mobilisation along class lines. The notion of an economically and socially distinct ethnic minority underclass, therefore, was undermined.

The debate on the underclass, however, enjoyed renewed momentum following Murray's account of the emerging British underclass (first published in as a specially commissioned article for the *Sunday Times* (1989) and subsequently re-published by the Institute for Economic Affairs (IEA) (1990)). Describing himself as 'a visitor from a plague area come to see whether the disease is spreading', Murray (1990: 3–4) argued that, 'Britain does have an underclass, still largely out of sight and still smaller than the one in the US. But it is growing rapidly. Over the next decade it will probably become as large (proportionately) as the United States' underclass. It could even become larger'. Again, Murray described an underclass of working-aged healthy people distinctive in terms of their behaviour: namely high rates of illegitimacy, rising crime and drop out from the labour market. He noted, for example, that illegitimacy (concentrated in the lower classes) had risen from 10.6 per cent in 1979 to 25.6 per cent in 1988. Murray blamed the rise of liberal society – softer penalties for crime and the loss of social stigma associated with illegitimacy – and the benefit system which had bred a dependency culture as the main causes of the underclass. Again, he emphasised that all these social problems were interconnected, and that incremental changes would not solve the problem. He advocated 'authentic self-government' if Britain is to avoid the bleak outlook he predicted (Murray 1990: 34–5). Five years later, Murray (1994) reiterated his main predictions. On the basis of rising illegitimacy, for example, he predicted the rise of a 'new rabble' as lower-class communities would degenerate into more crime, more abuse, more child neglect and so on undermining the social order of civil society (Murray 1994: 21–2). Once again, he called for the reduction in welfare – including economic penalties on single women who choose to be pregnant – as a way of reducing the growing underclass in Britain.

Murray's predictions generated widespread comment from politicians, journalists and academics. There was, at least, support for a structuralist account of the underclass if not for Murray's thesis of a culturally distinct underclass. Frank Field, Labour MP for Birkenhead, chairman of the House of Commons Select Committee on Social Security and previously Director of the Child Poverty Action Group (CPAG) argued that an underclass of people – the long-term unemployed, single-parent families and elderly pensioners all dependent on welfare benefits – was increasing in size in the 1980s. He argued that the underclass was the result of growing unemployment, widening class differentials, the exclusion of the very poorest from rapidly rising living standards and a significant change in public attitudes towards those people who have failed to 'make it' in Thatcher's Britain. In other words, Field painted a picture of increasing polarisation in which an emerging underclass 'loses out' and is left behind as a marginalised and isolated minority (Field 1989: 6). A similar position was taken by *The Guardian* and *Observer* journalist Melanie Phillips who argued that academic denial and ignorance was 'permitting the interrelated problems of our most disadvantaged citizens to fester and be transmitted down through our generations to even more disadvantaged children' (Phillips 1992). Indeed, she has increasingly expressed her concern about the growth of single parenthood across all social classes which leaves children having to face emotional chaos and fragmented lives (Phillips 1994: 60).

Academics, however, did not dismiss the underclass thesis out of hand (Dahrendorf 1987; Halsey 1987; Pahl 1988; Runciman 1990; Saunders 1990). Dahrendorf (1987), for example, charted the rise of an underclass in Britain. He argued that economic trends – the decline in manufacturing employment, the high cost of services in countries with 'sticky' wages and unemployment – explained the rise of the underclass. He estimated that it accounts for approximately 5% of the population whose members suffers from an accumulation of deprivations such as poor education, limited employment opportunities and inadequate housing. As in America, they are concentrated in the inner cities and many of them are black (Dahrendorf 1987: 13). For the young members of the underclass, their life-style embraces petty crime, crime against property and football hooliganism since they no longer live according to the norms of society. They, along with immigrants and the elderly, have found themselves excluded from the rest of society – by both institutions and people – in which the majority prosper. They have been denied citizenship in a society in which 'citizenship has become an exclusive rather than an inclusive status' (Dahrendorf 1987: 14). The implications for social policy, Dahrendorf argued, are far reaching. It is important, he emphasised to raise skills and general levels of education to abolish dependency and generate self-sufficiency. He also stressed the importance of local initiatives to redevelop deprived areas (citing American examples) in which local people become involved. It is imperative, therefore, that there is a 'new search for citizenship' for all, or otherwise, Dahrendorf warned, the consequences for the 'moral hygiene of British society' could be severe (Dahrendorf 1987).

In his review of social trends since the Second World War, Halsey (1987) also discussed an excluded minority. He argued that 'a new form of polarisation' is in evidence in that the gap in the distribution of income has increased. The bottom fifth of households, for example, dropped their share from 0.8 to 0.3 per cent and the top fifth moved up from 44.4 to 48.6 per cent between 1976 and 1984 (Halsey 1987: 17). Similar processes of social division could be seen in terms of wealth, housing and spatial polarisation in that 'deprived people (are) being left in the urban areas as the successful ones move out to middle Britain (Halsey 1987: 19). Thus, he effectively distinguished between 'a prosperous majority in secure and increasingly well remunerated employment' and a 'depressed minority of the unemployed, the sick and the unsuccessful ethnic minorities' (Halsey 1987: 17). Against the backdrop of Britain's changing economic fortunes, he concluded that:

> a pattern has emerged of a more unequal society as between a majority in secure attachment to a still prosperous country and a minority in marginal economic and social conditions, the former moving into the suburban locations of the newer economy of a 'green and pleasant land', the latter tending to be trapped into the old provincial industrial cities and their displaced fragments of peripheral council housing estates. (Halsey 1987: 19)

More recently, he has expressed his concerns about the growth of families without fathers (see Dennis and Erdos 1993) and the implications of the collapse of the family on social order.

Pahl (1984; 1988) and Saunders (1990a; 1990b) also commented on the trends towards polarisation between a relatively secure middle mass and an increasingly deprived minority. Pahl (1984), for example, distinguished between affluent home-owning work-rich households and poor council tenant work-poor households (Pahl 1984: 314). The trend towards polarisation results primarily from changes in work but they can also be attributed to the growing importance of home ownership and spatial polarisation. Similarly, Saunders (1990a; 1990b) discussed the growth of the underclass with reference to 'residualisation of the bottom stratum' (Saunders 1990a: 319)). He defined the underclass as 'a stratum of people who are generally poor, unqualified and irregularly or never employed. This underclass is disproportionately recruited today from among Afro-Caribbeans, people living in the north, those who are trapped in run down council estates or in single-parent families' (Saunders 1990b: 121). He argued that the underclass has four defining features: interrelated multiple deprivation, social marginalisation and exclusion, dependency on state benefits and, finally, a culture of fatalism embracing resignation and apathy. In time, Saunders noted, a minority 'grows accustomed to its dependency' which, in turn, contributes to its predicament. (Saunders 1990b: 125). Like Dahrendorf, Saunders argued that the underclass is likely to be a permanent feature of British society. Turning to policy initiatives, he called for a 'radical re-think' in social policy to alleviate the underclass and argued that they should be 'empowered' to make consumer choices through vouchers schemes for education, health and so forth. Not unlike Murray, therefore, Saunders called for a range of policies which lie outside current welfare state provisions rather than enhancing the declining value of welfare support.

Finally, Runciman (1990) addressed the issue of how many classes there are in contemporary Britain. Defining class in terms of economic power (or lack of it) according to three criteria of ownership, control and marketability, he concluded that there are seven classes including an underclass which consists of between 5–10 per cent of the population. He emphasised that the underclass does not include all those who occupy disadvantaged positions in the labour market but includes 'those members of British society whose roles place them more or less permanently at the economic level where benefits are paid by the state to those unable to participate in the labour market at all' (Runciman 1990: 388). He noted that many of its members are from ethnic minorities and single parents (many of whom are members of ethnic minorities). However, he stressed, ' it is not ethnicity or gender as such which defines their class position. They are typically the long-term unemployed . . . (and) they are 'the poor' of today'(Runciman 1990: 388). It is this institutional exclusion from the labour market (and subsequent dependency on welfare benefits for income support) that explains why members of the underclass have no economic power either in terms of ownership, control or marketability. This restricted definition of the underclass has found favour with others (Smith 1992).

However, Murray's thesis was also subject to fierce criticism (Brown 1990; Walker 1990; Deakin 1990; Alcock 1994; David 1994; Slipman 1994). Critics argued that the concept of the underclass was theoretically ill-defined and empirically imprecise (Brown and Scase 1991; Dean and Taylor-Gooby 1992). The analysis of single mothers, for example, overlooked the fact that the majority (75 per cent) of them were married before and only a quarter were single never-married mothers (Brown 1990: 43; Ermisch 1990; Hardey and Crow 1991). It also overlooked the fact that single mothers are less economically active than married mothers (49 per cent compared with 66 per cent in 1990) because they do not have childcare support. Nor is part-time employment a feasible option for those supporting a family on their own (Bartholomew *et al.* 1992). It was also noted that Murray's argument was tantamount to 'blaming the victim' for their poverty and distinguishing between the deserving and undeserving poor. Such a discourse, it was noted, has a 'long undistinguished history' in Britain (MacNicol 1987) and parallels were drawn with the 'cycle of deprivation' thesis promulgated by Keith Joseph in the 1970s. In an evaluation of the thesis, all the evidence suggested that poverty *per se* rather than the attitudes and behaviour of the poor accounted for the transmission of economic and social disadvantage from one generation to another (Brown and Madge 1982; Coffield *et al.* 1981; Rutter and Madge 1977). Bagguley and Mann (1992: 124) argued that the concept of the underclass 'is a set of ideological beliefs held by certain group among the upper and middle classes (which) helps them sustain certain relations of domination of class, patriarchy and race towards the unemployed, single mothers and blacks through the formation of state welfare policies'. Dean (1991: 33) also concluded that the underclass thesis has been used for 'dramatic effect' in an analysis of economic and social trends in the 1980s and 1990s.

Westergaard (1992; 1995) also concluded that the concept of the underclass was a 'colourful shorthand' of these trends which has been put to rhetorical use (Westergaard 1992). He levelled two further criticisms at the British version of the underclass thesis. First, he was critical of the crude dualistic model of the labour market which underpinned the thesis. Echoing Gallie's criticism of Giddens, Westergaard rejected the argument that employment opportunities have been structured to create a privileged elite on the one hand and a reserve army of labour on the other. Despite the popularity of the distinction between primary and secondary workers (Atkinson and Meager 1985; Hakim 1987), the empirical evidence suggests that employers have not actively recruited core and peripheral workers in response to increased competition (Hunter and MacInnes 1992; McGregor and Sproull 1992). Rather, the labour market is segmented along much more complex lines as the result of employer strategies, trade union action, the state and institutional factors (Burchill and Rubery 1989; Rubery 1988). Second, Westergaard (1992: 578) argued that the identification of the underclass rests on its separation from a classless majority 'included in society by broad common participation in rising prosperity' which is highly problematic. The data on income distribution shows that substantial gains which were made by the top earners have not been shared equally by those further down the occupational ladder. The growth of low pay in the 1980s and 1990s is stark, for example, when the statistics show that in 1992 the poorest tenth of men working in manual jobs earned 62.8 per cent of average (median) earnings compared with 68.3 per cent in 1979 (*The New Review* 1992). The boundary between the underclass and the prosperous middle mass, therefore, is far from clear. Westergaard (1992: 580) concluded that 'there is no such sharp, single line towards the bottom of the pile; and some lines of division appreciably further up have become all the more pronounced with the concentration of gains towards the top'. The evidence on wealth and income distribution and a range of other indicators showed that class inequalities had deepened rather than been eclipsed.

Against the background of high unemployment in Britain, a wide range of empirical research published in the 1990s has directly or indirectly challenged the underclass thesis with reference to the unemployed and long-term unemployed (Allatt and Yeandle 1991; Dean and Taylor-Gooby 1992; Jordan *et al.* 1992; McLaughlin *et al.* 1989). Allatt and Yeandle's (1991: 121) study of the young unemployed and their families in Newcastle-upon-Tyne in the North East found that young people were desperate to work because of the scarcity of jobs. They found little evidence of family breakdown since the family played an important role in helping the young unemployed to 'survive' their experiences and maintain their hopes and expectations for better times. It was a source of strength in sustaining the threatened values of hard work, rewards and justice (Allatt and Yeandle 1991: 140). Jordan *et al.*'s (1992) study of low-income families in Exeter in the South West found little evidence of extensive criminality among the unemployed either. While there was some 'bending of the rules' of the benefit system, there was a strong moral code as to why they engaged in informal work and the extent to which they did so. That is, they justified small amounts of undeclared cash work with reference to their family responsibilities in periods when their financial circumstances were especially dire. McLaughlin *et al.* (1991) also found that claimants were not passive victims, happy to accept their dependency on the welfare state, but active in their resilience and resourcefulness in coping with the circumstances in which they found themselves. Finally, in their study of social security claimants in Kent and South London, Dean and Taylor-Gooby (1992) found that the harsh conditions for claiming 'compounded the strains upon the expectations of social security claimants' (Dean and Taylor-Gooby 1992: 123). They found that, 'the social security system does not foster a dependency culture but it constructs, isolates and supervises a heterogeneous population of reluctant dependants (Dean and Taylor-Gooby 1992: 125).

Drawing on a local survey in Hartlepool in the North East, Morris (1995) also rejected the underclass thesis. Examining the employment histories of her predominately working-class sample, Morris and Irwin found a variety of relationships to the labour market – long-term unemployment, temporary bouts of employment and unemployment and relatively secure employment – not encapsulated in the concept. There was no clear division between the employed and unemployed (See also Harris 1987; Payne and Payne 1993). That said, they found that there was a tendency for skilled workers (especially those with credentials) to have chequered careers while skilled workers (without credentials) and unskilled workers were prone to long-term unemployment. They concluded;

> If long-term unemployment is a feature of this class position it seems inappropriate to assign them to a separate class location, that of the underclass. To separate those affected from their position when in work is to disguise the source of their vulnerability.
> (Morris and Irwin 1992a: 411)

Irwin and Morris (1993) also found little evidence of a dependency culture among the female partners of the sample who had little opportunity to earn a wage sufficient for household maintenance. Examining the social segregation of the long-term unemployed, Morris (1992) found that employment and unemployment was concentrated among family, friendship and neighbourhood networks. Given that informal means of getting a job were paramount (most notably from someone in employment), the long-term unemployed were disadvantaged in the job search process. Thus, rather than exhibit any specific cultural predispositions towards work, it was informal patterns of association which determined success or failure in the search for employment. Similarly, Morris and Irwin (1992b) found evidence of informal exchange with kin and friends across all employment status groups thereby undermining the notion of cultural distinctiveness still further. Overall, Morris (1995: 132) concluded that the residual concept of the underclass 'runs the risk of defining unemployment as in some sense separate from class' and excludes rather than includes the unemployed in the analysis of social class.

Finally, survey data from the Social Change and Economic Life Initiative (SCELI) (especially the 1986 Work Attitudes Survey and 1987 Household and Community Survey) indicate that the concept of the underclass is problematic in relation to the unemployed. Gershuny and Marsh (1993: 66) found that there has been 'a substantial growth in the social stratification of unemployment'. That is, unemployment is increasingly associated with manual working-class men and especially young manual workers in the 1970s and 1980s (see also Ashton 1986). They found no evidence of an 'unemployment underclass' of people permanently out of the labour market. However, they found that unemployment is concentrated among a small group of people in distinctive geographical and occupational locations. In this respect, the rise of unemployment has witnessed the emergence of 'unemployment careers' (Gershuny and Marsh (1993: 113). Turning to attitudes to work, Gallie and Vogler (1993: 124–6) found that the unemployed are more committed to employment than those in work. Two-thirds (66 per cent) of employees and the self-employed would continue working even if there was no financial necessity compared with three-quarters (77 per cent) of the unemployed. There was some variation between the different types of the unemployed ranging from 81 per cent among claimant seekers to 82 per cent among non-claimant seekers to a drop of 64 per cent among the non-seekers. However, the non-seekers were found to be older workers with problems of ill-health and younger mothers without adequate childcare support (Gallie and Vogler 1993a: 152). They also found that attitudes to work did not determine the position of the unemployed and nor did they determine how long it took them to find work. Gallie and Vogler concluded:

> Rather our evidence points to the importance for job chances of the availability of particular types of work, of the resources which can be provided by the household to facilitate job search, and of the structural misfit between the low qualifications possessed by the unemployed and the sharp rise in qualifications required by the changing nature of work in industry. (Gallie and Vogler 1993a: 152–3)

There was no evidence of a distinctive culture, therefore, among the unemployed which might contribute to their predicament.

Evidence was found to show that a husband's unemployment does have an effect on his wife's participation in the labour market. Davies et al. (1993) found that women married to unemployed men are often unemployed

Table 9.5. Employment commitment by type of unemployment (percentage)

Employment Commitment	Employed and self-employed	Unemployed				Non-employed	
		Claimant seekers	Claimant non-seekers	Non-claimant seekers	Total	Will return	Total
All Work somewhere	66	81	64	82	77	68	67
Remain jobless	34	19	36	19	23	32	33
	100	100	100	100	100	100	100
Significance .001 Gamma 0.2	(no.) (4,234)	(419)	(149)	(134)	(703)	421	(438)
Men Work somewhere	68	82	66	83	79	87	88
Remain jobless	32	19	34	17	21	13	13
	100	100	100	100	100	100	100
Significance 0.03 Gamma 0.05	(no.) (2,471)	(300)	(71)	(37)	(48)	(47)	(51)
Women Work somewhere	63	78	61	81	75	66	65
Remain jobless	38	22	39	19	25	34	35
	100	100	100	100	100	100	100
Significance 0.0001 Gamma 0.2	(no.) (1,764)	(119)	(78)	(97)	(294)	374	(386)

Source: Gallie and Vogler (1993a), Table 4.4, p. 125.

themselves so that the couple is dependent on the state. They found that married women are likely to give up work after approximately a year when their husbands would transfer from insurance based unemployment benefit to means-tested benefit. It is at this juncture that what amounts to a tax on the wife's earnings becomes very high. However, the incidence of 'cross-couple state dependence' is confined to areas of high unemployment where the prospects of re-employment are not very high. Long-term rather than short-term unemployment, in other words, is anticipated. The system of social security, therefore, did influence labour market behaviour in this respect (Davies *et al.* 1993: 184). Gallie and his colleagues (1993a: 262) found no evidence of a 'withdrawal into passivity and social isolation' in terms of patterns of leisure and sociability among the unemployed. They found comparable leisure patterns between the employed and unemployed although the unemployed did substitute expensive for less expensive leisure pursuits over time. There were some differences between the patterns of sociability between the employed and the unemployed but the differences were in terms of its nature rather than its extensiveness. As Morris (1995) also found, the unemployed were restricted to social networks whose other members were also unemployed. Gallie *et al.* (1993a: 263) concluded, 'They therefore had weaker social support systems to help with both psychological and material problems. These networks may be a significant factor locking the unemployed into a situation of labour disadvantage'.

Finally, the extent to which the underclass might be described as politically distinctive needs to be considered. Previously, Gallie (1988) had argued that the unemployed do not have a distinct socio-political identity. The experience of long-term unemployment is one of considerable financial deprivation which 'engenders a loss of sense of self-efficacy' (Gallie 1988: 471). This view was confirmed by Bagguley in a case study of an unemployed workers' centre in Brighton, who argued: 'Whilst the politically quiescent unemployed express a series of ideological beliefs to a limited degree, most important is the informed and rationalised fatalism about the efficacy of collective action. This is the major reason for the con-temporary quiescence of the unemployed (1991: 203). Similarly, Heath's (1992) analysis of the British Election Studies found little evidence of distinctive political attitudes and behaviour among the unemployed. Using data from SCELI, Gallie and Vogler (1993a) examined the extent to which changes in labour market conditions undermined collectivism and led to a polarisation of the political attitudes and behaviour of the economically secure and insecure. First of all, Gallie and Vogler established that those in insecure labour market conditions suffered from a number of disadvantages including financial difficulties, cuts in standards of living, a drop in the type and quality of housing psychological and physical ill-health (1993a:

334). The evidence showed that the unemployed and insecure low paid workers were more in favour of high benefits for the unemployed, more expenditure on council housing and a more redistributive tax and benefit system than the employed. There was a clear link, therefore, between unemployment and collectivism. Gallie and Vogler (1993a: 329) also found that the implications of labour market experience for collectivism varied considerably depending on people's political allegiances. That is, labour market experience had a stronger effect on the Conservatives than it did Labour. Gallie and Vogler (1993a:329) concluded that 'The effect of labour market experience is sharpest on those that have little exposure to more radical political ideologies'. Overall, however, they found no evidence of political polarisation as a result of the growth of collectivism among the securely employed in the mid 1980s.

Overall, therefore, the evidence suggests that there is a distinct group of people who have suffered the burden of unemployment and its associated poverty. The experience of unemployment increases the chances of further experiences of unemployment although that is not to say that a group of people are permanently out of the labour market. They often face cumulative disadvantages in terms of health, housing, psychological depression and so forth. However, there was little evidence to suggest that the unemployed are responsible for their predicament as implied by exponents of cultural explanations of the underclass. Their attitudes do not explain why they have been unable to find work. Most of the claimant unemployed were found to be actively seeking work and remarkably flexible about what job they would take. Gallie and his colleagues concluded that the unemployed do form a distinctive group at the bottom of the class structure who suffer from multiple deprivations but it is not their fault that they are at the bottom. The results, Gallie *et al.* suggested:

> that people may be caught in a spiral of disadvantage in which small events may have large repercussions. Through an initial accident of job loss, a person may get trapped in a cycle of further unemployment. Unemployment frequently leads to depression, family break-up, and social isolation, which in turn makes the next job more difficult to find. After the event, we may identify a group with a distinct life-style at the bottom of the heap, but they were not destined to be there, and under different labour market conditions . . . they would not have been there. (Gallie and Marsh 1993a: 30)

The concept of the underclass, therefore, has not proved a useful instrument for understanding the position of the poor in the class structure. What the evidence does show is that the life-chances of members of the working

Table 9.6. Labour market experience and items in the index of collectivism

Percentage claiming that	Unemployed		Insecure low-paid		Secure low-paid		Insecure higher-paid		Secure higher-paid		Self-employed		Insecure non-employed		Secure non-employed		Significance
	No	%	No	%	No	%	No	%	No	%	No	%	No	%	No	%	
Benefits for the unemployed are too low and cause hardship	157	83	117	62	168	57	81	65	273	59	41	45	48	78	141	61	0.01
The government should spend a great deal more on unemployment benefit	118	60	94	49	121	39	59	48	151	32	23	24	33	52	93	38	0.01
The government should spend a great deal more on council-house-building	132	68	128	70	169	53	74	58	224	47	33	33	37	63	119	50	0.01
Those with high incomes should pay most towards the cost of the welfare state	144	76	135	71	224	70	102	81	336	71	53	56	35	59	152	63	0.01
Increased state expenditure should be paid for by taxing the rich	123	64	121	64	187	58	70	54	256	55	44	44	29	50	136	55	0.05
Agree strongly that rich people should pay a greater share of taxes than they do now	86	44	71	37	112	35	48	38	135	28	20	20	25	42	71	28	0.01

Source: Gallie and Vogler (1993b), Table 10.10, p. 318–9.

class – to some extent between skilled and unskilled workers – have polarised in the last twenty years.

Finally, it is important to consider direct comparisons of poverty in America and Britain. Is poverty and inequality greater in the US than in Britain or vice versa? This question raises issues about the distribution of wealth and income which were previously discussed in Chapter Five (see also Atkinson 1993; Danziger and Gottchalk 1993; Papadimitriou and Wolff 1993). The trend towards the equalisation of wealth and income evident from the 1920s came to a halt in the 1970s and wealth and income became more unequal again in the 1980s and 1990s in both nations. Recent comparative research indicates that wealth is now more highly concentrated in the US than in Britain or other European nations. This finding led Wolff (1995: 21) to conclude that the situation between the 'new' and 'old' nations has 'completely reversed' so that European nations rather than the United States are the lands of opportunity and equality. Similarly, O'Higgins and his associates (1989) found that income inequality is now greater in the US than other industrialised economies including Britain while research on OECD countries (Atkinson *et al.* 1995) also shows that the US is the most unequal society in terms of income distribution although the US and the UK income distribution became notably worse over the 1980s. On the basis of this evidence, therefore, America is a more unequal society than Britain (see also George and Howards 1991; Scott 1994b).

The best source of comparative research on poverty, inequality and income distribution is the Luxembourg Income Study (LIS) (Smeeding *et al.* 1990). Data are held on seven nations (Canada, Israel, Norway, Sweden, West Germany) including America (employing data from the 1979 Current Population Survey) and Britain (using data from the 1979 Family Expenditure Survey). In terms of comparative income inequality, the United States (along with Israel and West Germany) was found to have the highest degree of inequality, the United Kingdom (and Canada and Norway) were less unequal nations while Sweden stood out as a significantly more equal nation in terms of share of income of the top and bottom quintiles (See Table 9.7). In terms of the distribution of family gross income among quintiles of families, for example, the lowest quintile had a 3.8 per cent share of income in the US compared with 4.9 per cent in the UK while the top quintile had a 44.5 per cent share in the US compared with 40.8 per cent in the UK. The share of the bottom quintile of income was especially low in the US in comparison to all the other nations of the research. Even after the effects of tax were considered, inequalities in the share of net income remained between the US and Britain (Smeeding *et al.* 1990:

Table 9.7. The distribution of income in seven nations

	Quintile shares (per cent) of income						
	Canada	United States	United Kingdom	West Germany	Sweden	Norway	Israel
Distribution of family gross income among quintiles of families							
Lowest quintile	4.6	3.8	4.9	4.4	6.6	4.9	4.5
Second quintile	11.0	9.8	10.9	10.2	12.3	11.4	10.5
Third quintile	17.7	16.6	18.2	15.9	17.2	18.4	16.5
Fourth quintile	25.3	25.3	25.3	22.6	25.0	25.5	24.9
Top quintile	41.4	44.5	40.8	46.9	38.9	39.8	43.6
Gini coefficient (%)	37.4	41.2	36.5	42.9	32.9	35.6	39.5
Revised West German gini				41.4			
Distribution of family net income among quintiles of families							
Lowest quintile	5.3	4.5	5.8	5.0	8.0	6.3	6.0
Second quintile	11.8	11.2	11.5	11.5	13.2	12.8	12.1
Third quintile	18.1	17.7	18.2	15.9	17.4	18.9	17.9
Fourth quintile	24.6	25.6	25.0	21.8	24.5	25.3	24.5
Top quintile	39.7	41.0	39.5	45.8	36.9	36.7	39.5
Gini co-efficient	34.8	37.0	34.3	40.9	29.2	31.1	33.8
Revised West German gini				38.9			
Distribution of family equivalent gross income among quintiles of persons							
Lowest quintile	6.7	5.1	7.2	7.9	9.4	8.1	6.1
Second quintile	12.6	11.4	13.0	12.1	14.6	13.6	10.3
Third quintile	17.5	17.1	17.9	16.0	18.5	17.9	15.9
Fourth quintile	24.0	24.2	23.7	21.3	23.3	23.4	23.7
Top quintile	39.2	42.1	37.5	43.4	34.2	37.0	44.0
Gini coefficient (%)	32.7	37.1	29.7	36.3	24.9	28.9	38.2
Revised West German gini				35.2			
Distribution of family equivalent net income among quintiles of persons							
Lowest quintile	7.6	6.1	9.0	7.5	10.6	9.9	7.5
Second quintile	13.3	12.8	13.5	12.7	16.1	14.8	11.7
Third quintile	17.9	18.1	18.0	16.1	19.1	18.4	16.8
Fourth quintile	23.8	24.4	23.4	20.7	23.1	22.9	23.7
Top quintile	37.4	38.6	36.1	43.0	31.1	34.1	40.3
Gini co-efficient	29.9	32.6	27.3	35.5	20.5	24.3	33.3
Revised West German gini				34.0			

Source: Smeeding *et al.* (1990), Table 2.2, pp. 34–5.

30). Smeeding and his colleagues (1990: 59) also found that the US has the greatest degree of poverty-creating inequality (along with Israel) followed by the UK (and Canada) while West Germany, Norway and Sweden have the least degree of poverty-creating inequality.

Smeeding *et al.* (1990) then went on to look at the composition of the poor and the likelihood of members of these different groups being in poverty. They focused on three groups: single parents, elderly, (both of whom are influenced by the social policy of the nation in question) and the two-parent families with children (whose fate is primarily determined by the vagaries of the labour market). They found that two-parent families who are poor in Britain tend to have larger families. Elderly families are more prone to poverty in the UK than in the US in that over half (48 per cent) were to be found in the bottom 20 per cent income quintile in the former in comparison with only a quarter (25.4 per cent) in the latter. America had over half (56.4 per cent) of single-parent families in the bottom quintile compared with just under half (45.3 per cent) in the UK. These high rates were only matched by Canada while the remaining nations had lower levels of single-parent families in poverty (Smeeding *et al.* 1990: 64–5). Examining the ability of the transfer system to prevent families falling into poverty, Smeeding *et al.* found that a high proportion of the elderly are pre-transfer poor. The high proportion of single-parent families who are pre-transfer poor in the US and UK, they argued, 'reflect low earnings and poor private alimony/child support arrangements'. Pre-transfer poverty among two-parent families was seen as a reflection of low wages and high unemployment. The United States is poor at pulling people out of poverty in comparison to Britain and all other countries of the study. Less than 20 per cent of pre-transfer poor persons in two-parent families are pulled out of poverty since welfare assistance is not 'enough to prevent widespread poverty among parents and children in families which experience long-term unemployment or low wages or both' (Smeeding *et al.* 1990: 69). Finally, in terms of the poverty gap, they found after transfers the average poor family in the US is 39.9 per cent away from the poverty line compared with the average UK poor families which is only 16 per cent away from its poverty line. The depth of poverty, therefore, is greater in the US than the UK.

Overall, Smeeding and his colleagues concluded that the US has the highest overall poverty rates followed by Israel, Canada, the UK, West Germany, Norway and Sweden. Poverty among the elderly is more notable in Britain than the US. Both nations have a high proportion of single-parent families in poverty who are not well served by welfare programmes. They also have high levels of two-parent families in poverty as a result of weak income support systems (US) or low earnings potential (UK). Overall, Smeeding and his associates (1990: 73) concluded that poverty rates varied between the seven nations as a result of three factors. First, expenditure on income transfers as a percentage of GDP help explain the overall effectiveness of the transfer system in alleviating poverty. Second, the universality of the transfer system effects poverty among certain groups. Third, the structure of pension schemes and of income are important in determining rates of income poverty across nations. Thus, the lack of universal income maintenance programmes – especially for children in two-parent families – goes a long way to explain why the US has the highest poverty rates of these seven advantaged industrialised nations while low wages and wide wage differentials explain the medium level of poverty in Britain.

More recent statistics largely confirm Smeeding *et al.*'s picture. Townsend's (1993) international analysis of poverty that America and Britain have experienced an exceptional trend towards polarisation. In terms of the share of total disposable income, he found that the rich 20 per cent in the US increased their share from 39 per cent in 1979 to 42.1 per cent in 1989 (an increase of 3.1 per cent) while the richest 20 per cent in the UK saw their share increased from 36 per cent in 1979 to 42 per cent in 1988 (an increase of 6 per cent). Turning to the poorest 20 per cent in the US, their share of total disposable income dropped from 6.4 per cent in 1979 to 5.6 per cent in 1989 (a decrease of 0.8 per cent) while in the UK the poorest 20 per cent saw their percentage share from 9 per cent in 1979 to 8 per cent in 1988 (a decrease of 1 per cent) (Townsend 1993: 15). In both nations, therefore, the rich became richer and the poor became poorer with British exhibiting the greatest percentages changes in each direction. That said, the lower share of total disposable income held by the poorest 20 per cent in the US in comparison to Britain confirms Smeeding *et al.*'s point that the depth of poverty is greater in the US than Britain. It is experienced most severely, as the Luxembourg team also noted, by families with children which has heightened concern about child poverty in the US. Overall, Townsend (1993: 3) argued that poverty is deep-seated in rich and poor countries and, therefore, poverty had to be understood in an international context and in terms of international trends.

Finally, comparative research (Kluegal *et al.* 1995; Marshall *et al.* 1996) has recently been conducted which determined whether or not the poor and long-term unemployed in America and Britain are culturally distinct from the rest of the population. Are they more fatalistic than their more affluent counterparts? Marshall and his associates asked the poor (defined at the bottom 5 per cent income group) and the long-term unemployed (unemployment spanning more than a year) a range of questions relating to such issues of fatalism and political disillusionment (see Table 9.8). The evidence showed there was little difference in the attitudes of the poor and the non-poor or the employed or unemployed in either the US or Britain.

Table 9.8. Fatalistic attitudes by poverty and by long term unemployment in the UK and the USA

(a)		Very often	Often	Sometimes	Rarely	Never
			(percentage by row, excludes 'don't know')			

Rich people are rich as a result of the economic system allowing them to take unfair advantages

		Very often	Often	Sometimes	Rarely	Never
UK	Poverty	24	26	26	10	02
	Non-poverty	15	29	36	14	02
	Employed	16	29	35	15	02
	Unemployed	19	22	31	12	03
USA	Poverty	23	27	26	15	02
	Non-poverty	13	25	38	21	02
	Employed	12	25	39	20	03
	Unemployed	17	22	49	12	00

Rich people are rich as a result of their having the right connections

		Very often	Often	Sometimes	Rarely	Never
UK	Poverty	45	36	12	04	02
	Non-poverty	32	45	20	01	00
	Employed	33	42	21	01	00
	Unemployed	39	39	16	01	00
USA	Poverty	44	34	18	03	00
	Non-poverty	31	44	22	03	00
	Employed	30	45	22	03	00
	Unemployed	49	27	24	00	00

(b)		Strongly agree	Somewhat agree	Neither	Somewhat disagree	Strongly disagree

People get rewarded for their effort

		Strongly agree	Somewhat agree	Neither	Somewhat disagree	Strongly disagree
UK	Poverty	06	37	14	29	12
	Non-poverty	03	45	16	35	05
	Employed	03	41	16	35	05
	Unemployed	07	49	08	22	14
USA	Poverty	21	46	01	16	12
	Non-poverty	13	58	07	17	05
	Employed	13	57	01	16	12
	Unemployed	17	46	07	17	05

People get rewarded for their intelligence and skill

		Strongly agree	Somewhat agree	Neither	Somewhat disagree	Strongly disagree
UK	Poverty	09	46	12	24	07
	Non-poverty	05	51	13	26	06
	Employed	05	48	13	26	06
	Unemployed	11	50	10	20	08
USA	Poverty	23	57	02	11	05
	Non-poverty	15	59	06	15	03
	Employed	16	59	07	15	04
	Unemployed	24	56	05	12	00

Table 9.8 (cont.)

(b)		Strongly agree	Somewhat agree	Neither	Somewhat disagree	Strongly disagree
		Public officials don't care much what people like me think				
UK	Poverty	33	33	13	14	02
	Non-poverty	18	47	12	20	02
	Employed	19	46	13	20	01
	Unemployed	30	27	19	15	04
USA	Poverty	25	33	07	20	12
	Non-poverty	21	44	08	20	06
	Employed	20	43	10	20	07
	Unemployed	22	49	02	12	15
		In elections in this country, voters have a real choice				
UK	Poverty	25	39	07	17	09
	Non-poverty	21	39	08	22	10
	Employed	19	36	10	25	10
	Unemployed	20	37	04	26	08
USA	Poverty	34	31	03	14	17
	Non-poverty	23	38	04	19	16
	Employed	23	39	03	18	15
	Unemployed	32	29	02	20	17

Source: Marshal *et al.* (1966), Tables IV and V, pp. 34–6.

While both disadvantaged groups were more prone to give the 'underclass view', the differences were relatively minor. Thus, there was little evidence of distinctive levels of fatalism, defeatism, mistrust or disillusionment among the disadvantaged in comparison to the advantaged in either nation (Marshall *et al.* 1996: 35). This finding was also upheld among the social groups most closely associated with the underclass; namely, single mothers, poorly-educated young people, ethnic minorities and the exceptionally long-term unemployed (two years or more) (Marshall *et al.* 1996: 39). They concluded that the concept of the underclass is fundamentally flawed with respect to either America or Britain. Marshall *et al.* (1996) have been criticised (Crompton 1996; Morris and Scott 1996) for elements in their analysis such as their dependence on income categories as a proxy indicator for the poor, their failure to identify the structural boundaries of the underclass from other social classes and their refutation of a simplistic argument on cultural distinctions arising out of more complex debates on the underclass. Their work, in other words, might offer an important empirical challenge to the underclass thesis but it does not provide a theoretical argument in relation to the concept of the underclass. These issues, however, raise question about the nature of class analysis which is beyond the remit of this chapter and which will be considered in the concluding chapter.

CONCLUSION

In this chapter, we have seen that poverty and inequality grew in America and Britain in the 1980s and 1990s. The evidence suggests that a sizeable minority of the American and British populations (as much as 20 per cent in each nation) are poor and they have grown poorer over time. In both nations, it is particular ethnic groups (African-Americans and Hispanics in the US and Pakistanis and Bangladeshis in Britain) who are prone to poverty. Women are also more prone to poverty than men, as single parents (whether never married or previously married) bringing children up on their own. In this respect, the American and British poor are similar in terms of their social characteristics. There are differences, however. In America, a disproportionate number of two-parents families with children are poor while in Britain, a disproportionate number of the elderly (more of whom are single women, of course, because they live longer than men) are poor. All of these groups suffer from multiple deprivations – poor education, poor housing and psychological and physical ill-health – to a greater or lesser degree. They are also spatially concentrated in areas of relatively high poverty within cities and towns which have borne the brunt of manufacturing decline in both nations. Their spatial concentration exacerbates the difficult predicament in which the poor find themselves in that they are isolated from networks of people in employment and distant from the locales where employment opportunities exist. It is extremely difficult, therefore, for these groups of people to find employment in order to sustain themselves and their families above the poverty line. This point testifies to the social isolation of the poor, their social exclusion from full participation in civil society and the extent to which they can be said to be fully-integrated citizens within contemporary society. The persistence of poverty in two affluent advantaged industrialised societies highlights the extent of social polarisation in America and Britain.

These trends generated a debate on the extent to which an underclass of permanently poor people has emerged and whether they are the perpetrators or victims of their own predicament. With reference to the US, we saw that Murray promulgated a cultural explanation of the rise of the underclass arguing that a culture of dependency, criminality and illegitimacy is the primary cause of poverty. With Herrnstein, he has subsequently developed this argument with reference to genetic intelligence as measured by IQ scores. Against this background, his policy recommendation was to cut welfare assistance. Murray's research, not surprisingly, has proved highly controversal in the US. In contrast, Wilson proffered a structuralist account of the underclass arguing that the poor are victims of manufacturing decline in the frostbelt cities of the North. He recommended policies to promote national economic renewal which would benefit all sections of society. More recently, however, Wilson distanced himself from the concept of the underclass since the political rhetoric which now surrounds the thesis has deflected attention away from theoretical developments and empirical research on the plight of the ghetto poor. The underclass thesis, therefore, has not proved helpful for understanding the position in the poor in the class structure of American society. Murray transported his cultural theory of the underclass to Britain, rehearsing the main arguments, promoting the same policy options and warning Britons of the dangers if the 'new rabble' if we did not heed his advice. His intervention met with considerable hostility although some commentators subscribed to structural explanations for the rise of the underclass. The most recent quantitative and qualitative research focusing on the employed and long-term unemployed, however, has undermined the underclass thesis. While it cannot be denied that the brunt of unemployment has been borne by a particular social group (the lower echolons of the working class) who also suffer from a multitude of other deprivations, there is no evidence to show that they are not culturally distinct from the employed and self-employed in British society. Again, therefore, the concept of the underclass has not proved very useful for understanding the plight of the poor and, indeed, has only detracted attention away from the class character of labour market insecurity in the 1980s and 1990s.

Finally, attention turned to direct comparative research on patterns and trends in poverty and inequality in America and Britain. Research indicates that both America and Britain exhibited exceptional trends towards polarisation in the 1980s in comparison to other nations. However, America has a greater level of wealth inequality and income inequality than Britain and other European nations. On this basis, America is a more unequal society than Britain. The depth of poverty – whether it is measured in terms of distance from the poverty line or the poor's share of income – is also greater in the US than the UK. The evidence shows that poverty is high among two-parent families with children and single-parent families with children in the US while in the UK it is high among single-parent families and the elderly. This evidence has led to much concern about child poverty in the US. The lack of a universal income maintenance programme, especially for children in two-parent families, explains the high poverty rates there in comparison to the UK and other advanced industrialised nations. The limitations of the

New Deal programmes for welfare assistance established in the 1930s in comparison to the tax and benefit system introduced under the auspices of the Welfare State (the limitations of which have also become readily apparent in the face of high unemployment) go a long way to account for the high rates of poverty in the US in comparison to Britain. Against this background, the concluding chapter returns to the central question of whether America's image of a classless society and Britain's image as a class-bound society stand up to systematic empirical investigation.

Chapter 10

Conclusion

This book opened with the debate among American and British sociologists over the extent to which social class is declining in importance or remains a significant form of structured inequality in the late twentieth century. In the US, Clark and Lipset (1991) and Clark *et al.* (1993) argued that class hierarchies have fragmented and new social divisions have emerged in a period of rapid economic, social and political change. In reply, Hout and his associates (1993) argued that class differences in income demonstrate the persistence of class despite the decline of a manufacturing-dominated industrial society and the rise of a service-based post-industrial society. In Britain, Pahl (1991; 1993) argued that class is an outmoded concept of little explanatory value in a world in which economic relations are global rather than national and where the nation state is no longer the arena of class struggle. In contrast, Goldthorpe and Marshall (1992) argued that class remains an important feature of contemporary society and the remarkable resilience of class relations to change should now dominate the research agenda of class analysis. The debate among sociologists on both sides of the Atlantic is strikingly similar and, as was noted previously, somewhat paradoxical since the US is frequently portrayed as a classless society and Britain is invariably characterised as a class-bound nation.

Against this background, this book examined whether popular stereotypes of the two nations stand up to systematic empirical scrutiny. Is America a class society? Was it a land of abundant opportunity in the past? Is it an open society today? Is Britain a class-bound society? Was it a closed society in the past? Is it still a closed society today? The overwhelming evidence from both nations indicates that America is not a classless society and Britain is not a class-bound society. Class origins influence people's class destinations in both countries, of course, although this is not to suggest that people never escape from their class origins. On the contrary, the evidence of considerable upward social mobility in both nations testifies to this fact. Popular stereotypes, therefore, have become misleading caricatures which are themselves notably static and outmoded in character. They tend to overstate differences and mask important similarities between the two countries. Neither nation, for example, is entirely open or entirely closed, and the degree of openness and closure of each nation varies according to the criteria on which they are being evaluated. Overall, it is argued that social class remains an important influence, to a greater or lesser degree, on people life-chances, collective identities and socio-political actions in America and Britain.

A number of general debates about social class in both nations were evaluated in the first part of the book. It was found that America and Britain have comparable class structures as a result of broadly similar experiences of industrial and occupational change in the economic sphere in the twentieth century. That said, the scale and pace of these changes have been greater in the US than Britain. Both nations, for example, have witnessed the decline of manufacturing industry and the rise of the service sector although the service sector is larger in the US than Britain. Both nations have seen the decline of manual occupations and the rise of low-level and high-level nonmanual work. Even so, both nations have also experienced the countertrend of growing low-level service jobs (especially in the US and unemployment (especially in Britain). These economic changes have fundamentally altered the shape of the class structure in America and Britain leading to the decline in the size of the working class and the rise of the (lower and upper) middle classes. The evidence suggests that these processes continued in the 1970s and 1980s despite the less favourable economic climate compared with the 1950s and 1960s. In the 1990s, however, there is increasing speculation as to whether structural change has come to a halt especially in the US in the face of economic restructuring, corporate downsizing and so forth. These issues are increasingly gaining attention in Britain as well. To date, however, the evidence suggests that demand for high-level occupations remains strong and it is low-level nonmanual jobs which might be disappearing in the face of computerisation and productivity gains. Overall, therefore, America and Britain have comparable class structures which have changed in broadly similar ways over the twentieth century.

The evolution of the class structure has had important implications for social mobility since its upward shift structure facilitated considerable upward mobility – including long-range mobility – in both nations. Again, the evidence suggests that the scale and pace of these changes varied between America and Britain. As a result of relatively late industrialisation, the pace of change was very rapid in the US and the extent of change was substantial in comparison to Britain. Practitioners in the 'status attainment' tradition in the US also noted the declning influence of origins on destinations. That said, these opportunities were enjoyed more by the white population than African Americans and other minority groups with disadvantaged class origins, and the return on their educational credentials was not as great as that for whites either. Nevertheless, researchers concluded that America was an exceptionally open society. Working in the 'class structural' perspective in Britain, researchers noted the continuing influence of origins on destinations for both men and women. Men have enjoyed upward mobility into high-level managerial and professional occupations while women of all origins have been confined to low-level clerical work. In this respect, Britain appears more closed than the US. However, direct comparative research suggests that America has experienced higher levels of absolute rates of mobility than Britain but in terms of relative rates – the degree of social fluidity – the patterns and trends have been similar in both nations. Again, therefore, the evidence points to differences between the two nations although it also highlights important similarities as well.

Finally, the extent to which class consciousness – especially working-class consciousness -has declined has long between debated in both the US and Britain. Commentators in both nations, for example, predicted the decline of working-class identification and the rise of middle-class identities in the 1950s and 1960s. However, subsequent research in the 1970s and 1980s has shown that an identification with the working class remains strong among sizeable proportions of the populations in both countries. In this respect, America and Britain are remarkably similar. However, class identification has not shaped socio-political attitudes and behaviour to the same degree in America as it has in Britain. Members of all classes are highly suspicious of federal government intervention in economic and social life and do not support redistributive measures which might create a fairer and more just society. Policies which promote equal opportunities rather than equal outcomes are preferred. Members of the working class have a greater propensity to support the Democrats than the Republicans but the Democratic Party is a moderate liberal party which has not mobilised its constituency on class lines. It is for this reason that class identities do not shape socio-political proclivities to a large degree in the US. In Britain, class identities continue to structure political attitudes and behaviour. Members of the working class, for example, express greater support for a more redistributive tax and benefit system than currently exists and they are not inherently suspicious of the role of government in creating a more equal society. In this respect, members of the working class have been mobilised along class lines by the Labour Party as the political vehicle which represents their interests. At the same time, this is not to suggests that members of the British working class are militant rebels for nothing could be further from the truth. They might share a relatively coherent view of the world in comparison to their American counterparts but the coherence of their socio-political attitudes and behaviour cannot be overstated.

Interestingly, recent research suggests that Americans have become more class conscious in the 1980s, and take a more oppositional stand than previously on a number of socio-political issues. The connection between class and politics, however, still remains weak. In Britain, the connection between class and politics remains strong although the extent to which oppositional views will prevail as the Labour Party continues to remodel itself (not unlike the Democrats in the US) remains an open question. The politics of the two nations, therefore, are different and this difference has effected the extent to which class identities have been mobilised into class consciousness, That said, similar trends in the nature of the democratic class struggle are also discernable. Thus, it has been established that America and Britain have comparable class structures. They have also witnessed similar patterns and trends in social mobility. Levels of class identity including working-class identification are high and class structures attitudes to a greater or less degree in both nations. However, class does not shape political attitudes and behaviour as strongly as it does in America and, undoubtedly, the culture and politics of the two nations continue to differ. The absence of a party system rooted in class, for example, accounts for the differential importance of subjective class on political identities in America and Britain.

Specific debates about each of the five major classes – the capitalist class, the upper middle (or service) class, the lower middle class, the working class and the underclass – were evaluated in the second half of this book. Turning to the capitalist class, the research showed that America and Britain experienced a rise of large corporations in the early twentieth century. Once again, the pace of change was faster in the US than in Britain and the scale of change – i.e. the size of modern bureaucracies – differed between the two countries. Moreover, there was a trend away from personal to impersonal control through a constellation of interests. Wealthy families remain an important feature of the British corporate world in comparison to America as a result of different historical social relations. In the US, financial institutions have a strong but not all-dominant position as a result of the huge scale of capital investment required by large multi-corporations. The alleged globalisation of the world economy has reinforced the importance of institutional shareholders in both nations but there is little evidence to suggest that a united transnational capitalist class has emerged. In relation to issues of wealth and income, empirical evidence shows that the wealthy became even more wealthy in the 1980s in both the US and Britain. The American wealthy saw the value of their corporate stock rise considerably over the decade while corporate managers and directors in both nations enjoyed substantial salary increases at a time when the tax burden on them was falling. In both America and Britain, the wealthy socialise in exclusive social circles – one of which, of course, includes members of the Royal Family. While their exclusivity might be less than it was in the past, it is difficult to judge whether America has more exclusive social circles than Britain or vice-versa. Any difference between them, however, is one of degree rather than kind. There are also important links to be found between the wealthy upper class and the business class of finance capitalists in both nations. Similarly, high-level businessmen and women are to be found in the world of politics. Indeed, business interests are forcefully represented in both nations – arguably more so in America than Britain relative to other interests such as organised labour – but it is not all powerful in either instance. In other words, neither America nor Britain can be said to be ruled by a capitalist class.

The rise of modern corporations characterised by bureaucratic forms of organisation has seen the phenomenal growth of high-level nonmanual employment in America and Britain over the twentieth century. Again, the increase in nonmanual occupations started somewhat earlier in America and also underwent a process of professionalisation earlier than in Britain. Today, however, the upper middle class (or service class) is broadly comparable in size and various forms of differentiation – between public and private sector employees, managers and professionals, old and new sections and so on – have been noted within this large formation. Despite the growth of professional and managerial jobs, however, opportunities have not been open to everyone. In both nations, ethnic minorities and women are still under-represented in high-level nonmanual occupations. The last thirty years has seen some progress as ethnic groups and women made inroads into the professions in the favourable climate of the 1960s. Discrimination against ethnic groups and women was challenged. However, it has been privileged ethnic minorities and women (of high social origins) who obtained the necessary educational credentials to benefit from change. Even so, recent evidence suggests that credentials facilitate entry into the labour market but they do not guarantee on-going career advancement. The top of the professions and high-level managerial positions – arguably where real power and authority lies – are still dominated by men. Subtle processes of social closure, therefore, are still in operation in both nations. Finally, the empirical evidence indicates that the middle class as a whole is a largely conservative force which tends to vote for the Republican Party in the US or the Conservative Party in Britain. That said, in both nations, public-sector professionals are more liberal on a range of social issues – civil rights, feminism, environmentalism, peace and so forth – and challenge the prevailing order in relation to these issues. The middle class as a whole, therefore, is conservative in inclination and supports the status quo although sections of it are liberal and a force for change in both nations.

America and Britain have also witnessed the growth of low-level nonmanual employment – namely, routine clerical work invariably performed by women – over the twentieth century. The growth of routine nonmanual occupations generated a debate as to whether clerical workers had been proletarianised to the extent that they are indistinguishable from the working class or whether they occupy a position in the class structure somewhere between the middle class and the working class. The evidence on the relative sizes of the different classes in the class structure and the mobility trajectories of individuals within them suggests that a process of proletarianisation has not taken place along the lines described by neo-Marxists. The division of labour of nonmanual work did not evolve as a result of the implementation of Scientific Management but as the result of the professionalisation of high-level clerical work and the redrawing of boundaries between it and routine white-collar work. Moreover, women entered the office prior to these developments and not after white-collar work was routinised. The existence of routine clerical work is not being denied although the processes by which it is said to have emerged are being challenged. Also, the terms and conditions of women in white-collar jobs are still favourable in comparison to semi and unskilled manual work undertaken by women. Finally, there is little evidence of socio-political proletarianisation among clerical workers in either country. Clerical workers tend to identify more with the middle class then the working class. Their collective identities are influenced by a range of factors including their social origins, their education, their current employment as well as their partner's social origins, education and current employment, There is little to indicate, therefore, that clerical workers align themselves within the working class. Indeed, the evidence from both nations suggests that routine nonmanual workers do not have a distinct socio-political identity at all precisely because many of its members straddle the middle class and the working class directly or indirectly through their own experiences of social mobility or those of their partners.

After the growth of manual employment in the first half of the twentieth century, it started to decline gradually in the 1960s and then more dramatically in the early 1980s in America and Britain. That is, the recession of the early 1980s experienced in both countries saw mass redundancies in the steel industry, the car industry and so forth on a scale never seen before. The size of the working class, in other words, has declined for much of the last thirty years in both nations. Economic restructuring also accounts to a large degree for the decline of trade unionisation in both nations. Anti-union sentiment was also dominant in the 1980s when Reagan and Thatcher were in power in America and Britain respectively. Of course, industrial collectivism has always been much weaker in the US than Britain for a variety of reasons including the strength of capital. Strong anti-union sentiments and harsh tactics undermined collective industrial action in the US in a way which has not been experienced in Britain for some time (although more so in the 1980s). The decline in trade union membership, therefore, started from different bases so that only 16 per cent of the American workforce belongs to a trade union compared with 39 per cent of the British workforce. It is not surprisingly, therefore, that there is much debate about the future of trade unionism in both countries although the evidence suggests workers still see collective action as the means of improving their position in the economy sphere. In neither America nor Britain, therefore, has industrial collectivism disappeared and it will be an important feature of industrial relations – whatever form it takes – into the foreseeable future.

The evidence suggests that the working class retains a distinctive cultural identity in terms of patterns of sociability and leisure. Moreover, working people's daily lives continue to shape their aspirations in distinctive ways and their experiences sustain a common sense of identity with other members of the working class. As was noted previously, working-class identification does not translate into political attitudes and behaviour to the same degree in the US as in Britain. Reflecting the political systems of each nation, centrist rather than left-wing political views prevail among American workers while members of the working class tend to hold beliefs and attitudes to the left of the political spectrum in Britain. However, the difference in political attitudes and behaviour of the American and British working classes cannot be over-stated not least since American working people have a great propensity to vote Democrat rather than Republican while the British working class have a greater propensity to vote Labour rather than Conservative. There is no evidence, therefore, of a general process of class dealigment across the two countries although there is considerable disillusionment with the political parties and national politics across the working classes of the two countries.

Finally, the US and Britain have seen the growth of poverty and inequality in the last twenty years as the trend towards the equalisation of wealth and income halted and went into reverse from the mid-1970s. Figures suggest that both nations have a poverty rate of approximately 20 per cent of the population. Indeed, Britain and especially the US stand out in comparative research as nations with a high concentration of wealth and income. In this respect, both countries are highly polarised. The evidence shows that the poor – who include a disproportionate number of young men of particular ethnic groups and single mothers – suffer from multiple deprivations which are exacerbated by their concentration in inner-city ghettos characterised by high rates of poverty overall. Why the poor have grown in number has been the source of much contention. In a debate which crossed the Atlantic, some commentators promulgated cultural explanations of the rise of the underclass while others proffered structural accounts of the underclass thesis. The evidence in both countries suggests that the poor are not the perpetrators of their own predicament. On the contrary, the rise of poverty needs to be located in a structural context; namely, manufacturing decline and substantial job loss in both the US and Britain. Moreover, the greater depth of poverty in America – especially among two-parent families with children – in comparison with Britain is the result of the absence of a universal income maintenance programme (although Britain, of course, has also seen a considerable reduction in levels of welfare assistance to the poor in the 1980s and 1990s). Once again, the similarities rather than the differences between the two nations are striking.

Overall, systematic enquiry suggests that neither America nor Britain conform to popular stereotypes. America is not a classless society and Britain is not a class-bound society. Popular stereotypes, therefore, have become misleading caricatures which are themselves static and outmoded in character. They tend to overstates differences and neglect important similarities between the two countries. It is, of course, always difficult to capture the differences and similarities between two countries simultaneously. No doubt, readers may feel that in stressing the similarities between America and Britain, the differences have been downplayed. Nevertheless, the central argument of this book is that social class remains an important influence, to a greater or lesser degree, on people life-chances, collective identities and socio-political actions in America and Britain. What, then, are the implications of this conclusion for the debate on class in the two countries? Despite rapid economic, social and political change, social class is not dead. On the contrary, social class has also proved remarkably resilient over the twentieth century. The challenge to American and British sociologists within the field of class analysis is to explain the processes by which classes are formed and reformed over time and space. The importance of comparative research within this remit cannot be denied.

This book was written with a student audience in mind. It reviewed a large body of sociological literature with reference to the general debate on social class and with reference to specific debates on different social classes in the two nations. The book drew on a wide range of empirical results from quantitative and qualitative research as a way of considering macro and micro sociological issues. As part of this endeavour, it would have been useful to have had more of a historical perspective on both nations. Similarly, it would have been helpful to know more about the politics of

America and Britain. However, to have delved into the history and politics of class in the two nations would have led to another book. If this book tempts students on both sides of the Atlantic to go in search of the answers to questions which it has not fully addressed, its purpose of developing a comparative perspective on social class will have been fulfilled.

Bibliography

Abbott, A. (1988) *The System of Professions*, Chicago: University of Chicago Press.

Abbott, P. and Sapsford, R. (1987) *Women and Social Class*, London: Tavistock.

Abercrombie, N. *et al.* (1980) *The Dominant Ideology Thesis*, London: Unwin Hyman.

Abercrombie, N. *et al.* (1986) *Sovereign Individuals of Capitalism*, London: Allen and Unwin.

Abercrombie, N. *et al.* (eds) (1990) *Dominant Ideologies*, London: Allen and Unwin.

Abercrombie, N. and Urry, J. (1983) *Capital, Labour and the New Middle Classes*, London: Allen and Unwin.

Acker, J. (1973) 'Women and social stratification: a case of intellectual sexism', *American Journal of Sociology*, 78 (4), 936–45.

Ahrne, G. (1990) 'Class and society: a critique of John Goldthorpe's model of social classes' in J. Clarke *et al.* (eds) *John H. Goldthorpe: Consensus and Controversy*, London: Falmer Press.

Aikenhead, M. and Liff, S. (1991) 'The effectiveness of equal opportunities policies', in J. Firth-Cozens and M. West (eds) *Women at Work*, Buckingham: Open University Press.

Albin, P. and Applebaum, E. (1988) 'The computer-rationalisation of work', in J. Jensen *et al.* (eds) *Feminisation of the Labour Force*, Cambridge: Polity.

Alcock, P. (1994) 'Back to the future: Victorian values for the 21st century', in C. Murray (ed.) *Underclass: The Crisis Deepens*, London: Institute for Economic Affairs.

Allatt, P. and Yeandle, S. (1991) *Youth Unemployment and the Family: Voices of Disordered Times*, London: Routledge.

Allcorn, D.H. and Marsh, C.M. (1975) 'Occupational communities – communities of what?', in M. Bulmer (ed.) *Working-Class Images of Society*, London: Routledge and Kegan Paul.

Allen, I. (1988) *Any Room at the Top?*, London: PSI.

Alves, W.M. and Rossi, P.H. (1978) 'Who should get what?: fairness judgements of the distribution of earnings', *American Journal of Sociology*, 84, 541–64.

Applebaum, E. (1988) 'Technology and the redesign of work in the insurance industry', in B. Wright (ed.) *Women, Work and Technology*, Ann Arbor: University of Michigan Press.

Applebaum, E. and Albin, P. (1989) 'Computer rationalisation and the transformation of work: lessons from the insurance industry', in S. Wood (ed.) *The Transformation of Work*, London: Unwin Hyman.

Argyris, C. (1972) *The Applicability of Organisational Sociology*, Cambridge: Cambridge University Press.

Ashton, D. (1986) *Unemployment Under Capitalism: The Sociology of British and American Labour Markets*, Brighton: Harvester.

Atkinson, A.B. (1983) *The Economics of Inequality*, 2nd edn, Oxford: Clarendon Press.

Atkinson, A.B. (1993) 'What is happening to the distribution of income in the UK?', *Proceedings of the British Academy*, 82, 317–51.

Atkinson, A. B. *et al.* (1995) *Incomes and the Welfare State*, Cambridge: Cambridge University Press.

Atkinson, J. and Meager, N. (1985) *Changing Working Patterns*, London: NEDO.

Auletta, K. (1982) *The Underclass*, New York: Random House.

Bagguley, P. (1991) *From Protest to Acquiescence? Political Movements of the Unemployed*, London: Macmillan.

Bagguley, P. (1995) 'Middle-class radicalism revisited', in T. Butler and M. Savage (eds) *Social Change and the Middle Classes*, London: UCL Press.

Bagguley, P. *et al.* (1990) *Restructuring: Place, Class and Gender*, London: Sage.

Bagguley, P. and Mann, K. (1992) 'Idle thieving bastards? Scholarly representations of the "underclass"', *Work, Employment and Society*, 6, 113–26.

Bain, C.S. and Price, R. (1983) *Social Stratification and Trade Unionism*, London: Heinemann.

Baker, D. *et al.* (1992a) 'More "classless" and less "Thatcherite"?: Conservative MPs and ministers after the 1992 election', *Parliamentary Affairs*, 45, 656–68.

Baker, D. *et al.* (1992b) 'Conservative MPs: a response', *Sociology*, 26, 695–97.

Baker, D. *et al.* (1995) 'The Conservative parliamentary elite 1964–1994: the end of social convergence?', *Sociology*, 29, 703–13.

Baran, B. (1988) 'Office automation and women's work: the technological transformation of the insurance industry', in R. Pahl (ed.) *On Work*, Oxford: Basil Blackwell.

Baron, J.N. (1994) 'Reflections on recent generations of mobility research', in D. Grusky (ed.) *Social Stratification*, Boulder: Westview Press.

Barbalet, J.M. (1980) 'Principles of stratification in Max Weber: an interpretation and critique', *British Journal of Sociology*, 31, 401–18.

Barnes, S.H. and Kaase, M. (1983) *Political Action*, London: Sage.

Bartholomew, R. *et al.* (1992) 'Lone parents and the labour market: Evidence from the Labour Force Survey', *Employment Gazette*, November, 559–579.

Baxter, J. (1994) 'Is a husband's class enough?: class location and class identity in the United States, Norway, and Australia', *American Sociological Review*, 59, 220-35.

Beard, M. (1989) *English Landed Society in the Twentieth Century*, London: Routledge.

Beckett, J.V. (1988) *The Aristocracy in England, 1766–1914*, Oxford: Basil Blackwell.

Beeghley, L. and Cochran, J.K. (1988) 'Class identification and gender role norms among employed married women', *Journal of Marriage and the Family*, 50, 546–66.

Bell, D. (1979) 'The new class: a muddled concept', in B. Bruce-Briggs (ed.) *The New Class?*, New Brunswick, NJ: Transaction Books.

Bell, D. (1973) *The Coming of Post-Industrial Society*, New York: Basic Books.

Bell, D. (1976) *The Cultural Contradictions of Capitalism*, London: Heinemann.

Bell, W. and Robinson R.V., (1980) 'Cognitive maps of class and racial inequalities in England and the United States', *American Journal of Sociology*, 86, 320–49.

Bellah, R.N. *et al.* (1985) *Habits of the Heart*, Berkeley: University of California Press.

Bensman, D. and Lynch, R. (1988) *Rusted Dreams*, Berkeley: University of California Press.

Benson, L. (1978) *Proletarians and Parties*, London: Tavistock Publications.

Berelson, B.R. *et al.* (1954) *Voting*, Chicago: University of Chicago Press.

Beresford, P. (1990) *The Sunday Times Book of the Rich*, London: Weidenfield and Nicolson.

Berger, B.M. (1968) *Working-Class Suburb*, Berkeley: University of California Press.

Berle, A.A. and Means, G.C. ((1932) 1968) *The Modern Corporation and Private Property*, New York: Harcourt Brace and World Inc.

Beynon, H. (1984) *Working for Ford*, 2nd edn, Harmondsworth: Penguin.

Beynon, H. (ed.) (1985) *Digging Deeper*, London: Verso.

Beynon, H. and Blackburn, R.M. (1972) *Perceptions of Work*, Cambridge: Cambridge University Press.

Binns, D. (1977) *Beyond the Sociology of Conflict*, London: Macmillan.

Bird, E. (1980) *Information Technology in the Office*, Manchester: Equal Opportunities Commission.

Blackburn, R. and Mann, M. (1979) *The Working Class in the Labour Market*, London: Macmillan.

Blau, P. and Duncan, O.D. (1967) *The American Occupational Structure*, New York: John Wiley.

Blauner, R. (1964) *Alienation and Freedom*, Chicago: University of Chicago Press.

Blossfeld, H.P. and Shavit, Y. (eds) (1993) *Persisting Inequality*, Boulder: Westview Press.

Bluestone, B. and Harrison, B. (1982) *The Deindustrialisation of America*, New York: Basic Books.

Bonney, N. (1988a) 'Gender, household and social class', *British Journal of Sociology*, 39, 28–45.

Bonney, N. (1988b) 'Dual earning couples: trends of change in Great Britain', *Work, Employment and Society*, 2, 89–101.

Borthwick, G. *et al.* (1991) 'The social background of British MPs', *Sociology*, 25, 713–17.

Boston, T. (1988) *Race, Class and Conservatism*, London: Unwin Hyman.

Bott, E. (1957) *Family and Social Networks*, London: Tavistock Publications.

Bottomore, T. (1989) 'The capitalist class', in T. Bottomore and R. Byrm (eds) *The Capitalist Class*, Hemel Hempstead: Harvester Wheatsheaf.

Bottomore, T. (1991) *Classes in Modern Society*, 2nd edn, London: HarperCollins.

Bradshaw, J. and Holmes H. (1989) *Living on the Edge: A Study of Living Standards of Families on Benefit in Tyne and Wear*, London: Tyneside Child Poverty Action Group.

Braverman, H. (1974) *Labour and Monopoly Capital*, New York: Monthly Review Press.

Braverman, H. (1994) 'The Making of the U.S. working class', *Monthly Review*, 46 (6), 1–14, Special Issue.

Breen, R. and Rottman, D.B. (1995a) *Class Stratification*, Hemel Hempstead: Harvester Wheatsheaf.

Breen, R. and Rottman, D.B. (1995b) 'Class analysis and class theory', *Sociology*, 29, 453–73.

Brieger, R. (1990) *Social Mobility and Social Structure*, Cambridge: Cambridge University Press.

Brint, S. (1984) "New Class" and cumulative trend explanations of the liberal political attitudes of professionals', *American Journal of Sociology*, 90, 30–71.

Brint. S. (1985) 'The political attitudes of professionals', *American Review of Sociology*, 11, 389–414.

Brint, S. (1987) 'Classification struggles: reply to Lamont', *American Journal of Sociology*, 92, 1,506–9.

Brody, D. (1993) *Workers in Industrial America*, 2nd edn, Oxford: Oxford University Press.

Brooks, C. (1994) 'Class consciousness and politics in comparative perspective', *Social Science Research*, 23, 167–195.

Brooks, C. and Manza, J. (1994) 'Do changing values explain the new politics?: a critical assessment of the postmaterialist thesis', *Sociology Quarterly*, 36, 541–70.

Brown, C. (1984) *Black and White Britain: The Third PSI Survey*, Aldershot: Gower/PSI.

Brown, J.C. (1990) 'The focus on single mothers', in C. Murray (ed.) *The Emerging British Underclass*, London: IEA.

Brown, M. and Madge, N. (1982) *Despite the Welfare State*, London: Heinemann.

Brown, P. (1995) 'Cultural capital and social exclusion: some observations on recent trends in education, employment and the labour market', *Work, Employment and Society*, 9, 29–51.

Brown, P. and Scase, R. (eds) (1991) *Poor Work, Disadvantage and the Division of Labour*, Milton Keynes: Open University Press.

Brown, P. and Scase, R. (1994) *Higher Education and Corporate Realities*, London: UCL Press.

Brown, R. (1973) 'Sources of orientations in work and employment', in J. Child (ed.) *Man and Organisation*, London: George Allen and Unwin.

Brown, R. *et al.* (1983) 'Changing attitudes to employment?', *Department of Employment Research Paper 40*, London: Department of Employment.

Brown, R.K. (1992) *Understanding Industrial Organisations*, London: Routledge.

Bruce-Briggs, B. (1979) *The New Class?*, San Diego: Harcourt Brace Jovanovich.

Bryne, P. (1988) *The Campaign for Nuclear Disarmament*, London: Croom Helm.

Bulmer, M. (1975) *Working-Class Images of Society*, London: Routledge and Kegan Paul.

Burchill, B. and Rubery, J. (1989) *Segmented Jobs and Segmented Workers*, Social Change and Economic Life Initiative, Working Paper Number 13, Oxford: Nuffield College.

Burnham, J. (1941) *The Managerial Revolution*, New York: Day.

Buroway, M. (1979) *Manufacturing Consent*, London: Verso.

Buroway, M. (1985) *The Politics of Production*, London: Verso.

Burris, V. (1986) 'The discovery of the new middle class', *Theory and Society*, 15, 317–49.

Burtless, G. (ed.) (1990) *A Future for Lousy Jobs?*, Washington, DC: Brookings Institute.

Butler, T. and Savage, M. (eds) (1995) *Social Change and the Middle Classes*, London: UCL Press.

Campbell, P.E. *et al.* (1960) *The American Voter*, New York: Wiley.

Cannadine, D. (1990) *The Decline and Fall of the British Aristocracy*, London: Picador.

Cannadine, D. (1994) *Aspects of Aristocracy*, Yale: Yale University Press.

Carter, R. (1985) *Capitalism, Class Conflict and the New Middle Class*, London: Routledge and Kegan Paul

Carter, R. (1986) 'Review of *Classes*', *Sociological Review*, 34, 686–8

Caton, C.L.M. (1989) *Without Dreams*, New York: Oxford University Press. *1991 Census Report for Great Britain, Part 2.*

Centers, R. (1949) *The Psychology of Social Classes*, Princeton: Princeton University Press.

Chandler, A.F. (1977) *The Visible Hand*, Cambridge, MA: Harvard University Press.

Charles, N. (1990) 'Women and class – a problematic relationship?', *Sociological Review*, 38, 43–89.

Chase, I.D. (1975) 'A comparison of men's and women's intergenerational mobility in the United States', *American Sociological Review*, 40, 483–505.

Chinoy, E. (1955) *Automobile Workers and the American Dream*, New York: Doubleday.

Clark, T.N. and Lipset, S.M. (1991) 'Are social classes dying?', *International Sociology*, 6, 397–410.

Clark, T.N. *et al.* (1993) 'The declining political significance of class', *International Sociology*, 8, 293–316.

Clarke, J. *et al.* (eds) (1990) *John H. Goldthorpe: Consensus and Controversy*, London: Falmer Press.

Clawson, D. *et al.* (1986) 'The logic of business unity: corporate contributions to the 1980 congressional elections', *American Sociological Review*, 51, 797–811.

Clegg, S. (1990) *Modern Organisations*, London: Sage.

Cockburn, C. (1991) *In the Way of Women*, London: Macmillan.

Coffield, F. *et al.* (1981) *A Cycle of Deprivation?*, London: Heinemann Educational Books.

Cohn, S. (1985) *The Process of Occupational Sex Typing*, Philadelphia: Temple University Press.

Coleman, and Rainwater, L. (1978) *Social Standing in America*, London: Routledge and kegan Paul.

Collins, S.M. (1993) 'Black on the Bubble: the vulnerability of black executives in white corporations', *The Sociological Quarterly*, 34, 429–47.

Coser, L.A. (1975) Presidential address: 'Two methods in search of a substance', *American Sociological Review*, 40, 691–700.

Converse, P.E. (1964) 'The nature of belief systems in mass politics', in D.E. Apter (ed.) *Ideology and Discontent*, New York: Free Press.

Corcoran, M. *et al.* (1985) 'Myth and reality: the causes and persistence of poverty', *Journal of Policy Analysis and Management*, 4, 506–39.

Coyle, A. and Skinner, J. (1988) *Women and Work*, London: Macmillan.

Crewe, I. (1973) 'The politics of "affluent" and "traditional" workers in Britain: an aggregate data analysis', *British Journal of Political Science*, 3, 29–52.

Crewe, I. (1986) 'On the death and resurrection of class voting: some comments on *How Britain Votes*', *Political Studies*, 34: 620-38.

Crewe, I. (1987) 'A new politics of class', *The Guardian*, 15 June.

Crewe, I. and King. A. (1996) *The SDP*, Oxford: Oxford University Press.

Crompton, R. (1980) 'Class mobility in modern Britain', *Sociology*, 14, 117–19.

Crompton, R. (1991) 'Three varieties of class analysis: comment on R.E. Pahl', *International Journal of Urban and Regional Research*, 15, 108–13.

Crompton, R. (1992) 'Patterns of social consciousness amongst the middle classes', in R. Burrows and C. Marsh (eds) *Consumption and Class*, London: Macmillan.

Crompton, R. (1993) *Class and Stratification*, Cambridge: Polity.

Crompton, R. (1995) 'Women's employment and the "middle class"', in T. Butler and M. Savage (eds) *Social Change and the Middle Classes*, London: UCL Press.

Crompton, R. (1996) 'The fragmentation of class', *British Journal of Sociology*, 47, 56–67.

Crompton, R. and Gubbay, J. (1977) *Economy and Class Structure*, London: Macmillan.

Crompton, R. and Jones, G. (1984) *White-Collar Proletariat*, London: Macmillan.

Crompton, R. and Mann, M. (eds) (1986) *Gender and Stratification*, London: Macmillan.

Crompton, R. and Sanderson, K. (1990) *Gendered Jobs and Social Change*, London: Unwin Hyman.

Crompton, R. and Le Feuvre, N. (1992) 'Women in finance in Britain and France , in M. Savage and A. Witz (eds) (1992) *Gender and Bureaucracy*, Oxford: Basil Blackwell.

Crow, G. and Allan, G. (1990) 'Constructing the domestic sphere: the emergence of the home in post-war Britain', in H. Corr and L. Jamieson (eds) *Politics of Everyday Life*, London: Macmillan.

Crow and Allan, G. (1994) *Community Life*, Hemel Hempstead: Harvester Wheatsheaf.

Dahl, R. (1961) *Who Governs?*, New Haven, CT: Yale University Press.

Dahrendorf, R. (1959) *Class and Class Conflict in Industrial Society*, London: Routledge and Kegan Paul.

Dahrendorf, R. (1987) 'The erosion of citizenship and its consequences for us all', *New Statesman*, 12 June, 12–15.

Dale, A. (1986) 'Social class and the self-employed', *Sociology*, 20, 430-4.

Dale, A. *et al.* (1986) 'Integrating women into class theory', *Sociology*, 19, 384–409.

Daniel, W.W. (1969) 'Industrial behaviour and orientations to work – a critique', *Journal of Management Studies*, 6, 366–75.

Daniel, W.W. (1971) 'Productivity bargaining and orientations to work – a rejoinder to Goldthorpe', *Journal of Management Studies*, 8, 329–35.

Daniel, W.W. (1987) *Workplace Industrial Relations and Technical Change*, London: Frances Pinter.

Danziger, S. and Gottschalk, P. (eds) (1993) *Uneven Tides*, New York: Russel Sage Foundation.

David, M. (1994) 'Fundamentally flawed', in C. Murray (ed.) *Underclass: The Crisis Deepens*, London: Institute for Economic Affairs.

Davies, M. (1979) 'Women's place is at the typewriter: the feminisation of the clerical labour force' in Z.R. Eisenstein (ed.) *Capitalisat Patriarchy and the Case for Socialist Feminism*, New York: Monthly Review Press.

Davies, R.B. *et al.* (1993) 'The relationship between a husband's unemployment and his wife's participation in the labour force', in D. Gallie *et al.* (eds) *Social Change and the Experience of Unemployment*, Oxford: Oxford University Press.

Davis, J.A. (1986) 'British and American attitudes: similarities and contrasts' in R. Jowell *et al.* (eds) *British Social Attitudes: The 1986 Report*, Aldershot: Gower.

Davis, N.J. and Robinson, R.V. (1988) 'Class identification of men and women in the 1970s and 1980s', *American Sociological Review*, 51, 168–83.

Davis, R.L. and Cousins, J. (1975) 'The "new working class" and the old', in M. Bulmer (ed.) *Working-class Images of Society*, London: Routledge and Kegan Paul.

Daye, S. (1994) *Middle-Class Blacks in Britain*, London: Routledge.

Deakin, N. (1990) 'Mr Murray's ark', in C. Murray (ed.) *The Emerging British Underclass*, London: Institute for Economic Affairs.

Dean, H. (1991) 'In search of the underclass', in P. Brown and R. Scase (eds) *Poor Work, Disadvantage and the Division of Labour*, Milton Keynes: Open University Press.

Dean, H. and Taylor-Gooby, P. (1992) *Dependency Culture: The Explosion of a Myth*, Hemel Hempstead: Harvester Wheatsheaf.

De Graaf, N.D. and Heath, A. (1992) 'Husbands' and wives' voting behaviour in Britain: class-dependent mutual influence of spouses', *Acta Sociologica*, 35, 311–22.

De Kadt, M. (1979) 'Insurance: a clerical work factory', in A. Zimbalist (ed.) *Case Studies in the Labour Process*, New York: Monthly Review Press.

Delgrado, H.L. (1993) *New Immigrants, Old Unions*, Philadelphia: Temple University Press.

Delphy, C. (1981) 'Women in stratification studies', in H. Roberts (ed.) *Doing Feminist Research*, London: Routledge and Kegan Paul.

Dennis, N. *et al.* (1956) *Coal is Our Life*, London: Tavistock.

Dennis, N. and Erdos, G. (1993) *Families Without Fatherhood*, London: Institute for Economic Affairs.

Dent, M. (1993) 'Professionalism, educated labour and the state: hospital medicine and the new managerialism', *Sociological Review*, 41, 244–273.

Devine, F. (1992) *Affluent Workers Revisited*, Edinburgh: Edinburgh University Press.

Devine, F. (1992a) 'Social identities, class identity and political perspectives', *Sociological Review*, 40, 229–52.

Devine, F. (1992b) 'Gender segregation in the engineering and science professions: a case of continuity and change', *Work, Employment and Society*, 6, 557–75.

Devine, F. (1992c) 'Working-class evaluations of the Labour Party', in I. Crewe *et al.* (eds) *British Elections and Parties Yearbook*, Hemel Hempstead: Harvester Wheatsheaf.

Devine, F. (1996a) 'The "new structuralism" and class politics', in N. Kirk (ed.) *Social Class and Marxism*, London: Scolar Press.

Devine, F. (1996b) 'The stability of class in contemporary society: studying the processes of class mobility and immobility', in W. Bottero (ed.) *Post-Class Society?*, Cambridge: Cambridge Sociological Research Group Publications.

Dex, S. (1985) *The Sexual Division of Labour*, Brighton: Wheatsheaf.

Dex, S. (1987) *Women's Occupational Mobility*, London: Macmillan.

Dex, S. (1990) 'Goldthorpe on class and gender: the case against', in J. Clarke *et al.* (eds) *John H. Goldthorpe: Consensus and Controversy*, London: Falmer Press.

Dex, S. and Shaw, L.B. (1986) *British and American Women at Work*, London: Macmillan.

DiPrete, T.A. (1987) 'The professionalisation of Administration and equal opportunity policy in the U.S. Federal Government, *American Journal of Sociology*, 93, 119–40.

DiPrete, T.A. (1988) 'The upgrading and downgrading of occupations: status redefinition vs deskilling as alternative theories of change', *Social Forces*, 66, 725–46.

DiPrete, T.A. (1989) *The Bureaucratic Labour Market: The Case of the Federal Civil Service*, New York: Plenum Press.

DiPrete, T.A. (1993) 'Industrial restructuring and the mobility response of American workers in the 1980s', *American Sociological Review*, 58, 74–96.

DiPrete, T.A. and Grusky, D.B. (1990) 'Structure and trend in the process of stratification for American men and women', *American Journal of Sociology*, 96, 107–43.

Domhoff, G.W. (1967) *Who Rules America?*, Englewood Cliffs, NJ: Prentice Hall Inc.

Domhoff, G.W. (1970) *The Higher Circles*, New York: Random House.

Domhoff, G.W. (1980) *Power Structure Research*, Beverley Hills: Sage.

Domhoff, G.W. (1983) *Who Rules America Now?*, Englewood Cliffs, NJ: Prentice Hall Inc.

Domhoff, G.W. (1991) 'A critique of Skocpol's state autonomy theory', *Berkeley Journal of Sociology*, 91, 1–49.

Downs, A. (1957) *An Economic Theory of Democracy*, New York: Harper Row.

Dubin, R. (1956) 'Industrial workers' worlds: a study of the central life-interests of industrial workers', *Social Problems*, 3, 131–41.

Dudley, K.M. (1994) *The End of the Line*, Chicago: University of Chicago Press.

Duncan, G. *et al.* (1984) *Years of Poverty, Years of Plenty*, Michigan: University of Michigan.

Dunleavy, P. (1980a) The political implications of sectoral cleavages: the growth of state employment: part 1, the analysis of production cleavages', *Political Studies*, 28, 364–83.

Dunleavy, P. (1980b) 'The political implications of sectoral cleavges and the growth of state employment: part 2, cleavage structures and political alignment, *Political Studies*, 28, 527–49.

Dunleavy, P. and Husbands, C. (1985) *British Democracy at the Crossroads*, London: Allen and Unwin.

Durkheim, E. (1938) *The Rules of Sociological Method* (ed. G.E.G. Caitlin), Chicago: University of Chicago Press.

Eckersley, R. (1989) 'Green politics and the new class: selfishness or virtue?', *Political Studies*, 37, 205–223.

Eder, K. (1993) *The New Politics of Class*, London: Sage.

Edgell, S. (1993) *Class*, London: Routledge.

Edgell, S. and Duke V. (1991) *A Measure of Thatcherism*, London: HarperCollins.

Edsall, T. (1984) *The New Politics of Inequality*, New York: Norton.

Edsall, T. and Edsall, M. (1991) *Chain Reaction*, New York: Norton.

Edwards, R. (1979) *Contested Terrain*, London: Heinemann.

Ehrenreich, B. (1989) *Fear of Falling*, New York: Pantheon.

Ehrenreich, J. and Ehrenreich, B. (1979) 'The professional-managerial class', In P. Walker (ed.) *Between Labour and Capital*, Boston: South End.

Ellwood, D.T. (1988) *Poor Support*, New Year: Basic Books.

Emmison, M. and Western, M. (1990) 'Social class and social identity: a comment on Marshall *et al.*', *Sociology*, 24, 241–53.

England, P. and Farkas, G. (1986) *Households, Employment and Gender*, New York: Aldine Press.

Erikson, R. (1984) 'Social class of men, women and families', *Sociology*, 18, 400-14.

Erikson, R. *et al.* (1979) 'Intergenerational class mobility in three western European societies: England, France and Sweden', *British Journal of Sociology*, 30, 415–41.

Erikson, R. *et al.* (1982) 'Social fluidity in industrial nations', *British Journal of Sociology*, 33, 1–34.

Erikson, R. and Goldthorpe, J.H. (1985) 'Are American rates of social mobility exceptionally high?: New evidence on an old question', *European Sociological Review*, 1, 1–15.

Erikson R. and Goldthorpe, J.H. (1988) 'Women at class crossroads: a critical note', *Sociology*, 22, 545–53.

Erikson, R. and Goldthorpe, J.H. (1992a) *The Constant Flux*, Oxford: Clarendon Press.

Erikson, R. and Goldthorpe, J.H. (1992b) 'Individual or family? results from two approaches to class assignment', *Acta Sociologica*, 35, 95–105.

Erikson, R. and Goldthorpe, J.H. (1992c) 'The CASMIN project and the American dream', *European Sociological Review*, 8, 283–29?

Ermisch, J. (1990) 'Divorce: economic antecedents and aftermath', in H. Joshi (ed.) *The Changing Population of Britain*, Oxford: Blackwell.

Esping-Andersen, G. (1990) *The Three Worlds of Welfare Capitalism*, Cambridge: Polity.

Esping-Andersen, G. (1993) *Changing Classes*, London: Sage.

Evans, G. (1992a) 'Testing the validity of the Goldthorpe class schema', *European Sociological Review*, 8, 211–32.

Evans, G. (1992b) 'Is Britain a class-divided society? A re-analysis and extension of Marshall *et al.*'s study of class consciousness', *Sociology*, 26, 233–58.

Evans, G. (1993a) 'Class conflict and inequality', in R. Jowell *et al.* (eds) *International Social Attitudes: The 10th British Social Attitudes Report*, Aldershot: Dartmouth.

Evans, G. (1993b) 'The decline of class divisions in Britain? Class and ideological preferences in the 1960s and the 1980s', *British Journal of Sociology*, 44, 449–71.

Evans, G. (1996) 'Putting men and women into classes: an assessment of the cross-sex validity of the Goldthorpe class schema', *Sociology*, 30, 309–34.

Fantasia, R. (1988) *Cultures of Solidarity*, Berkeley: University of California Press.

Fantasia, R. (1995) 'Class consciousness in culture, action and social organisation', *Annual Review of Sociology*, 21, 269–87.

Farley, R. (1984) *Blacks and Whites*, Cambridge, MA: Harvard University Press.

Farley, R. and Allen, W. (1989) *The Colour Line and the Quality of Life in America*, New York: Oxford University Press.

Farley, R. and Frey, W. (1994) 'Changes in the segregation of whites from blacks during the 1980s', *American Sociological Review*, 59, 23–45.

Featherman, D.L. *et al.* (1975) 'Assumptions of social mobility research in the United States: the case of occupational status', *Social Science Research*, 4, 329–60.

Featherman, D.L. and Hauser, R.M. (1978) *Opportunity and Change*, New York: Academic Press.

Fendrich, J.M. (1993) *Ideal Citizens*, New York: State University of New York Press.

Field, F. (1989) *Losing Out*, Oxford: Basil Blackwell.

Filson, M. and Knoke, D. (1974) 'Social status and the married woman', *Journal of Marriage and the Family*, 36, 516–21.

Fine, L.M. (1990) *Souls of the Skyscraper*, Philadelphia: Temple University Press.

Fisher, J. (1994a) 'Political donations to the Conservative Party', *Parliamentary Affairs*, 47, 61–72.

Fisher, J. (1994b) 'Why do companies make donations to political parties?', *Political Studies*, 42, 75–99.

Fisher, J. (1995) 'The institutional funding of British political parties', in D. Broughton *et al.* (eds) *British Elections and Parties Yearbook* 1994, London: Frank Cass.

Flynn, A. (1992) 'Manager markets: consumers and producers in the NHS' in R. Burrows and C. Marsh (eds) *Consumption and Class*, London: Macmillan.

Form, W. (1985) *Divided We Stand*, Urbana: University of Illinois Press.

Form, W. (1987) 'On the degradation of skills', *Annual Review of Sociology*, 13, 29–47.

Francis, A. (1980) 'Families, firms and finance capital', *Sociology*, 14 (1), 1–27.

Franklin, A. (1989) 'Working-class privatism: an historical case study of
   Bedminster, Bristol', *Society and Space*, 7, 93–113.
Franklin, M.N. (1985) *The Decline of Class Voting in Britain*, Oxford:
   Clarendon Press.
Franklin, M.N. *et al.* (1992) *Electoral Change*, New York: Cambridge
   University Press.
Fraser, S. (ed.) (1995) *The Bell Curve Wars*, New York: Basic Books.
Frazier, E.F. (1957) *The Black Bourgeoisie*, New York: Macmillan.
Friedson, E. (1986) *Professional Powers*, Chicago: University of Chicago Press.
Fritzell, J. (1993) 'Income inequality trends in the 1980s: a five-country
   comparison', *Acta Sociologica*, 36, 47–62.
Galbraith, J.K. (1967) *The New Industrial State*, Boston, MA: Houghton
   Mifflin.
Gallie, D. (1983) *Social Inequality and Class Radicalism in France and Britain*,
   Cambridge: Cambridge University Press.
Gallie, D. (1988) 'Employment, unemployment and social stratification',
   in D. Gallie (ed.) *Employment in Britain*, Oxford: Basil Blackwell.
Gallie, D. (1989) 'Trade union allegiance and decline in British urban
   labour markets', *The ESRC Social Change and Economic Life Initiative
   Working Paper 9*, Oxford: Nuffield College.
Gallie, D. (1974) 'Pattrens of skill change: upskilling, deskilling, and
   polarization', in R. Penn *et al.* (eds) *Skill and Occupational Change*,
   Oxford: Oxford University Press.
Gallie, D. and Marsh, C. (1993) 'The experience of unemployment', in D.
   Gallie, C. Marsh and C. Vogler (eds) *Social Change and the Experience
   of Unemployment*, Oxford: Oxford University Press.
Gallie, D. and Vogler, C. (1993a) 'Unemployment and attitudes to work', in
   D. Gallie *et al.* (eds) *Social Change and the Experience of Unemployment*,
   Oxford: Oxford University Press.
Gallie, D. and Vogler, C. (1993b) 'Labour market deprivation, welfare and
   collectivism', in D. Gallie *et al.* (eds) *Social Change and the Experience
   of Unemployment*, Oxford: Oxford University Press.
Gamble, A. (1990) *Britain in Decline*, 3rd edn, London: Macmillan.
Gans, H.J. (1967) *The Levittowners*, London: Allen Lane.
Gans, H.J. (1988) *Middle American Individualism*, New York: Free Press.
Gans, H.J. (1990) 'Deconstructring the underclass: the term's danger as
   a planning concept', *Journal of the American Planning Association*, 56,
   271–349.
Ganzeboom, H.B.G. *et al.* (1989) 'Intergenerational class mobility in
   comparative perspective', *Research in Social Stratification and Mobility*,
   8, 229–52.
Ganzeboom, H.B.G. *et al.* (1991) 'Comparative intergenerational stratification
   research: three generations and beyond', *Annual Review of Sociology*,
   17, 277–302.
Gardner, H. (1995) 'Cracking open the IQ box' in S. Fraser (ed.) *The Bell
   Curve Wars*, New York: Basic Books.
Gates, H.L. Jr (1995) 'Why now?', in S. Fraser (ed.) *The Bell Curve Wars*,
   New York: Basic Books.
George, V. and Howards I. (1991) *Poverty Amidst Affluence: Britain and
   the US*, Aldershot: Edward Elgar.

Gershuny, J. (1983) *Social Innovation and the Division of Labour*, Oxford: Clarendon Press.

Gershuny, J. (1993) 'Post-industrial career structures in Britain', in G. Esping-Andersen (ed.) *Changing Classes*, London: Sage.

Gershuny, J. and Marsh, C. (1993) 'Unemployment in work histories', in D. Gallie *et al.* (eds) *Social Change and the Experience of Unemployment*, Oxford: Oxford University Press.

Giddens, A. (1973) *The Class Structure of the Advanced Societies*, London: Hutchinson.

Giddens, A. (1980) *The Class Structure of the Advanced Societies*, 2nd edn, London: Unwin Hyman.

Gilbert, D. and Kahn, J.A. (1993) *The American Class Structure*, 4th edn, Belmont, CA: Wadsworth.

Gilder, G. (1982) *Wealth and Poverty*, New York: Buchan and Enright.

Glass, D. (ed.) (1954) *Social Mobility in Britain*, London: Routledge and Kegan Paul.

Glass, D. and Hall, J.R. (1954) 'Social mobility in Britain: a study of intergenerational changes in status', in D. Glass (ed.) *Social Mobility in Britain*, London: Routledge and Kegan Paul.

Glendinning, C. and Millar, J. (1992) *Women and Poverty in Britain*, 2nd edn, Hemel Hempstead: Harvester Wheatsheaf.

Glenn, E.N. and Feldberg, R.L. (1979) 'Proletarianising clerical work: technology and organisational control in the office', in A. Zimbalist (ed.) *Case Studies in the Labour Process*, New York: Monthly Review Press.

Glenn, E.N. and Feldberg, R.L. (1995) 'Clerical work: the female occupation', in J. Freeman (ed.) *Women: A Feminist Perspective*, Palo Alto, California: Mayfield Publishing Company.

Glenn, N.D. *et al.* (1974) 'Patterns of intergenerational mobility of females through marriage', *American Sociological Review*, 39, 633–99.

Goldfield, M. (1987) *The Decline of Organised Labour in the US*, Chicago: University of Chicago Press.

Goldthorpe, J.H. (1970) 'The social action approach to industrial sociology: a reply to Daniel', *Journal of Management Studies*, 7, 199–208.

Goldthorpe, J.H. (1972) 'Daniel on orientations to work: a final comment', *Journal of Management Studies*, 9, 266–73.

Goldthorpe, J.H. (1978) 'The current inflation: towards a sociological account in J.H. Goldthorpe and F. Hirsch (eds) *The Political Economy of Inflation*, London: Martin Robertson.

Goldthorpe, J.H. (1980) 'Class mobility in modern Britain: a reply to Crompton', *Sociology*, 14, 121–3.

Goldthorpe, J.H. (1982) 'On the service class: its formation and future', in A. Giddens and G. Mackenzie (eds) *Social Class and the Division of Labour*, Cambridge: Cambridge University Press.

Goldthorpe, J.H. (1983) 'Women and class analysis: in defence of the conventional view', *Sociology*, 17, 465–88.

Goldthorpe, J.H. (1984) 'Women and class analysis: a reply to the replies', *Sociology*, 18, 491–9.

Goldthorpe, J.H. (1990) 'A response', in J. Clarke *et al.* (eds) *John H. Goldthorpe: Consensus and Controversy*, London: Falmer Press.

Goldthorpe, J.H. (1995) 'The service class revisited', in T. Butler and

M. Savage (eds) *Social Change and the Middle Classes*, London: UCL Press.

Goldthorpe, J.H. *et al.* (1968a) *The Affluent Worker: Industrial Attitudes and Behaviour*, Cambridge: Cambridge University Press.

Goldthorpe, J.H. *et al.* (1968b) *The Affluent Worker: Political Attitudes and Behaviour*, Cambridge: Cambridge University Press.

Goldthorpe, J.H. *et al.* (1969) *The Affluent Worker in the Class Structure*, Cambridge: Cambridge University Press.

Goldthorpe, J.H. and Llewellyn, C. (1977) 'Trends in inter-generational class mobility in England and Wales, 1972–1983', *Sociology*, 20, 229–252.

Goldthorpe, J.H. (in association with C. Llewellyn and C. Payne) (1980) *Social Mobility and Class Structure in Modern Britain*, Oxford: Clarendon Press.

Goldthorpe, J.H. (in association with C. Llewellyn and C. Payne) (1987) *Social Mobility and Class Structure in Modern Britain*, 2nd edn, Oxford: Clarendon Press.

Goldthorpe, J.H. and Payne, C. (1986a) 'Trends in inter-generational class mobility in England and Wales 1972–1983', *Sociology*, 20, 1–24.

Goldthorpe, J. H. and Payne, C. (1986b) 'On the class mobility of women: results from different approaches to the analysis of recent British data', *Sociology*, 20, 531–55.

Goldthorpe, J.H. and Marshall, G. (1992) 'The promising future of class analysis: a response to recent critiques', *Sociology*, 26, 381–400.

Gordon, D. *et al.* (1982) *Segmented Work, Divided Workers*, Cambridge: Cambridge University Press.

Gould, S.J. (1995) 'Curveball', in S. Fraser (ed.) *The Bell Curve Wars*, New York: Basic Books.

Gouldner, A.W. (1979) *The Future of Intellectuals and the Rise of the New Class*, New York: Continuum.

Granovettor, M. (1995) *Getting a Job*, 2nd edn, Chicago: University of Chicago Press.

Grant, W. (ed.) (1985) *The Political Economy of Corporatism*, London: Macmillan.

Grant, W. (1987) *Business and Politics*, London: Macmillan.

Grant, W. and Marsh, D. (1977) *The Confederation of British Industry*, London: Hodder and Stoughton.

Greatz B. (1991) 'The class location of families: a refined classification and analysis', *Sociology*, 25, 101–18.

Greed, C. (1991) *Surveying Sisters*, London: Routledge.

Green, P. (1990) *The Enemy Without*, Milton Keynes: Open University Press.

Greenstone, J.D. (1977) *Labour in American Politics*, Chicago: University of Chicago Press.

Gregson, N. and Lowe, M. (1994) *Servicing the Middle Classes*, London: Routledge.

Grieco, M. (1987) *Keeping It in the Family*, London: Tavistock Publications.

Grusky, D.B. (1994) *Social Stratification*, Boulder: Westview Press.

Grusky, D.B. and Hauser, R.M. (1984) 'Comparative social mobility revisited: models of convergence and divergence in 16 countries', *American Sociological Review*, 49, 19–38.

Guest, A.M. *et al.* (1989) 'Intergenerational occupational mobility in the late 19th century United States', *Social Forces*, 68, 351–78.

Guttsman, W.L. (1974) 'The British political elite and the class structure', in P. Stanworth and A. Giddens (eds) *Elites and Power in British Society*, Cambridge: Cambridge University Press.

Hakim, C. (1987) 'Trends in the flexible workforce', *Employment Gazette*, November, 549–60.

Halford, S. and Savage, M. (1995a) 'Restructuring organisations, changing people: gender and careers in banking and local government', *Work, Employment and Society*, 9, 97–122.

Halford, S. and Savage, M. (1995b) 'The bureaucratic career: demise or adaption?', in T. Butler and M. Savage (eds) *Social Change and the Middle Classes*, London: UCL Press.

Halle, D. (1984) *America's Working Man*, Chicago: University of Chicago Press.

Halle, D. and Romo, F. (1991) 'The blue collar working class', in A. Wolfe (ed.) *America at Century's End*, Berkeley: University of California Press.

Halsey, A.H. (1987) 'Social trends since World War II', *Social Trends*, 17, 11–19.

Halsey, A.H. (1992) *Decline of Donnish Dominion*, Oxford: Clarendon Press.

Halsey, A.H. (1995) 'Preface', in N. Dennis and G. Erdos, *Families Without Fatherhood*, London: Institute of Economic Affairs.

Halsey, A.H. *et al.* (1980) *Origins and Destinations*, Oxford: Clarendon Press.

Hamilton, M. and Hirszowicz, M. (1993) *Class and Inequality*, Hemel Hempstead: Harvester Wheatsheaf.

Hamilton, R. (1972) *Class and Politics in the United States*, New York: Wiley.

Hammond, J.L. (1987) 'Wife's status and family social standing', *Sociological Perspectives*, 30, 30:71–92.

Handel, G. and Rainwater, L. (1964) 'Changing family roles in the working class', in A. Shostak and W. Gomberg (eds) *Blue-Collar World*, Englewood Cliffs, NJ: Prentice-Hall.

Hannah, L. (1983) *The Rise of the Corporate Economy*, 2nd edn, London: Methuen.

Hansard Society (1990) *The Report of the Hansard Society Commision on Women at the Top*, London: The Hansard Society.

Harbury, C. and Hitchens, D.M.W.N. (1979) *Inheritance and Wealth Inequality in Britain*, London: George Allen and Unwin.

Hardey, M. and Crow, G. (1991) *Lone Parenthood*, Hemel Hempstead: Harvester Wheatsheaf.

Harrington, M. (1979) 'The new class and the left', in B. Bruce-Biggs (ed.) *The New Class?*, New Brunswick, NJ: Transaction Books.

Harris, C.C. *et al.* (1987) *Redundancy and Recession in South Wales*, Oxford: Basil Blackwell.

Harrison, B. and Bluestone, B. (1988) *The Great U-Turn*, New York: Basic Books.

Hartmann, H. (ed.) (1986) *Computer Chips and Paper Clips*, Washington, DC: National Research Council.

Hauser, R.M. and Featherman, D.L. (1977) *The Process of Stratification*, New York: Academic Press.

Hayes, B. and Jones, F. (1992a) 'Marriage and political partisanship in Australia: do wives' characteristics make a difference?', *Sociology*, 26, 81–101.

Hayes, B. and Jones, F. (1992b) 'Class identification among Australian couples: are wives' characteristics irrelevant?', *British Journal of Sociology*, 43, 463–83.

Heath, A. (1981) *Social Mobility*, London: Fontana.

Heath, A. (1992) 'The attitudes of the underclass', in D.J. Smith (ed.) *Understanding the Underclass*, London: PSI.

Heath, A. and Britten, N. (1984) 'Women's jobs do make a difference', *Sociology*, 18, 475–90.

Heath, A. *et al.* (1985) *How Britain Votes*, Oxford: Pergamon Press.

Heath, A. and Evans, G. (1988) 'Working-class Conservatives and middle-class socialists', In R. Jowell *et al.* (eds,) *British Social Attitudes: The 5th Report*, Aldershot: Gower.

Heath, A. *et al.* (1991) *Understanding Political Change*, Oxford: Pergamon Press.

Heath, A. *et al.* (1994) 'Towards meritocracy: recent evidence on an old problem,' in C. Crouch and A. Heath (eds) *Social Research and Social Reform*, Oxford: Clarendon Press.

Heath, A. *et al.* (1994) *Labour's Last Chance?*, Aldershot: Dartmouth.

Heath, A. and Savage, M. (1994) 'Middle-class politics', in R. Jowell *et al.* (eds) *British Social Attitudes: The 11th Report*, Aldershot: Gower.

Heath, A. and Savage, M. (1995) 'Political alignments and the middle classes', in T. Butler and M. Savage (eds) *Social Change and the Middle Classes*, London: UCL Press.

Herman, E.S. (1981) *Corporate Control, Corporate Power*, Cambridge: Cambridge University Press.

Herring, C. (1989) *Splitting the Middle*, New York: Praeger.

Herrnstein, R.J. and Murray, C. (1994) *The Bell Curve*, New York: The Free Press.

Hewitt, P. (1974) 'Elites and the distribution of power in British society', in P. Stanworth and A. Giddens (eds) *Elites and Power in Britain*, Cambridge: Cambridge University Press.

Hill, S. (1976) *The Dockers*, London: Heinemann.

Hiller, D.V. and Philliber, W.W. (1978) 'The derivation of status benefits from occupational attainments of working wives', *Journal of Marriage and the Family*, 4, 63–9.

Hirsch, S.G. (1978) *Roots of the American Working Class*, Philadelphia: University of Pennsylvania Press.

Hochschild, J. (1981) *What's Fair?*, Cambridge, MA: Harvard University Press.

Hochschild, J. (1995) *Facing Up to the American Dream*, Chicago: University of Chicago Press.

Hodge, R.W. and Treiman, D.W. (1968) 'Class identification in the United States', *American Journal of Sociology*, 73, 535–47.

Holton, R. and Turner, B. (1994) 'Debate and pseudo debate in class analysis', *Sociology*, 28, 799–804.

Hout, M. (1984) 'Occupational mobility of black men in the United States: 1962–1973,' *American Sociological Review*, 49, 308–22.

Hout, M. (1986) 'Opportunity and the minority middle class: a comparison of blacks in the United States and Catholics in Northern Ireland', *American Sociological Review*, 51, 308–22.

Hout, M. (1988) 'More universalism less structural mobility: the American occupational structure in the 1980s', *American Journal of Sociology*, 93, 1,358–400.

Hout, M. *et al.* (1993) 'Classes in post-industrial society', *International Sociology*, 8, 259–77.

Hout, M. *et al.* (1996) 'The democratic class struggle in the US, 1948–1992, *American Sociological Review*, 60, 805–828.

Howe, L. (1977) *Pink-Collar Workers*, New York: G.P. Putman's Sons.

Huber, J. and Form, W.H. (1973) *Income and Ideology*, New York: Free Press.

Huckfeldt, R. and Kohnfeld, C.W. (1989) *Race and the Decline of Class in American Politics*, Champaign, Illinois: University of IL: Press.

Hunter, L. and MacInnes, J. (1992) Employers and labour flexibility: the evidence from case studies', *Employment Gazette*, June, 307–15.

Ingham, G. (1984) *Capitalism Divided*, London: MacMillan.

Inglehart, R. (1977) *The Silent Revolution*, Princeton: Princeton University Press.

Inglehart, R. (1990) *Culture Shift in Advanced Industrial Society*, Princeton: Princeton University Press.

Institute for Employment Research (1995) *Review of the Economy and Employment*, Coventry: University of Warwick.

Jackman, M. (1994) *The Velvet Glove*, Berkeley: University of California Press.

Jackman, M. and Jackman, R. (1983) *Class Awareness in the United States*, Berkeley: University of California.

Jacobs, J.A. (1989) *Revolving Doors*, Stanford, CA: University of California Press.

Jacobs, J.A. (1993) 'Careers in the US service economy', in G. Esping-Andersen (ed.) *Changing Classes*, London: Sage.

Jargowsky, P.A. and Bane, M.J. (1991) 'Ghetto poverty in the United States, 1970-1980' in C. Jencks and P.E. Peterson (eds) *The Urban Underclass*, Washington, DC: The Brookings Institute.

Jaynes, G.D. and Williams, M. (1989) *A Common Destiny*, Washington, DC: National Academy Press.

Jencks, C. (1991) 'Is the American underclass growing?' in C. Jencks and P.E. Peterson (eds) *The Urban Underclass*, Washington, D.C.: The Brookings Institute.

Jencks, C. (1993) *Rethinking Social Policy*, New York: Harper Perennial.

Jencks, C. (1994) *The Homeless*, Cambridge, MA: Harvard University Press.

Jencks, C. *et al.* (1972) *Inequality*, New York: Basic Books.

Jencks, C. *et al.* (1979) *Who Gets Ahead?*, New York: Basic Books.

Jencks, C. and Peterson, P.E. (eds) (1991) *The Urban Underclass*, Washington, DC: The Brookings Institute.

Jones, T. (1993) *Britain's Ethnic Minorities*, London: PSI.

Jordan, A.G. and Richardson, J.J. (1987) *Government and Pressure Groups in Britain*, Oxford: Clarendon Press.

Jordan, B. *et al.* (1992) *Trapped in Poverty: Labour Market Decisions in Low Income Households*, London: Routledge.

Jordan, B. *et al.* (1994) *Putting the Family First*, London: UCL Press.

Kahl, J.A. and Davis, J.A. (1955) 'A comparison of indexes of socio-economic status', *American Sociological Review*, 20, 317–25.

Kander, R. (1977) *Men and Women of the Corporation*, New York: Basic Books.

Kasarda, J.D. (1989) 'Urban Industrial Transition and the underclass', *The Annals of the American Academy of Political and Social Science*, 501, 26–47.

Katz, M. (1989) *The Undeserving Poor*, New York: Pantheon.

Katznelson, I. (1981) *City Trenches*, New York: Pantheon.

Katznelson, I. and Zolberg, A.R. (eds) (1986) *Working-class Formation*, Princeton: Princeton University Press.

Kelly, M.P. (1980) *White-Collar Proletariat*, London: Routledge and Kegan Paul.

Kent, R.A. (1981) *A History of British Empirical Sociology*, Aldershot: Gower.

Kerchoff, A.C. *et al.* (1985) 'Social mobility in Great Britain and the United States', *American Journal of Sociology*, 92 (2), 281–308.

Kimeldorf, H. (1988) *Reds or Rackets?*, Berkeley: University of California Press.

Kirschenman, J. and Neckerman, K.M. (1991) 'We'd love to hire them, but . . .': the meaning of race for employers" in C. Jencks and P.E. Peterson (eds) *The Urban Underclass*, Washington, DC: The Brookings Institute.

Klein, M. (1965) *Samples From English Culture, Volume 1*, London: Routledge and Kegan Paul.

Kleugal, J.R. and Smith, E.R. (1986) *Beliefs about Inequality*, New York: Aldine De Gruyter.

Kleugal, J.R. *et al.* (eds) (1995) *Social Justice and Political Change*, New York: Aldine de Gruyter.

Knottnerus, J.D. (1987) 'Status Attainment Research and its image of society', *American Sociological Review*, 52, 113–21.

Kocko, J. (1980) *White-Collar Workers in America 1890-1940*, London: Sage.

Kohn, M.L. (1987) 'Cross-national research as an analytical strategy', *American Sociological Review*, 52, 713–31.

Komarsovsky, M. (1962) *Blue-Collar Marriage*, New York: Vintage.

Kornblum, W. (1974) *Blue-Collar Community*, Chicago: University of Chicago Press.

Kotz, D. (1978) *Bank Control of Large Corporations in the United States*, Berkeley: University of California Press.

Kristol, I. (1972) 'About inequality', *Commentary*, 54, 41–7.

Ladd, E.C. (1978) 'The new lines are drawn: class and ideology', *Public Opinion*, 1, 14–20.

Lamont, M. (1987) 'Cultural capital and the liberal political attitudes of professionals: comment on Brint', *American Journal of Sociology*, 92, 1,501–6.

Lamont, M. (1992) *Money, Morals and Manners*, Chicago: University of Chicago Press.

Landry, B. (1987) *The New Black Middle Class*, Chicago: University of Chicago Press.

Landry, B. (1991) 'The enduring dilemma of race in America', in A. Wolfe (ed.) *America at Century's End*, Berkeley: University of California Press.

Lane, C. (1988) 'New technology and clerical work', in D. Gallie (ed.) *Employment in Britain*, Oxford: Blackwells.

Lane, T. (1996) 'Foreign fuel, foreign ships and disorganised trade unionism: an alternative interpretation of the defeat of the miner's strike in 1984–5', *Working, Employment and Society*, 10, 57–84.

Larson, S.L. (1977) *The Rise of Professionalism*, Berkeley: University of California Press.

Lash, S. and Urry, J. (1987) *The End of Organised Capitalism*, Cambridge: Polity Press.

Lee, D. (1994) 'Class as a social fact', *Sociology*, 28, 397–416.

Leggett, J.C. (1968) *Class, Race and Labor: Working-class Consciousness in Detroit*, New York: Oxford University Press.

Leiulfrud, H. and Woodward, A. (1987) 'Women at class crossroads: repudiating conventional theories of family class', *Sociology*, 21, 393–412.

LeMasters, E.E. (1975) *Blue-Collar Aristocrats*, Madison: University of Wisconsin Press.

Lester, J. (ed.) (1971) *The Seventh Son*, New York, Vintage Books.

Levy, F. (1987) *Dollars and Dreams*, New York: Russell Sage.

Lewis, O. (1969) *La Vida*, London: Panther Books.

Liff, S. (19860 'Technical change and occupational sex-typing', in D. Knights and H. Willmott (eds) *Gender and the Labour Process*, London: Gower.

Lindblom, C. (1977) *Politics and Markets*, New York: Basic Books.

Linder, M. and Houghton, J. (1990) 'Self-employment and the petty bourgeoisie: comments on Steinmetz and Wright', *American Journal of Sociology*, 96, 727–35.

Lipset, S.M. (1991) 'American exceptionalism reaffirmed', in B. Shafer (ed.) *Is America Different?*, Oxford: Oxford University Press.

Lipset, S.M. and Bendix, R. (1954) *Class, Status and Power*, London: Routledge and Kegan Paul.

Lipset, S.M. and Bendix, R. (1959) *Social Mobility in Industrial Society*, Berkeley: University of California Press.

Lipset, S. M. and Zetterberg, H.L. (1956) 'A theory of social mobility', *Transactions of the Third World Congress of Sociology*, 3, London: International Sociological Association.

Lisle-Williams (1985) 'Beyond the market: the survival of family capitalism in the English merchant banks', *British Journal of Sociology*, 35, 241–73.

Lister, R. (1991) 'Concepts of poverty', *Social Studies Review*, 6 (5), 192–5.

Lockwood, D. (1958) *The Blackcoated Worker*, London: Allen & Unwin.

Lockwood, D (1975) 'Sources of variation in working-class images of society', in M. Bulmer (ed.) *Working-Class Images of Society*, London: Routledge and Kegan Paul.

Lockwood, D. (1989) *The Blackcoated Worker*, 2nd edn, Oxford: Clarendon Press.

Lowe, G.S. (1987) *Women in the Administrative Revolution*, Cambridge: Polity Press.

Lynd, R.S. and Lynd, H.M. (1929) *Middletown*, New York: Harcourt Brace Jovanovich.

Lynd, R.S. and Lynd, H.M. (1937) *Middletown in Transition*, New York: Harcourt Brace Jovanovich.

McAdam, D. (1988) *Freedom Summer*, Oxford: Oxford University Press.

McDermott, J. (1991) *Corporate Society*, Boulder: Westview Press.

McGregor, A. and Sproull, A. (1992) 'Employers and the flexible workforce', *Employment Gazette*, May, 225–53.

MacGregor, S. and Pimlott, B. (1990) *Tackling the Inner Cities*, Oxford: Clarendon Press.

Mack, J. and Lansley, S. (1993) *Breadline Britain in the 1990s*, London: HarperCollins.

MacKenzie, G. (1973) *The Aristocracy of Labour*, Cambridge: Cambridge University Press.

MacKie, I., and Marsh, D. (1995) 'The comparative method', in D. Marsh and G. Stoker (eds) *Theory and Methods in Political Science*, London: Macmillan.

MacKinnon, M.H. (1980) 'Work instrumentalism reconsidered', *British Journal of Sociology*, 31, 339–74.

McLaughlin, E. *et al.* (1989) *Work and Welfare Benefits*, Aldershot: Avebury.

MacLeod, J. (1987) *Ain't No Making It*, Boulder: Westview Press.

McNally, F. (1979) *Women for Hire*, London: Macmillan.

McNally, S.G. *et al.* (1991) *Bringing Class Back In*, Boulder: Westview Press.

MacNicol, J. (1987) 'In pursuit of the underclass', *Journal of Social Policy*, 16, 293–318.

McRae, S. (1986) *Cross-class Families*, Oxford: Clarendon Press.

McRae, S. (1990) 'Women and class analysis', in J. Clarke *et al.* (eds) *John H. Goldthorpe: Consensus and Controversy*, London: Falmer Press.

Mann, K. (1992) *The Making of an English Underclass?*, Buckingham: Open University Press.

Mann, M. (1970) 'The social cohesion of liberal democracy', *American Sociological Review*, 35, 423–39.

Mann, M. (1973) *Consciousness and Action among the Western Working Class*, London: Macmillan.

Mann, M. (1986) *The Sources of Social Power*, Cambridge: Cambridge University Press.

Manza, J. *et al.* (1995) 'Class voting in capitalist democracies since World War II: dealignment, realignment, or trendless fluctuation?,' *Annual Review of Sociology*, 21, 137–62.

Marcus, G.E. (1992) *Lives in Trust*, Boulder: Westview Press.

Marsh, C. (1986) 'Social class and occupation', in R. Burgess (ed.) *Key Variables in Sociological Investigation*, London: Routledge and Kegan Paul.

Marsh, C. and Blackburn, R.M. (1992) 'Class differences in access to higher education', in R. Burrows and C. Marsh (eds) *Consumption and Class*, London: Macmillan.

Marsh, D. (1992) *The New Politics of British Trade Unionism*, London: Macmillan.

Marshall, G. (1988) 'Some remarks on on the study of working-class consciousness', in D. Rose (ed.) *Social Stratification and Economic Change*, London: Hutchinson.

Marshall, G. (1990) *In Praise of Sociology*, London: Unwin Hymen.

Marshall, G. (1991) 'In defence of class analysis: a comment on R.E. Pahl', *International Journal of Urban and Regional Research*, 15, 114–18.

Marshall, G. *et al.* (1988) *Social Class in Modern Britain*, London: Hutchinson.

Marshall, G. and Rose, D. (1989) 'Reply to Saunders', *Network*, 44, 4–5.

Marshall, G. and Rose, D. (1990) 'Out-classed by our critics', *Sociology*, 24, 255–67.

Marshall, G. and Swift, A. (1993) 'Social class and social justice', *British Journal of Sociology*, 44, 187–211.

Marshall, G. and Swift, A. (1996) 'Merit and mobility: a reply to Peter Saunders', *Sociology*, 30, 375–86.

Marshall, G. *et al.* (1995) 'Class, gender and the asymmetry hypothesis', *European Sociological Review*, 11, 1–15.

Marshall, G. *et al.* (1996) 'Social class and the underclass in Britain and
  the USA', *British Journal of Sociology*, 47, 22–44.
Martin, J and Roberts, C. (1984) *Women and Employment*, London: HMSO.
Mayer, K. (1963) 'The changing shape of the American class structure',
  Social Research, 30, 458–68.
Mead, L.M. (1986) *Beyond Entitlement: The Social Obligations of Citizenship*,
  New York: Free Press.
Miliband, R. (1969) *The State in Capitalist Society*, London: Weidenfeld
  and Nicolson.
Milkman, R. (1991) 'Labour and management in uncertain times: renegotiating
  the social contract', in A. Wolfe (ed.) *America at Century's End*, Berkeley:
  University of California Press.
Miller, S.M. (1960) 'Comparative social mobility', *Current Sociology*, 9, 1–89.
Mills, C. (1994) 'Who dominates whom? Social class, conjugal households
  and political identification', *Sociological Review*, 42, 639–63.
Mills, C. (1995) 'Managerial and professional work-histories', in T. Butler
  and M. Savage (eds) *Social Change and the Middle Classes*, London:
  UCL Press.
Mills, C.W. (1951) *White Collar*, New York: Oxford University Press.
Mills, C.W. (1956) *The Power Elite*, Oxford: Oxford University Press.
Mintz, B. and Schwartz, M. (1981) 'Interlocking directorates and interest
  group formation', *American Sociological Review*, 46, 851–69.
Mintz, B. and Schwartz, M. (1985) *The Power Structure of American Business*,
  Chicago: University of Chicago Press.
Mintz, B. (1989) 'United States of America', in T. Bottomore and R. Brym
  (eds) *The Capitalist Class*, Hemel Hempstead: HarvesterWheatsheaf.
Mishel, L. and Bernstein, J. (1993) *The State of Working America 1992–3*,
  New York: M.E. Sharp.
Mizruchi, M. and Koenig, T. (1986) 'Corporate political consensus',
  American Sociological Review, 51, 482–91.
Mogey, J.M. (1956) *Family and Neighbourhood*, Oxford: Oxford University Press.
Moorhouse, B. (1983) 'American automobiles and workers' dreams',
  Sociological Review, 31, 403–26.
Moran, M. (1984) *The Politics of Banking*, London: Macmillan.
Morris, L. (1992) 'The social segregation of the long-term unemployed in
  Hartlepool', *Sociological Review*, 38, 344–69.
Morris, L. (1994) *Dangerous Classes*, London: Routledge.
Morris, L. (1995) *Social Divisions*, London: UCL Press.
Morris, L. and Irwin, S. (1992a) 'Employment histories and the concept
  of the underclass', *Sociology*, 26, 401–20.
Morris, L. and Irwin, S. (1992b) 'Employment and informal support:
  dependency, exclusion or participation', *Work, Employment and Society*,
  6, 185–207.
Morris, L. and Scott, J. (1996) 'The attenuation of class analysis: some
  comments on G. Marshall, S. Roberts and C. Burgoyne, "Social class
  and the underclass in Britain and the USA"', *British Journal of Sociology*,
  47, 45–55.
Moynihan, D.P. (1972) 'Equalising education: in whose interest?', *The
  Public Interest*, 29, 69–89.
Mullins, C. (1991) 'The identification of social forces in development as

a general problem in Sociology', *International Journal of Urban and Regional Research*, 15, 119–29.

Murtgatroyd, L. (1982) 'Gender and occupational stratification', *Sociological Review*, 30, 573–601.

Murgatroyd, L. (1984) 'Women, men and the social grading of occupations', *British Journal of Sociology*, 35, 473–97.

Murray, C. (1984) *Losing Ground: American Social Policy 1950-1980*, New York: Basic Books.

Murray, C. (1990) *The Emerging British Underclass*, London: IEA.

Murray, C. (1994) *The Underclass: The Crisis Deepens*, London: Institute for Economic Affairs.

Murray, C. (1995) 'The next British revolution', *The Public Interest*, 118, 3–39.

Neckerman, K. *et al.* (1988) 'Family structure, black unemployment and American social policy', in M. Weir *et al.* (eds) *The Politics of Social Policy in the United States*, Princeton: Princeton University Press.

Nelson, J.I. (1995) *Post-Industrial Capitalism*, London: Sage.

Newman, K. (1988) *Falling from Grace*, New York: Free Press.

Newman, K. (1991) 'Uncertain seas: cultural turmoil and the domestic economy', in A. Wolfe (ed.) *America at Century's End*, Berkeley: University of California Press.

Newman, K. (1993) *Declining Fortunes*, New York: Basic Books.

Nie, N.H. *et al.* (1981) *The Changing American Voter*, Cambridge, MA: Harvard University Press.

Nisbett,R. (1995) 'Race, IQ and scientism', in S. Fraser (ed.) *The Bell Curve Wars*, New York: Basic Books.

Ogburn, T. (1955) 'Technology and the standard of living in the United States', *American Journal of Sociology*, 60, 529–52.

O'Hare, W.P. *et al.* (1991) 'African Americans in the 1990s', *Population Bulletin*, 46, 1–6.

Oppenheim, C. (1993) *Poverty: The Facts*, London: CPAG.

Owen, D. (1992) 'Ethnic minorities in Great Britain: settlement patterns', *1991 Census Statistical Paper No. 1*, University of Warwick: Centre for Research in Ethnic Relations.

Oyen, E. (ed.) (1990) *Comparative Methodology*, London: Sage.

Pahl, R.E. (1984) *Divisions of Labour*, Oxford: Basil Blackwell.

Pahl, R.E. (1988) 'Some remarks on informal work, social polarisation and the social structure', *International Journal of Urban and Regional Research*, 12, 247–67.

Pahl, R.E. (1989) 'Is the emperor naked? some questions on the adequacy of sociological theory in urban and regional research', *International Journal of Urban and Regional Research*, 13, 711–20.

Pahl, R.E. (1993) 'Does class analysis without class theory have a future?: a reply to Goldthorpe and Marshall', *Sociology*, 27, 253–8.

Pakulski, J. and Waters, M. (1996) *The Death of Class*, London: Sage.

Papadimitriou, D.B. and Wolff, E.N. (eds) (1993) *Poverty and Prosperity in the USA in the Late Twentieth Century*, London: Macmillan.

Parkin, F. (1968) *Middle-Class Radicalism*, Manchester: Manchester University Press.

Parkin, F. (1971) *Class Inequality and Political Order*, London: Paladin Books.

Parkin, F. (1979) *Marxism and Class Theory*, London: Tavistock Publications.
Patterson, J. (1981) *America's Struggle Against Poverty*, Cambridge, MA: Harvard University Press.
Pawson, R. (1989) *A Measure for Measures*, London: Routledge.
Pawson, R. (1990) 'Half-truths about bias', *Sociology*, 24, 229–40.
Pawson, R. (1993) 'Social mobility', in D. Morgan and L. Stanley (eds) *Debates in Sociology*, Manchester: Manchester University Press.
Payne, G. (1986) *Mobility and Change in Modern Society*, London: Macmillan.
Payne, G. (1987) *Employment and Opportunity*, London: Macmillan.
Payne, G. (1990) 'Social mobility in Britain: a contrary view', in J. Clark *et al.* (eds) *John H. Goldthorpe: Consensus and Controversy*, London: Falmer Press.
Payne, G. (1992) 'Competing views of contemporary social mobility and social divisions' in R. Burrows and C. Marsh (eds) *Consumption and Class*, London: Macmillan.
Payne, G. and Abbott, P. (eds) (1990) *The Social Mobility of Women*, London: Falmer Press.
Payne, J. (1987) 'Does unemployment run in families? Some general findings from the general household survey', *Sociology*, 21 (2), 199–214.
Payne, J. and Payne, C. (1993) 'Recession, restructuring and the fate of the unemployed: evidence in the underclass debate', *Sociology*, 27, 1–22.
Penn, R. (1981) 'The Nuffield class categorisation', *Sociology*, 15, 265–71.
Penn, R. (1983) 'Theories of skill and class structure', *Sociological Review*, 31, 22–88.
Penn, R. (1986) 'Where have all the craftsmen gone?', *British Journal of Sociology*, 37, 569–80.
Peterson, P.E. (1991) 'The urban underclass and the poverty paradox' in C. Jencks and P.E. Peterson (eds) The Urban Underclass, Washington, DC The Brookings Institute.
Phillips, D. and Sarre, P. (1995) 'Black middle-class formation in contemporary Britain', in T. Butler and M. Savage (eds) *Social Change and the Middle Classes*, London: UCL Press.
Phillips, K. (1990) *The Politics of Rich and Poor*, New York: Random House.
Phillips, K. (1993) *Boiling Point*, New York: Random House.
Phillips, M. (1992) 'Nothing for the outcast generation', *The Guardian*, 4 December.
Phillips, M. (1994) 'Where are the new Victorians?', in C. Murray (ed.) *Underclass: The Crisis Deepens*, London: Institute for Economic Affairs.
Piore, M.J. and Sabel, C. (1984) *The Second Industrial Divide*, New York: Basic Books.
Piven, F.F. (eds) (1992) *Labour Parties in Post-industrial Societies*, Park: Pennsylvannia State University Press.
Pomper, G.M. (1989) *The Election of 1988*, New Jersey: Chatham House.
Pomper, G.M. (1993) *The Election of 1992*, New Jersey: Chatham House.
Pond C. (1989) 'The changing distribution of income, wealth and poverty', in C. Hamnett *et al.* (eds) *The Changing Social Structure*, London: Sage.
Poutlantzas, N. (1973) *Political Power and Social Classes*, London: New Left Books.
Poutlantzas, N. (1975) *Class in Contemporary Capatilism*, London: New Left Books.

Prandy, K. *et al.* (1983) *White-Collar Unionism*, London: Macmillan.

Pringle, R. (1989) *Secretaries Talk*, London: Verso.

Proctor, I. (1990) 'The privatisation of working-class life: a dissenting view', *British Journal of Sociology*, 41, 158–80.

Przeworski, A. (1985) *Capitalism and Social Democracy*, New York: Cambridge University Press.

Przeworski, A. and Sprague, J. (1986) *Paper Stones*, Chicago: University of Chicago Press.

Przeworski, A. and Teune, H. (1970) *The Logic of Comparative Social Inquiry*, New York: Wiley.

Quadagno, J. (1984) 'Welfare capitalism and the Social Security Act of 1935', *American Sociological Review*, 49, 632–47.

Quadagno, J. (1985) 'Two models of welfare state development', *American Sociological Review*, 50, 575–8.

Ragin, C.C. (1987) *The Comparative Method*, Berkeley: University of California Press.

Ragin, C.C. (ed.) (1991) *Issues and Alternatives in Comparative Social Research*, Berkeley: University of California Press.

Reid, I. (1989) *Social Class Differences in Britain*, 3rd edn, London: Fontana.

Reskin, B. and Hartmann, H. (1986) *Women's Work, Men's Work*, Washington, DC: National Academy Press.

Reskin, B.F. and Padavic, I. (1994) *Women and Men at Work*, London: Pine Forge Press.

Rex, J. (1986) *Race and Ethnicity*, Milton Keynes: Open University Press.

Rex, J. (1988) *The Ghetto and the Underclass*, Aldershot: Avebury.

Rex, J. and Tomlinson, S. (1979) *Colonial Immigrants in a British City*, London: Routledge and Kegan Paul.

Rex, J. and Moore, R. (1967) *Race, Community and Conflict*, London: Institute of Race Relations.

Richie, J. (1990) *Thirty Families*, London: SCPR.

Rieder, J. (1985) *Canarsie*, Cambridge, MA: Harvard University Press.

Ritter, K. and Hargens, L. (1975) 'Occupational positions and class identifications of married working women: a test of the asymmetry hypothesis', *American Journal of Sociology*, 80, 934–48.

Roberts, H. and Barker, R. (1989) *The Sociological Classification of Women*, London: City University Social Statistics Research Unit.

Roberts, K. (1995) *Youth and Employment in Modern Britain*, Oxford: Oxford University Press.

Roberts, S. and Marshall, G. (1995) 'Inter-generational class processes and the asymmetry hypohesis', *Sociology*, 29, 43–58.

Robinson, R.V. (1983) 'Explaining perceptions of class and racial inequality in England and the United States of America', *British Journal of Sociology*, 34, 344–66.

Robinson, R.V. and Bell, W. (1978) 'Equality, success and social justice in England and the United States', *American Sociological Review*, 43, 125–43.

Robinson, R.V. and Kelley, J. (1979) 'Class as conceived by Marx and Dahrendorf: effects of income inequality, class consciousness and class conflict in the United States and Great Britain', *American Sociological Review*, 44, 38–58.

Robinson, V. (1988) 'The new Indian middle class in Britain', *Ethnic and Racial Studies*, 11, 456–73.

Robinson, V. (1990) 'Roots to mobility: the social mobility of Britain's black population', *Ethnic and Racial Studies*, 13, 1971–87.

Rodman, H. (1963) 'The lower class value stretch', *Social Forces*, 42, 206–15.

Rose, D. (1995) *A Report on Phase 1 of the ESRC Review of OPCS Social Classifications*, Swindon: ESRC.

Rose, D. and Birkelund, G.E. (1991) 'Social class and occupational segregation', *Working Papers of the ESRC Research Centre on Micro-Social Change, Occupational Paper No. 1*, Colchester: ESRC Research Centre on Micro-Social Change.

Rose, D. and Marshall, G. (1986) 'Constructing the (W)right classes', *Sociology*, 20, 440-5.

Rosemer, J. (1982) *A General Theory of Exploitation and Class*, Cambridge, MA: Harvard University Press.

Rosen, E.I. (1987) *Better Choices*, Chicago: University of Chicago Press.

Rossi, P. (1989) *Down and Out in America*, Chicago: University of Chicago Press.

Rossi, P. *et al.* (1974) 'Measuring household social standing', *Social Science Research, 3,.* 169–90.

Rostella, F. (1981) *From Home to Office*, Ann Arbor: UMI Research Press.

Rothman, R.A. (1993) *Inequality and Stratification*, Englewood Cliffs, NJ: Prentice Hall Inc.

Routh, G. (1987) *Occupations of the People of Great Britain, 1801–1981*, London: Macmillan.

Rubery. J. (1988) 'Employers and the labour market' in D. Gallie (ed.) *Employment in Britain*, Oxford: Basil Blackwell..

Rubin, B.A. (1986) 'Class struggle American style: unions, strikes and wages', *American Sociological Review*, 51, 618–31.

Rubin, L. (1976) *Worlds of Pain*, New York: Basic Books.

Rubinstein, W.D. (ed.) (1980) *Wealth and the Wealthy in the Modern World*, London: Croom Helm.

Rubinstein W.D. (1981) *Men of Property*, London: Croom Helm.

Rubinstein, W.D. (1986) *Wealth and Inequality in Britain*, London: Faber and Faber.

Rubinstein, W.D. (1993) *Capitalism, Culture and Decline in Britain, 1750-1990*, London: Routledge.

Rudig, W. *et al.* (1991) *Green Party Members: A Profile*, Glasgow: Delta Publications.

Runciman, W.G. (1966) *Relative Deprivation and Social Justice*, Harmondsworth: Penguin.

Runciman, W.G. (1990) 'How many classes are there in contemporary British society?', *Sociology*, 24, 377–96.

Rutter, M. and Madge, N. (1977) *Cycles of Disadvantage*, London: Heinemann.

Salaman, G. (1986) *Working*, London: Tavistock Publications.

Sarlvik, B. and Crewe, I. (1983) *Decade of Dealignment*, Cambridge: Cambridge University Press.

Sarre, P. (1989) 'Race and the class structure', in C. Hamnett *et al.* (eds) *The Changing Class STructure*, London: Sage.

Saunders, P. (1989) 'Left write in Sociology', *Network*, 44, 3–4.

Saunders, P. (1990a) *A Nation of Home Owners*, London: Unwin Hyman.

Saunders, P. (1990b) *Social Class and Stratification*, London: Tavistock.

Saunders, P. (1995) 'Might Britain be a meritocracy?', *Sociology*, 29, 23–41.

Saunders, P. (1996) 'Social mobility in Britain: an empirical evaluation of two competing explanations', in W. Bottero (ed.) *Post-Class Society?*, Cambridge: Cambridge Sociological Research Group Publications.

Saunders, P. and Harris, C. (1994) *Privatisation and Popular Capitalism*, Buckingham: Open University Press.

Savage, M. (1992) 'Women's expertise, men's authority: gendered organisation and the contemporary middle classes', in M. Savage and A. Witz (eds) *Gender and Bureaucracy*, Oxford: Blackwell.

Savage, M. (1996) 'Social mobility the the survey method', in D. Bertaux and P. Thompson (eds) *Pathways to Social Class*, Oxford: Oxford University Press.

Savage, M. *et al.* (1992) *Property, Bureaucracy and Culture*, London: Routledge.

Sawhill, I. (1989) 'The underclass: an overview', *The Public Interest*, 96, 3–15.

Scase, R. (1992) *Class*, Buckingham: Open University Press.

Schwartz, M. and Mintz, B. (1987) *The Structure of Power in America*, New York: Holms and Meier.

Scott, J. (1979) *Corporations, Classes and Capitalism*, London: Hutchinson.

Scott, J. (1982) *The Upper Classes*, London: Macmillan.

Scott, J. (1985) *Corporations, Classes and Capitalism*, 2nd edn, London: Hutchinson.

Scott, J. (1986) *Capitalist Property and Financial Power*, Brighton: Wheatsheaf.

Scott, J. (1988) 'Ownership and employee control', in D. Gallie (ed.) *Employment in Britain*, Oxford: Basil Blackwell.

Scott, J. (1990) 'Corporate control and corporate rule: Britain in an international perspective', *British Journal of Sociology*, 41, 351–73.

Scott, J. (1991) *Who Rules Britain?*, Cambridge: Polity.

Scott, J. (1994a) *Poverty and Wealth*, Harlow: Longman.

Scott, J. (1994b) 'Class analysis: back to the future', *Sociology*, 28, 933–42.

Scott, J. (1996) *Stratification and Power*, Cambridge: Polity.

Sewell, W. *et al.* (eds) (1976) *Schooling and Achievement in American Society*, New York: Academic Press.

Seyd, P. and Whitley, P. (1992) *Labour's Grass Roots*, Oxford: Clarendon Press.

Shafer, B.E. (1991) *Is America Different?*, Oxford: Oxford University Press.

Shostak, A.B. and Gomberg, W. (eds) (1964) *Blue-Collar World*, Englewood Cliffs, NJ: Prentice Hall.

Shorrocks, A.F. (1987) 'UK wealth distribution: current evidence and future prospects', in E.N. Wolff (ed.) *International Comparisons of the Distribution of Household Wealth*, Oxford: Clarendon Press.

Sigelman, L. and Welch, S. (1991) *Black Americans' Views of Racial Inequality*, Cambridge: Cambridge University Press.

Simpson, I.H. *et al.* (1988) 'Class identification of married, working men and women', *American Sociological Review*, 53, 284–93.

Singlemann, J. and Tienda, M. (1985) 'The process of occupational change in a service society: the case of the United States', in B. Roberts *et al.* (eds) *New Approaches to Economic Life*, Manchester: Manchester University Press.

Sklair, L. (1991) *Sociology of the Global System*, Hemel Hempstead: Harvester Wheatsheaf.

Skocpol, T. (1981) 'Political response to capitalist crisis: neo-Marxist theories of the state and the case of the New Deal', *Politics and Society*, 10, 155–201.

Skocpol, T. and Amenda, E. (1985) 'Did capitalists shape social security?', *American Sociological Review*, 50, 572–5.

Skocpol, T. and Campbell, J.L. (1995) *American Society and Politics*, New York: McGraw Hill.

Skocpol, T. and Finegold, K. (1982) 'State capacity and economic interaction in the early New Deal', *Political Science Quarterly*, 97, 255–78.

Skocpol, T. and Ikenberry, J. (1983) 'The political formation of the American welfare state in historical and comparative perspective', *Comparative Social Research*, 6.

Slipman, S. (1994) 'Would you take one home with you?', in C. Murray (ed.) *Underclass: The Crisis Deepens*, London: Institute for Economic Affairs.

Small, S. (1994) *Racialised Barriers*, London: Routledge.

Smeeding, T. *et al.* (1990) *Poverty, Inequality and Income Distribution in Comparative Perspective*, Hemel Hempstead: Harvester Wheatsheaf.

Smeeding, T.M. *et al.* (1995) *Income Distribution in OECD Countries*, Paris: OECD.

Smith, D.J. (1992) 'Defining the underclass', in D.J. Smith (ed.) *Understanding the Underclass*, London: PSI.

Smith, J.D. (1987) 'Recent trends in the distribution of wealth in the US: data, research problems and prospects', in E.N.Wolff (ed.) *International Comparisons of the Distribution of Household Wealth*, Oxford: Clarendon Press.

Smith, T.W. (1989) 'Inequality and welfare', in R. Jowell *et al.* (eds) *British Social Attitudes: Special International Report*, Aldershot: Gower.

Social Focus on Women (1995), London: HMSO.

Social Trends (1994), London: HMSO.

Social Trends (1995), London: HMSO.

Sombart, W. (1906) 1976 *Why is there Socialism in the United States?*, London: Macmillan.

Sorensen, A. (1994) 'Women, family and class', *Annual Review of Sociology*, 20, 27–47.

Sorensen, A.B. (1977) 'The structure of inequality and the process of attainment', *American Sociological Review*, 42, 965–78.

Sorensen, A.B. (1986) 'Theory and methodology in social stratification', in U. Himmelstrand (ed.) *Sociology: From Crisis to Science?*, London: Sage.

Sorensen, A.B. (1991) 'On the usefulness of class analysis in research on social mobility and socio-economic inequality', *Acta Sociologica*, 34, 71–87.

Sorensen, A.B. and Kalleberg, A.L. (1981) 'An outline of a theory of the matching of persons to jobs', in I. Berg (ed.) *Sociological Perspectives on Labour Markets*, New York: Academic Press.

Sorokin, P.A. (1927) *Social Mobility*, New York: Harper and Brothers.

Sorokin, P.A. (1964) *Social and Cultural Mobility*, Glencoe, IL: Free Press.

Sowell, T. (1995) 'Ethnicity and IQ', in S. Fraser (ed.) *The Bell Curve Wars*, New York: Basic Books.

Stacey, M. (1960) *Tradition and Change*, London: Oxford University Press.

Stanworth, M. (1984) 'Women and class analysis: a reply to Goldthorpe', *Sociology*, 18, 159–70.

Stanworth, P. and Giddens, A. (1974) 'An economic elite: a demographic profile of company chairmen', in P. Stanworth and A. Giddens (eds) (1974) *Elites and Power in British Society*, Cambridge: Cambridge University Press.

Stark, T. (1987) 'The changing distribution of income under Mrs Thatcher', in F. Green (ed.) *The Restructuring of the UK Economy*, Hemel Hempstead: Harvester Wheatsheaf.

Statistical Abstract of the United States 1994.

Steinmetz, G. and Wright, E.O. (1989) 'The fall and rise of the petty bourgeoisie: changing patterns of self-employment in the postwar United States', *American Journal of Sociology*, 94 (5), 973–1,018.

Steinmetz, G. and Wright, E.O. (1990) 'Reply to Linder and Houghton', *American Journal of Sociology*, 96, 736–40.

Stewart, A. *et al.* (1980) *Social Stratification and Occupations*, London: Macmillan.

Stockman, N. *et al.* (1995) *Women's Work in East and West*, London: UCL Press.

Strobel, F.R. (1993) *Upward Dreams, Downward Mobility*, Lanham, MD: Rowman and Littlefield.

Strom, S.H. (1992) *Beyond the Typewriter*, Chicago: University of Illinois Press.

Szymanski, A. (1984) *Class Structure*, New York: Praeger.

Taylor-Gooby, P. (1989) 'Attachment to the welfare state', in R. Jowell *et al.* (eds) *British Social Attitudes: The 8th Report*, Aldershot: Dartmouth.

Taylor-Gooby P. (1991) *Social Change, Social Welfare and Social Science*, Hemel Hempstead: Harvester Wheatsheaf.

Taylor-Gooby, P. (1993) 'What citizens want from the state', in R. Jowell *et al.* (eds) *International Social Attitudes: The 10th BSA Report*, Aldershot: Dartmouth.

Testa, M. *et al.* (1989) 'Employment and marriage among inner-city fathers', *Annals of the American Academy of Political and Social Science*, 501, 79–91.

Thurow, L. (1984) *Generating Inequality*, 2nd edn, London: Macmillan.

Tienda, M. (1989) 'Puerto Ricans and the underclass debate', *Annals of the American Academy of Political and Social Science*, 501, 105–19.

Tocqueville de, A. (1948) *Democracy in America*, New York: Knopf.

Townsend, P. (1976) *Poverty in the United Kingdom*, Harmondsworth: Penguin.

Townsend, P. (1979) *Poverty in the United Kingdom*, Harmondsworth: Penguin.

Townsend, P. (1993) *The International Analysis of Poverty*, New York: Harvester Wheafsheaf.

Townsend, P. and Gordon, D. (1989) *Memorandum laid before the Social Services Committee on Minimum Income*, London: HMSO.

Thompson, F.M.L. (1994) *Landowners, Capitalists and Entrepreneurs*, Oxford: Clarendon Press.

Thompson, P. (1989) *The Nature of Work*, London: Macmillan.

Treiman, D.J. (1977) *Occupational Prestige in Comparative Perspective*, New York: Academic Press.

Treiman, D.J. and Ganzeboom, H.B.G. (1990) 'Cross-national comparative status-attainment research', *Research in Social Stratification and Mobility*, 9, 105–27.

Tryee, A. and Treas, J. (1974) 'The occupational and marital mobility of women', *American Sociological Review*, 39, 293–302.

Urry, J. (1981) *The Anatomy of Capitalist Society*, London: Macmillan.

Useem, M. (1984) *The Inner Circle*, Oxford: Oxford University Press.

Valentine, C.A. (1968) *Culture and Poverty*, Chicago: University of Chicago Press.

Van de Pijl, K. (1989) 'The international level', in T. Bottomore and R. Brym (eds) *The Capitalist Class*, Hemel Hempstead: Harvester Wheatsheaf.

Vanneman, R. (1980) 'US and British perceptions of class', *American Journal of Sociology*, 85, 769–90.

Vanneman, R. and Cannon, L.W. (1987) *The American Perception of Class*, Philadelphia: Temple University Press.

Vanneman, R. and Pampel, F. (1977) 'The American perception of class and status, *American Sociological Review*, 42, 422–37.

Van Velson, E. and Beeghley, L. (1979) 'The process of class identification among married women: a replication and reanalysis', *Journal of Marriage and the Family*, 41, 771–8.

Vidich, A.J. (1995) *The New Middle Classes*, London: Macmillan.

Vogel, D. (1978) *Lobbying the Corporation*, New York: Basic Books.

Vogel, D. (1989) *Fluctuating Fortunes*, New York: Basic Books.

Wacquant, L.J.D. and Wilson, W.J. (1989) 'The cost of racial and class exclusion in the inner city', *Annals of the American Academy of Political and Social Science*, 8–25.

Waddington, D. *et al.* (1991) *Split at the Seams*, Milton Keynes: Open University Press.

Walby, S. (1986) *Patriarchy at Work*, Oxford: Blackwell.

Walker, A. (1990) 'Blaming the victims', in C. Murray (ed.) *The Emerging British Underclass*, London: Institute for Economic Affairs.

Walker, A. and Walker, C. (1987) *The Growing Divide: A Social Audit 1979–1987*, London: CPAG.

Ward, R. and Cross, M. (1991) 'Race, employment and economic change', in P. Brown and R. Scase (eds) *Poor Work, Disadvantage and the Division of Labour*, Buckingham: Open University Press.

Warner, W.L. and Lund, P. (1941) *The Social Life of a Modern Community*, New Haven, CT: Yale University Press.

Warner, W.L. *et al.* (1949) *Social Class in America*, New York: Science Research Associates.

Warwick, D. and Littlejohn, G. (1992) *Coal, Capital and Culture*, London: Routledge.

Waters, M. (1995) *Globalisation*, London: Routledge.

Weakliem, D. (1989) 'Class and party in Britain, 1964–1989', *Sociology*, 23, 285–97.

Weakliem, D. (1993) 'Class consiousness and political change: voting and political attitudes in the British working class, 1964 to 1970', *American Sociological Review*, 58, 382–97.

Webster, J. (1990) *Office Automation*, London: Macmillan.

Wellman, D. (1995) *The Union Makes Us Strong*, New York: Cambridge University Press.

West, J. (1984) *Work, Women and the Labour Market*, London: Routledge and Kegan Paul.

Westergaard, J. (1992) 'About and beyond the "underclass": some notes on influences of social climate on British sociology today', *Sociology*, 26, 575–87.

Westergaard, J. (1995) *Who Gets What?*, Cambridge: Polity.

Westergaard, J. and Resler, H. (1976) *Class in a Capitalist Society*, Harmondsworth: Penguin.

Westergaard, J. *et al.* (1989) *After Redundancy*, Cambridge: Polity.

Whelan, C.T. (1976) 'Orientations to work: some theoretical and methodological problems', *British Journal of Industrial Relations*, 14, 142–58.

Whitley, R. (1974) 'The city and industry: the directors of large companies: their characteristics and connections', in P. Stanworth and A. Giddens (eds) *Elites and Power in British Society*, Cambridge: Cambridge University Press.

Wilensky, H.L. (1960) 'Work, careers and social integration', *International Social Science Journal*, 12, 543–60.

Willmott, P. and Hutchinson, R. (1992) *Urban Trends 1*, London: PSI.

Wilson, W.J. (1978) *The Declining Significance of Race*, Chicago: University of Chicago Press.

Wilson, W.J. (1987) *The Truly Disadvantaged*, Chicago: University of Chicago Press.

Wilson, W.J. (ed.) (1989) 'The ghetto underclass: social science perspectives', *Annals of the American Academy of Political and Social Science*, 501, January.

Wilson, W.J. (1990) *The Truly Disadvantaged*, 2nd edn, Chicago: Chicago University Press.

Wilson, W.J. (1991) 'Public policy research and *The Truly Disadvantaged*', in C. Jencks and P.E. Peterson (eds) *The Urban Underclass*, Washington, DC: The Brookings Institute.

Wilson, W.J. (ed.) (1993) *The Ghetto Underclass*, London: Sage.

Winchester, D. (1988) 'Sectoral change and trade union organisation', in D. Gallie (ed.) *Employment in Britain*, Oxford: Basil Blackwell.

Winterton, J. and Winterton, J.H. (1989) *Coal, Crisis and Conflict*, Manchester: Manchester University Press.

Witz, A. (1992) *Professions and Patriarchy*, London: Routledge.

Witz, A. (1995) Gender and service-class formations', in T. Butler and M. Savage (eds) *Social Change in the Middle Classes*, London: UCL Press.

Witz, A. and Savage, M. (1992) *Gender and Bureaucracy*, Oxford: Basil Blackwell/Sociological Review.

Wolfe, A. (1995) 'Has there been a cognitive revolution in America? The flawed sociology of *The Bell Curve*', in S. Fraser (ed.) *The Bell Curve Wars*, New York: Basic Books.

Wolff, E.N. (1987) *International Comparisons of the Distribution of Household Wealth*, Oxford: Clarendon Press.

Wolff, E.N. (1995) *Top Heavy*, New York: The Twentieth Century Fund Press.

Woodward, J. (1958) *Management and Technology*, London: HMSO.

Wright, E.O. (1978) *Class, Crisis and the State*, London: Verso.

Wright, E.O. (1979) *Class Structure and Income Determination*, London: Academic Press.

Wright, E.O. (1985) *Classes*, London: Verso.

Wright, E.O. (1989a) *The Debate on Classes*, London: Verso.

Wright E.O. (1989b) 'Women in the class structure', *Politics and Society*, 17, 35–66.

Wright, E.O. (1994) *Interrogating Inequality*, London: Verso.

Wright, E.O. and Martin, B. (1987) 'The transformation of the American class structure, 1960-1980', *American Journal of Sociology*, 93, 1–29.

Wright, E.O. and Singlemann, J. (1982) 'Proletarianisation in the American class structure', *American Journal of Sociology*, 93, 176–209.

Young, M. and Willmott, P. (1957) *Family and Kinship in East London*, London: Routledge and Kegan Paul.

Zeitlan, M. (1974) 'Corporate ownership and control: the large corporation and the capitalist class', *American Journal of Sociology*, 79, 1073–1119.

Zeitlan, M. (1983) *How Mighty a Force*, Los Angeles: University of California Institute of Industrial Relations.

Zeitlan, M. (1989) *The Large Corporation and Contemporary Classes*, Cambridge: Polity Press.

Zimbalist, A. (ed.) (1979) *Case Studies in the Labour Process*, New York: Monthly Review Press.

Zwieg, F. (1961) *The Worker in an Affluent Society*, London: Heinemann.

Index